P
95.82
U6
G57
1980

California Maritime Academy Library (CSU)

D0093031

WITHDRAWN

The Whole World Is Watching

The Whole World

mass media in the making

Todd Gitlin

Is Watching

& unmaking of the new left

University of California Press / Berkeley, Los Angeles, London

LIBRARY
CALIFORNIA MARITIME ACADEMY
P. O. BOX 1392
VALLEJO, CA 94590

WITHDRAWN

University of California Press
Berkeley and Los Angeles, California

University of California Press, Ltd.
London, England

ISBN 0-520-04024-4 (alk. paper)
Library of Congress Number: 78-68835

© 1980 by
The Regents of the University of California

Printed in the United States of America

9   10   11   12   13   14   15

The paper used in this publication is both acid-free
and totally chlorine-free (TCF). It meets the
minimum requirements of American Standard
for Information Sciences—Permanence of Paper
for Printed Library Materials, ANSI Z39.48-1984. ∞

To my parents and my sister

Contents

Acknowledgments

We think in society; authorship is always indebted, always a process that takes place in an historical situation, on ground prepared by many hands. The ideas in this book are mine, but directly and indirectly, in extrapolation and in critique, they draw on many writings by many people, many conversations about politics and culture.

I wish especially to thank the following former SDS and other antiwar workers for submitting to interviews: Mike Davis, R. G. Davis, Douglas Dowd, Nick Egleson, Daniel Ellsberg, Richard Flacks, Helen Garvy, Alan Haber, David Hawk, Glenn Hirsch, Michael Klare, Michael P. Lerner, Ken McEldowney, James Russell, Maria Varela, and Susan Werbe.

Equally I want to thank my informants in the media: Lawrence M. Bensky, Fred Powledge, Kirkpatrick Sale, and Daniel Schwartz, each formerly of the *New York Times*; Adam Hochschild, formerly of the *San Francisco Chronicle*; Ben H. Bagdikian, formerly of the *Washington Post*; Carolyn Craven, formerly of ABC News and KQED-TV Newsroom; and the following former and present reporters, producers, executives, and staff of CBS News: Russ Bensley, Ron Bonn, Blair Clark, the late Louis G. Cowan, Stanhope Gould, Mary Halloran, Alexander Kendrick, Stephen Lighthill, Michael Nolan, Cynthia Samuels, and Daniel Schorr. All were gracious to sit still for the arduous and sometimes embarrassing business of historical retrieval, as were others at CBS News and the *Times* who prefer to remain anonymous.

Many conversations and amenities filtered into my ideas

and accounts: thanks to Thomas R. Brooks, Connie Brown, Paul Cowan, Rachel Cowan, Jon D. Cruz, Tom Engelhardt, Nancy Garrity, Timothy Haight, Carol Hatch, Lorraine Kahn, Leo Lowenthal, Terry Lunsford, David Matza, Mark Osiel, Frances Fox Piven, my mother Dorothy Renik, Pamela Roby, Kirkpatrick Sale, Neil Smelser, Barbara Spark, David Wellman, and Paul E. Willis. Thanks also to the following for reading and commenting on pieces of drafts: Paul Booth, Greg Calvert, Dave Dellinger, Robert Gottlieb, and Daniel C. Hallin, the last of whom also placed at my disposal the copious notes he took on TV ne⋯·s broadcasts at Vanderbilt University and the National Archives. Robert Wuthnow made helpful comments on the whole manuscript. Robert J. Ross made a decisive contribution to my reworking of Part III, for which I am deeply grateful. Carol S. Wolman helped in many ways. Footnotes record many other intellectual debts. Needless to say, none of these people bears personal responsibility for my conclusions.

Glenn Hirsch gave me leads, did archival research, and typed part of an early draft. Iris Rosenberg did some follow-up research in the CBS archives in New York. Malin Persson was my research assistant, tracking down articles on movements against nuclear power and nuclear weapons, and helping distill an analysis from them. Pamela Ellis and Margaret Oakley typed the final draft of the earlier dissertation version. Ernest Callenbach has been a clear and supportive editor, for which relief much thanks.

The Laras Fund and the Foundation for National Progress subsidized my research at CBS News in New York, and helped me afford the manifold materials that flow into a work of scholarship. A research fellowship at the Institute for Race and Community Relations bought me the time for writing the doctoral dissertation on which this book is based. Thanks to Mary Anna Colwell and Troy Duster, respectively. And thanks to the Committee on Research at the University of California, Berkeley, for research funds to help in revising and updating.

The members of my dissertation committee were appropriate in provocation, challenging in criticism, and encouraging—not least!—when the going got tough. My deepest thanks to Arlie Hochschild, to Michael Paul Rogin, and especially to William Kornhauser, without whose steady encouragement none of this would have gotten onto the page.

Finally: After many revisions of several drafts, successive approximations to the hoped-for book that would state exactly what one thinks one has to say, this writer, like others, tends to see his work take on the opacity of a blocklike mass. At this point in revising, one wants the aid of the ideal reader and critic: one who reads with exquisite care; who grasps the purposes of the book perhaps even more clearly than the author; who knowledgeably criticizes shaky arguments and strengthens strong ones; and who wants the prose to be transparent. In making the final revisions, I had the inestimable help of just this reader, Clare Spark. She read the manuscript line by line, challenging the argument at a number of points, working with me to clarify it in the course of long discussions; her lucidity leaves its mark throughout. I am immensely grateful, immensely pleased to honor her generosity.

Introduction

This book is about the mass media, the New Left, and their complex relations in historical time. It tells of one fateful conflict over control of the public cultural space in a society saturated with mass media.

Since the advent of radio broadcasting half a century ago, social movements have organized, campaigned, and formed their social identities on a floodlit social terrain. The economic concentration of the media and their speed and efficiency in spreading news and telling stories have combined to produce a new situation for movements seeking to change the order of society. Yet movements, media, and sociology alike have been slow to explore the meanings of modern cultural surroundings.

People directly know only tiny regions of social life; their beliefs and loyalties lack deep tradition. The modern situation is precisely the common vulnerability to rumor, news, trend, and fashion: lacking the assurances of tradition, or of shared political power, people are pressed to rely on mass media for bearings in an obscure and shifting world. And the process is reciprocal: pervasive mass media help pulverize political community, thereby deepening popular dependence on the media themselves. The media bring a manufactured public world into private space. From within their private crevices, people find themselves relying on the media for concepts, for images of their heroes, for guiding information, for emotional charges, for a recognition of public values, for symbols in general, even for language. Of all the institutions of daily life, the media specialize in orchestrating everyday consciousness —by virtue of their pervasiveness, their accessibility, their centralized symbolic capacity. They name the world's parts, they certify reality *as* reality—and when their certifications are doubted and opposed, as they surely are, it is those same certifications that limit the terms of effective opposition. To put it simply: the mass media have become core systems for the distribution of ideology.

That is to say, every day, directly or indirectly, by statement and omission, in pictures and words, in entertainment and news and advertisement, the mass media produce fields of definition and association, symbol and rhetoric, through which ideology becomes manifest and concrete. One important task for ideology is to define—and also define away—its opposition. This has always been true, of course. But the omnipresence and centralization of the mass media, and their integration into the dominant economic sector and the web of the State, create new conditions for opposition. The New Left of the 1960s, facing nightly television news, wire service reports, and a journalistic ideology of "objectivity," inhabited a cultural world vastly different from that of the Populist small farmers' movement of the 1890s, with its fifteen hundred autonomous weekly newspapers, or that of the worker-based Socialist Party of the early 1900s, with its own newspapers circulating in the millions. By the sixties, American society was dominated by a *consolidated* corporate economy, no longer by a *nascent* one. The dream of Manifest Destiny had become realized in a missile-brandishing national security state. And astonishingly, America was now the first society in the history of the world with more college students than farmers. The social base of radical opposition, accordingly, had shifted—from small farmers and immigrant workers to blacks, students, youth, and women. What was transformed was not only the dominant *structures* of capitalist society, but its *textures*. The whole quality of political movements, their procedures and tones, their cultural commitments, had changed. There was now a mass market culture industry, and opposition movements had to reckon with it—had to operate on its edges, in its interstices, and against it. The New Left, like its Populist and Socialist Party predecessors, had its own scatter of "underground" newspapers, with hundreds of thousands of readers, but every night some twenty million Americans watched Walter Cronkite's news, an almost equal number watched Chet Huntley's and David Brinkley's, and over sixty million bought daily newspapers which purchased most of their news from one of two international wire services. In a floodlit society, it becomes extremely difficult, perhaps unimaginable, for an opposition movement to define itself and its world view, to build up an infrastructure of self-generated cultural institutions, outside the dominant culture.[1] Truly, the process of making meanings in the world of centralized commercial culture has become comparable to the process of making value in the world through labor. Just as people *as workers* have no voice in what they make, how they make it, or how the product is distributed and used, so do people *as producers of meaning* have no voice in what the media make of what they say or do, or in the context within which the media frame their activity. The resulting meanings, now mediated, acquire an eery substance in the real world, standing outside their ostensible makers and confronting them as an alien force. The social meanings of intentional action have been deformed beyond recognition.

In the late twentieth century, political movements feel called upon to rely on large-scale communications in order to *matter*, to say who they are and what they intend to publics they want to sway; but in the process they become "newsworthy" only by submitting to the implicit rules of newsmaking, by conforming to journalistic notions (themselves embedded in history) of what a "story" is, what an "event" is, what a "protest" is. The processed image then tends to *become* "the movement" for wider publics and institutions who have few alternative sources of information, or none at all, about it; that image has its impact on public policy, and when the movement is being opposed, what is being opposed is in large part a set of mass-mediated images. Mass media define the public significance of movement events or, by blanking them out, actively deprive them of larger significance. Media images also become implicated in a movement's self-image; media certify leaders and officially noteworthy "personalities"; indeed, they are able to convert leadership into *celebrity*, something quite different. The forms of coverage accrete into systematic framing, and this framing, much amplified, helps determine the movement's fate.

For what defines a movement as "good copy" is often flamboyance, often the presence of a media-certified celebrity-leader, and usually a certain fit with whatever frame the newsmakers have

1. This point is made by Walter Adamson, "Beyond Reform and Revolution: Notes on Political Education in Gramsci, Habermas and Arendt," *Theory and Society* 6 (November 1978): 429–460.

construed to be "the story" at a given time; but these qualities of the image are not what movements intend to be their projects, their identities, their goals. Yet while they constrict and deform movements, the media do amplify the issues which fuel these same movements; as I argue at length in Part III, they expose scandal in the State and in the corporations, while reserving to duly constituted authority the legitimate right to remedy evils. The liberal media quietly invoke the need for reform—while disparaging movements that radically oppose the system that needs reforming.

The routines of journalism, set within the economic and political interests of the news organizations, normally and regularly combine to select certain versions of reality over others. Day by day, *normal* organizational procedures define "the story," identify the protagonists and the issues, and suggest appropriate attitudes toward them. Only episodically, in moments of political crisis and large-scale shifts in the overarching hegemonic ideology, do political and economic managers and owners intervene directly to re-gear or reinforce the prevailing journalistic routines. But most of the time the taken-for-granted code of "objectivity" and "balance" presses reporters to seek out scruffy-looking, chanting, "Viet Cong" flag-waving demonstrators and to counterpose them to reasonable-sounding, fact-brandishing authorities. Calm and cautionary tones of voice affirm that all "disturbance" is or should be under control by rational authority; code words like *disturbance* commend the established normality; camera angles and verbal shibboleths ("and that's the way it is") enforce the integrity and authority of the news anchorman and commend the inevitability of the established order. Hotheads carry on, the message connotes, while wiser heads, officials and reporters both, with superb self-control, watch the unenlightened ones make trouble.

Yet these conventions originate, persist, and shift in historical time. The world of news production is not self-enclosed; for commercial as well as professional reasons, it cannot afford to ignore big ideological changes. Yesterday's ignored or ridiculed kook becomes today's respected "consumer activist," while at the same time the mediated image of the wild sixties yields to the image of the laid-back, apathetic, self-satisfied seventies. Yesterday's revolutionary John Froines of the Chicago Seven, who went to Washington in 1971 to shut down the government, goes to work for it in 1977 at a high salary; in 1977, Mark Rudd surfaces from the Weather Underground, and the sturdy meta-father Walter Cronkite chuckles approvingly as he reports that Mark's father thinks the age of thirty is "too old to be a revolutionary"—these are widely publicized signs of presumably calmer, saner times. Meanwhile, movements for utility rate reform, for unionization in the South, for full employment, for disarmament, and against nuclear power—movements which are not led by "recognized leaders" (those whom the media selectively acknowledged as celebrities in the first place) and which fall outside the prevailing frames ("the New Left is dead," "America is moving to the right")—are routinely neglected or denigrated—until the prevailing frame changes (as it did after the accident at Three Mile Island). An activist against nuclear weapons, released from jail in May 1978 after a series of demonstrations at the Rocky Flats, Colorado, factory that manufactures plutonium triggers for all American H-bombs, telephoned an editor he knew in the *New York Times*'s Washington bureau to ask whether the *Times* had been covering these demonstrations and arrests. No, the editor said, adding: "America is tired of protest. America is tired of Daniel Ellsberg." Blackouts do take place; the editorial or executive censor rationalizes his expurgation, condescendingly and disingenuously, as the good shepherd's fair-minded act of professional news judgment, as his service to the benighted, homogenized, presumably sovereign audience. The closer an issue is to the core interests of national political elites, the more likely is a blackout of news that effectively challenges that interest. That there is safety in the country's nuclear weapons program is, to date, a core principle; and so news of its menace is extremely difficult to get reported—far more difficult, for example, than news about dangers of nuclear power after Three Mile Island. But if the issue is contested at an elite level, or if an elite position has not yet crystallized, journalism's more regular approach is to *process* social opposition, to control its image and to diffuse it at the same time, to absorb what can be absorbed into the dominant structure of definitions and images and to push the rest to the margins of social life.

The processed message becomes complex. To take a single example of a news item: on the CBS Evening News of May 8, 1976, Dan Rather reported that the FBI's burglaries and wiretaps began in the thirties and continued through World War II and the Cold War; and he concluded the piece by saying that these activities reached a peak "during the civil disturbances of the sixties." In this piece we can see some of the contradictory workings of broadcast journalism—and the limits within which contradictory forces play themselves out. First of all, Rather was conveying the information that a once sacrosanct sector of the State had been violating the law for decades. Second, and more subtly—with a clipped, no-nonsense manner and a tough-but-gentle, trustworthy, Watergate-certified voice of technocracy—he was deploring this law-breaking, lending support to those institutions within the State that brought it to the surface and now proposed to stop it, and affirming that the media are integral to this self-correcting system as a whole. Third, he was defining a onetime political opposition *outside* the State as "civil disturbance." The black and student opposition movements of the sixties, which would look different if they were called, say, "movements for peace and justice," were reduced to nasty little things. Through his language, Rather was inviting the audience to identify with forces of reason within the State: with the very source of the story, most likely. In a single news item, with (I imagine) no deliberate forethought, Rather was (a) identifying an abuse of government, (b) legitimating reform within the existing institutions, and (c) rendering illegitimate popular or radical opposition outside the State. The news that man has bitten dog carries an unspoken morality: it proposes to coax men to stop biting those particular dogs, so that the world can be restored to its essential soundness. In such quiet fashion, not deliberately, and without calling attention to this spotlighting process, the media divide movements into legitimate main acts and illegitimate sideshows, so that these distinctions appear "natural," matters of "common sense."[2]

What makes the world beyond direct experience look natural is a media *frame*.[3] Certainly we cannot take for granted that the world depicted is simply the world that exists. Many things exist. At each moment the world is rife with events. Even within a given event there is an infinity of noticeable details. Frames are principles of selection, emphasis, and presentation composed of little tacit theories about what exists, what happens, and what matters. In everyday life, as Erving Goffman has amply demonstrated, we frame reality in order to negotiate it, manage it, comprehend it, and choose

2. For further analysis of the meaning of this and other television news items, see Todd Gitlin, "Spotlights and Shadows: Television and the Culture of Politics," *College English* 38 (April 1977): 791–796.

3. On media frames, see Gaye Tuchman, *Making News* (New York: The Free Press, 1978); and Stuart Hall, "Encoding and Decoding in the Television Discourse," mimeographed paper, Centre for Contemporary Cultural Studies, University of Birmingham, England, 1973.

appropriate repertories of cognition and action.[4] *Media* frames, largely unspoken and unacknowledged, organize the world both for journalists who report it and, in some important degree, for us who rely on their reports. *Media frames are persistent patterns of cognition, interpretation, and presentation, of selection, emphasis, and exclusion, by which symbol-handlers routinely organize discourse, whether verbal or visual.* Frames enable journalists to process large amounts of information quickly and routinely: to recognize it as information, to assign it to cognitive categories, and to package it for efficient relay to their audiences. Thus, for organizational reasons alone, frames are unavoidable, and journalism is organized to regulate their production. Any analytic approach to journalism—indeed, to the production of any mass-mediated content—must ask: What is the frame here? Why this frame and not another? What patterns are shared by the frames clamped over this event and the frames clamped over that one, by frames in different media in different places at different moments? And how does the news-reporting institution regulate these regularities?

And then: What difference do the frames make for the larger world?

The issue of the influence of mass media on larger political currents does not, of course, emerge only with the rise of broadcasting. In the Paris of a century and a half ago, when the commercial press was young, a journalistic novice and littérateur-around-town named Honoré de Balzac was already fascinated by the force of commercialized images. Central to his vivid semiautobiographical novel, *Lost Illusions*, was the giddy, corroded career of the journalist. Balzac saw that the press degraded writers into purveyors of commodities. Writing in 1839 about the wild and miserable spectacle of "A Provincial Great Man in Paris," Balzac in one snatch of dinner-party dialogue picked up the dispute aborning over political consequences of a mass press; he was alert to the fears of reactionaries and the hopes of Enlightenment liberals alike:

"The power and influence of the press are only at their dawn," said Finot. "Journalism is in its infancy, it will grow and grow. Ten years hence everything will be subjected to publicity. Thought will enlighten everything, it—"

4. Erving Goffman, *Frame Analysis: An Essay on the Organization of Experience* (New York: Harper and Row, 1974), pp. 10–11 and passim.

"Will blight everything," interposed Blondet.

"That's a *bon mot*," said Claude Vignon.

"It will make kings," said Lousteau.

"It will unmake monarchies," said the diplomat.

"If the press did not exist," said Blondet, "we could get along without it; but it's here, so we live on it."

"You will die of it," said the diplomat. "Don't you see that the superiority of the masses, assuming that you enlighten them, would make individual greatness the more difficult of attainment; that, if you sow reasoning power in the heart of the lower classes, you will reap revolution, and that you will be the first victims?" [5]

Balzac's ear for hopes and fears and new social tensions was acute; he was present at the making of a new institution in a new social era. Since then, of course, radio and now television have become standard home furnishings. And in considerable measure broadcast content has become part of the popular ideological furniture as well. But while researchers debate the exact "effects" of mass media on the popularity of presidential candidates and presidents, or the "effects" on specific patterns of voting or the salience of issues, evidence quietly accumulates that the texture of political life has changed since broadcasting became a central feature of American life. Media certainly help set the agendas for political discourse; although they are far from autonomous, they do not passively reflect the agendas of the State, the parties, the corporations, or "public opinion." [6] The centralization and commercialization of the mass media of communication make them instruments of cultural dominance on a scale unimagined even by Balzac. In some ways the very ubiquity of the mass media removes media *as a whole system* from the scope of positivist social analysis; for how may we "measure" the "impact" of a social force which is omnipresent within social life and which has a great deal to do with

5. Honoré de Balzac, *Lost Illusions*, trans. G. Burnham Ives (Philadelphia: George Barrie, 1898), Vol. 2, p. 112.

6. Least of all, public opinion. Evidence is accumulating that the priorities conveyed by the media in their treatment of political issues lead public opinion rather than following it. See Maxwell E. McCombs and Donald L. Shaw, "The Agenda-Setting Function of Mass Media," *Public Opinion Quarterly* 36 (1972): 176–187; Jack M. McLeod, Lee B. Becker, and James E. Byrnes, "Another Look at the Agenda-Setting Function of the Press," *Communication Research* 1 (April 1974): 131–166; Lee B. Becker, Maxwell E. McCombs, and Jack M. McLeod, "The Development of Political Cognitions," in Steven H. Chaffee, ed., *Political Communication* (Beverly Hills, Calif.: Sage Publications, 1975), pp. 21–63, especially pp. 38–53; and Jay G. Blumler and Denis McQuail, *Television in Politics: Its Uses and Influence* (London: Faber, 1968).

constituting it? I work from the assumption that the mass media are, to say the least, a significant social force in the forming and delimiting of public assumptions, attitudes, and moods—of ideology, in short. They sometimes generate, sometimes amplify a field of legitimate discourse that shapes the public's "definitions of its situations," and they work through selections and omissions, through emphases and tones, through all their forms of treatment.

Such ideological force is central to the continuation of the established order. While I defer a fuller statement of this position until Part III, I take it for now that the central command structures of this order are an oligopolized, privately controlled corporate economy and its intimate ally, the bureaucratic national security state, together embedded within a capitalist world complex of nation-states. But the economic and political powers of twentieth-century capitalist society, while formidable, do not by themselves account for the society's persistence, do not secure the dominant institutions against the radical consequences of the system's deep and enduring conflicts. In the language of present-day social theory, why does the population accord legitimacy to the prevailing institutions? The goods are delivered, true; but why do citizens agree to identify themselves and to behave as consumers, devoting themselves to labor in a deteriorating environment in order to acquire private possessions and services as emblems of satisfaction? The answers are by no means self-evident. But however we approach these questions, the answers will have to be found in the realm of ideology, of culture in the broadest sense. Society is not a machine or a thing; it is a coexistence of human beings who do what they do (including maintaining or changing a social structure) as sentient, reasoning, moral, and active beings who experience the world, who are not simply "caused" by it. The patterned experiencing of the world takes place in the realm of what we call ideology. And any social theory of ideology asks two interlocking questions: How and where are ideas generated in society? And why are certain ideas accepted or rejected in varying degrees at different times?

In the version of Marxist theory inaugurated by Antonio Gramsci, *hegemony* is the name given to a ruling class's domination through ideology, through the shaping of popular consent.[7] More recently, Raymond Williams has transcended the classical Marxist

7. Antonio Gramsci, *Selections from the Prison Notebooks,* ed. and trans. Quintin Hoare and Geoffrey Nowell Smith (New York: International, 1971).

base–superstructure dichotomy (in which the "material base" of "forces and relations of production" "gives rise" to the ideological "superstructure"). Williams has proposed a notion of hegemony as "not only the articulate upper level of 'ideology,'" but "a whole body of practices and expectations" which "constitutes a sense of reality for most people in the society."[8] The main economic structures, or "relations of production," set limits on the ideologies and commonsense understandings that circulate as ways of making sense of the world—without mechanically "determining" them. The fact that the networks are capitalist corporations, for example, does not automatically decree the precise frame of a report on socialism, but it does preclude continuing, emphatic reports that would embrace socialism as the most reasonable framework for the solution of social problems. One need not accept all of Gramsci's analytic baggage to see the penetrating importance of the notion of hegemony—uniting persuasion from above with consent from below—for comprehending the endurance of advanced capitalist society. In particular, one need not accept a strictly Marxist premise that the "material base" of "forces of production" in *any* sense (even "ultimately") precedes culture.[9] But I retain Gramsci's core conception: those who rule the dominant institutions secure their power in large measure directly *and indirectly*, by impressing their definitions of the situation upon those they rule and, if not usurping the whole of ideological space, still significantly limiting what is thought throughout the society. The notion of hegemony that I am working with is an active one: hegemony operating through a complex web of social activities and institutional procedures. Hegemony is done by the dominant and collaborated in by the dominated.

Hegemonic ideology enters into everything people do and think is "natural"—making a living, loving, playing, believing, knowing, even rebelling. In every sphere of social activity, it meshes with the "common sense" through which people make the world seem intelligible; it tries to *become* that common sense. Yet, at the same time, people only partially and unevenly accept the he-

8. Raymond Williams, "Base and Superstructure in Marxist Cultural Theory," *New Left Review*, No. 82 (1973), pp. 3–16. See also Williams, *Marxism and Literature* (New York: Oxford University Press, 1977), especially pp. 108–114.

9. For a brilliant demonstration of ways in which culture helps *constitute* a given society's "material base," and in particular the way in which the bourgeois concept of utility conditions capitalism's claims to efficiency, see Marshall Sahlins, *Culture and Practical Reason* (Chicago: University of Chicago Press, 1976), Part 2.

gemonic terms; they stretch, dispute, and sometimes struggle to transform the hegemonic ideology. Indeed, its contents shift to a certain degree, as the desires and strategies of the top institutions shift, and as different coalitions form among the dominant social groups; in turn, these desires and strategies are modified, moderated by popular currents. In corporate capitalist society (and in state socialism as well), the schools and the mass media specialize in formulating and conveying national ideology. At the same time, indirectly, the media—at least in liberal capitalist society—take account of certain popular currents and pressures, symbolically incorporating them, repackaging and distributing them throughout the society. That is to say, groups out of power—radical students, farm workers, feminists, environmentalists, or homeowners groaning under the property tax—can contest the prevailing structures of power and definitions of reality. One strategy which insurgent social movements adopt is to make "news events."

The media create and relay images of order. Yet the social reality is enormously complex, fluid, and self-contradictory, even in its own terms. Movements constantly boil up out of the everyday suffering and grievance of dominated groups. From their sense of injury and their desire for justice, movements assert their interests, mobilize their resources, make their demands for reform, and try to find space to live their alternative "lifestyles." These *alternative* visions are not yet *oppositional*—not until they challenge the main structures and ideas of the existing order: the preeminence of the corporate economy, the militarized State, and authoritarian social relations as a whole. In liberal capitalist society, movements embody and exploit the fact that the dominant ideology enfolds contradictory values: liberty versus equality, democracy versus hierarchy, public rights versus property rights, rational claims to truth versus the arrogations and mystifications of power.[10] Then how does enduring ideology find its way into the news, absorbing and ironing out contradictions with relative consistency? How, in particular, are rather standardized frames clamped onto the reporting of insurgent movements? For the most part, through journalists' routines.

These routines are structured in the ways journalists are socialized from childhood, and then trained, recruited, assigned, edited, rewarded, and promoted on the job; they decisively shape the

10. I adapt this argument from my "Prime Time Ideology: The Hegemonic Process in Television Entertainment," *Social Problems* 26 (February 1979): 264–265.

ways in which news is defined, events are considered newsworthy, and "objectivity" is secured. News is managed routinely, automatically, as reporters import definitions of newsworthiness from editors and institutional beats, as they accept the analytical frameworks of officials even while taking up adversary positions. When reporters make decisions about what to cover and how, rarely do they deliberate about ideological assumptions or political consequences.[11] Simply by doing their jobs, journalists tend to serve the political and economic elite definitions of reality.

But there are disruptive moments, critical times when the routines no longer serve a coherent hegemonic interest. The routines produce news that no longer harmonizes with the hegemonic ideology, or with important elite interests as the elites construe them; or the elites are themselves so divided as to quarrel over the content of the news. (In the extreme case, as in Chile in 1973, the hegemonic ideology is pushed to the extremity of its self-contradiction, and snaps; the dominant frame then shifts dramatically, in that case toward the Right.) At these critical moments, political and economic elites (including owners and executives of media corporations) are more likely to intervene directly in journalistic routine, attempting to keep journalism within harness. To put it another way, the cultural apparatus normally maintains its own momentum, its own standards and procedures, which grant it a certain independence from top political and economic elites. In a liberal capitalist society, this bounded but real independence helps legitimate the institutional order as a whole and the news in particular. But the elites prefer not to let such independence stretch "too far." It serves the interests of the elites as long as it is "relative," as long as it does not violate core hegemonic values or contribute too heavily to radical critique or social unrest. (It is the elites who determine, or establish routines to determine, what goes "too far.") Yet when elites are themselves at odds in important ways, and when core values are deeply disputed—as happened in the sixties—journalism itself becomes contested. Opposition groups pressing for social and political change can exploit self-contradictions in hegemonic ideology, including its journalistic codes. Society-wide

11. As Gaye Tuchman writes, "news both draws upon and reproduces institutional structures" (*Making News*, p. 210). For particulars, see Leon V. Sigal, *Reporters and Officials: The Organization and Politics of Newsmaking* (Lexington, Mass.: D. C. Heath, 1973); Bernard Roshco, *Newsmaking* (Chicago: University of Chicago Press, 1975); and most fully, Herbert Gans, *Deciding What's News* (New York: Pantheon, 1979).

conflict is then carried into the cultural institutions, though in muted and sanitized forms. And then ideological domestication plays an important part—along with the less visible activities of the police[12]—in taming and isolating ideological threats to the system.

The test of such a line of argument, of course, is whether it makes sense of evidence, whether it comprehends historical truth. Most of this book sorts out evidence in the course of telling the particular story of major media and the New Left in the 1960s. One set of questions I ask addresses *the nature of media coverage*. Just how did major media respond to the emergence of student radicalism? Which events and rhetorical gestures were considered newsworthy, and what were the reasons? What were the major themes and tones of this coverage, and how did they shift over time? To what extent were these shifts determined by shifts in the actual policies and actions of the movement? (Methodological difficulties notwithstanding, there is no avoiding the attempt to discover and describe *what actually happened*.) I try first to locate the central emphases in coverage of the movement, and then to reach behind them to grasp the media's central—usually unspoken—assumptions about the political world and about political opposition in particular.[13] For

12. Very little has been written on direct relations between police agencies and the mass media. Gans (*Deciding What's News*, p. 121) makes the valuable point that "perhaps the most able sources are organizations that carry out the equivalent of investigative reporting, offer the results of their work as 'exclusives,' and can afford to do so anonymously, foregoing the rewards of publicity." For a survey of the FBI's COINTELPRO media operations, especially active in New York, Chicago, Los Angeles, and Milwaukee, at least between 1956 and 1971, and a few extant details of direct cooperation between the FBI and reporters, see Chip Berlet, "COINTELPRO: What the (Deleted) Was It? Media Op," *The Public Eye* 1 (April 1978): 28–38. I know of no evidence of cooperation between the FBI and either CBS News or the *New York Times*, but this entire field is *terra incognita*.

13. A fine precedent for thematically analyzing media coverage of a movement's activities, and the sources of this coverage in the organizational activities and assumptions of news-gatherers, is James D. Halloran, Philip Elliott, and Graham Murdock, *Demonstrations and Communication: A Case Study* (Harmondsworth, England: Penguin Books, 1970), which closely follows British newspaper and television coverage of the giant October 1968 anti–Vietnam War demonstration in London. Also relevant is Stanley Cohen's study of the media-aided "social construction" of Mod and Rocker teenage gangs in the early sixties, *Folk Devils and Moral Panics* (London: MacGibbon and Kee, 1972). Several of the essays in Stanley Cohen and Jock Young, eds., *The Manufacture of News: A Reader* (London: Constable, 1973; and Beverly Hills, Calif.: Sage Publications, 1973) give useful informal textual analyses of media frames for deviant activities; see also Charles Winick, ed., *Deviance and Mass Media* (Beverly Hills, Calif.: Sage Publications, 1978). The existence of systematic news frames for political events is demonstrated empirically in Harvey

before messages can have "effects" on audiences, they must emanate outward from message-producers and then into the audience's minds, there to be interpreted. The recent flurry of concern with "the effects of television" selects out certain aspects of the message (violence, say) as *the* content, then masks this selectivity with the trappings of quantitative methodology. Since the media aim at least to influence, condition, and reproduce the activity of audiences by reaching into the symbolic organization of thought, the student of mass media must pay attention to the symbolic content of media messages before the question of effects can even be sensibly posed. These questions about how the media treated the movement constitute the agenda of Part I, tested on the case of Students for a Democratic Society (SDS)—and, for comparison, other segments of the antiwar movement—in the year SDS first became public, 1965. I organize this discussion chronologically to call attention to both regularities and shifts of journalistic frame.

But the movement was far from the passive object of media attentions. The study of mass communications effects has had quite enough of Pavlovian stimulus-response psychology, along with its pluralist opposite. Although I may sometimes adopt the convenient language of a single cause producing a single effect, I am talking not about determined objects "having impacts" on each other, as if movements and media were billiard balls, but about an *active* movement and *active* media pressing on each other, sometimes deliberately, sometimes not, in a process rich with contradiction and self-contradiction, a process developing in historical time.

A second set of questions, then, concerns *what the New Left did*

Molotch and Marilyn Lester, "News as Purposive Behavior: On the Strategic Use of Routine Events, Scandals, and Rumors," *American Sociological Review* 39 (1974): 101–112, and is extended to media treatment of opposition movements in Molotch's "Media and Movements," unpublished paper, 1977. Several essays by Stuart Hall also contain rich semiological "readings" of media programs, especially in television; see especially his "Encoding and Decoding in the Television Discourse," and Stuart Hall, Ian Connell, and Lidia Curti, "The 'Unity' of Public Affairs Television," *Working Papers in Cultural Studies* 9 (Spring 1976): 51–93, both forthcoming in Stuart Hall, *Reproducing Ideologies* (London: Macmillan). An attempt at a more systematic interpretive scheme for television programs may be found in John Fiske and John Hartley, *Reading Television* (London: Methuen, 1978); see also my review in *Theory and Society*, forthcoming. My earlier discussions of television's frames for the New Left may be found in Gitlin, "Fourteen Notes on Television and the Movement," *Leviathan* 1 (July–August 1969): 3–9; "Sixteen Notes on Television and the Movement," in George Abbott White and Charles Newman, eds., *Literature in Revolution* (New York: Holt, Rinehart and Winston, 1972) pp. 335–366; and "Spotlights and Shadows" (note 2, above).

about media treatment. Once floodlit, from 1965 on, the New Left found it necessary to take the media into account in planning actions, choosing leaders, responding to those leaders, and articulating positions. What tensions developed within the movement about how to approach the media, and how were they resolved or surpassed? How did the New Left's approach to the media change over time, and from leadership generation to leadership generation?

And here we fade into a third set of questions. *What were the consequences of media coverage for the movement—for its structure, its leadership, its politics, its strategy and tactics—for the history, the texture, and the feeling tone of the New Left?* This second and third set of questions, applied mostly to SDS between 1965 and 1970, constitute the agenda for Part II.

Two general questions hover beneath the surface of these particular accounts. First, *why did the media do what they did?* In reporting the movement, how important were routine journalistic practices, organizational arrangements, the specific (and changing) institutional interests of the news media, the society's wider (and also changing) political and economic structures, and the ideological surroundings, needs, and consequences of those structures? How was the media treatment of movements like, and how unlike, their treatment of any other social happening accorded the dignity of a continuing story? These issues filter back into the question of structure: What is the place of the cultural apparatus and its ideological constructions among the major social institutions in ensemble?

And no less important: *Why did the movement do what it did?* Just how important was media treatment in turning the movement in this or that political direction, and how important were class identity, ideology, organizational structure, State repression, and the play of political events and deliberate choices? All these shaped the New Left, and each mattered in the context of the others. I am most emphatically not propounding a new single-factor political analysis; but I am scrutinizing one feature of a whole history in order to cast light on the whole. I want to ask, finally: How far can the SDS experience with the media be generalized to other movements at other times? These questions are the business of Part III.

This is a study of the nature, sources, and consequences of news. It is also one point of entry into a rethinking of the New

Left's moment in history. I aim to contribute to a new reckoning with the much-mythologized sixties, already fast receding either into oblivion or into convenient distortion. For neo-conservative historiography and the unreconstructed Nixonian Right, the New Left was a catastrophic upsurge of adversary culture gone anti-American and wild. For fashionable popular writers, it was a moment of puerility, adolescent enthusiasm, and naivete, a fad at last discarded. For the current generation of Marxist-Leninists, it was a petit bourgeois adventure needing to be purged of its "moralistic," "idealist," "reformist" elements before the true road to revolution could emerge into clean, hard, twentieth-century light. For many who participated, and their younger brothers and sisters, it was perhaps a noble crusade that failed, perhaps a vaguely interesting or dangerous tumult. For the younger still, nothing remains but the shadow of a reputation, a rumor conditioned by media images of something that mysteriously came, made trouble, and went. Without writing a memoir, a collective biography, or a political chronicle, I hope to show something of the New Left as a movement, a motion in history: that is, a coherent process wherein organizations and individuals, making choices in specific situations, mattered. I approach this history as the story of a movement in its lived richness; at the same time, I distill from this story analytic categories which extend beyond the particular events of a particular decade.

I cannot do justice to the whole of the movement. Since my point of entry is the movement's collision with the large-scale commercial media, there are very important dimensions of the movement's history and cultural identity which I do not discuss at all. Not least, there are the movement's *own* media, the hundreds of weekly photo-offset "underground" papers that sprang up in the later sixties and early seventies. Nor do I discuss the role of other cultural and communication institutions that served the movement: its own internal newspapers and magazines; political weeklies like *The Guardian*; monthlies like *Ramparts*; the Liberation News Service; or Newsreel filmmaking and film distributing collectives. I do not trace the movement's ideological career in much detail, nor many of its political choices and settings, nor the contingencies of political developments outside the largely white, largely youthful sector of the New Left. *I never mean to suggest that the movement's interior culture was purely the creature of media images, or that movement people were wholly or even largely dependent on them for information and bearings.* I offer *one* approach to a recomprehending of the New Left's experience; and I would like it to take its place among others, together to give the sixties their due.

In looking at the movement-media dance, of course, I had to limit my attention within each domain. The reader who wishes fuller information about my choices and procedures should consult the Appendix. But briefly: as for the movement, I've drawn most of my particulars from the history of Students for a Democratic Society during the half-decade it operated under the media spotlight. At points I've supplemented this history with information about other New Left groups during the same period. SDS was the main national organization of the white New Left during most of this period; it was also the major field of my own political work in the mid-sixties. Much reflected upon and reconsidered, my experience in SDS primed me to ask questions about the movement-media relation, about the nature of media coverage, and about its consequences for the movement. I participated in demonstrations— and helped organize them—and then followed the television and newspaper and newsmagazine versions; the disjuncture, the shock of nonrecognition, raised wrenching questions about media frames. I worked in a movement and watched it construed as something quite other than what I thought it was. Living with the discrepancy became one characteristic experience of my generation; we had, after all, grown up to take on faith what was in the newspapers, and to believe with Walter Cronkite that "that's the way it is." This continuing experience of disjuncture gave me my agenda for research; it did not give me answers.

As for the media, I was also compelled to make choices. As is usually the case in social research, theoretical considerations and practical exigencies intertwined to create my field of exploration, my "data base." For several reasons I centered on CBS News and the *New York Times*: they were influential in powerful circles *and* inside the movement, they were in some sense the best of the mainstream media (and we expected the best of them), and their archives are relatively accessible. So most of my reflections on the sources of news treatment concern these institutions in particular. I take up the reasons, the limits of my samples and conclusions, and the problems of extending them in the Appendix.

One more prefatory note. I study news here, except for brief digressions into TV documentary and film. News is one component of popular culture; the study of news should ultimately be enfolded within a more ample study of all the forms of cultural production and their ideology. Television entertainment is also an ideological field, and must have played a part in formulating and crystallizing the cultural tendencies of the sixties; surely it deserves extensive treatment of its own.[14] So do other cultural forms, including popular songs, popular fiction (genre novels as well as magazine stories), jokes, and popular films (which are not necessarily the acclaimed films which critics prefer to see and to analyze); so do the careers of pop stars like Bob Dylan and Joan Baez, the San Francisco bands and hip heroes who stood somewhere on the thin and fluid boundary between the New Left and the counterculture. Let popular culture have its analytic due: we live in it.

14. Considering the great amount of time Americans and others spend watching TV entertainment, there is a great imbalance in sociological attention: many more studies have been done of the production and meanings of news, which is more transparently available for political understandings, than of everyday fiction. I have sketched some preliminary categories for the analysis of TV entertainment conventions in "Prime Time Ideology," (note 10, above). On TV entertainment and its evolution in general, there is abundant material in Erik Barnouw's *The Image Empire* (New York: Oxford University Press, 1970), *Tube of Plenty* (New York: Oxford University Press, 1975), and *The Sponsor* (New York: Oxford University Press, 1978); in Fiske and Hartley, *Reading Television*, and Hall, "Encoding and Decoding in the Television Discourse," both cited in note 13, above; and in Rose K. Goldsen, *The Show and Tell Machine* (New York: Dial Press, 1977), though many analytic questions remain. On the content and history of specific shows and types of show, see Danny Czitrom, "Bilko: A Sitcom for All Seasons," *Cultural Correspondence* 4 (Spring 1977): 16–19; Todd Gitlin, "The Televised Professional," *Social Policy*, November–December 1977, pp. 94–99; Pete Knutson, "Dragnet: The Perfect Crime?" *Liberation* 18 (May 1974): 28–31; Michael R. Real, *Mass-Mediated Culture* (Englewood Cliffs, N.J.: Prentice-Hall, 1977), pp. 118–139 (on medical shows); and Bob Schneider, "Spelling's Salvation Armies," *Cultural Correspondence*, No. 4 (Spring 1977): 27–36 (on police shows). On soap operas, see Dennis Porter, "Soap Time: Thoughts on a Commodity Art Form," *College English* 38 (April 1977): 782–788. On the production process, see Muriel G. Cantor, *The Hollywood TV Producer* (New York: Basic Books, 1971); Les Brown, *Television: The Business Behind the Box* (New York: Harcourt Brace Jovanovich, 1971); and Gaye Tuchman, "Assembling a Network Talk-Show," in Tuchman, ed., *The TV Establishment* (Englewood Cliffs, N.J.: Prentice-Hall, 1974), pp. 119–135.

I Images of a Movement

1 Preliminaries

At the beginning of 1965, Students for a Democratic Society consisted of fewer than fifteen hundred paid-up members and a few dozen more or less active chapters on campuses in the United States. Within a year the membership had tripled, and the number of active chapters had also grown considerably. This boom was the most dramatic in the organization's history: never before or afterward did SDS grow so fast. But numbers only begin to suggest the change. SDS was becoming a mass student organization and a public political fact. By numbers, by spirit, by the acclamation of friends and enemies alike, SDS was the central student organization in a rising New Left.

The year 1965 was a pivotal one in the history of SDS, and in the student movement as a whole: pivotal both in reality and in the realm of publicity. SDS organized the first major national demonstration against the Vietnam war, and then failed to lead the antiwar movement that was burgeoning. Politically, SDS moved away from its social-democratic progenitors, eliminating its anti-Communist exclusion principle for members. Organizationally, SDS was tense with generational conflict as a new ideological and geographical wave began to displace the founding generation.

Also during 1965, SDS was discovered by the national media. As SDS became a famous and infamous national name and the germ of a national political force, publicity came to be a dimension of its identity, a component of its reality. By the end of that year, an SDS program that barely existed was front-page news all over the country, and SDS was being denounced by members of the Senate and by the attorney general of the United States. In 1965, SDS changed irreversibly from an organization that recruited its elites and communicated its ideas face to face, to an organization that lived in the glare of publicity and recruited both elites and members on the basis of reputations refracted in large part through the channels of mass media. The nature of that publicity changed too, over time; but the spotlight remained, an invariant fact that for the rest of the movement's life had to be taken into account. For the next several years, the student movement faded in and faded out—even the cinematic language seems appropriate—under the globular eye of the mass media. Its actions were shaped in part by the codes of mass media operations. It conducted its activities in a social world that recognized it, liked it, and disliked it through media images, media versions of its events and rhetoric. To some extent the movement even recognized *itself* through mass-mediated images. In 1965, then, the spotlight was turned on for good. As different filters were clamped onto the floodlamp, it changed colors; the movement tried, at times, to place its own filters onto the lamp, or to set up its own; but the spotlight was there to stay.

Because 1965 was the year in which media discovered SDS and the national New Left, I examine that year's media coverage in considerable detail. I look at every *New York Times* story about SDS and antiwar activity in general, and every CBS News piece to be found in the sole remaining archive. My approach is historical and detailed because the process was historical and singular. It was not simply—as is implied if not stated in some analyses—a predictable reflex of invariant media *structures* or movement structures, or a preordained interaction between them. As movement and media discovered and acted on each other, they worked out the terms with which they would recognize and work on the other; they developed a grammar of interaction. This grammar then shaped the way the movement-media history developed over the rest of the decade, opening certain possibilities and excluding others. As the movement developed, so did the media approaches to it, so that the media's structures of cognition and interpretation never stayed entirely fixed. The analysis must therefore attend closely to the precise historical experience.

It bears emphasis that the media treatment of the movement and the movement approach to the media were themselves *situated*, sewn into an historical context. Movements and media are not creatures of each other; they work on each other, but, as Marx said in another connection, not in conditions of their own making. In the accounts that follow, I have tried to insist on the larger context, especially where I could do so without violence to the flow of the narrative argument. But let me insist at the start on the importance of the national political situation. It must never be forgotten that the period I am talking about in Part I is Lyndon B. Johnson's administration; it is particularly and emphatically the time when the administration dramatically escalated the war in Vietnam and, simultaneously, opened up the Great Society program at home. My discussion of publicity's effects on the movement in Part II is equally inseparable from the history of the Johnson and Nixon years, from the continuing war abroad and the blockage of liberal reform at home.

Chapter 1 summarizes the early history of SDS, and the nature of the frames—the core principles of selection, exclusion, emphasis, and valuation—which major media used to cover SDS in 1965. Chapter 2 is devoted to specific analyses of every extant CBS and *New York Times* treatment of SDS in the spring of that year, especially in covering the sit-in against Chase Manhattan Bank loans to South Africa in March and the first substantial national demonstration against the Vietnam war in April. Chapter 3 continues the narrative into the fall, and then proceeds to widen the analytic scope. The issue is no longer simply the media version of SDS, but SDS's struggle to repossess its image. That fall, the media helped amplify right-wing and Johnson administration attacks on SDS. Vulnerable, SDS tried to go onto the offensive. For the first time, the movement's image became an object of contestation. Chapter 3 examines the first phases of that contestation.

Especially in Chapter 2, the details are profuse for several reasons; most will be found in the methodological Appendix, but one deserves a note here. The historical record has value and interest in itself. The early history of the New Left has already sunk into oblivion; popular belief has it that the antiwar movement began in the late sixties, and that protest against American corporate support of South African apartheid began in the mid-seventies. In many quarters, not only the journalistic but the academic, "the New Left" has become synonymous with the wilder actions of the late sixties and early seventies, or with one or another tendency in Marxist thought. The earlier, more original New Left vanishes, or is annexed, after the fact, to the era of trashing, bomb blasts, and Leninist organizations. And what is forgotten along with the makeup and the objectives of the original New Left is the nature of its reception. I had myself taken part in the events discussed here; I had read some of the newspapers and watched some of the broadcasts at the time; but as a researcher reading through the old clippings and screening the old film-clips, I was sometimes astounded to see what the New York Times or CBS News had been saying about SDS in 1965. A few times I was impressed by accuracy or sensitivity, but more often by derogation. If my own sense of what the media had been doing in 1965 needed a series of confrontations with documented fact, I reasoned, my readers might also find the recollection illuminating.

THE STRUGGLE OVER IMAGES

What was the course of the media-movement relation in 1965?

For their different reasons, the media and the movement needed each other. The media needed stories, preferring the dramatic; the movement needed publicity for recruitment, for support, and for political effect. Each could be useful to the other; each had effects, intended and unintended, on the other. As Herbert Gans has written more generally: "In any modern society in which a number of classes, ethnic and religious groups, age groups and political interests struggle among each other for control over the society's resources, there is also a struggle for the power to determine or influence the society's values, myths, symbols, and information." [1] The struggle of movement groups with reporters and media institutions was one instance of a larger and constant struggle; so was, and is, the continual jockeying in which elements of the State intervene to shape or constrict media content. The interaction not only existed in history, it *had* a history. At times, movement and media were symbiotic, at times antagonistic. We can even detect distinct, though overlapping, phases. At first the mass media disregarded the movement; then media discovered the movement; the movement cooperated with media; media presented the movement in patterned ways; the quality and slant of these patterns changed; different parts of the movement responded in different ways; elements of the State intervened to shape this coverage. These were "moments" in a single, connected process, in which movement participants, media institutions and the State—them-

1. Herbert Gans, "The Politics of Culture in America: A Sociological Analysis," in Denis McQuail, ed., *Sociology of Mass Communications* (Harmondsworth, England: Penguin Books, 1972), p. 373.

selves internally conflicted—struggled over the terms of coverage: struggled to define the movement and the nature of political reality around it.

In the single pivotal year 1965, the media-movement relationship went through a number of transformations. For each phase, the central questions are: Who took the initiative? Why? How was each move received by the other side and countered? What conflicts developed within each side? Why did the phase end? To clarify the historical account, I first summarize, schematically, these earlier phases of media-movement history.

In the struggle over the right and the power to define the public images of the movement in 1965, one can discern five essential phases:

I. Starting in 1960, and up through the late winter of 1965, SDS was not covered by major news media. For its part, SDS did not actively, forcefully, or consistently seek major media coverage. That was not the way a political organization got started. As SDS's first president and national secretary Alan Haber says about the period 1960–62: "The coverage wasn't much and I didn't feel much about it. The kind of stuff we did wasn't organizing demonstrations where we'd look and see what they said about it. . . . SDS was not media-oriented." [2] And for their part, the media were simply not interested in an organization so small and tame. SDS had 19 chapters on paper (of which 6 were real) and 610 members in October 1963; 29 chapters and almost 1,000 members in June 1964; but 80 chapters and more than 2,000 members in June 1965; and 124 chapters and 4,300 members by the end of 1965. [3]

In SDS's early days, organizers visited campuses and expounded SDS's declaration of values, its political analysis and programs. *The Port Huron Statement*, adopted by SDS at its 1962 convention, argued from the human capacity for reason to the necessity of participatory democracy: "People should make the decisions that affect their lives." The analysis centered on the failure of corporate liberalism, the bankruptcy of both the Old Left and the New Deal, the inadequacy of the welfare state, and the destructiveness and obsolescence of the Cold War; it celebrated the promise of the civil rights movement and the breakdown of the Cold War consensus; and it proclaimed the need for "local insurgency"

2. Interview, Alan Haber, December 9, 1976.
3. These figures are taken from Kirkpatrick Sale's extraordinarily accurate *SDS* (New York: Random House, 1973), pp. 119, 122, 193, 246.

and the special role of students as galvanizers of radical activity. SDS mimeographed and distributed dozens of its own publications and sought to move liberals and local activists toward a more radical, coherent understanding of the world. One SDS leader from that time, Richard Flacks, remembers "there was a general assumption that since we weren't part of the Establishment, we wouldn't be covered by the Establishment media." Rather, SDS gradually became a distinct voice of campus radicalism, known for ideas summed up in phrases like "participatory democracy" and "the issues are interrelated," associated with the force and presence of some of its leaders. If it was a small voice, why should it be otherwise? This was a "network of individuals." As Flacks recalls, "We didn't have much pretension about being a mass organization":

Instead, there was a general sense of progress being made in expanding the circle of people hearing the message. Partly, of course, through our activity on campuses, but also because of our increasing access to liberal organizations. We could go to the peace movement or the civil rights movement and get a hearing from those groups and influence the way they looked at the issues.

To get its ideas across to a fragmented, scattered left and to left-liberal groups, "what SDS wanted was to get written up in left oriented small circulation things," not the mass press. If anything, the prevailing attitudes toward mass media were disdain and suspicion. Celebrities were distrusted. "We weren't even in that world," as Flacks says. "Why would any of the media be interested in SDS?"[4]

For their part, the media paid little attention. SDS did not perform photogenically; it did not mobilize large numbers of people; it did not undertake flamboyant actions. It was not, in a word, newsworthy.

II. In the late winter of 1965, after the independent upwelling of the Berkeley Free Speech Movement, the media discovered SDS. A few reporters took the initiative, and, SDS, for its part, cooperated actively. That winter, a sympathetic reporter, Fred Powledge of the *New York Times*, on his own initiative, wrote at length and respectfully about SDS's politics and approach, heralding the emergence of a "new student left." Powledge's article, published in the

4. Interview, Richard Flacks, January 9, 1977.

Times of March 15, 1965, certified student radicalism as a live national issue. The SDS leadership of 1964–65 showed a growing interest in large-scale student organization and in publicity, but was far from organizing actions or propounding slogans for the sake of "how they would look." Under National Secretary C. Clark Kissinger, the National Office began to send out press releases more regularly, and, especially after the steady bombing of North Vietnam started in February, members of the SDS elite began for the first time to entertain thoughts of a *mass* student movement.[5] Still, SDS did not envisage a central role for the press in the process. Indeed, its own communications were scanty and improvised. The National Office published an irregular mimeographed monthly *Bulletin*, and sent newsy biweekly "Work List" mailings to key local and national activists; there were phone and mail contacts with chapters and individual members, and occasional visits by "campus travelers" and speechmakers; but SDS did not publish its own weekly newspaper until January 1966.

III. With the SDS March on Washington on April 17, 1965, student antiwar protest—and SDS activity in particular—became big news. Now reporters began to seek out SDS leaders and to cover protest events. That spring, major articles on the New Left appeared in newsmagazines (*Newsweek*, *Time*, *U.S. News & World Report*), large-circulation weeklies (the *Saturday Evening Post*, the *New York Times Magazine*), and liberal weeklies (the *Nation*, the *New Republic*, the *Reporter*); and television news produced its own survey pieces. The movement was amplified.

But which movement? The observer changed the position of the observed. The amplification was already selective: it emphasized certain themes and scanted others. Deprecatory themes began to emerge, then to recur and reverberate. The earliest framing devices were these:

- *trivialization* (making light of movement language, dress, age, style, and goals);
- *polarization* (emphasizing *counter*demonstrations, and balancing the antiwar movement against ultra-Right and neo-Nazi groups as equivalent "extremists");
- *emphasis on internal dissension*;
- *marginalization* (showing demonstrators to be deviant or unrepresentative);

5. Ibid.; and telephone interview, Mike Davis, February 15, 1977.

- *disparagement by numbers* (under-counting);
- *disparagement of the movement's effectiveness*.

In the fall, as parts of the antiwar movement turned to more militant tactics, new themes and devices were added to the first group:

- *reliance on statements by government officials and other authorities;*
- *emphasis on the presence of Communists;*
- *emphasis on the carrying of "Viet Cong" flags;*
- *emphasis on violence in demonstrations;*
- *delegitimizing use of quotation marks* around terms like "peace march";
- *considerable attention to right-wing opposition to the movement,* especially from the administration and other politicians.

Some of this framing can be attributed to traditional assumptions in news treatment: news concerns the *event*, not the underlying condition; the *person*, not the group; *conflict*, not consensus; the fact that *"advances the story,"* not the one that explains it. Some of this treatment descends from norms for the coverage of deviance in general: the archetypical news story is a crime story, and an opposition movement is ordinarily, routinely, and unthinkingly treated as a sort of crime. Some of the treatment follows from organizational and technical features of news coverage—which in turn are not ideologically neutral. Editors assign reporters to beats where news is routinely framed by officials; the stories then absorb the officials' definitions of the situation.[6] And editors and reporters also adapt and reproduce the dominant ideological assumptions prevailing in the wider society. All these practices are anchored in organizational policy, in recruitment and promotion: that is to say, in the internal structure of institutional power and decision. And when all these sources are taken into account, some of the framing will still not be explained unequivocally; some must be understood as the product of specifically political transactions, cases of editorial judgment and the interventions of political elites. The proportion of a given frame that emanates from each of these sources varies from story to story; that is why stories have to be scrutinized

---

6. See Leon V. Sigal, *Reporters and Officials: The Organization and Politics of News-making* (Lexington, Mass.: D. C. Heath, 1973), p. 47 and chap. 6; Harvey Molotch and Marilyn Lester, "Accidental News: The Great Oil Spill as Local Occurrence and National Event," *American Journal of Sociology* 81 (September 1965): 235–260; and Herbert Gans, *Deciding What's News* (New York: Pantheon, 1979), chap. 4.

one by one, as concretely as possible, before we can begin to compose general theories.

When we examine stories closely, we discover that there were exceptional moments of coverage within both the *Times* and CBS News. Not only was there—within the boundaries of the norms—some latitude for expressions of individual idiosyncrasy, for random perturbations within the general terms of the code; there were also larger conflicts within the news organizations about how to cover the movement, conflicts that were fought and resolved in different ways at different times. The overall effect of media coverage was blurred and contradictory; there was not a single voice. But increasingly the impression was conveyed that extremism was rampant and that the New Left was dangerous to the public good.

In short, the media were far from mirrors passively reflecting facts found in the real world. The facts reported were out there in the real world, true: out there *among others*. The media reflection was more the active, patterned remaking performed by mirrors in a fun house.

IV. As media actively engaged the movement, an adversary symbiosis developed. Within the movement, arguments emerged about how best to cope with the new situation. Some groupings within the movement stayed on the defensive; others turned to the offense. In neither case was it possible to ignore the media spotlight, or to turn it at will to the movement's own uses.

Some movement organizers responded casually, at first, to the media's attentions. Their commitment to face-to-face organization remained primary; in their view, the press would play a secondary role in transmitting news and images to uncommitted publics. They were working within a pre-spotlight organizational form; they were eager to maintain the movement's own distinct communication channels. But in the fall of 1965, media attention and right-wing attacks caught them by surprise. The strategy they improvised called for a sort of judo operation: using the weight of the adversary to bring him down. They would use the unsought media attention to amplify the antiwar message. They began to speak into the symbolic microphone.

Others, committed to an antiwar movement before all else, and operating mostly outside SDS, began to organize symbolic events deliberately to attract the media spotlight. Very small groups of draft-card burners could leap to national prominence. Three pacifists, trying to awaken a national conscience, immolated themselves and died. Some within SDS proposed attention-getting actions—later called "media events"—that would, they hoped, place the issue of the war at the focus of national politics. Galvanizing opposition, even repression, from the administration or from the political Right could be a means to that end.

V. As the spotlight kept on burning, media treatment entered into the movement's internal life. The media helped recruit into SDS new members and backers who expected to find there what they saw on television or read in the papers. The flood of new members tended to be different from the first SDS generation—less intellectual, more activist, more deeply estranged from the dominant institutions. Politically, many of them cared more about antiwar activity than about the broad-gauged, long-haul, multi-issued politics of the earlier SDS. They were only partially assimilated into the existing organization; they viewed the SDS leaders, the remnants of the founding generation, with suspicion. The newcomers overwhelmed SDS's fragile institutions, which had been created for a tiny organization, a network of so-called Old Guard elite clusters living in intense political and personal community. The fragile person-to-person net of organizational continuity was torn.

This new generation coursed into SDS in the wake of the April 1965 antiwar march, and by June 1966 they had moved into the key positions of leadership. They were known as the Prairie Power people, underscoring—and at times exaggerating—their non-Northeastern, non-elite origins. True, this generation *did* differ from the founders in many ways; the distinction cannot be laid purely and simply at the door of the media and their selectivities. For one thing, the Old Guard elite had already graduated from college, many from elite colleges at that; many had moved into Northern ghettoes as community organizers. Most of the new leaders, by contrast, were still students at state universities. Coming from more conservative regions, Texas and the Great Plains primarily, many of the new generation had become radical quickly, because even mild rebellion against right-wing authority—hair grown slightly long, language grown obscene, or the like—provoked repression. If one were to be punished for small things, it was only a small step to declaring oneself an outlaw in earnest, a communist, a revolutionary: as soon be hanged for a sheep as a goat. So, as cultural rebels, they tended to skip the stage of consciousness that marked the Old Guard generation and informed its politics: a *radical disappointment* with existing liberal institutions, liberal promises, and liberal hopes. In style, too, they declared their deep disaffection from the prevailing culture: many were shaggy in appearance, they smoked dope, they had read less, they went for broke. Even Northeastern members of the Prairie Power leadership shared the new style.

The media not only helped produce and characterize this sharp break within SDS, but they proceeded to play it up; in so doing, they magnified its importance—both to the outside world and inside the organization. When it happened that, as the former SDS National Secretary wrote in December 1965, "chapters, regional offices, and members find out what the organization is doing by reading the newspapers," [7] mass-mediated images were fixing (in the photographic sense) the terms for internal debate; they were helping define the organization's situation for it. Again, none of this happened in a vacuum. The drastic escalation in the war was at the same time pushing many people, both in and out of SDS, toward greater militancy, greater estrangement from dominant American values. The default of liberal forces isolated the whole generation of radical youth, pushing them toward the left. Larger cultural forces were nourishing the possibility of a deviant counterculture. But the media blitz, by amplifying and speeding all these processes, prevented SDS from assimilating them. The organization tried—and failed. Thus the internal frailties that were later to undo the organization were already built in at the moment of its greatest growth and vigor. In its beginning as a mass organization was its end.

7. C. Clark Kissinger, quoted in Sale, *SDS*, p. 255.

2 Versions of SDS, Spring 1965

DISCOVERING SDS

The *New York Times*'s frames for the New Left shifted in the course of 1965. At the beginning, the *Times* set out a respectful exposition of SDS's activities and goals; then it proceeded to trivialize and denigrate the movement. By the fall, unflattering themes had become prominent: SDS was now viewed as extremist, deviant, and dangerous. Though there was no straight-line evolution from respect to hostility, there was a definite tilt in the emphasis and proportions. As for CBS News, the other major news operation I examined closely, extant records of its coverage are fragmentary (see Appendix), but among the newsfilm pieces that survive for analysis there is a somewhat different mixture of framing themes, ranging from the quietly respectful to the ambiguously sensational and the deprecatory.

When the *Times* first discovered SDS, in February 1965, the organization had existed for some five years.[1] In 1960, as a small network of radical and left-liberal students, it had helped coordinate support activity on Northern campuses for the Southern civil rights movement. In 1962, it had promulgated a statement of principles and politics, the Port Huron Statement, which gained a significant degree of respect among activists on campuses throughout the country—and tumultuous opposition from SDS's parent organization, the social-democratic League for Industrial Democracy. SDS had organized conferences on civil rights and poverty. In the

1. See Kirkpatrick Sale, *SDS* (New York: Random House, 1973), pp. 15–172.

summer of 1965, it had placed into the field eight or ten community organizing projects in the slums of Northern cities. It had helped organize (with Campus Americans for Democratic Action) left-liberal caucuses at the summer conventions of the National Student Association. It had organized national support and arranged speaking tours for the Berkeley Free Speech Movement. During this entire period, the SDS national headquarters had been located in Manhattan.

On January 2, 1965, SDS sent out a brief press release announcing its sponsorship of an April 17 march in Washington against "American intervention in the Vietnamese civil war." The *Times* did not pick it up.

On February 7, 1965, the administration of Lyndon B. Johnson launched into the systematic bombing of North Vietnam. Almost immediately, students around the country were moved to demonstrate. Seeing a need to centralize information about these demonstrations, and an opportunity to boost SDS's prominence as a coordinator of student antiwar activities, SDS National Secretary C. Clark Kissinger (no relation to the future Secretary of State) sent out, on February 11, a lengthy press release itemizing student protests and repeating that SDS planned an April 17 March on Washington to End the War in Vietnam. Reporting this action in a Work List mailing to the SDS hard core, Kissinger explained:

The first phase of our activities was an attempt to break through the almost total black-out at the national level of the dozens of student protest demonstrations which were going on about the country. Acting as a clearing house for information, SDS sent out several hundred press releases to organizations, wire-services, and all major campus newspapers.[2]

Perhaps as a response to this publicity operation, the *Times*, on Saturday, February 18, 1965, printed what was—at least according to the *New York Times* index[3]—its first mention of Students for a Democratic Society. The page 2 story by Martin Arnold, a general assignment city reporter, was headlined "14 ARRESTED HERE IN VIETNAM MOVE." In the tenth paragraph of a story about the logis-

2. SDS Work List Mailing, Vol. 2, No. 3½, February 13, 1965.
3. The index is not flawless. The important March 15, 1965, feature by Fred Powledge is not cited there, for example. But Kirkpatrick Sale, in his exhaustive chronicle *SDS*, agrees that the *Times* did not report on SDS before 1965. See also Sale, "Myths as Eternal Truths," *More*, June 1973, p. 3.

tics of a demonstration at the U.S. Mission to the United Nations, we read:

> During the day, the Students for a Democratic Society, 119 Fifth Avenue, held a news conference at the Overseas Press Club.
> "It's quite clear," said Clark Kissinger, 24 years old, its national secretary, "that the major foreign intervening power in Vietnam is the United States."
> Mr. Kissinger said that the group had 1,500 members on 40 college campuses and that it planned a march on Washington April 17 "to end the war in Vietnam."

After a subhead, "Reaction at College Cited," the story goes on: "U.S. policy on Vietnam seems to have caused concern to students in many colleges, a sampling showed yesterday. . . ." There followed a report of sentiment at Columbia, City College of New York, Barnard, Fordham, and Yale. The treatment of SDS was neutral enough; it is worth noting that since the SDS paragraphs were contained within the arrest story, the impression conveyed was that SDS was an antiwar organization. This image was to become progressively more prominent throughout 1965, though it was always crucially inaccurate. SDS put itself forward in no uncertain terms as a multi-issue organization which worked in university reform, civil rights, and community organizing, as well as against war and corporate domination of foreign policy. That same spring, SDS was putting a good deal of energy and resources into organizing a sit-in at the Chase Manhattan Bank to protest the bank's involvement in a revolving credit arrangement that had helped bail out the government of South Africa after the Sharpeville massacre of 1960. The bank had taken this seriously enough to seek a prior injunction barring not only a sit-in on or abutting its property, but also the distribution of buttons proclaiming: CHASE MANHATTAN, PARTNER IN APARTHEID. (A New York City judge granted the bank an injunction against a sit-in on Chase property, but threw the rest of Chase's suit out of court.) Articles in the January and February issues of the SDS Bulletin (sent routinely to SDS members) not only discussed the projected March on Washington and the sit-in at Chase, but reported on SDS chapter and community organization activities and conferences (none of them flamboyant); and it contained a list of seventy SDS publications on universities, civil rights and community organizing, economics, peace, foreign policy, and politics.

Already, in what Martin Arnold did *not* mention, we encounter an essential fact about the American press: the news "peg" required an *event* deemed, within the news organization, *significant*. The event made significant then projects a sort of gravitational field which sucks in information that the reporter and editors construe to be related. Thus, in this case, the demonstration (event) projected a field (the issue of student opposition to the war) which framed as subsidiary the SDS press conference illustrating the growing student opposition. When the frame has been chosen, the reporter does not, in general, want to confront or complicate it by adducing other more complex material. Extending the news story would entail hard and unaccustomed work, outside normal news-gathering routines, going beyond the given scene, the given press conference, and the given press release. Deadlines increase the pressure to keep the story simple, using what is at hand. In general, then, a single story—provoked by a single event—projects only a single field. *The crucial, unintended ideological effect is to undermine whatever efforts movements may make to present a general, coherent political opposition; the effect is to reinforce the image that reform movements focus, and in the nature of things ought to focus, on single grievances which the system, however reluctantly, can correct without altering fundamental social relations.* The media thus support the dominant system's claim to general legitimacy and its ability to fragment opposition.

Only the longer, more exploratory background story, extending beyond the newsworthy "peg," contains even the technical potential for overcoming the fragmenting, denaturing effect of the topical, single-event, single-issue piece. The background story serves to place on the agenda a social change, a "trend," a "phenomenon," and automatically—since the background piece is relatively rare—confers on it a certain importance. Such was the background piece by Fred Powledge which began on page 1, column 1, of the *Times* of Sunday, March 15, 1965, headlined: "THE STUDENT LEFT SPURRING REFORM: New Activist Intelligentsia Is Rising On Campuses." It ran to thirty-nine column inches, the first four on page 1, the rest on page 26 under the headline "The New Student Left: Movement Represents Serious Activists In Drive For Changes." It began:

On a recent Saturday night, a group of University of Chicago students gathered at an apartment for a party. There was no liquor and no dancing and no talk about basketball, student politics, or sex.

Instead, the young men, in sport coats and without ties, and the young women, in skirts and black stockings, sat on the floor and talked about such things as "community organization," "powerlessness," and "participatory democracy."

The story went on to quote a few paragraphs from five individuals (four of them active in SDS, one in the Northern Student Movement), on radical goals, strategies, and political beliefs. It called these people "part of a new, small, loosely bound intelligentsia that calls itself the new student left and that wants to cause fundamental changes in society." It mentioned a range of activities: a picket in favor of academic tenure; a school boycott; civil rights demonstrations and sit-ins; community organization; demonstrations against the draft, against the war, and for disarmament. It suggested "new student left" beliefs in the form of key words:

Some of them, who liken their movement to a "revolution," want to be called radicals. Most of them, however, prefer to be called "organizers." Others reply that they are "democrats with a small 'd' or socialists with a small 's.'" A few like to be called Marxists. . . .

And it offered some fuller formulations:

Although a few displayed a tendency to defend the Soviet Union as an example of the sort of society they want to create, the great majority of those questioned said they were as skeptical of Communism as they were of any other form of political control.

It quoted a key paragraph on goals from the Port Huron Statement: "We seek the establishment of a democracy of individual participation. . . ."

All in all, the Powledge piece derived its information from within the radical student orbit, and conveyed respect and a certain distanced sympathy. It cited the movement's own preferred labels, and not those of opponents; it took at face value the radicals' own statements of belief; and it spoke from the perspective of the students, even when it proceeded toward balance. For example:

They are mindful that their numbers are tiny in comparison with the total in the nation's colleges. Now, as before, the great majority of their fellow students are primarily interested in marriage, a home, and a job.

The words *They are mindful* signaled that the radicals were self-aware and realistic. Without those words, the statement that "their numbers are tiny in comparison with the total in the nation's colleges" would have suggested that the radicals were deviant and insignificant. Powledge's method connoted the writer's respect for the New Left vantage.

Finally, Powledge's piece did not go through the motions of looking outside the student world for the sake of balancing opinions. It did not report on the attitudes of university officials, city officials, faculty, hostile or indifferent students, or professional experts on youth. It took SDS seriously at face value, as conventional news stories take seriously every day the proclamations and activities of government officials, corporate leaders, and university officials. In other words, it conferred legitimacy; it imparted significance. No wonder SDS reprinted this piece and used it for recruiting.

How did this exceptional survey (or, in journalists' jargon, "takeout") find its way into the *Times*?[4] Fred Powledge recalls lobbying to get the assignment. A white Southerner who had covered the civil rights movement, Powledge in the winter of 1964–65 "wondered what had happened to the minds of all those people who went to Mississippi." He knew about the Free Speech Movement in Berkeley, and the role played there by Mississippi veterans. The *Times*'s executive editor (Clifton Daniel), the managing editor (Turner Catledge), and the national editor (Claude Sitton) were interested too, and the idea was approved. Like any *Times* reporter assigned to a story, Powledge then went out on his own, decided where to go and whom to interview.[5] Powledge believes that the editors' interest was conditioned by their class experience and their children's:

New York Times editors are white and upper-middle-class and consider themselves intellectuals; some of *their* offspring were running around yelling "Fuck" and threatening to change the world, and this got to the editors of *The Times* a lot more than did the actions (and the assassinations) of any number of illiterate black Southerners. It was almost like the caricature of the middle-class white family whose kid ran away during the summer of love, and who sits around the kitchen table asking "Where did we go wrong?"

4. The following account, including all quotations, comes from Powledge's letter to me, July 1, 1977, and a telephone interview of October 2, 1977. Powledge worked at the *Times* from August 1963 through the end of December 1965.

5. Sigal (*Reporters and Officials* [Lexington, Mass.: D. C. Heath, 1973], p. 16) concludes that at the *Times* and the *Washington Post*, at least, once an assignment is made, "information-gathering is largely left to a reporter's own initiative."

Powledge saw himself as a newsroom deviant: "I felt like the mysterious stranger in the city room, at least until the *Times* got around to hiring some blacks; I was as exotic as a Jew would be in a Southern newsroom." Because he had covered race, and had just started to cover the war on poverty, "I was deemed to be something of an expert on what best can be categorized as 'what these people want' (though I never felt very expert on it)." So the assignment was reasonably general: more or less (in Powledge's words), "Find out what these young people are up to and write us a takeout on it."

After months of traveling and interviewing, Powledge came in with the piece; it was cut for length and subjected only to minor, routine copy-editing. Powledge argues that when the *Times* invests a large amount of money and time in a major piece like this, the editors run the piece and they run it prominently—whether the editors like it a little or a lot. As he puts it, "They were honorable enough to print what I'd written." But over the next nine months that Powledge was at the *Times*, the editors never again sent him out to report at length on the radical movement. They sent other reporters instead; and Powledge recalls that the others came back confirming the accuracy of his own account. One of them, Homer Bigart, whom Powledge calls "the world's best reporter," found essentially what Powledge had found, and asked the editors, "Why did you send me?" Powledge believes

they were hoping that somebody would find this wasn't a good homespun American movement. When I found Bettina Aptheker at Berkeley, and a few others [Communists] like that, I thought they were a minor element in the whole story: what would really count in the long run would be what the rest of the young people did.

In Powledge's current view, the *Times*'s subsequent search for a Red menace emanated silently and decisively from the editors' class position. Not that there was a deliberate conspiracy—"and nobody looks harder for a conspiracy than a reporter." Rather:

It's a state of mind, I think, that comes of being an editor or a publisher: you know you can send your kids to college, you know you have a pension plan waiting for you; you have lunch with department store owners and you know they're not the enemy.

The rules were transmitted to reporters through recruitment, evaluation, reward, promotion, and an array of informal control techniques: a "real Timesman" (and most *were* males) had to be conspicuously loyal. "If you worked for the *Times*, you were expected to give all your loyalty, all your energy, to the *Times*; it's almost like a military organization."

Powledge's is not just a view from the bottom. Turner Catledge, in his memoir of seventeen years as a top *Times* editor, writes that he customarily asserted "strong leadership" over "a chain of command," that he sought in his subordinates both "talent" and "loyalty—not to myself, but to the office I held and to the *Times*." Catledge, who was next in line to the publisher in 1965, wanted what he calls "independent, creative men, thoroughbreds, . . . not the sort who could be bossed or browbeaten. *I had to make them do what I wanted done, often by making them think it was what they wanted done.*" [6] How could the art of organizing hegemony be more nicely defined?

Yet Catledge in turn had been groomed by publisher Arthur Hays Sulzberger, and Sulzberger was in the habit of "making his likes and dislikes known" to his managing editor by firing off all manner of memoranda on matters large and small.[7] If one of Sulzberger's memos criticized a reporter's work, and Catledge thought the point valid, he would

pass it on to the reporter as my own comment, for insofar as possible I wanted our reporters and editors to do their work without feeling that the publisher was constantly looking over their shoulders. In truth, however, he was. He read the paper closely and he had a very personal feeling about what he saw there—if the *Times* looked silly, he felt that he looked silly.[8]

Catledge was a good organization man; he knew his place. Sulzberger "had unerring good judgment on the big issues," he writes. "In that, he reminded me of Harry Truman."[9]

Yet, at the same time, a *Times* publisher still has to respect journalistic conventions, or at least not rupture them flagrantly. Reporters and editors must still be permitted—indeed, encouraged—to define and discover the news, though not in ideological circumstances of their own making. In their daily conversations with each other in the newsroom and on the beat, in their entangling associations with sources, and in their reading of their actual product—the daily newspaper itself—they interpret the traditions and work

6. Turner Catledge, *My Life and The Times* (New York: Harper and Row, 1971), p. 188 (emphasis added).
7. Ibid., p. 189.   8. Ibid., p. 190.   9. Ibid., p. 189.

out their sense of what journalism is.[10] The publisher's "very personal feeling" does allow considerable latitude for reporters' initiative; and many reporters would say that *they* write the news without interference from above. Yet by now it is well established that they do not make the bureaucratic rules which condition their writing.[11]

Turner Catledge is to be taken seriously when he writes:

[Arthur Hays] Sulzberger did not want to be an aggressive, dominating publisher, hurling thunderbolts at an awed staff. His style was more reserved, more subtle, and I think more effective. He sought executives who shared his general outlook, and he tried, by word and deed, to set a tone for the paper.[12]

To set a tone: that is what Fred Powledge is talking about. And his own story probed to the limits of that set tone. Frames, angles, assumptions about what is salient and what is not, all flowed through the *Times* bureaucracy with both subtlety and persistence; the newsroom was soaked in them. When this kind of communication is "done by smart people," Powledge says, "it's never done in so many words."

FRAMING AN ACTION, I:
THE CHASE MANHATTAN DEMONSTRATION

Friday afternoon, March 19, after months of planning by SDS, several hundred people demonstrated at the world headquarters of the Chase Manhattan Bank near Wall Street; forty-one sat in and were hauled off in paddy wagons to jail. Chase Manhattan was one of ten American banks which had joined in a major revolving credit to South Africa in 1960—just after the South African police had opened fire on unarmed African demonstrators, killing sixty-nine, wounding 178, and in the process shaking the regime's international standing.

All through the winter of 1965, the SDS National Office in New York had been working to recruit new members and to boost its reputation on campuses. Accordingly, the office had been (in the words of a staff member) "persistent about finding ways to get

10. See Sigal, *Reporters and Officials*, p. 39.
11. The classic account is Warren Breed, "Social Control in the Newsroom," *Social Forces* 33 (May 1955): 326–335. The best accounts of the *Times*'s news-gathering and writing processes in particular are in Sigal, *Reporters and Officials*, and Robert Darnton, "Writing News and Telling Stories," *Daedalus* 104 (Spring 1975): 175–194.
12. Catledge, *My Life and The Times*, p. 189.

publicity." [13] So it went for the Chase Manhattan project too, though publicity was not the primary goal. The strategy was two-fold: (1) to put the issue of corporate investment in apartheid—and, by extension, in racism generally—on the agenda of the American Left, including civil rights and church groups; and (2) to reveal, for a broader public, the tarnish on the liberal image of the Rockefellers' bank. Both goals required coverage in the mainstream daily media. Direct action could not dispense with media coverage, since only through mass-mediation could a large audience be notified, let alone aroused.

Still, SDS was new at the game of getting media attention. An inexperienced staff did not seek many direct contacts with reporters. Especially after the North Vietnam bombing started, the National Office was diverting effort to organizing and publicizing the April antiwar march. But Mike Davis and Clark Kissinger of the SDS staff sent out "the usual number of press releases" in advance, using a standard press list compiled by the Student Non-violent Coordinating Committee. There had been one press release some days in advance of the demonstration, and another one announcing a pre-demonstration rally—attended enthusiastically by hundreds—at the Community Church in Manhattan. Most of all, National Secretary Kissinger and the rest of the staff had naively expected that the size of the demonstration itself would attract the press. How many demonstrations, after all, took place on working days in the narrow streets of the world's financial center, at least in 1965?

The *Times* covered the Friday demonstration on Saturday, March 20, on page 11, in fifteen column inches under the headline: "49 Arrested at Chase Building in Protest on South Africa Loans." The rather straightforward article, by Theodore Jones, continued Powledge's tone of respect, though it was less thorough and its frame more mixed. It took SDS seriously enough in giving three paragraphs to SDS President Paul Potter's account of his meeting with a bank official; then there followed four paragraphs quoting the bank's laissez-faire defense of its lending policy. The Jones piece began, however, with the theme trumpeted in the headline:

13. Telephone interview, Mike Davis, February 15, 1977. Davis worked in the National Office from October 1964 through June 1965, and was the prime mover there of the Chase Manhattan project. My discussion of the project is indebted to Davis's recollections, as well as to my own files and to the discussion in Sale, *SDS*, pp. 182–183.

"49 Arrested." Only in the second paragraph did Jones mention the picket line of "400 persons." There was no mention of the bank's attempt to enjoin the demonstration or to prohibit the distribution of buttons, leaflets, and research papers. No word appeared of SDS's research into the decisiveness of the role of American banks in keeping the Verwoerd regime afloat after the Sharpeville massacre. What was most distinctly newsworthy was sharp clash and arrests.

Throughout the sub-society of news reporters, arrests certify protest events. According to a reporter who covered the Berkeley beat for the *San Francisco Chronicle* in 1965–66, stories about student activities at the University of California were routinely disqualified as news unless there had been arrests.[14] I do not argue that *Times* editors imposed such a policy directly. But on reading through *Times* coverage of both civil rights and antiwar movements, one is struck with the great proportion of stories that begin with the fact of arrests, in both headlines and leads. Editors take arrests as a sign that something significant has taken place—something "out of the ordinary," even though during a lengthy civil disobedience campaign the fact of arrests day after day might itself become ordinary. Arrests are dramatic; yet they can be reported routinely. They have around them the aura of human interest, since there are particular people arrested; they take place sharply and clearly on a given day, and in numbers at least are unequivocal; thus they can be assimilated to the publishing timetable. Not least, they are unusual: people are *voluntarily* getting arrested.

The practice of taking arrests as the "handle" on the story and the threshold for newsworthiness descends from the operational code of crime news coverage and the police beat. Very often it was police reporters who were assigned to cover the student movement. Indeed, most *Times* reporters learn the news-reporting trade on a police beat,[15] where they can rely on the police to dig up "the facts" and, actually, to decree just what constitutes a relevant fact. So reporting arrests, which can be easily counted and processed by the police, helps a reporter cope with complexity and deadlines, and lightens his or her load. For all these reasons, the media place arrest reports at the center of their coverage of a movement. But this routine news-gathering operation has the effect of assigning

14. Interview, Adam Hochschild, December 22, 1976.
15. Darnton, "Writing News and Telling Stories."

newsmaking power to police, in the first instance, and then to activists who learn how to turn the tables by strategically getting arrested. Arrests allow non-celebrities to become newsmakers: they are, in fact, one of the few mechanisms available for certifying a social issue. Arrests, in other words, help democratize access to news for powerless and dissident groups. But not even activists bent on arrest for publicity's sake can get arrested unless the police authorities *decide* to make the arrests. (Even the grammar of the passive voice shows that the activists remain passive in the situation: they must *get* arrested.) When the power to define news is, in effect, turned over to the police, the media are serving to confirm the existing control mechanisms in society. Of course, the State's de facto determination of news may well backfire; this is the gamble of nonviolent demonstrations making the most of their dependent situation.[16]

CBS, meanwhile, did not report the Chase Manhattan demonstration at all; so far as I could discover, they did not even film it.[17] The fact that the sit-in—itself only part of the total demonstration—took place in the afternoon would have sufficed to keep *it* off the Friday evening news, since developing and editing time exclude almost all late-breaking news (except assassinations, hijack-

16. The Chase Manhattan story was also framed, somewhat misleadingly, as a civil rights piece. Just to its left appeared a Cleveland dispatch headlined "36 SEIZED IN OHIO RACIAL DISPUTE." Beneath it came a smaller piece: "Broadcaster Says Klan Is Forcing Him Off Air." The *Times* had already begun framing civil rights stories as fragments of a larger story, "the civil rights story."

Below a two-column photo which conveyed the image of a tiny picket line vastly outnumbered by bystanders, the caption read: "Members of several civil rights groups marching outside Chase Manhattan Bank's downtown headquarters to protest the bank's investments in South Africa, where segregation is rigid." Framing SDS as "civil rights" made it comprehensible by relating it to an already established story. But framing it to make it familiar stripped the event of its uniqueness: the linking of race issues with American corporate power abroad. This was, after all, the first distinctly anti-imperialist demonstration of the sixties: a foreshadowing of later campaigns against Dow Chemical and other companies. And more: the same day, March 19, SDS chapters and cooperating groups around the country had organized a number of other demonstrations against a range of corporations and banks involved in South Africa. An inquiring reporter not confined to a police-centered beat could have discovered this by interviewing SDS staff or reading SDS's copious reports. Discovering the simultaneous demonstrations would have meant discovering a new frame for the Chase Manhattan story. But it was easier and less time-consuming for beat-ridden reporters and hasty caption-writers, all working on deadline, to locate the event within the established frame of "the continuing civil rights story."

17. At least no film of it exists in the CBS Newsfilm Archives, and no file card or log note records the existence of any film.

ings, and the like). SDS had not planned the sit-in to capture the spotlight, or else they might have scheduled it for the morning. But the bad timing of the sit-in, from a network point of view, could not account for CBS overlooking the earlier picket line of five hundred or one thousand people, itself no common sight on Wall Street. For television, as for print, a large picket line was not judged newsworthy unless it resulted in a large number of arrests. (Thus, a few weeks later, on April 16, the arrest of *six* antiwar demonstrators sitting in at the State Department—the entire number demonstrating—got on the CBS Evening News, albeit for only thirty-five seconds.) Possibly the New York film crews and correspondents—there were only a handful—were busy elsewhere that day. All of which is to say that CBS News didn't think the Chase Manhattan demonstration was much of a story.

Or suppose for a moment, for the sake of argument, that CBS News *did* film the picket line. What could in principle compensate for the lack of arrests might be a producer's decision to lump the story with another batch of stories, to present a common theme which would then resituate the demonstration story, and in resituating it magnify its importance. Thus the individual story would then become defined by its context as "part of a developing story." For example, the April 16 sit-in story was inserted between a piece about student riots in South Korea and another about anti-Americanism in the Philippines. So the State Department sit-in could be understood as thematically linked to a worldwide, Asia-centered phenomenon of student revolt. No such context evidently occurred to the producers of the March 19 Evening News—if, indeed, they did film the Chase Manhattan demonstration—and thus no story was formulated. Moreover, although ordinarily the Morning News presents a second chance for a previous day's story, CBS did not—and does not—broadcast a Morning News show on Saturdays. Since a hard news story is judged to have a shelf life of twenty-four hours or less, the Chase Manhattan story, once omitted, remained omitted. No organ of the media likes to admit fallibility by running a story late; television news, by committing itself to the visual representation, gives itself a built-in one-day-at-a-time immediacy, which serves the organizational purpose of clearing the decks for the next broadcast, eliminating backlogs, and thereby making decisions easier.

To put it another way: the simple scarcity of news time on television drastically limits what gets on the air. This is precisely the common sense of CBS News reporters and managers: whether any given piece gets on the air depends in part on what else is new. They point to the well-known fact that television news in the United States is limited to about twenty-two minutes (thirty minutes minus commercial time), whereas in a pinch a newspaper can always add extra pages. True enough. But it is also true that any given quantum of time is somewhat flexible; it can bend to accommodate more or fewer words, more or fewer pictures, depending on the pace of the anchor's voice, the correspondent's voice, the particular choices made by film editors, and other operational decisions.[18] The shortage of film crews, correspondents, air time—all these scarcities matter, and as I argue in Chapter 8, they have a distinctly ideological meaning; but they don't themselves explain *what* will be omitted.

More to the point, the Chase Manhattan story was in important ways unprecedented, and thus a poor candidate for CBS coverage. To say this sounds paradoxical, yet it follows from the bureaucratic organization and ideological assumptions of news. News must be timely, unambiguous, intense, predictable, culturally familiar—and precedented. The more of these criteria an event meets, the more likely it will be covered. As the first explicitly anti-imperialist demonstration, attempting to link Wall Street loans with South African apartheid (itself of low salience to most Americans, including most journalists), the Chase Manhattan demonstration suffered from being unusual. The *Times* framed it as a civil rights story, CBS didn't cover it at all: these were alternate responses to the story's strangeness. Or as Johan Galtung and Mari Holmboe Ruge put it, "'news' are actually 'olds,' because they correspond to what one expects to happen."[19]

18. The point is beautifully illustrated in a 1968 Public Broadcast Laboratory documentary, "Journalism—Mirror, Mirror on the Wall?" PBL covered five news organizations covering the January 1968 Jeanette Rankin Brigade women's antiwar demonstration in Washington: the *New York Times*, the *Washington Post*, UPI, NBC News, and PBL itself. At one point on camera, David Brinkley blames the brevity of TV news pieces for their superficiality. PBL then demonstrates that in the fifty-two seconds allotted to Brinkley's NBC piece, much more information could have been conveyed about the demonstration—which is not to deny that the time squeeze is an obstacle to thorough reporting. But an obstacle is not an all-purpose, all-determining alibi; and the shortage of time cannot by itself account for the prevalence of a *particular* frame, a *particular* version of the superficial.

19. Johan Galtung and Mari Holmboe Ruge, "The Structure of Foreign News," *Journal of International Peace Research* 1 (1965): 64–90, reprinted in Jeremy Tunstall, ed., *Media Sociology: A Reader* (Urbana: University of Illinois Press, 1970), pp. 259–298. I quote from p. 264. Galtung and Ruge propound a quasi-structuralist model,

FRAMING AN ACTION, II:

THE MARCH ON WASHINGTON TO END THE WAR IN VIETNAM

The *Times* next mentioned SDS in a brief, poker-faced page 3 story on Saturday, April 17, the day of the antiwar March on Washington, stating simply: "More than 10,000 students from all over the country are expected to descend on the capital tomorrow to protest against Administration policies in Vietnam." What is most interesting is the *Times*'s restrained and vague handling of a critical statement issued by a group of peace luminaries:

> Support for efforts to obtain peace in Vietnam was expressed yesterday by Norman Thomas, the Socialist leader, and ten other persons.
> They said in a statement that they sympathized with the student march in Washington although they disagreed with positions expressed "by some of the elements" in the protest.

Thus did this item read in its entirety. Those disagreeable "positions" and "elements" went unspecified.[20] The effect was one of formal balance, yielding the benefit of the doubt to the March; the Thomas statement was deprived of impact by being quoted so scantily. The *Times* was evidently refusing to be inflamed against the demonstration.

But more subtly, the *Times*'s coverage of the March itself compounded the serious and the shallow. The story trivialized the March; it balanced presumably equivalent antiwar and ultra-Right forces; and it began to construe the student movement as freakish deviancy.[21]

---

complete with quantified criteria, to explain how certain events become news, and I draw on their account in the preceding paragraph. But I owe to a graduate seminar presentation by Nicole Biggart (Fall 1978) the point that the Galtung-Ruge criteria for newsworthiness leave out the historical origins of these criteria and the way in which a news organization enforces them. The criteria are also more ambiguous and flexible than Galtung and Ruge's strict categorical account allows for. Even if their factors were more precisely stated, naming a set of factors is not the same as accounting for a specific decision.

20. By contrast, on the eve of the March, the liberal afternoon *New York Post* ran an editorial lauding this statement and warning against unattributed "attempts to convert the event into a pro-Communist production" and "a frenzied, one-sided anti-American show" (Sale, *SDS*, p. 179). It may well be that the statement's signers, organized by LID board member Robert Gilmore, had more pull with the liberal *Post* than with the less accessible, more mandarin *Times*. (Sale shows, by the way, how faulty the red-scare predictions were, on pp. 181–182.)

21. As for CBS News, its incomplete archives make any useful analysis impossible. Two pieces were broadcast, both by Bruce Morton of the Washington bureau: one on April 17 itself, the third piece on the Saturday News; and one follow-up

The lead story in the April 18 Sunday *Times*, running down the right-hand column, was headlined: "JOHNSON REFUSES TO HALT BOMBING; AGAIN ASKS TALKS." Below the fold, stretching across columns 5–7, ran a less conspicuous headline: "15,000 White House Pickets Denounce Vietnam War." Immediately beneath it ran a large three-column photo showing the White House at the top, the anti-war demonstration across the center, and an equivalent number of other pickets at the bottom. The caption to this United Press International telephoto read: "Students protesting Vietnam policy march outside White House while, in foreground, a counter demonstration is carried on by others on the sidewalk along Lafayette Square." (See p. 50.)

In the normal run of things, editors could choose among a range of photos from both their own photographers (if assigned) and the wire services; they *chose* this particular picture. Indeed, a look at the other photos UPI sent out that day to its subscribers, including the *Times*, throws the *Times'* choice into especially sharp relief. I retrieved the five other April 17 photos from UPI's archives. Two show a mass of antiwar pickets carrying signs bearing readable slogans (one of these is reproduced on p. 51); one shows a large mass at the antiwar rally at the Washington Monument; and the other two give an accurate sense of the degree to which the antiwar people outnumbered the counterdemonstrators. All five were, in formal terms, printable; the pictures of the picketers with their signs were even elegantly composed, with high contrast and good formal balance. But the effect of the photo the *Times* chose was

---

about demonstrators who stayed in Washington over the weekend, this one broadcast on Monday morning, April 19. The former piece is to be found neither in CBS Newsfilm Archives nor in CBS Audio Archives. The April 19 piece is one minute and twenty seconds long, and does not even mention the April 17 demonstration: it treats a small Sunday demonstration as a self-enclosed event in which a few students are "willing to brave bad weather" in order to try to see the President. Morton begins: "Nobody ever said April rains make good weather for picketing." He closes: "This is a hard way to spend your vacation. These students seem determined to stick it out." The demonstration is framed as improbable, hardy, and quixotic—virtually a "human interest" story, appropriate to the format of the Monday Morning News. At one level, it tenders respect to the hardy demonstrators; but simultaneously it depoliticizes the demonstration. It substitutes the frame people-against-the-elements for the frame people-in-a-political-situation. Through such devices political speech is denatured and replaced by journalistic wryness. The wryness conveys the correspondent's privileged position above and outside the messy quarrels of the committed; it is a common distancing voice for journalists assigned to cover activities they do not comprehend and cannot easily enclose within a certified category.

visually to equate the antiwar and right-wing demonstrations, and to give the impression—since the photographed segment of the two picket lines were identical in length—that they were equally large. In fact, according to the article itself, the counterdemonstration, by American Nazis and the Delaware Valley Citizens for Victory Over Communism, included a little over *one hundred* pickets. So the photo showed almost all of the right-wing pickets and only a tiny fragment of the antiwar picket line. Though outnumbered one hundred and fifty to one by the *Times's* own account, the counterdemonstrators were accorded equal photographic space.[22] Such equations were also, and remain, a staple of TV coverage of the Left; as one television reporter told Herbert Gans, "at anti-war demonstrations, we shot the Viet Cong supporters and the Nazis because they were interesting, and also because they are what sells. You always go after the extremes; the same in the South, where we shot the black militants and the Ku Klux Klan."[23]

22. The significance of news photographs has been argued with great force by Stuart Hall in "Determinations of News Photographs," in Stanley Cohen and Jock Young, eds., *The Manufacture of News* (Beverly Hills, Calif.: Sage Publications, 1973). The following passage (p. 188) is apropos: "News photos have a specific way of passing themselves off as aspects of 'nature.' They repress their ideological dimensions by offering themselves as literal visual-transcriptions of the 'real world.' News photos witness to the *actuality* of the event they represent. Photos of an event carry within them a message: 'this event really happened and this photo is the proof of it.' Photos of people—even the 'passport' type and size—also support this function of *grounding and witnessing*: 'this is the man we are talking about, he really exists.' Photos, then, appear as records, in a literal sense, of 'the facts' and speak for themselves. This is what Barthes calls the 'having-been-there' of all photographs. News photos operate under a hidden sign marked, 'this really happened, see for yourself.' Of course, the choice of *this* moment of an event as against that, of *this* person rather than that, of *this* angle rather than any other, indeed, the selection of this photographed incident to represent a whole complex chain of events and meanings, is a highly ideological procedure. But, by appearing literally to reproduce the event as it *really* happened, news photos suppress their selective/interpretive/ideological function. They seek a warrant in that ever pre-given, neutral structure, which is beyond question, beyond interpretation: the 'real world.' At this level, news photos not only support the credibility of the newspaper as an accurate medium. They also guarantee and underwrite its *objectivity* (that is, they neutralize its ideological function). This 'ideology of objectivity' itself derives from one of the most profound myths in the liberal ideology: the absolute distinction between fact and value, the distinction which appears as a commonsense 'rule' in newspaper practice as 'the distinction between facts and interpretation': the empiricist illusion, the utopia of naturalism."
    For other illustrations of the connotations of photographs, see Roland Barthes, "Photography and Electoral Appeals," in *Mythologies* (New York: Hill and Wang, 1972), and "Rhetoric of the Image," in *Image—Music—Text* (New York: Hill and Wang, 1977).
    23. Herbert Gans, *Deciding What's News* (New York: Pantheon, 1979), p. 176.

The story itself had no by-line, probably a sign that it was assigned to a lower-ranking, general assignment reporter. It began:

More than 15,000 students and a handful of adults picketed the White House in warm spring sunshine today, calling for an end of the fighting in Vietnam. Walking three and four abreast in orderly rows and carrying printed white signs, the students clogged the sidewalk. The principal occupant of the White House was at his ranch in Texas.

Thus emerged a major theme in mass media coverage of SDS and the antiwar movement: the movement's absurd ineffectuality. [24]

The article went on to describe SDS as "left-leaning but noncommunist." Jumping to page 3, the article mentioned the names of some co-sponsoring organizations, and went on:

Many marchers appeared to be newcomers to the "peace movement" and some had only a hazy idea of how they might go about ending the fighting in Vietnam.

It quoted from five rank-and-file marchers, and then from Paul Booth, an SDS spokesman. After the subhead "Holiday From Exams," it characterized the demonstrators' dress as "beards and blue jeans mixed with ivy tweeds and an occasional clerical collar"; then reported two arrests of right-wing counter-pickets; and concluded with two paragraphs on the Washington Monument rally. One paragraph mentioned the speech (quoting half a sentence) of Senator Ernest Gruening, urging a halt to the bombing of North Vietnam. The second paragraph mentioned two other speakers: the journalist I. F. Stone, and Yale professor Staughton Lynd, "who recently announced that he was refusing to pay part of his Federal income tax as a protest against the war." There followed a subsidiary article, datelined Ithaca, under the subhead "Cornell Marchers in Melee." In considerable detail, this story reported how counterdemonstrators had tried to block the buses of Washington-bound antiwar marchers. In all, the main story on the Washington March ran seventeen and one-half inches, the Cornell sequel nine and three-fourths inches.

Media are mobile spotlights, not passive mirrors of the society; selectivity is the instrument of their action. A news story adopts a certain frame and rejects or downplays material that is discrepant. A story is a choice, a way of seeing an event that also amounts to a

24. See the further example of CBS's coverage of the November antiwar march, in Chapter 3, pp. 120–121, below.

... south of here. ab...   ... sihanouk maintains he in international ce...   ... over F-105 made a low pass at a ... pass. The

Continued on Page 6, Column 1 | Continued on Page 18, Column 1 | Continued on Page 4, Column 1

ptians—
British
'gan to
emen to
iey had
offen-
ording
to re-
across
Shah

ng to

imn 1

'S

by Bob
0 Wood
at Aque-
sidor Bie-
Derby
ay in the
vent for

the 1½-
/5 and
bet to
atched
s final
candi-
ivorite,

one hit
igs and
io pace
s to a
New
ium.
er lost
or the
ith a
itcher
crifice
; and
i the

owing
rs of
ws in
) for
race

porta
Vietna
Dong, o
last N
four-p
nized
nation
Pre
gested
troops
nam i
that
of th

Cont

T

Sectic
Sectic

Sectic
Sectic
Sectio
Sectio
Sectio
Sectio
Section
Section
*Inclu
metropo.

Ind

Art
Book R
Boating
Bridge
Camera
Chess
Coins
Dance
Drama
Editori
Educati
Fashio
Financ
Food
Gardens
Home F
Home R
Letters t
Music
News S
Obituari
Puzzles
Radio-T
Real E
Records
Resorts
Revie
Scien
Screen
Ships
Societ
Stamp
Weatl

15,000 White House Pickets Denounce Vietnam War

United Press International Telephoto

Students protesting Vietnam policy march outside White House while, in foreground, a counter demonstration is carried on by others on the sidewalk along Lafayette Square.

Special to The New York Times
WASHINGTON, April 17— More than 15,000 students and a handful of adults picketed the White House in warm spring sunshine today, calling for an end of the fighting in Vietnam. Walking three and four abreast in orderly rows and carrying printed white signs, the students clogged the sidewalk. The principal occupant of the White House was at his ranch in Texas. In early afternoon, the marchers paraded to the Sylvan Theater, on the grounds of the Washington Monument, for a series of speeches. Then they walked down the Mall to the Capitol, bearing a petition for Congress The demonstration was initiated by Students for a Democratic Society, a left-leaning but non - Communist group with chapters on 63 campuses throughout the coun-

Continued on Page 3, Column 5

From the *New York Times*, Sunday, April 18, 1965, page 1.

One of the April 17, 1965, photos sent out by United Press International and not chosen by the *New York Times*. Note the visible proportion between the antiwar demonstrators in the foreground and the few counter-demonstrators in the background, across Pennsylvania Avenue.

way of screening from sight. The *Times* relayed—and continues to relay—a hegemonic frame; which is not to say that it straightforwardly excluded alternative or discrepant information. As Raymond Williams rightly insists, hegemony "does not just passively exist as a form of dominance. It has continually to be renewed, recreated, defended, and modified. It is also continually resisted, limited, altered, challenged by pressures not at all its own. . . . [I]t is never either total or exclusive. . . . [A]ny hegemonic process must be especially alert and responsive to the alternatives and opposition which question or threaten its dominance." [25] The hegemonic frame thus incorporates some information which might tend to call into question the adequacy or the completeness of the

25. Raymond Williams, *Marxism and Literature* (New York: Oxford University Press, 1977), pp. 112–113.

established system of power and knowledge. Indeed, just as the hegemony of the powers that be rests on their claim to wise stewardship of the general good ("the national interest," "the American Dream"), so the legitimacy of hegemonic news rests on its claim to objectivity. It cannot afford to be seen as grossly incomplete by the publics who accord it legitimacy. Serving the political and economic elites as it does, the *Times* must function as a distant early warning system, an instrument of general surveillance; it cannot afford to overlook disagreeable facts, at least not for long.[26] The world it reports is in flux, and much of that flux challenges those in charge; at times it may suggest that they are not, perhaps, capable of staying in charge, or even that their system of values and truths is not the best imaginable. So the *Times* incorporates discrepant information—within a frame that minimizes and muffles its significance; at the same time, it tends to leave out a great deal of other information which would lend weight to an oppositional sense of things. (Again, it does this through journalistic routines, through standard practices enshrined as objectivity or at times experienced as "technical.") The *Times*, like any other news organization, has discretion. Even mainstream news-gathering— the unpublished UPI newsphotos, at the very least—produces a range of information within a certain range of frames; on April 17, 1965, the *Times* screened out discrepant information to which its own routines gave access.

How else could the March on Washington have been reported? One way into the question is to see how it *was* handled from other points of view.[27] The left-wing weekly *National Guardian*, with considerably lengthier coverage, gave one alternate reading of the reality. In another way, so did SDS's own announcements and propaganda. Their readings alert us to aspects of the March reality that could have been chosen for mention by the *Times*, but were not. The *Times*'s reading then takes its place as one angle among angles, whose meaning is thrown into relief against the background of what it excluded. Thus the *Guardian* coverage is interesting here

26. On the surveillance function of mass communications, see Charles Wright, *Mass Communications*, 2nd edition (New York: Random House, 1975) pp. 8 ff. I am using *surveillance* here to refer to the needs of specific elites; Wright in his functionalism roots surveillance in the social system as a whole and is unclear about just who needs surveillance over whom, and why.

27. This approach derives from the fascinating methodical study by James D. Halloran, Philip Elliott, and Graham Murdock, *Demonstrations and Communication: A Case Study* (Harmondsworth, England: Penguin Books, 1970).

not as a model of the unexceptionable or as a neglected story option at the *Times* (the *Guardian*, after all, was a weekly without the *Times*'s technical strictures on Saturday coverage), but as a model of a rival cognitive possibility. It would be *de rigueur* to observe that the *Guardian* coverage was ideological. The *Times*'s coverage was no less so.

The *Guardian* of April 24, 1965, printed two major stories on the March on Washington: a general descriptive story by Jack A. Smith (43¼ column inches), and a background story by William A. Price (22 column inches). It also printed a page of excerpts from two rally speeches, primarily Staughton Lynd's. By comparing the *Guardian* stories (supplemented by materials printed by SDS) with the *Times* piece, we observe the following themes neglected by the *Times*:

1. *The content of the call printed by SDS.* This one-page document contained a rudimentary analysis of the nature of the Vietnam War. Hundreds of thousands of copies had been distributed on campuses since SDS had decided to organize the March the previous December. It presented an alternative if inadequate point of view about the nature of the war (as a "civil war" in which the United States was intervening aggressively), not simply a "denunciation" of the "fighting." The call was not mentioned by the *Times*. Why? Generally, the coverage of unorthodox politics descends from the conventions of crime news. Journalism has traditionally equated insurgency and protest with deviance—which is interesting because problematic. The style of the human interest story also deprecates collective motivations in favor of personal, idiosyncratic reasons. When reporters (and editors) ask demonstrators, "Why are you here?" they are looking for singular reasons, not political logic. (Demonstrators may themselves embrace this hegemonic sense of motives, and give reporters the answers they seek.) It is not that the SDS call was deliberately and consciously suppressed: the reporter simply did not mention it. Just so, political positions— even the establishmentarian positions adopted during elections— are rarely treated in the media; journalists often scorn them as mere rhetoric. Sometimes movement positions *are* rhetorical; they are also competing frames for the event, rivaling not only the lore of the newsroom but the common understanding of reporters sharing a beat. They say: Look, we think the world is *this* way, not the way you have learned to see it, not the way the President says it is; and it drives us to these actions. But most reporters derive their pictures of the world from factions of the government; to ac-

cord legitimacy to an alternate reading of a policy issue would cast doubt on the adequacy of the reporter's usual sources. It would make everyday journalistic life quite different—unless the usual sources, government and semiofficial agencies, are themselves divided. In this case, an outsider's statement might acquire standing as a reportable fact. In 1965, however, SDS's political analysis was out of bounds. And not because it was deeply radical: its main critique was moral; and it called the war "civil," not "imperialist." In early 1965, SDS was prematurely antiwar.

2. *A listing of the picket sign slogans.* SDS had decided to print signs with standardized slogans, and asked attending groups to carry only the approved signs along with placards identifying the campuses and locales from which the groups had come. The slogans were easily observable on the scene: "I Won't Fight in Vietnam," "Negotiate," "Withdraw from Vietnam," "Unconditional Negotiations Yes—Killing Vietnamese Children No," "Get U.S. Troops Out," "Stop the Killing," "War on Poverty, Not on People," "One Man One Vote—Selma or Saigon," "End the War in Vietnam Now," "Ballots, Not Bullets in Vietnam," "Stop World War III Now," "Escalate Freedom in Mississippi," "Our Hope Is Human Freedom." The *Times* mentioned none of these, although several slogans were plainly legible in two of the photographs sent to subscribers by United Press International and not used by the *Times*.

The slogans suggested a diversity of critical approaches to the war; they embodied SDS's actual ecumenism. But SDS's statements of purpose were screened away from the *Times*'s hegemonic vision. Why? No technical reason could account for the omission, and so we must look beyond the technical to the tacitly ideological. To have quoted the slogans would have been to permit SDS to articulate its own positions; it would have detracted from the hegemonic frame's implied claim to comprehensiveness.

3. *Unprecedented cooperation between white and black movements.* To those of us within the student movement, and to sensitive observers on the periphery, the participation of a large number of blacks in a peace demonstration was worthy of note. The *Guardian* estimated that almost ten percent of the demonstrators were black. *Guardian* reporter William A. Price wrote: "The most important new liaison was that between the young, vibrant freedom workers of the South and the peace-oriented students of the North. . . ." One of the main rally speeches was delivered by Bob (Moses) Parris, a leader of the Student Nonviolent Coordinating Committee

(SNCC). Bob Parris talked about the men who ran the Vietnam war as the same men who were letting racist violence in Mississippi take its course. Jack Smith of the *Guardian* wrote that Parris "sought to outline the connection between Vietnam and the civil rights movement." Two years before Martin Luther King, Jr.'s first public speech on an antiwar platform, an important civil rights leader was lending his considerable prestige to interracial alliance on the Left. And a singing group of three SNCC field secretaries, the Freedom Voices, sang to the rally.

If news incorporates aspects of a "developing story" which were not present or not evident to the reporter and editors on previous days, or in previous versions of the given event, then the cooperation of black and white movements was news. There is also evidence (after the fact) that the political elite later felt deeply threatened by growing cooperation between the movements. For example, in Air Force Undersecretary Townsend Hoopes's retrospective account, by 1967 the political chiefs were worried "above all" that "through riots, protests, *and the fateful merging of antiwar and racial dissension,* [the war] was polarizing U.S politics, dividing the American people from their government, and creating the gravest American political disunity in a century." [28] These were the political counselors who after the Tet offensive in early 1968 urged President Johnson to retrench. So presumably they would have been attuned to news of this "fateful merging," and their interest in information cannot explain why the *Times* scanted the interracial aspect of the April 1965 story. Quite the contrary: if national elite interests explained everything about the news, we would have expected the *Times* to pay direct attention.

The most plausible explanation is that, in April 1965, the *Times* did not yet construe the continuing, whole movement as "a story." "The story" was a set of isolated facts lying on the surface of a single event. Most likely the unnamed *Times* reporter was not close enough to the radical movement to notice that there was anything extraordinary about the racial composition in front of the White House. Interracialism or its absence was not yet a salient fact. The movement's own frame for the March was not so much *ruled* out of bounds as it was routinely *omitted*, unintentionally left outside the reporter's frame of reference.

28. Townsend Hoopes, *The Limits of Intervention* (New York: David McKay, 1969), p. 57 (emphasis added). A similar point is made in Chester Cooper's inside account, *The Lost Crusade: America in Vietnam* (New York: Dodd, Mead, 1970), p. 263.

4. But *other aspects of the March composition* were salient to the *Times*. As I've already mentioned, the lead to the *Times* Late City edition story read: "More than 15,000 students and a handful of adults picketed the White House in warm spring sunshine today, calling for an end of the fighting in Vietnam." One implication is that this is what happens to students when they are not adequately supervised by their elders. In an earlier edition, curiously, the lead began: "More than 15,000 students and a number of their elders. . . ." (A *Times* staff member must have intervened to change the lead this far—but not farther: not one other line was changed.)[29] The frame, in other words, was *generational*.

By contrast, the *Guardian* estimated that "almost one-fourth of the participants were not students"; *Guardian* reporter Price wrote:

The participants in the demonstration represented an amazing amalgam of forces, mostly young, on the move. They included Iowa farmers, students from innumerable campuses, peace workers, pacifists, socialists, revolutionaries, freedom workers from the South, the "old Left," and a new Left searching for a firm footing in a world in which they felt oppressed from all sides.[30]

5. *The Potter speech*. To the SDS elite and to a considerable proportion of the crowd, SDS President Paul Potter's speech closing the rally was a major event in itself. For it was the first public and eloquent articulation of a radical position on the war, insisting that because the war had been generated by the entire American social order, therefore the whole system had to be uprooted:

We must name that system. We must name it, describe it, analyze it, understand it and change it. For it is only when that system is changed and brought under control that there can be any hope for stopping the forces that create a war in Vietnam today or a murder in the South tomorrow. . . .

To many in the audience, this speech was to become both frame and inspiration for the antiwar movement: a way to think about the

29. On April 19, the *Times* unaccountably lowered its estimate to "more than 10,000." SDS, the *National Guardian*, and one police official estimated 25,000.

30. The *Guardian* adds this information on other press accounts: The *New York Herald Tribune* referred to the march "as the largest civil rights rally" since August 1963. The *Tribune* also reported that "some of [the demonstrators] wore beards, tweeds and dark glasses." (On an extremely sunny day, dark glasses are rather common, one would think.) The *Washington Star's* "seven individual photos of marchers" showed three beards and a mustache. Its accompanying "color" story emphasized "long hair and stovepipe tight pants" and referred to the marchers moving down the Capitol Mall as a "herd of tranquilized sheep."

war and the movement against it. It was not mentioned in the *Times*'s account. Even the fact that it was given was not mentioned.

Why? Both technical and ideological-cognitive factors came into play. The omission could be traced partly to the *Times*'s operating procedure: specifically, the early deadline for the Sunday edition. Kirkpatrick Sale has pointed out:

> Part of the problem, one that would persist through every single other Washington march, was that these marches were held on Saturday, so the reporters filing early for the Sunday A.M. deadlines rarely stayed around to see what went on in the afternoon or to hear the major speeches delivered during the afternoon rallies. Hence the effective, reasoned, inspired presentations—Paul Potter's during this April rally, Carl Oglesby in November—almost never got covered.[31]

Potter was rewriting his speech up to the hour of the rally, so the advance text which makes the reporter's task easier was not available. (For a Saturday rally, most reporters like to have a text on Friday.) Brash, inexperienced SDS was not concerned about such niceties: SDS was not wise, or practical, or even ambitious in the ways of amplifying its messages through the media. But this could have been only part of the problem. The early deadline and the absence of an advance text could not account for the omission of the very fact that Potter was to give a speech, when other speakers were named, at least in passing. What could account for the *Times*'s omission was Potter's obscurity as president of SDS. Most likely, the *Times* had no morgue file on Potter. Like an uncertified movement, an uncertified person whom reporters don't encounter in the everyday rounds of a beat is likely to be, precisely, offbeat. Noteworthiness, in the eyes of the *Times*, is like money: it takes some to get some.

Finally, it would not have been impossible for the *Times* to run a subsequent story on Potter's speech, or, indeed, on any of the neglected angles of the March; just such a follow-up piece on Carl Oglesby's speech at the November 1965 antiwar demonstration was Ward Just's astute "Student Radicals Challenge Liberals: Leader States Aims," which appeared in the *Washington Post* a full *two weeks after* the November rally. But such reflectiveness was unusual. The normal code of press operations insists on the transitory quality of news: unless, that is, it permits an exception.

6. *The tactical dispute.* After the Washington Monument rally,

31. Sale, "Myths as Eternal Truths," p. 3.

most of the demonstrators moved en masse toward the Capitol. According to the *Guardian* account:

> As the Capitol dome loomed larger, the sporadic singing of peace and freedom songs—at least in the front ranks—changed into sharp and angry chants. "Get out, get out." The chant died, replaced by another, "End the war."
>
> According to plan (and law), the marchers were to stop about 500 feet from the Capitol grounds, at the statue of Grant, from whence a token delegation would proceed to the Capitol to deliver the petition. As the front ranks reached the statue, the shout "Let's all go, let's all go" arose from hundreds of throats. Four hundred students marched across the cement walk that was to have signified a barrier to the march.
>
> "Let's all go," they shouted from across the walk, attempting to encourage others, dozens of whom continued to cross the cement barrier, heading toward the Capitol and an eventual confrontation with outnumbered police. At this point, several students identified with SDS began trying to restrain the rest of the group in the front ranks from crossing—and succeeded without difficulty. . . .
>
> About 300 students eventually sat down in front of the door to the Capitol, but dispersed after a half-hour when a police captain received the petition in lieu of anyone else.

This incident prefigured a central dispute in the antiwar movement between those who wanted to act more militantly and those who wanted to expand the movement's political base toward the center. Again, the *Times*'s early deadline would account for its neglecting this incident in its April 18 edition; and the newspaper's bias toward the immediate, toward yesterday's facts, accounts for subsequent neglect. Yet notice: in this incident, the *Times* had an opportunity to report an important division in the movement. It missed the opportunity. Or to put the matter differently: in this case, *the conventions of news-reporting overcame the paper's political interest in reporting divisions on the Left.*

In sum, the *Times* piece *deprecated* the size and significance of the march (the photo, the reference to "the principal occupant of the White House"); *marginalized* it by identifying it with youthful deviance ("a handful of adults," "a number of their elders," "beards and blue jeans"); *trivialized* it by failing to cover the call, the picket signs, or the speeches; and *polarized* it to its ostensible right-wing equivalent by choosing a wire-service photo that likened Left to Right. The frame was also *generational*. Meanwhile, the story failed to report politically significant interracialism or internal divisions in the movement.

Was this the *Times*'s standard treatment of demonstrations as such? How much did this coverage of the April 17 march follow from their normal journalistic practice (the model of crime news, the importance of deadlines, etc.), and how much was it the creature of more special ideological treatment? Happily, the *Guardian* compared this *Times* story with the *Times*'s treatment of the Selma-to-Montgomery civil rights march three weeks earlier, on March 26. Below a five-column, three-tiered, 36-point headline, and what the *Guardian* called "a panoramic photo of the massed march in Montgomery," the Selma lead read: "The Reverend Dr. Martin Luther King, Jr. led 25,000 Negroes and whites to the shadow of the state Capitol here today and challenged Alabama to put an end to racial discrimination." *Shadow* implied there was something menacing about Alabama authority: thus the civil rights challenge was to be taken seriously, at face value, as a moving and dramatic act of bravery. Compare: "More than 15,000 students and a handful of adults picketed the White House in warm spring sunshine today, calling for an end of the fighting in Vietnam." On April 17, there was an implication that students were not adults; perhaps this was valid and sufficient reason why (as we learn in the third sentence) "the principal occupant of the White House was at his ranch in Texas." "In warm spring sunshine" was an accurate description—but also, implicitly, a commendation of the hospitality, the welcoming air, of Washington, D.C. The phrase conveyed the sense that there was nothing much to fear from the White House, as if to say: "How could anybody get riled up in the warm glow? No shadows there." Or alternatively: "The frivolity of marching around on a beautiful day!" It's no wonder that only a handful of adults (chaperones?) could be found to accompany the young ones as they picketed the White House.

I have no way of knowing whether the *Times* writer meant to convey so much with a condescending phrase. But intention is not the issue. The issue is meaning, and the meaning of the lead emerges clearly in contrast with the meaning of the Montgomery lead. The Washington lead established the tone—discounting the demonstration and trivializing it. It is fair to conclude, as the *Guardian* did, that opposition to the Vietnam war was as illegitimate for the *Times* as civil rights was legitimate. And more: what shall we make of the fact that distinguishing sharply between legitimate and illegitimate movements was exactly the policy of Lyndon Johnson? Strikingly, in important ways the *Times* was covering demonstrations as the Johnson administration saw the world.[32] Shortly, we shall consider why this might have been.

IDENTIFYING SDS

Three weeks after the march, CBS broadcast a "takeout" on SDS—a longer assessment piece, not pegged to any particular event. This story ran over three minutes on the Evening News of May 6; it was narrated by the veteran correspondent Alexander Kendrick, attached to the New York bureau.

Kendrick recalls that, as usual when he got an assignment,

I was doing the interview; I devised the questions; I wrote and spoke the narration. The story as shot was under my control. What the editors and other processors did with it afterwards was not in my control, nor were the action pictures. . . . But for a reporter working out of the New York office it was very rare for a story to be edited without some sort of consultation, and at least tacit agreement. Technically any story, after being turned in by the reporter and film crew, belonged to CBS and they could do with it what

32. The *Time*'s follow-up story, on April 19, page 6, continues the mode of deprecation and trivialization even further. This time we have three very short stories under a single headline, "PICKETING KEPT UP AT THE WHITE HOUSE." Two of the stories are AP dispatches, one a *Times* Washington dispatch without a by-line. The lead of the Washington story reads: "A score of student opponents of the Government's policies in Vietnam, leftovers from the more than 10,000 who paraded yesterday, picketed in front of the White House today." The number has shrunk, unaccountably, to "more than 10,000." The picketers are "leftovers," not, say, "students who stayed in Washington at the cost of their studies." The third paragraph of this 2¼ column-inch item reads: "Mr. Woywod [a student] said the students did not plan to cause trouble, but hoped to present a petition tomorrow to a White House official." It seems a fair inference that the reporter asked Woywod the equivalent of "Do you plan to cause trouble?" and framed the event thereby.

The second short item, another 1¾ column inches from AP, is datelined Stonewall, Texas: "Demonstrators called off an Easter vigil this afternoon after having failed to give President Johnson himself a petition protesting United States actions in Vietnam. The petition was accepted by an aide." The AP here continues the *Times*'s own theme of the aloof President who does not let his vacation be disturbed by political interlopers, thereby consigning demonstrators to automatic ineffectuality. The uncounted demonstrators are "failures." The second and final paragraph describes them as "sunburned and weary."

The *Times*'s final bit reports that two Queens College students obtained 2,000 signatures on a pro-Johnson petition.

It is interesting that the well-known conservatism of the Associated Press works out in practice not substantially differently from the "objective" thematizing of the august *Times*. On AP, see the classic article by David Manning White, "The 'Gatekeeper': A Case Study in the Selection of News," *Journalism Quarterly* 27 (Fall 1950): 383–390.

they wished. As I say, in reality, there had to be consultation, if only to prevent mutiny. [As for the SDS story in particular] certainly there was no tension with the producer over its contents; in fact it was probably the producer who thought of the story in the first place.[33]

Like Fred Powledge of the *Times*, Kendrick himself was sympathetic to the New Left, and unusually well-informed. "My personal feeling," he writes,

having just returned after 20 solid years abroad and a close-up view of the decline of British, French, Belgian and other colonialism, was that Vietnam was both a moral and political American catastrophe.

In general, he "tended to read to the left"; he had read SDS's Port Huron Statement, for example. As head of the CBS London bureau from 1954 through early 1965, he had covered the Campaign for Nuclear Disarmament, and viewed it favorably: "When a guy like [Left Labourite M.P.] Michael Foot marches from Aldermaston to London [against British nuclear weapons]," he recollects, "you take it seriously."[34] Back in the States now for the first time in decades, Kendrick brought with him an uncommon distance from administration policies and an uncommon knowledgeability and experience. As one of the "Murrow boys" (the first generation of radio and then TV reporters who worked under Edward R. Murrow at CBS News), he had started out as a newspaper foreign correspondent in the days when a good deal of personal initiative went with the calling; later on, he had helped invent the conventions of television journalism. Unlike most TV reporters, he commanded his own regular radio program. In short, Kendrick was an old pro. And in this case, the sensibility and news sense of the correspondent matched the sensibility and news sense of the field producer in charge of the piece. Both were inclined to see the story in a large political frame.

A takeout, or feature—or as they called it at CBS, an "enter-priser"—was automatically more ample than the event-centered daily news piece. Far from being confined by an imminent deadline, the takeout was deliberately explanatory. There was less time pressure, and the form was less rigid. The organizational system

33. This quotation and the first one in the following paragraph come from Kendrick's letter to me, January 3, 1977. Kendrick adds: "But whatever reporting I did I like to think was based on the merits of a story, not on what I thought about the story."

34. Interview, Alexander Kendrick, November 17, 1976.

for producing takeouts was even partitioned off from the hard news operation: the takeout field producer was responsible to a CBS Evening News producer, at that time Russ Bensley, while hard news had its own top producer. True, as Kendrick says, editors, co-producers, the executive producer, anchorman Cronkite, and even (though rarely) higher management could intervene at various stages to shape the final piece. But once the decision was made to proceed on a subject, the field producer and the correspondent, working together, had their way—subject, of course, to their sense of what the organization permitted.[35]

The May 6 takeout on SDS began with a medium shot of Kendrick standing before a campus building, facing into the camera in the habitually distanced, authoritative manner and asking, "Whatever happened to the conformist student generation? There has been a participation explosion. College students are in ferment— or it seems that way." As Kendrick went on speaking, the screen showed a montage of scenes of student groups, in demonstrations, rallies, singing—all high-spirited, all determinedly nonviolent. Kendrick labeled the phenomenon "the new student left. Its slogan is, 'We protest inadequate everything.'" (In fact, this was the half-joking—but only half—slogan of the Cleveland community organizing project of SDS's Economic Research and Action Project, ERAP). "Some," Kendrick went on, "are the new left. Some are linked to the old left, including the Communist Party. Most have no ideology. One such organization is Students for a Democratic Society." With this, the scene changed to a close-up of SDS President Paul Potter, dressed in a suit and tie. (No pretext for a youthful deviance frame here!) Potter spoke of the Chase Manhattan demonstration and the March on Washington, and their objectives. Kendrick asked: "You say you're not affiliated politically. Aren't you really taking a political line?" Potter: "We're searching. . . . Political liberalism is not doing the job." A more muted version of Potter's Washington speech, this was a fair representation of the dominant SDS mood: the fear of rigidity, the spirit of search, experiment, risk—all of which angered Marxists as well as liberals inside and outside SDS.

As the camera showed SDS office staff mimeographing and printing pamphlets, and panned the office walls to show the stick-

35. On the general workings of network news, see Edward Epstein, *News from Nowhere* (New York: Random House, 1973), Gaye Tuchman, *Making News* (New York: The Free Press, 1978), and Gans, *Deciding What's News*.

ers "Register to Vote" and "Free Speech Movement," Kendrick's voice-over said: "At its New York headquarters, SDS writes and disseminates pamphlets on civil rights, free speech, university reform, poverty, the draft, and nuclear war." Then the summary, Kendrick once more reading into the camera:

Their own paid organizers are not paid much—a mere subsistence. Admittedly a small minority, the student left may have bitten off more than it can chew. Its aims may spring more from the heart than from any defined program of legislation. But it has brought to the surface many of the doubts and uncertainties of American youth—and its desires. And by engaging itself it has engaged many others in new appraisals. Alexander Kendrick, CBS News, Tufts University.

The theme of the small movement was prominent; so was the difficulty a man of Kendrick's generation had comprehending the programless left. But what was more striking was Kendrick's tribute to SDS's *intellectual* sweep (the publications), its *moral* seriousness (low pay), and its larger *meaning* (as a provoker of "new appraisals"). As a house intellectual, Kendrick had caught on to SDS's importance as the crest of a larger social movement. Like Powledge's feature for the *Times*, Kendrick's piece broke through the standard hard-news frame.[36] But so far as I can tell, it was one of a kind. Paradoxically, the freedom accorded the takeout can serve *within the news organization* to relieve the hard story of the responsibility to be substantively intelligible. If explanation ("the 'why' of a story") was consigned to the realm of the "in-depth" feature, then the hard-news story ("the 'what' of the story") cannot so easily be faulted for its shallowness. Similarly, when network news is accused of superficiality, its defenders routinely cite the pressure of time, and then refer the critic to documentaries or newsmagazine shows for "depth."

And speaking of documentaries, it is worth pausing briefly to consider the fate of CBS's only documentary of the year on the

36. On CBS's frames, see note 21, above, and the discussion of Bruce Morton's coverage of the November 1965 SANE March, in Chapter 3, pp. 119–122, below. Notice, likewise, that *Times* coverage of the women's liberation movement later was far more thorough, regular, and sympathetic in the women's pages than in the news section. (See Gaye Tuchman, "Ridicule, Advocacy, and Professionalism: Newspaper Reporting about a Social Movement," paper delivered to the American Sociological Association meeting, New York, August 1976.) The difference, of course, is that the *Times*'s women's section is a continuing feature capable of giving regular coverage. The television takeout is a one-shot.

New Left, Arthur Barron's *The Berkeley Rebels*. Barron's detailed account of the editing imposed on him by high CBS officials gives us a rare glimpse into the ways in which media elites enforce normal journalistic operations, and the occasions when high political interests overcome the producer's workaday autonomy.[37]

Barron, who had a Ph.D. in sociology, had already written and produced six documentaries for CBS when he went to work for CBS Reports in 1965. CBS wanted a documentary about youth, taking off from "the trouble at Berkeley." Barron traveled to Berkeley, and then proposed to CBS Reports a film about four people: a political rebel, a graduate disenchanted with the university, and "a young unmarried couple who had rebelled against their parents and were living together, and represented a kind of new search for values."[38] Barron further proposed that his film "evoke the world of the students," that it not be "factual" or "objective reporting." CBS agreed, and Barron went on to produce a film full of *cinéma vérité* devices, "evocative sequences," including some that were staged for effect.

The president of CBS News, Fred Friendly, and the vice-president in charge of news documentaries told Barron to delete the staged sequences; network policy strictly prohibits staging. Barron made the deletions, and his superiors approved the film. And then, three weeks before broadcast, CBS Chairman William S. Paley and President Frank Stanton ordered new changes—over Friendly's protest. What they ordered out included an orgiastic fraternity party sequence shot in order to contrast Joe College self-indulgence with the rebels' disaffection; the executives called this "a slander against nice kids." They also cut a sequence demonstrating the use of television in university lecture halls ("too extreme"). In the name of balance, they ordered Barron "to fly out to Berkeley and interview professors analyzing the revolt and saying things like, 'The kids are immature and impatient. It will all blow over,' that kind of thing." They forced him to insert "two or three minutes from a speech [University President] Clark Kerr made in the Greek Theatre in Berkeley." And most damaging to the *vérité* film

37. The account that follows derives from an interview with Arthur Barron by Alan Rosenthal, printed in Rosenthal's *The New Documentary in Action: A Casebook in Film Making* (Berkeley: University of California Press, 1971), especially pp. 139–148. I am grateful to Professor Lawrence Lichty of the University of Wisconsin for alerting me to this material.
38. Ibid., p. 141.

he had set out to make, Paley and Stanton forced him to write a deprecating introduction and conclusion for CBS correspondent Harry Reasoner, with Reasoner voice-overs to be superimposed over each sequence. Where the film had depicted a political bull session without narrative comment, for example, now Barron wrote a voice-over statement along these lines: "The bull session—an old and true ritual of young people, wherein much heat but little light is shed."[39] In this domesticated form, *The Berkeley Rebels* was aired.

CBS Reports knew from the beginning that Barron's idea was unorthodox, that it violated the normal strictures of balance and objectivity. There was, in the beginning, enough slack in the documentary norms to permit a daring exception to the routine. Then why the last-minute intervention from a higher level? Barron's theory is tantalizing:

I was told later [Barron does not say by whom] that what had happened was that Clark Kerr, the president of the University of California, had written a letter to Frank Stanton saying in effect that he hadn't seen the picture but had been told that it was very dangerous and unfair; that it was distorted and full of lies; that I had paid people to say things; and that there were various erotic scenes in the film—in short, that the whole thing was going to be a disaster and would be very embarrassing to the university and to CBS. As far as I understand, Stanton didn't interview Kerr and got no expert testimony. He just bought the story, hook, line, and sinker. So, I was told to make these changes. I can't really tell you what they were; there were too many.[40]

The high network command intervened, in other words, when they were jarred by a prominent and influential class ally. Barron's story testifies to the rising influence of the university elite; it also illustrates the principle that the media elite actively construe and alter their world view and enforce their standards, *even—if necessary—against the normal workings of journalistic routines.* This intervention, if it happened as Barron was told, was an early portent. Barron had departed from the conventions; this was unusual in itself. As American politics heated up through the later sixties, as the elite political consensus on the war and on the American destiny broke apart, more reporters broke more often—fitfully, partially, inconsistently, but in earnest—from hegemonic assump-

39. Ibid., p. 147.
40. Ibid., p. 146.

tions. Then normal news routines failed to accomplish their task of reinforcing social stability, of cooling out opposition, of suggesting through subtle frames that the institutional structure of the society was deservedly superior to—and in control of—everything but the weird. Later, alternative news frames crystallized, to corroborate, to make sense of—and to domesticate—the spreading opposition movement. An administration committed to prosecuting a divisive war had to crack down on both the movement and its far-from-enthusiastic amplifier (it could barely tell the difference between the two). By the time the Nixon White House took to exercising the heavy hand, the media elite were hard-pressed to choose between what the journalism they had cultivated told them was true, and what the President told them was right.

But in 1965, the routine journalistic procedures still sufficed, almost always, to keep news coverage of the New Left aligned with the assumptions of the elite political consensus. That consensus was only now congealing. Fred Powledge's treatment belonged to a past that preceded the hardening of the dominant frame. The movement was now regularly reported as trivial and deviant; increasingly it was seen as dangerous as well.

We see the hegemonic frame at work again in the *New York Times*'s coverage of the SDS convention, in two pieces by Natalie Jaffe, June 13 and 14.[41] This first report of the organization's inner workings—indeed, the first intimation that the organization might *have* inner workings—began on page 77 of the Sunday edition with the headline: "STUDENT SOCIETY WORKS ON AIMS: Finds Meeting Can Be More Trouble Than Campaign." The story begins:

KEWADIN, Michigan, June 12—The executive secretary of Students for a Democratic Society climbed on a picnic table today and addressed more than 300 delegates to the organization's annual convention on its third day.

"How many think the food is lousy?" he asked. A loud chorus of yeas.

"How many think there's not enough?" More loud yeas.

"How many would put up a couple of extra bucks to improve things?" Vehement boos.

"In that case, when you complain, please think of this in the context of the problem," concluded the speaker, Clark Kissinger.

A University of Texas student in blue jeans and boots muttered, "And

41. There was actually a third, unsigned article in the *Times*'s convention series, on June 16, but it was brief and not worth analyzing: a strictly matter-of-fact report, on page 28, of the election of Carl Oglesby as SDS President.

they wonder why we spent all morning discussing how to create and operate the participatory democracy?''

This exchange, which took place on a grassy, maple-strewn hillside
here in northern Michigan, illustrates a major problem of Students for a
Democratic Society, an organization that has taken a leading role in the
movement known as the new student left.

Already in these opening paragraphs, the frame is unambiguous: the organization is ambitious beyond its means. The unifying tone is ridicule. The remarks as quoted are ludicrous. Even the
syntax is garbled to guarantee senselessness. (No one in SDS ever
spoke of *"the"* participatory democracy.) The rest of the piece continued in this manner, interspersing laughable physical details
among pieces of the SDS program, conveying the impression that
SDS's ambitions were absurd. For example:

> Standing on the lawn outside the big main house here at Camp Maple-
> hurst, and shouting over the clamor for more breakfast from the dining
> room, Mr. Kissinger said: "Maybe when all the forces finally get together,
> the country will remember this as the beginning of a real left opposition."
> He looked down the rows of bunkhouses, where many of the delegates
> were still rolled up in their sleeping bags.

And so on. Jaffe's scorn for the proceedings was bolstered by
faulty statements about SDS activities—distorted in such a way as
to seem not so much dangerous as incoherent, senseless, and, in
their own way, absurd. Every subsequently adduced fact was absorbed into the general mockery, and seemed to warrant it. For
example:

> Unlike the civil rights and the university reform groups, the society has
> chosen its causes less to get results than to dramatize what it considers
> basic errors of national principle. From its national office comes an endless
> flow of documents analyzing these errors.

It was difficult to imagine that this "endless flow" could contain
anything of substance or worth. It was an image of SDS's production of literature quite different from Kendrick's.

Jaffe's mood piece was consigned to the far reaches of the Sunday news section, and its impact was probably weakened thereby.
But her report the next day appeared on page 16, under the headline: "Student Group Proposes Major Protest Against Vietnam Policy." Now the image of SDS graduated from absurd pretension to
militancy and menace.

The entire story hinged on a proposal by SDS National Secretary Clark Kissinger that the organization encourage antiwar soldiers to desert en masse, and thereby challenge the government to suppress SDS under the Espionage Act of 1917. Kissinger had in mind a Nuremberg-type legal defense, a political trial. He had been promoting this scheme for several months; within the inner circles of SDS it had become known, less than enthusiastically, as "the Kamikaze plan." The success of the scheme would depend on publicity: in theory, publicity would push the government into a corner and force it to prosecute. The Kamikaze proposal loomed large at the convention because SDS leaders did not know how else to follow the March on Washington, what part to play in the antiwar movement. No specific counterproposals emerged. The convention overall was confused and confusing. So it made sense that Jaffe should latch onto the Kamikaze plan: if nothing else, it was a definite proposal, a peg amidst incoherence. But in focusing on Kissinger's flamboyant announcement, she garbled the politics of the proposal and effectively overstated SDS's commitment to it. One jumbled sentence late in the story was her sole attempt to represent an SDS political position:

The issues, according to the society, involve the prevention of the Vietnamese people from exercising their right of self-determination, which is not justified by Washington's desire to contain Communism.

But the greater misrepresentation had to do with the status of the Kissinger plan itself. The headline—"Student Group Proposes Major Protest"—made it sound as if SDS had decided to go ahead with the Kamikaze plan. (It never did.) The second paragraph, however, more accurately denoted something more vague:

The 300 delegates to the group's national convention here at Camp Maplehurst expressed their willingness to stake the survival of their 2000 member organization on support of such a protest. But they deferred a decision on whether they would take a place in the front line.

All the way down the page, in the penultimate paragraph, came the convention's actual decision about the proposal:

Since such a campaign would require all the resources of the society, which has been primarily concerned with domestic affairs and community organization, a final decision on student participation was left until a general referendum of all the members.

This buried fact—which threw the earlier account into question—now flowed into the concluding paragraph:

The 5-day conference ends today. The society still seems evenly divided between those who want to concentrate on local issues and those who prefer involvement in national issues.

"... *still seems evenly divided.*" Yet neither in this piece nor the previous one had there been an account of that "even divide"—a live tension in SDS between the community organizers and the campus-based. This was one of the animating issues of the convention, and Jaffe had mentioned it only in passing. On the face of it, such an "even division" should have considerably diminished the significance of Kissinger's Kamikaze plan. Jaffe did not try to resolve the discrepancy. By stating the qualification only in her final sentence, she preserved the unadopted Kamikaze plan as the story's determining frame.

The theme was militancy, a sort of freestanding tactical emphasis severed from SDS's political understanding, from its hesitations and divisions, and from its actual organizational life. The frame, again, is always a principle of rejection as well as a principle of selection. Most likely it determines how the article is read; only the closest of readings will detect the qualifications tacked on at the end of the story. The subtlest and most accurate reporting will incorporate complication in the heart of the story, precisely to overcompensate for the power of the frame. Leaving the significant qualification for the end, on the other hand, amounts to admitting that the frame will not hold the available evidence—while retaining it nevertheless.

The *Times*'s major frame was shifting, from Powledge's serious, respectful coverage to April's mixture of deprecation, marginalization, trivialization, and polarization. In the June convention coverage, SDS was introduced as a dangerous, extreme political force. These turns could be attributed only partly to actual turns in SDS policy. But when we look closely, we can see a kind of *internal*, textual unity in these later phases of coverage: trivialization and the attribution of menace are not such different frames of reference as they may appear to be. Far from being mutually exclusive, they are alternating expressions of a more fundamental notion: *SDS as the deviant other*. The marginality and menace themes were united by a subterranean logic: they were conjoint ways of evading the substantive political challenge proposed and embodied by the New Left.[42] When dissidents were "muttering," "rolled up in sleeping bags," "bearded," disheveled, and at the same time planning massive illegality, they themselves became the issue. Seeing opposition this way, respectable opinion—reporters, editors, and respectable readers alike—avoided having to take seriously any fundamentally opposed view of the free society that was raining napalm upon a small nation in revolution.

But if triviality and menace were compatible and functionally related frames, why did the *Times* consistently move over time from one to the other? Why a progression from the marginal and trivial to the menacing; why not, say, a random oscillation? Here a purely formal interpretation of the two frames runs up against its limit, and a textual analysis of cultural artifacts must move outside journalism proper into the larger realm of politics and history. For the way the nation's most influential and prestigious newspaper covers an opposition movement—whatever else it may be—is also a political fact: the outcome of a complex interaction in which the political assumptions and strategies of editors and publisher combine with conventions of newsworthiness and technical factors of news production, as well as the particular approach of the reporter, to generate a frame and a story.

The general community of interest between top political leaders and top media owners and executives seems obvious: they share a common education, common social contacts, much common experience in relation to subordinate groups, a commonly nurtured world view—a common class position, in a word. One wonders, then, about possible routes of direct influence and coordination. How and when could specific cues be transmitted from the State to the media when there is a taboo on acknowledging them? If political interventions do shape the news, they are likely to be concealed, if for no other reason than that they violate the canons of journalistic autonomy. Therefore, the scarcity of hard-and-fast evidence for such interventions—whether in memoirs or interviews—cannot be taken as conclusive disproof of the hypothesis. No research can establish sharply just what took place in the minds of *Times* editors and *Times* reporters, or between them, in

42. On a similarly split image of the deviant other, see Frank Pearce, "How to Be Immoral and Ill, Pathetic and Dangerous, All at the Same Time: Mass Media and the Homosexual," in Cohen and Young, eds., *Manufacture of News*, pp. 284–301.

the spring of 1965. Nor have I uncovered anything more than fragmentary and (at times) hearsay evidence of any direct communications from the Johnson White House to the *New York Times*, or of editors consciously or unconsciously aligning their coverage to harmonize with the goals of the Johnson administration.

In fact, I plunged into this examination of the 1965 events assuming that there was no coherent political orchestration of the slant of *Times* coverage. Impressed by the *Times*'s reputation for independence, I was decidedly skeptical that reporters and editors would be swayed by anything so crude as the political policy of the moment. True, the *Times* had on one famous occasion permitted itself to be swayed, holding up an advance report on the CIA-sponsored Bay of Pigs invasion in April 1961. Then, in 1966, *Times* managing editor Clifton Daniel had performed public self-criticism for the *Times*'s censorship. After the embarrassment of 1961, presumably the *Times* would have stood firmer against White House pressure; President Kennedy himself had taken Turner Catledge aside to tell him, "Maybe if you had printed more about the operation you would have saved us from a colossal mistake." (When Catledge had pointed out that earlier information had previously appeared in the *Nation*, Kennedy said: "But it wasn't news until it appeared in the *Times*.")[43] In 1963, David Halberstam later recounted, President Kennedy had complained to *Times* publisher Sulzberger about Halberstam's reporting from Vietnam, and had suggested to Sulzberger (jocularly, he later insisted) that Halberstam be moved elsewhere; but Sulzberger had stood firm.[44] When the *Times* cares so much about its reputation for autonomy, and when indeed its usefulness to readers depends in good measure on that reputation, why speculate about political orchestration?

But close observation of the pattern of *Times* coverage of the movement throughout 1965 led me to wonder about the sources of shifts in frame—shifts which could not be explained conclusively by fixed journalistic practice. True, it remains possible that the variations I have recorded could be attributed to the vagaries of reportorial style. The possibility cannot be dismissed. Yet it is worth entertaining the hypothesis that the progression in *Times* images of SDS from (a) serious movement (Powledge in March), to (b) marginal, ineffectual, contested oddity (April), to (c) a mixture of absur-

43. Catledge, *My Life and The Times*, p. 264.
44. David Halberstam, *The Making of a Quagmire* (New York: Random House, 1965), p. 268.

dity and menace (Jaffe in June), and subsequently to (d) undoubted menace (October), was partly the professional, informal, unreflective, "free" response of *Times* reporters to their editors' responses, in turn, to the Johnson administration's escalation of the Vietnam war; and partly their political response to the unsettling emergence of a radical movement.

In the first four months of 1965, the Johnson administration unleashed unremitting air war on North and South Vietnam, and landed 200,000 ground troops in the South. We know now that President Johnson took steps to influence media coverage of the war; I broach and interpret the evidence in Part III, below. It stands to reason that Johnson was also interested in dampening media coverage of the budding antiwar movement, and turning what coverage there was to his own uses. Johnson, like Nixon after him, understood that any coverage of the war that stretched outside the official frame, even if it didn't directly contradict that frame, was likely to damage the war effort through its weak link: American public opinion.[45] Anything less than an uncritical relay of the administration point of view was, in the long run at least, dangerous to the administration prosecuting the war. In order to make the huge American expeditionary force and the new air war "credible," Johnson and Nixon both needed a docile public, or at least a confused and accepting one, if they could not have one that was sufficiently enthusiastic. The very existence of the antiwar movement, then, was tantamount to political sabotage of the war effort.

45. In *The Time of Illusion* (New York: Alfred A. Knopf, 1976), Jonathan Schell has shown the centrality of image-management, "credibility," in the war planning of three administrations, from Kennedy through Nixon. Although he exaggerates somewhat for the sake of the point (Woodrow Wilson, less concerned to keep hidden *his* war agenda, needed no such rationale to justify repressing the movement against American intervention in World War I), Schell's argument does bolster the point I am making. For example: "When a government has founded the national defense on the national image, as the United States did under the doctrine of credibility, it follows that any internal dissensions will be interpreted as an attack on the safety of the nation. . . . If the Vietnam war was one aspect of the nation's image, then the political process at home was the very essence of the nation's image. . . . What better way is there to oppose a public-relations war than with a public-relations insurrection? The anti-war movement was often taken to task for its 'theatricality.' The fact is that it was precisely in its theatricality that its special genius lay. The war had been conceived as theatre—as a production for multiple 'audiences'—and the anti-war movement was counter-theatre, and very effective counter-theatre. . . . The fact is that the demonstrations at home struck at the very foundation of the larger aims for which the war was being fought. They struck a crippling blow at the credibility on which the whole strategy was based" (pp. 368–369).

As Johnson acknowledged when he renounced his second term on March 31, 1968, he had never been wrong to fear the potential of his opposition.

We have no evidence that Johnson directly attempted to manage news of the antiwar movement. But images of the antiwar movement hinged significantly on images of the war; messages about how to handle the movement could be conveyed quietly, tacitly, piggyback, as corollaries to messages about how to handle the war. Nothing conspiratorial here, necessarily; at CBS News, for example, a top producer explained to me that the antiwar movement and student radicalism in general were routinely seen as part of the larger story of the Vietnam war.[46] Or there may have been no direct White House attempts to influence treatment of the movement at all. Or there may have been attempts which failed. All we know for certain is that the administration did maneuver to affect the slant of war coverage. We know that the deceptive public information policies of the military in Saigon ("the five o'clock follies") were not invented at low echelons but were centrally decreed. There is this piece of documentary evidence, for one: On April 6, 1965, McGeorge Bundy, the Special Assistant to the President, recorded in a memorandum that, on April 1, Johnson had approved the sending of eighteen to twenty thousand more troops to Vietnam. Even more important, Johnson had approved, in Bundy's words, "a change of mission for all Marine Battalions deployed to Vietnam to permit their more active use." Their mission was no longer "static defense" but "ground combat." Johnson had given the first official, across-the-board presidential clearance for offensive military action in Vietnam. At the same time, Bundy wrote:

The President desires that . . . premature publicity be avoided by all possible precautions. The actions themselves should be taken as rapidly as practicable, but in ways that should minimize any appearance of sudden changes in policy. . . . The President's desire is that these movements and changes should be understood as being gradual and wholly consistent with existing policy.[47]

Only within Johnson's war plan was his change of orders to the Marines "gradual" and "wholly consistent with existing policy."

46. Interview, Russ Bensley, November 16, 1976. Bensley was telling me why he thought student activism *in 1976* was being underreported: it lacked the handle of the war.

47. Memo NSAM 328, Document 254 in *The Pentagon Papers*, Gravel Edition, Vol. 3 (Boston: Beacon Press, 1972), pp. 702–703.

But high administration officials held to this frame, and most reporters went along. Officials had more than one standard method for misleading reporters. Obviously they could monopolize information, at least for long periods of time. They could easily resort to the "background" briefing, whose ground rules pledged reporters not to disclose the source of official remarks. The "backgrounder" was thus a marvelous device for dispensing administration versions—including lies, half-truths, and strategic omissions—without having to stand publicly behind them. Less inquisitive reporters were prone to rely on the administration version, while the more inquisitive could be stalled, befuddled, and warded off. CBS's diplomatic correspondent Marvin Kalb recalled that it took "an entire month . . . of trying to get various spokesmen for both the White House and the State Department and the Pentagon" before they would "acknowledge what in fact McGeorge Bundy's memo says, that there has been a change of mission."[48]

Evidence abounds that the Johnson administration routinely lied to reporters about the nature and purposes of the war.[49] What is less well understood, and more relevant to coverage of the antiwar movement, is that the lie often took the form of *minimizing* the magnitude of the enemy's forces and actions. Daniel Ellsberg, who in 1965 was Special Assistant to John McNaughton, Robert McNamara's top aide in the Pentagon, recalls that the Brink Hotel, an American Army barracks in Saigon, was destroyed by NLF fire on Christmas day 1964, and that the Joint Chiefs of Staff and Ambassador Maxwell Taylor wanted to start bombing North Vietnam in retaliation right then. But Johnson was not yet ready for the major escalation that was to be justified by the much smaller NLF attack on the Pleiku base in February 1965; and so he took steps (which the press did not contravene) to minimize reports of the damage to the Brink Hotel.[50] The explanation for this bizarre project in news management, according to Ellsberg, lies in *the administration's fear of*

48. Transcript, CBS News Special Report, "The Pentagon Papers: What They Mean" (broadcast Tuesday, July 13, 1971, 10:00–11:00 P.M.), p. 17. © 1971 CBS Inc. All rights reserved.

49. See, for example, David Halberstam, *The Best and The Brightest* (New York: Random House, 1972); William McGaffin and Erwin Knoll, *Anything But the Truth* (New York: Putnam's, 1968); and Ben H. Bagdikian, *The Effete Conspiracy* (New York: Harper and Row, 1972). According to Daniel Ellsberg (interview, March 2, 1977), Johnson went so far as to have Ambassador Ellsworth Bunker in Saigon send him specially concocted false cables bearing high classifications, which he could then leak to reporters as evidence from the field.

50. Interview, Daniel Ellsberg, March 2, 1977.

arousing a McCarthyite public opinion which it conceived to be lurking in the wings to its Right. Official "optimism" about the war effort was one way of managing a public construed as prone to stampede: if the light was visible at the end of that famous tunnel, the administration could not be attacked for failing to take more extreme military measures—measures which Johnson thought were dangerous, unnecessary, and expensive. Minimizing the NLF's threat to American troops was part of this Machiavellian strategy.[51]

Interestingly, *Times* editors had parallel reasons to shy away from covering the antiwar movement too sympathetically and the war too critically. According to a reporter who worked there between 1966 and 1968, the editors were bending over backward to avoid handing the Right any pretext for charging the paper with sympathy for Communism.[52] McCarthyism "had cut a wide swath through the *Times*" in the fifties. Turner Catledge recalls that, in 1955, Senator James O. Eastland's Senate Internal Security Subcommittee had held hearings on Communists in American newspapers. Eastland had called thirty-eight witnesses, of whom twenty-five were from the *New York Times*. Sixteen of these held positions in the news or editorial departments; six had admitted having once belonged to the Communist Party. Catledge records that publisher Sulzberger's "deep personal abhorrence of Communism" warred with "his protective and paternal feeling toward employees of the *Times*." In the end, although *Times* editors decided a reporter's exercise of the Fifth Amendment against self-incrimination was not to be taken as prima facie evidence of the reporter's guilt, the editors called all the named ex-Communists to account—in the *Times*'s own investigation. "When our employees were named as former Communists," in Catledge's words, "they had an obligation to give the *Times* management a full, candid accounting of their political histories. Only by so doing could they maintain the trust and confidence both of management and their fellow workers that were essential if our newspaper was to

51. For more along this line of argument, see Ellsberg's *Papers on the War* (New York: Simon and Schuster, 1972), especially the essay "The Quagmire Myth and the Stalemate Machine."

52. Interview, Lawrence M. Bensky, February 14, 1977. Also see Godfrey Hodgson, *America in Our Time* (Garden City, N.Y.: Doubleday, 1976), pp. 374–375: the majority of producers and news editors at NBC News when Edward Epstein interviewed there (Jewish, middle- to upper-middle-class in origin, urban-educated) were "precisely the people who had learned in the McCarthy period to fear the dormant right-wing anger of the sleeping beast, the great American majority."

function effectively on the course we had set." After questioning all the accused, *Times* editors fired three of them—two copy-editors and an assistant book-review editor—for "choosing not to cooperate."[53]

Ten years later, the Red scare had receded; but *Times* editors had not forgotten how to be afraid of looking excessively critical of government policy. And how could reporters be insulated from this fear and its history? Like high-level definitions of balance, objectivity, and newsworthiness, high-level editorial fear (to use Catledge's words) "set a tone." And as Fred Powledge says, fear of being labeled left-wing does not need to be spread "in so many words." A workplace can be soaked in it; timidity can become an occupational tradition.

Both the administration and the *Times*, in other words, feared that the antiwar movement would trigger a right-wing backlash; that they could be blamed, after the fact, for "losing Vietnam." A few years later, Vice-President Spiro Agnew enlisted the White House in just such a crusade against the "effete snobs" of the media; and media people breathed many sighs of relief when Richard Nixon went down in flames. Their fears may have been self-serving; they were also far from unrealistic. But in all the appropriate furor about the machinations of the Nixon White House—about which more below—the *Johnson* administration's forays into news management tend to be eclipsed. In any event, who knows what specific combination of assignments, editing, and editorial gestures took place in 1965? Although there is plenty of evidence of direct management of war news, I have no firm evidence that the White House deliberately and directly attempted to influence *Times* treatment of the antiwar movement in particular. It seems more likely that the New Left had taken the *Times* by surprise in the first place. Fred Powledge's treatment filled a vacuum before hegemonic policy had been formulated. After the paper's early hesitations between respectful and trivializing coverage, the theme of the *dangerous* movement now arose "spontaneously" in the minds of reporters—it arose, that is, in the crucible of Cold War ideology, in editorial policy transmitted to staff in a thousand quiet ways, and in the course of routine dependence on official news sources. In the spring of 1965, all this began to crystallize in response to the dra-

53. Catledge, *My Life and The Times*, pp. 225–236. The quotations are from pp. 226–227 and 233.

matic turn in the Johnson administration's war policy. The details of the *Times*'s turn toward a hegemonic understanding of the New Left remain murky; but in an important way the details do not matter. What remains clear is that (1) the *Times* was shifting frames, (2) the shift was toward alignment with government policy, and (3) the shift had a coherence that cannot be explained by actual changes in the New Left over so short a time.

And yet that shift of frame did, in the end, correspond to something real in the society: not accurately, as a mirror image corresponds to a reflected object, but as a distortion of something actual. The movement *was* becoming more radical, more disaffected, and more militant; it *was* spreading; for all the trivial signs that journalists seized upon as tokens of this radicalization, this growing anti-imperialism, the movement was beginning to loom up as something more than a narrow, transitory phenomenon. Rather, it was now appearing to be a profound challenge to the core principles which the dominant institutions sustain. The government and the *Times* shared a fear so general and all-pervading, so deeply lodged in routine assumptions about the way things ought to be done, that it had to have shaped reporting of the movement. They feared all mass movements *as such*, because mass movements threaten to get out of control and disrupt the rationales of their power and privilege. The New Left in particular disrupted decorum and professional roles; it threatened the prerogatives of the powerful, the adequacy of their ideological self-justifications and their very discourse; it disputed their claims to systematic and beneficent knowledge of the world. Only later did the media managers come to understand that they had an interest in embracing the moderate wing of the movement, in order to avert what they construed to be the far greater evil of unending social uproar. (See Chapter 7.) The antiwar movement *was* coming to reject the core hegemonic principles of the American system, and it was beginning to find allies at every class and race layer of the society. As established journalism had opposed the Populist and Socialist movements at earlier historical moments, now it wheeled its routines around to confront the new incarnation of a traditional nemesis.

3 SDS in the Spotlight, Fall 1965

SDS IN THE SEMI-DARK

Throughout the summer and into the fall of 1965, the antiwar movement spread throughout the country, grew more various and at times more militant. In August, a loose coalition of civil rights and peace activists organized an Assembly of Unrepresented People (AUP) to march on the Congress demanding peace: if Congress failed to end the war, the march would stream into the chambers to *declare* peace, carrying out the uncompleted militancy of the tail end of the April 17 march. Afterward there were two main foci of antiwar action: the first nationally coordinated actions of the International Days of Protest, October 15 and 16, and then the moderate March on Washington organized by SANE for November 27.

SDS was involved in all this only in a backhanded and lurching way. Despite the hopes of Berkeley's new Vietnam Day Committee, just beginning to work toward the International Days of Protest, SDS failed to generate *any* antiwar organizing program at the Kewadin convention in June. At Kewadin, the leadership proved reluctant to convert SDS into a single-issue organization, no matter how urgent the issue; it was distant from campus concerns and moods, it despaired of the practical prospects of a narrow antiwar movement, and in the crevices of consciousness it feared it could jeopardize the organization's safety if SDS, in wartime, threw itself into the leadership of a movement for peace. So although Carl Oglesby, the newly elected SDS president, and other SDS activists worked on the Assembly of Unrepresented People, the organization refused to endorse it and even discouraged members from attending, while cynics both inside and outside SDS highlighted the Assembly's symbolic putschist connotations by derisively—and bemusedly—calling it the *Congress* of Unrepresented People, or COUP. In the end, these internecine issues were veiled by the widely circulated newsphoto of the demonstration, which relayed a colorful, heroic battlefield image of organizers Staughton Lynd, Dave Dellinger, and Bob Parris just after they had been splashed with red paint by a right-wing disrupter.[1]

The vacuum left by SDS's inability to lead the nascent antiwar movement was quickly filled by the newly formed National Coordinating Committee to End the War in Vietnam (NCCEWV), which sponsored the AUP. On their own, many of the SDS chapters worked up local antiwar projects and hooked up with the NCCEWV, which set up its own national coordinating office in Madison, Wisconsin. But in the midst of the International Days of Protest in October, mass media bent on exposure and investigation pushed a bewildered and incoherent SDS to the center of attention; SDS was suddenly outfitted with a reputation for activity that drastically outdistanced its political reality. To study the meteoric rise of SDS itself as an object of publicity, and the techniques SDS improvised to work in the media spotlight, is to move toward understanding the power of the media over an opposition movement and, dialectically, the nature and limits of a movement's response. For this sequence of events helped push SDS toward a new course and, in no small sense, a new identity. Such episodes of crisis and direct pressure deserve special attention; they often establish, and often prefigure, shifts in the balance of political forces, the emergence of new patterns of relation, new structures of cognition, new opportunities for being in the political world. In the movement-media dance, they create some new steps and the occasion for others—all of which may end up transforming the dance and the political situation as a whole.

Throughout the summer, while SDS was dormant, the war reached a new pitch of violence, and antiwar militancy intensified to suit. The AUP was one sign; in Berkeley and Oakland, meanwhile, the Vietnam Day Committee (VDC) tried to block warbound troop trains, to a fanfare of publicity. *New York Times*

1. On the Assembly of Unrepresented People, see Kirkpatrick Sale, *SDS* (New York: Random House, 1973), pp. 219–221, and the debates recorded in *Liberation* 10 (June–July 1965), especially Staughton Lynd, "Coalition Politics or Nonviolent Revolution?" pp. 18–21.

coverage now tended to link increased militancy with political extremism. The *Times* did not invent this increased militancy, of course, but accentuated it as a troubling social problem severed from the escalation of the war. Thus an October 4 story,[2] headlined "More Student Demonstrations Over Vietnam Policy Planned," turned out to be an account of the Berkeley police chief's speech to the Miami Beach convention of the International Association of Chiefs of Police, describing "last year's student riots" as "revolutionary activity" and warning that "individuals dedicated to the promotion of Communist ideology" would be exploiting "youthful restlessness." The word *riots* in the reporter's account was not neutralized by quotation marks: it was presented as objective description.

This story manifested another new element in the *Times*'s approach to antiwar stories; *increasing reliance on statements by government officials and other certified authorities.*[3] Despite the conventional claim that news objectivity requires a balance of opposing views, few of the *Times*'s stories turned to antiwar or New Left voices for conflicting opinions, even when the subject of the story was New Left activity itself. In the first two weeks of October—that is to say, through the eve of the International Days of Protest—the *Times* ran seven pieces touching on student antiwar action. Four of these consisted entirely of antagonistic statements by authorities: two

2. This was actually a *New York Times* News Service piece. From September 17 through October 10, the *Times* was on strike and the newspaper was not published in New York; but the wire service continued to function, producing stories for syndication, for the international edition, and for the *Times*'s New York radio station, WQXR.

3. In general, newspaper reliance on government statements, especially federal ones, has been well documented. Leon V. Sigal, *Reporters and Officials: The Organization and Politics of Newsmaking* (Lexington, Mass.: D. C. Heath, 1973), p. 124, found that in all stories appearing in the *New York Times* and the *Washington Post* between 1949 and 1969, 46.5 percent of all information sources were U.S. officials and agencies. In staff stories published in the *Times* alone, 42.3 percent of all sources were U.S. officials and agencies, but the *Times*'s use of government sources increased markedly from 38.8 percent in 1949 to 47.9 percent by 1969 (p. 128). Studying newspaper coverage of the 1969 Santa Barbara oil spill, Harvey Molotch and Marilyn Lester found that "access to newspapers clearly was centered in the hands of the federal executive branch, including its departments and appointed agencies. Congress, the oil companies, and state politicians, in that order, were the next most significant groups. Local Santa Barbara groups, conservation associations, and local politicians had least access to the nonlocal papers" ("Accidental News: The Great Oil Spill as Local Occurrence and National Event," *American Journal of Sociology* 81 [September 1975]: 244).

university presidents (Kerr of the University of California and Brewster of Yale), the aforementioned police chief, and the attorney general of the United States. The composite effect was that students produce actions while authorities have thoughts.

A fifth article, "Berkeley Faculty Group Protests U.S. Policy in Vietnam," began with a reference to "a group calling itself the Faculty Peace Committee." (I shall speak later on about the use of quotation marks to delegitimate the Left.) A sixth article concerning a minor, abortive antiwar action—"A Vietnam Protest Dies in Planning Stage"—balanced an antiwar organizer's hangdog admission of failure against the triumphant statement of a pro-war student.

During this two-week period, there was no advance notice of the International Days of Protest from the point of view of its organizers or advocates.

The only article that mentioned these plans at all, in fact, was an October 11, page 7 piece by the *Times*'s chief Bay Area correspondent, Wallace Turner, displaying a full panoply of denigrating techniques. Turner referred to the impending "peace march"—the only phrase removed from the realm of objective action by quotation marks. He was at pains to stipulate that most of the leaders of the Vietnam Day Committee were "former students"—a fact of significance to Berkeley administrators but of dubious meaning to students or to national politics. He declared that "[t]he Berkeley students appear interested but uncommitted"—a claim not heard again later in the week, after the enormous Friday march. He wrote of the newly organized Faculty Peace Committee: "Some observers thought it was organized to provide a respectable organization for faculty members to join." These "observers" were not named. (The citing of unnamed "observers" or "experts" is conventionally a way for reporters to adduce either their own opinions or the opinions of other reporters, officials, or cronies they credit.) Having denigrated the Faculty Peace Committee, Turner elaborated: the Vietnam Day Committee had acquired "a bad name" with its summer and fall "activist talk." Both groups were plainly out of bounds. The rest of the article went on to illustrate the purported marginality of the two groups. "[No] one has been able to find an issue with which to flay the university administration"; the new rules for political conduct on campus were permissive (the implication is that only the most deviant would complain). And finally, there was deprecation by number: "The attendance at Vietnam Day Committee meetings has appeared to disappoint its directorate";

The Faculty Peace Committee drew the biggest crowd of the year last week, perhaps 600 at the peak. The total enrollment of the Berkeley campus is about 27,000, so that these 600 represented less than 3 per cent of the student body, if all had been students, which many were not.

Turner did not go on to compare the size of this rally with the size of any other political rallies; there was no sense of political proportion or process in this single snapshot. Turner quoted from the demonstration organizers only to reveal that "demonstrations have been promised in three Iron Curtain countries," and to mention (in the seventh paragraph) a few of the other American cities where demonstrations were expected.

Thus did the *Times* prepare its readers for the demonstrations of October 15 and 16.

As for CBS: during the entire month of September, the network ran only a single report on antiwar activity—less than two minutes about anti-draft demonstrations, on September 22. But the spotlight was turning up again, anticipating the new wave of demonstrations. In the second week of October, CBS devoted a goodly amount of coverage to anti-draft activity. Within a week afterward, Attorney General Katzenbach and President Johnson were calling for investigations of SDS; Senator Stennis was denouncing an SDS "conspiracy"; and the front page of the *Times* was running news of antiwar demonstrations and official responses for six straight days.

To grasp the irony of the process through which SDS became front-page news, we must back up for a moment and look in some detail first at SDS's activity in those weeks and then at the exact sequence of media images and official maneuvers.

As I have said, SDS had stumbled into the fall without a coherent antiwar program: indeed, without much of a program at all. Clearly the organization did not want to lead the antiwar movement, did not want to submerge its multi-issue generalism in antiwar specificity. The hypothetical risk and extremity of Clark Kissinger's "Kamikaze plan" were only the other side of an actual default: SDS was defaulting in the name of no program at all. After the heady day of April 17, no one knew what to do. SDS's failure followed from the leadership group's loss of cohesion and confidence. The first-generation elite had stalled. Those of its cadre committed to campus-based organizing were unwilling or unable to decide on a new antiwar program; they despaired of the possibility of effective action against the war and tended to leave antiwar matters to isolated or less experienced organizers. (Carl Oglesby chose, and I endorsed, a quotation from a Beckett novel—something about a man on his deathbed still eagerly looking for diagnoses of his ailment—as epigraph to the workshop agenda on foreign policy issues.) The rest of the elite—including many of the most experienced and skilled organizers—were committed to local organizing work among the underclass on domestic issues. By the time of the Kewadin convention, energy was pouring, helter-skelter, into personal affairs: this was both cause and effect of the Old Guard's uncertainty. Divided, bewildered by the influx of new and younger members, lacking a clear commitment to bring them into common rituals, the original elite were abdicating. Even their institutions were decomposing. The national ERAP staff in Ann Arbor—with the approval of the local staffs—decided to abandon its office and to meld into the Chicago JOIN project. The Peace Research and Education Project office in Ann Arbor, which had contributed greatly in initiative, research, and planning to the Chase Manhattan and Washington demonstrations, also emptied out and closed down in the name of localism.

To redeem their bond with the student organization, some of the original elite ("Ann Arbor," or the Old Guard as they came to be called) had decided to push—to offer up?—one of their number, Paul Booth, to be the next year's National Secretary. When, in a private letter before the convention, a reluctant Booth had mustered arguments against his "nomination," he sought to clinch his case with the localist point:

I think we want to make national guys like me into regional and local-based guys, and make the new generation of local-regional people into national people. I want to be localized. So Pardun, Brecher, et al. [campus organizers from Texas and Oregon, respectively] would be suitable. Here the point that I have vast contacts is part of a self-defeating syndrome—the people in the middle *always* have them. NEW BLOOD!![4]

The entire convention had been imbued with the localist, anti-authoritarian spirit. There had been a serious and popular proposal to

4. Paul Booth to Todd Gitlin, May 29, 1965; author's file.

abolish the offices of President and Vice-President.[5] Old Guard and Prairie Power groups alike doubted the founding group's right to lead.

One result was that the National Office (NO) stumbled through the summer without a competent staff. The Acting National Secretary had little experience in SDS and none in administering it.[6] This antibureaucratic bureaucracy, without a clear program to proclaim and propagate, barely took care of the elementary business of the organization: it had trouble keeping up with correspondence and sending out membership cards. A skeletal and inexperienced sub-staff did send out one newsletter containing proposals for antiwar work, including one proposal—by the author and Mike Locker—for anti-draft activity, but it attracted little attention within the summer-dispersed organization, and gathered no organizational support. It was in this organizational world of disarray and stagnation that Paul Booth was prevailed upon to move to Chicago and to become the new National Secretary. Only in September, then, did the National Office begin to function in anything like a coherent way. Now it was given something to do.

The National Council meeting in September empowered the office to hold a membership conference in December, to discuss key and now-controversial issues in SDS politics: the politics of anti-Communism, national coalitions versus "local insurgency," the vision of a democratic society, and the like. At the behest of some of the Old Guard, the organization would shift back to first principles. Maybe talk about political ideals could reinstate the common political culture that had crumbled when the Old Guard slipped away from the student organization and the Prairie Power insurgency percolated through SDS. But the National Council's proposals for antiwar action were jumbled, and lacked a justifying logic.[7] At a loss to conceive its own program, the meeting finally endorsed the impending October 15–16 International Days of Protest. SDS also settled on "deepening/radicalizing the campus constituency"; it urged local chapters to work locally, in unspecified ways, against the draft; and it directed the National Office to pre-

5. It actually went to a membership referendum in October. At the very moment when Evans and Novak, Katzenbach, and Stennis were discovering SDS plots, SDS was in the process of voting whether to deprive itself of a good part of its formal leadership and public representation. The referendum, conducted through the October *SDS Bulletin*, was finally defeated.

6. For details, see Sale, *SDS* pp. 217–222.

7. Ibid., pp. 226–227.

pare a draft-counseling program (again unspecified) to "mobilize opposition to the war among draft-age people"—*this program to be submitted to a membership referendum* before going into effect. By early October, in accordance with its mandate, the NO had proposed a legal anti-draft program for the members, including: (1) large-scale filing of claims as conscientious objectors; (2) organizing against the Selective Service System's new system (endorsed by almost all colleges) of ranking male students to establish draft priorities; (3) demonstrating against and debating military recruiters and ROTC officials; and (4) exposing the class-limited composition and unfair practices of local draft boards.[8] The mandated referendum was being readied. In the days just before October 15–16, Booth had little to say to the chapter leadership but this routine note:

We know of about 40 chapters with specific plans for October 15–16. It looks to be an important event in bringing the anti-war movement back into the public eye.[9]

SDS, in short, was crawling around in the semi-dark. It expected no spotlights.

THE SPOTLIGHT SWITCHES ON

But the spotlight was switching on again, anticipating a big turnout on October 15 and 16. Although the *New York Times* was for the most part ignoring the coming demonstrations, other media organizations were interested.

Monday, October 11, and Tuesday, October 12, the CBS Evening News ran two long takeouts—feature stories—on anti-draft activity. The initiative came from Stanhope Gould, a young, long-haired, brash, inventive field producer who had gone to work for the Cronkite show in 1964. Gould knew a hot story when he ran across one, and for him the news judgment at this moment was obvious: "This is when it started to be clear that there was political resistance to the draft." Routinely, Gould got clearance from his superior, Russ Bensley, the producer in charge of all takeouts. The anti-draft story would be a "grabber." Gould remembers that he often proposed "going with a grabber"; he would not propose the mundane, wearisome subject of SDS as a radical group, say, but "SDS in the high schools," expecting to draw the reaction, "What?

8. Ibid., pp. 227–228.
9. SDS Work List Mailing, No. 22, October 12, 1965.

Those fuckers are in the high schools?"[10] Gould wanted to stoke
up public anger, thinking that whatever "punched through" the
public apathy would produce a *reasoned* anger. Such flamboyant
choices were not, according to Gould, controversial within CBS
News; they were not even discussed, let alone challenged. "A dramatic piece is a dramatic piece. You wanted to get what Fred
Friendly [then president of CBS News] used to call 'fire in the belly,'
an emotional event with emotional people. You knew that people
don't watch television in the same way they read a newspaper or
go to a movie, with undivided attention. Our fear was that people
would tune out. Everybody [at CBS News] was looking for that
[dramatic] kind of stuff."[11] From this point of view, the draft-resistance story would be a good one precisely *because* it would fly in the
face (or the gut) of the audience.

Once Bensley had agreed to cover draft resistance, the New
York bureau assigned the veteran correspondent Alexander Kendrick to work on the story. As usual, it was the correspondent
who devised the questions, conducted the interviews, and wrote
and spoke the narration. Also as usual, there was consultation up
and down the line: CBS reporters and producers all insist that the
news-generating process—planning, shooting, editing—is a collaboration from start to finish. And my observations confirm that
there is collectivity enough to scotch any nice attempt to locate the
specific contributions of particular individuals in an orderly "structure" of decision-making."[12] Nonetheless, as with Kendrick's SDS
story in May, it was probably not irrelevant that, as Kendrick says,
"When I interviewed draft-card burners, I was sympathetic." Kendrick thinks his sympathy worked in two ways: he asked particularly probing questions, and he sustained his lines of questioning

10. Interview, Stanhope Gould, November 13, 1976.
11. Telephone interview, Stanhope Gould, April 5, 1977.
12. In a critical review of Edward J. Epstein's *News from Nowhere* (Stanhope
Gould, "The Trials of Network News," *More* 3 [May 1973]:8–11, Gould himself
insists on the fluidity of the editorial process, a fluidity imposed partly by the hectic
pace and high volume of network news. Of course, a takeout, not being tied to a
particular deadline, is more susceptible to deliberate control than a hard news story.
Indeed, the second part of Gould's takeout on Watergate in 1972 was directly censored by the CBS hierarchy after the White House was enraged by the first part, and
not long afterward he left to head NBC's investigative unit; later he became special
assignment field producer for ABC News. (On the Watergate incident, see Daniel
Schorr, *Clearing the Air* [Boston: Houghton Mifflin, 1977], pp. 51–57; Gary Paul
Gates, *Air Time: The Inside Story of CBS News* [New York: Harper and Row, 1978],
pp. 303–306; and David Halberstam, *The Powers That Be* [New York: Alfred A.
Knopf, 1979], pp. 652–663.)

rather than dashing off to the next question on a preconceived, discontinuous list. [13]

The actual October 11 and 12 takeouts do not survive for analysis. [14] But Gould remembers a segment on resisters at Columbia University: this would, he thought, "grab" a middle-class audience inclined to associate draft evasion with lowlife. There was a sequence showing a draft counselor teaching students at the Alternate University to check "yes" on a question about homosexuality—and then to erase the check. The piece began and ended with verses from Phil Ochs's hilarious and didactic song, "Draft Dodger Rag."

Gould fought with SDS over his symbolic choices. In effect, he had staked out a new beat, the antiwar movement, defined it as a legitimate object of news for CBS; and, like any good beat reporter outside the corridors of power, he had developed a certain tension with his sources and *their* sense of what the news was. Gould recalls that "for the sake of impact, I probably tended to portray SDS as a sort of monolithic organization," unambiguously committed to organizing draft resistance. He was not interested, he grants, in showing "the fine points of SDS organization. Subtlety and nuance doesn't go on television. SDS was like a peg. SDS or no SDS, there was a relatively large number of young men who didn't want to go." [15] He clashed with Booth, who wanted SDS's politics spelled out; Gould argued that "you can get only one symbolic idea across, to get people's attention." [16] In this struggle, Booth's loyalty to SDS's complexity was no match for the momentum of the CBS operation. The "story" was draft evasion, not SDS's program. And it was broadcast as big news. The first piece ran over six minutes on the Cronkite show; the second, over five. By TV news standards, those are long pieces.

13. Alexander Kendrick, letter to the author, January 3, 1977.

14. No record exists of them—even in audio form—in the CBS Newsfilm Archive. Evidently no one at CBS thought they were important enough to keep. If any record at all remains, it lies buried in the videotape air-check, a copy of which would have to be bought—at great expense—in order to be studied. So, for all the furor they generated at the time, the draft resistance stories survive only in memory and political consequence. But my feel for the styles and work routines of Gould, Kendrick, and Bensley makes me fairly confident that I have decently reconstructed the story and the process of producing it. I qualify my conclusions, but they are nonetheless conclusions. For more on CBS's archives, see Appendix.

15. Telephone interview, Stanhope Gould, April 5, 1977; and Gould's lecture, University of California, Berkeley, April 16, 1979.

16. Interview, Stanhope Gould, November 13, 1976.

To what extent was this story the product of Stanhope Gould and Alexander Kendrick in particular, and to what extent was it the predictable product of impersonal organizational procedures? Gould thinks he was more likely to have done the piece than the other producers. He had cultivated the movement "beat." He had "hung out" for days at the SDS office in Chicago, steeped himself in the movement world, looking for stories. (Later it was there that he heard about draft resisters seeking refuge in Canada, and produced the first media report on the new exiles. All told, he did seven to nine stories on draft resistance over the years.) He had rapport with Paul Booth. And his opinion of the movement was "influenced by events. I was sympathetic. I wasn't that old myself." Indeed, once the piece was broadcast, Gould remembers that, around the newsroom, "I was accused of being the Scarlet Pimpernel of the draft movement." A lower-level CBS News employee recalls that, at the time, Gould "was known as a 'leftie' and 'troublemaker.'" During the 1972 presidential campaign, Timothy Crouse called him "defiantly hip." [17] And we have already learned about Kendrick's personal sympathies.

So Gould's personal predilections, along with his news sense, led him to *propose* the draft story. How did he find himself in a position to propose? The riddle of his standing in the CBS News operation is solved when we understand the routine organizational procedures and codes. It was not that CBS News President Fred Friendly (or later Richard Salant) or Chairman William S. Paley were "nattering nabobs of negativism," as Vice-President Agnew later strained to say, but that *Gould's sympathies harmonized with the institutional definition of good TV news*. The aforementioned employee points out that Gould "wasn't only political; he was *good* [i.e., competent], he was fast." [18] Gould's technical proficiency and productive intelligence gave him a limited latitude—as long as he held to routine assumptions about newsworthiness, and as long as he made the organization's need his own. Defiant hipness or no, CBS News standards made the anti-draft story a premium story; they created the occasion for Gould. And once the organization had decided to go after the story, Gould's particular interests and sympathies played only a minor part in shaping the final film. In

17. Timothy Crouse, *The Boys on the Bus* (New York: Random House, 1973), p. 172. For more on Gould, see Gates, *Air Time*, pp. 188–189.
18. Interview, Michael Nolan, December 28, 1976.

Gould's words: "Given the parameters, the institutional barriers, it all comes out pretty predictable. You're going to come out with a homogenized piece."[19]

Gould's news sense was impeccable. The "grabber" grabbed—and it grabbed, first of all, the Right.

On Thursday, October 14, the syndicated columnists Rowland Evans and Robert Novak, whose most prominent outlets were the *New York Herald Tribune* and the *Washington Post*, accused SDS of organizing a national "draft-dodging" campaign. How had they conjured up this sensation? Evans and Novak had culled some speculative proposals from SDS's August Vietnam newsletter—all of which had been rejected, explicitly, by the National Council meeting in September—to prove that SDS had a "calculated" and "illegal" "master plan" to "sabotage the war effort."[20] As usual, Evans and Novak did not cushion the force of their exposé by asking SDS to confirm or deny their story, or by asking for any comment whatsoever. The National Office would have told them, of course, that the "master plan" did not exist. Perhaps with regret; in any event accurately.

As was their habit, Evans and Novak, longtime Communist-hunters, were relaying a bigger right-wing campaign. The day before, Senator Thomas Dodd of the Senate Internal Security Sub-committee had published his report on the antiwar movement, asserting:

The control of the anti-Vietnam [*sic*] movement has clearly passed from the hands of the moderate elements, who may have controlled it at one time, into the hands of Communists and extremist elements who are openly sympathetic to the Viet Cong and openly hostile to the United States. . . . This is particularly true of the national Vietnam protest movement scheduled for October 15–16.[21]

Most of the news media now proceeded to amplify attacks from the Right. The theme of a menacing movement, already creeping into

19. For a succinct discussion of the relative irrelevance of personal opinions in the production of network news, see Edward J. Epstein, *Between Fact and Fiction* (New York: Vintage Books, 1975), pp. 199–201.

20. Sale, *SDS*, p. 229. Evans and Novak must have had an informer on the SDS Work List, or someone with access to the SDS National Office. It is not inconceivable that the story was suggested to them by the FBI or by someone on Senator Dodd's staff.

21. Ibid., p. 228.

news accounts late the previous spring, now became the main media leitmotif.

This was the stuff of dramatic reporting. Keep in mind that the traditional narrative structure of a news story selects for dramatic (preferably melodramatic) conflict. With the antiwar Left mobilizing and the pro-war Right counterattacking, the media's usual interest in conflict found a "news peg," a "handle." Political polarization made good copy—for both Gould on the Left and Evans and Novak on the Right, independently. Counterposed extremisms set up the sort of balances that journalists routinely equate with "good stories."

The CBS draft-resistance stories did not catch on directly; network takeouts are less than urgent for print journalists, and they are broadcast, moreover, rather late in the day to catch the interests of reporters working on evening deadlines for morning papers. But the day that Evans and Novak's column appeared, a *Chicago Sun-Times* reporter, Art Petacque, invited Paul Booth to the *Sun-Times* office for an interview, probably in response (though Booth was unaware of it at the time) to the Dodd broadside.[22] To refute Evans and Novak's claim of an anti-draft "master plan," Paul Booth gave Petacque a copy of SDS's actual referendum proposal. The next day, Friday, October 15, Petacque's story dominated the tabloid's front page under the thick headline, "U.S.-WIDE DRIVE TO BEAT DRAFT IS ORGANIZED HERE." Booth later told the SDS Work List that this story was "accurate in tone and detail, except that it underplayed very slightly the war context of our program."[23] From the *Sun-Times*, this amplification of the SDS quasi-program went out over the UPI wire—before any of it had been officially endorsed by the SDS membership.

MAKING THE MOST OF THE GLARE

Booth and SDS's National Administrative Committee (NAC)—dominated by the Old Guard—now decided that the best defense was a strong offense. In the hectic days that followed, in the midst of the Days of Protest and the government denunciations, they called press conferences in Chicago and Washington, sent out press releases on a revised anti-draft program, and spoke to a swarm of reporters. SDS had not started out seeking the spotlight;

22. Paul Booth, letter to the author, September 15, 1977; Sale, *SDS*, p. 230.
23. SDS Work List Mailing, No. 23, October 22, 1965.

but, caught in the glare, the SDS responsibles decided to make the most of it. Booth wrote of the prevailing spirit: "The cardinal principle to follow is that we must always try to argue against the war, using the public attention we now have for all it's worth." [24] A fuller statement of the SDS strategy came in an article written at the last minute for the October *SDS Bulletin* by NAC members Richard Rothstein and Jeff Shero. Rothstein, a New Yorker, was one of the Old Guard, Shero, a Texan associated with Prairie Power, and they often disagreed about how much the National Office should do and how tightly organized it should be; but now they were united by the opportunity to use the switched-on spotlight:

First, we in the office view the publicity as the greatest *opportunity* the anti-war movement has yet had. In the guise of scandalous exposure, we have seen anti-war leaflets photostated on the front page of newspapers with circulations in the millions. We could have been at the mimeograph for ten years, and not reached as many draftable young men with our program as the press has reached for us in five days.

Even the attacks on us are an opportunity for a response of anti-war statements. The important thing is never to let our critics get us debating about communists in the movement, the reactions of Hanoi to marches, the wisdom or legality of draft-card burning. The issue is the war, and we must not let anyone forget it. When Booth was asked today in Washington about draft-card burnings, he answered on national TV that it was a trivial point when compared to the burning of villages of South Vietnam. When LBJ and Katzenbach attacked SDS [see below], we in Chicago announced a press conference to "respond to Johnson." A very large turn-out of reporters and cameramen resulted; we said that LBJ wasn't going to deter our anti-war program, and then spent an hour talking about the issues of the war: self-determination, Right-wing dictator Ky, lies by the Administration, etc. In short, every attack by the opposition can be used as the occasion for an attack on the war by us, cleverly disguised as a response to the original attack. . . .

They went on, in high excitement, to note one of the ironies of the publicity process:

All reports seem to indicate that SDS has grown fantastically in the last few days. Our new visibility on campus seems to have brought people flocking to SDS. Our Harvard organizer reports that he walked into Harvard Yard with 30 membership cards and had to go back for more ½ hour later on the day after the first press. He wasn't lying. We just got 50 new membership cards from him special delivery. (Plus $100.)

24. Ibid.

In this light, we think that this period should be treated as a prime re-cruiting period. . . .[25]

And indeed it was. One thousand new national memberships came into the office, pushing the national membership over 4,000: some in the office estimated that membership in the chapters dou-bled in those weeks to over 10,000.[26] National Office staff felt, in short, that this unsought publicity was all to the good. As one for-mer staff member told me: "Sure, [the publicity] was hostile, but it was kind of like P. T. Barnum's saying, 'I don't care what they say about me, as long as they get the name right.'. . . The fact that someone is calling you terrible means that other people might re-act and say, 'If they are calling you terrible, then you must be good.'"[27]

But peripheral groups in SDS, groups left out of last-minute, under-the-glare decisions, were uneasy, even angry. For the force of publicity was straining the organization at its weak seams. If access to media was now a source of power, it was also a source of dissension. Now that mass-mediated image had willy-nilly be-come a political resource, who within SDS was going to control it? And toward what end? We shall see in Chapter 4 how this conflict tore at an unprepared SDS, and with what serious consequences.

THE MEDIA, THE RIGHT, AND THE ADMINISTRATION

To those who contend in the internecine battles of the Left, the stakes often seem global. They fight for control over a known ob-ject, an organization of manageable extent and vast significance, whose shadow seems to eclipse the rest of the world. Ferocious in their myopia, the contenders are often oblivious to the concrete po-litical implications of their actions—the impacts their factional differences have on the policies of political adversaries. And the working press are in their own way as insular as movement fac-tions, protected as they are from the implications of their actions by an ideology of objectivity and a belief in their own autonomy, as well as a real uncertainty about the consequences of what they write. Ideologies and professional norms help protect both parties

25. SDS *Bulletin*, Vol. 4, October 1965, inside front cover; emphasis in original. (This issue was mailed in such haste, with its printing information page cut out at the last minute to make room for the Rothstein-Shero memo, that it did not have an issue number.)

26. Sale, *SDS*, pp. 231–232.

27. Interview, James Russell, January 19, 1977.

from becoming confused, immobilized, or overwhelmed by the political consequences of their actions; their working conventions permit them to calculate moves, to process information, in businesslike fashion. Thus, in the fall of 1965, by force of circumstance the interplay of movement and media was helping mobilize the repressive forces of the State.

The political Right was "grabbed" first. Senator John Stennis of Mississippi, a key member of the Senate Armed Services Committee, was quick to exploit CBS's sensational coverage of anti-draft activity. An Associated Press dispatch, printed in the *Times* on October 16, was headlined "Stennis Attacks Anti-draft Drive as 'Conspiracy': Senator Says Attempt to Balk Induction is a Violation of Federal Law," and it read:

WASHINGTON, Oct. 15 (AP)—Senator John Stennis called on the administration today to pull the anti-draft movement up "by the roots and grind it to bits."

The Mississippi Senator told the Senate that the "unwarranted and disgraceful campaign" to encourage and instruct youths to avoid military service in Vietnam amounted to an "unlawful conspiracy."

Senator Stennis added that reports carried by the Columbia Broadcasting System's television network on the activities by the Students for a Democratic Society, to disrupt the Selective Service System, added up to "a Federal offense punishable by fine or imprisonment."

The Senator, who is chairman of the Senate Preparedness subcommittee, said he was sure that CBS had presented its program in good faith to call public attention to what he called "this deplorable and shameful activity on the part of those who have no regard for duty, honor, or their country."

But he said that the publicity of "a nationwide television documentary gives them great encouragement and stimulation to continue their unwarranted and disgraceful campaign."[28]

Senator Stennis said it was imperative for the Administration, acting through the Justice Department or other agencies, "to immediately move to jerk this movement up by the roots and grind it to bits before it has the opportunity to spread further and to be nourished by further publicity."

He said that the CBS program has presented interviews direct from some of the schools of instruction that are conducted to teach young Americans how to evade military service.

The films, he added, showed leaders of the organized effort attempting

---

28. Stanhope Gould, the producer, acknowledges that Senator Stennis accurately grasped the link between coverage and amplification (telephone interview, April 5, 1977).

to spread the philosophy that "every American has the right to refuse to fight in any war or military action that he does not personally approve."

The Senator later told a reporter that he had no plans for an investigation by his subcommittee because "it is more a matter for the Justice Department. . . ."

The day after this article appeared, reporters were asking Attorney General Nicholas deB. Katzenbach what was being done about the SDS "conspiracy" (see below). What was happening? Parts of the media apparatus, for their own reasons, had discovered draft resistance and linked it with SDS; now the ostensible SDS-draft link was a certified "story," a tissue of false presumptions and stray facts with a secondhand life of its own. Turning this presumably hard-and-fast story to their own uses, politicians of the Right were drawing their own conclusions, pushing the administration into a combative response and driving the movement pell-mell onto the defensive. All this time, the media proceeded to muckrake the movement as if the movement, not the war, were the scandal. The story of SDS-and-the-draft was now fused with the story of the October 15–16 demonstrations, forming a single organizing frame.

Coverage was voluminous and prominent: front-page stories in the *Times* from October 16 through 21, and virtually all of the CBS Evening News of Monday, October 18. Some of this reportage was poker-faced and straightforward; but much of it continued the deprecatory framing of the spring. In reporting demonstrations, the *Times* and CBS[29] emphasized *violence, counterdemonstrations,* and *official statements.* In Douglas Robinson's roundup story about the International Days of Protest on October 16, for example, the *Times* devoted one-third of forty-two paragraphs to counterdemonstrators or to administration statements. On page 2, by contrast, the Associated Press story on Senator Stennis's attack contained no balancing statement from SDS. This was routine for stories that relayed the canned news of politics: SDS's was not a certified "other opinion." The *Times* antiwar stories that week devoted between one-quarter and almost one-half their length to counterdemonstrations. Photos, chosen for drama, displayed the same slant. On October 17, the front-page photo showed police grabbing a counterpicket who had attacked an antiwar demonstrator; the inside page

29. Alas again for bad archives: I have to extrapolate from the few CBS News stories I was able to view.

photo showed police holding an anti-demonstration Hell's Angel in Oakland. Yet, by the *police* estimates cited in the New York demonstration story, there were 10,000 antiwar demonstrators to 1,000 supporting the war.[30]

The most curious item of framing, though, was the *Times's* October 18, page 1 account of the attorney general's press conference, magnifying Katzenbach's own attack on SDS. Up to this point, the *Times* had framed stories about the movement as tales of marginality; now the *Times's* commitment to the drama of polarization colored its treatment of the administration. In this case, the *Times's* frame for movement-administration relations seems not to have been strictly determined by administration policy. To the contrary: acting on their own, the media probably helped change the administration's course of action, at least in the short run. The *Times's* version moved to the right of the administration.[31]

ITEM: THE KATZENBACH PRESS CONFERENCE

Memories have faded, and evidence of just what happened at Attorney General Katzenbach's press conference is hard to come by. To assess the media version of the event when the only definite trace of the event is the media version itself, one is forced to rely on scrutiny of that version's internal structure. But this structure reveals conventions all its own. And since we know the conventions which routinely distill news stories from events, we can "read back" from the published story and strongly infer some features of the event.

The *Times's* front-page report of the Katzenbach press conference appeared under the headline: "u.s. INVESTIGATES ANTI-DRAFT GROUPS: Katzenbach Says Reds are Involved in Youth Drive." The

30. The fact that this figure of 10,000—reported in the headline *and* the lead—was a police estimate showed up only in the sixteenth paragraph, on the jump page, where the reporter also reported that other (unspecified) estimates had ranged "as high as 20,000." The next day, October 18, a more respectful piece—also by Douglas Robinson—relayed the insistence of moderate demonstration leaders that, indeed, the figure had been closer to 20,000, and that many had been non-radicals. Several antiwar organizers had evidently visited the *Times* to complain about Robinson's coverage. But this after-the-fact piece, as "softer" news, ended up on page 7.

31. There has been very little scholarly attention to specific political functions of news coverage in the circles of power. In their well-known article on "the agenda-setting function of the press," Maxwell E. McCombs and Donald L. Shaw speak of the press impact on diffuse publics, not on political elites ("The Agenda-Setting Function of the Mass Media," *Public Opinion Quarterly* 36 [Summer 1972]: 176–187). The subsequent literature has preserved this emphasis.

headline defined the issue unambiguously: Communist infiltration. The reporter was Chicago correspondent Austin C. Wehrwein. The story began:

CHICAGO, Oct. 17—Attorney General Nicholas B. Katzenbach told a news conference here today that the Justice Department had started a national investigation of groups behind the anti-draft movement.

Mr. Katzenbach, here for a speaking engagement, said:

"There are some Communists in it." He also said: "We may very well have some prosecutions."

Mr. Katzenbach was questioned chiefly about the Students for a Democractic Society, a group of the "new left" that has headquarters here. But he said it was "one of many" that the Justice Department was investigating.

Wehrwein went on to quote a denial from Paul Booth, interviewed *before* the Katzenbach press conference: "The one basic thing is that we take a very principled civil liberties position. It sounds like a Red-baiting smear. [Presumably Booth had been notified in advance of the Katzenbach statement.] The real issue is the war in Vietnam. This is a kind of smokescreen. We are going right ahead. Our program is legal." Booth, interviewed for balance, was trying to contest Katzenbach's frame.

But Wehrwein's story defeated Booth's judo strategy; the draft-dodging-and-Communism theme dominated. Thus, to underscore the illegitimacy of SDS, Wehrwein went on to deny "that the society [SDS] was the instigator of the demonstrations in many cities over the weekend. But [Booth] said that 50 of its campus charters had staged demonstrations." Wehrwein was not about to let an SDS officer redefine the situation. Instead, Wehrwein went on about Booth:

He said the society was "in communication" with the National Coordinating Committee to End the War in Vietnam, which has headquarters in Madison, Wis., and which did claim to be the instigator of the demonstrations.

One would only "claim to be the instigator" if one were admitting culpability. (The root means to goad, provoke; the Latin *instigare* stems from the Greek for tattoo.) Rarely is the White House reported as "claiming to be the instigator" of policies or wars; rarely is the Army reported to be the "instigator" of its maneuvers. And SDS, being "in communication" with the claimed "instigator," now shared in its imputed wrongdoing.

Wehrwein could have cleared up the mystery he had created—of just who was responsible for the demonstrations, and just what was SDS's part in them—by explaining that SDS chapters were autonomous and that the National Coordinating Committee had been founded precisely because SDS refused to lead the antiwar movement. He did not. Rather, he went on to attribute an aura of immoral conduct to SDS by relaying the report earlier circulated by Evans and Novak and echoed elsewhere in the media. The article continued:

Mr. Booth declared that the society had put a "low priority" on demonstrations and denied it had anything to do with a mimeo sheet passed out in Berkeley, California, called "Brief Notes on the Ways and Means of Beating and Defeating the Draft."

Wehrwein proceeded to describe at length the very thing whose connection to SDS Booth was denying. After a subhead inserted by an editor, "Bribes Advocated," Wehrwein's piece continued:

The Berkeley document advised, besides taking a conscientious objector's stand, such things as faking homosexuality, arriving at Selective Service examinations drunk or "high" on narcotics and bribing doctors for certificates of disability. Mr. Booth declared that the society was interested only in claims of conscientious objectors, which it wanted to encourage, and said he was a conscientious objector himself.

Having discharged his obligations to formal balance by citing Booth's denials of multifarious immorality, Wehrwein now returned to the Katzenbach press conference. Note that the formal obligation to balance does not prohibit the reporter from tilting the coverage toward one or another party. The conventions of objectivity may be bent without much trouble. Wehrwein: "At the news conference, Mr. Katzenbach left the impression that the Justice Department did associate the society with the Berkeley 'Beat the Draft' document. However, he did not elaborate on this point. . . ." and so on.

Katzenbach hesitated to charge SDS with treason, Wehrwein continued; the attorney general declared that there was, after all, a constitutionally protected right to expression. Only now, in the last four paragraphs of the story, on the jump page, did Wehrwein recount Katzenbach's response to the Communist issue:

Asked about Communist influence, he said that in such groups "you are likely to find some Communists involved." Asked specifically about the so-

ciety, he said that the identities of some Communists in the society and some Communists who claim association with it were known.

Asked if Communists were leaders in the society, he replied: "By and large, no."

Mr. Katzenbach said he thought the danger was that the demonstrations might be misunderstood abroad, particularly in Peking and Hanoi. He said that "an overwhelming majority of the American people stand with President Johnson's policy in Vietnam." [Emphasis added.]

Here the story ended.

Two features of the genesis of the Communist issue are worth pausing over:

1. The effect of the headline—"Katzenbach Says Reds are Involved in Youth Drive"—was quite different from the tenor of Katzenbach's actual statement. The headline elevated the Communist issue to major proportions, which it did not assume even in Wehrwein's account of Katzenbach's own words. That is, the promotion of the Communist issue was a *Times* editorial decision.

2. Probably it was reporters, not Katzenbach, who first brought up the Communist issue.[32] We do not know which reporters. We do not know how many other issues were brought up at the press conference but downplayed by Wehrwein. Possibly the fingers were pointed by reporters with an explicit political interest, from right-wing newspapers like the *Chicago Tribune*. What is interesting in this case is that newspapers with carefully guarded reputations for objectivity, such as the *New York Times* (and the *Washington Post* and the then-publishing *New York Herald Tribune*), were framing the SDS-draft story from the Right.

How did this frame come to prevail so widely? News stories spread from medium to medium, from newsroom to newsroom, by chain reactions. Reporters covering the same event find it convenient to borrow angles, issues, and questions from each other. Borrowed frames help them process a glut of facts—on deadline. Especially when reporters are in unfamiliar social territory, and when enough of them are clustered in that unfamiliar territory to constitute a social group, they are liable to become a *hermetic* group, looking around the circle of reporters, rather than outward to the event, for bearings. In the pure hermetic situation—Amer-

32. Occasionally, officials—from the President on down—do plant questions with friendly reporters (see Sigal, *Reporters and Officials*, p. 110). But in this instance planting seems unlikely, although the possibility cannot be ruled out entirely.

ican reporters in Saigon, or a presidential campaign—they are especially prone to what Timothy Crouse memorably calls "pack
journalism." [33] To begin with, reporters are rarely expert on the
subject at hand. In the networks, vast parts of the country may be
assigned to a bureau of three or four correspondents. On short
notice from an assignment editor or a producer, a correspondent
may have to fly into a city he or she has never seen before, film a
story, and fly out the next morning to edit a piece for broadcast that
night. (Abroad, he or she may be flying into an unknown country
where people speak an apparently impenetrable language.[34]) But
even at the larger and more prestigious newspapers, daily deadlines, budgetary limits, and the unspecified quality of "news"
combine to drop reporters into situations where information is
abundant and understanding is scarce. Automatically, reporters
are going to take their cues from their peers, from respected col-
leagues among the competition.

Editors, for their part, also function as something of a pack—at
least in their judgments of newsworthiness. They confer great
prestige on the wire services and the elite newspapers. So many
editors and reporters read and esteem the *New York Times* that the
Times alone can become the critical mass that certifies a story's
significance—and even its frame. Likewise, the wire services by
themselves can certify the story, leading editors to assign reporters
to it. Less often, the *Washington Post*, or widely syndicated columnists like Evans and Novak, or one of the two major newsmagazines, or one of the networks can certify and define a key story by
covering it. Then reporters and assignment editors in other newsrooms recognize an occurrence as a story; they look for their own
continuations, their own (often local) angles. If they lack a version
of the occurrence, an editor is likely to notice and to query a reporter: "Why don't we have anything on X?" If the *Times* does

33. Timothy Crouse, *The Boys on the Bus*, passim.
34. At CBS News in November 1976, I saw a report come in by satellite of
Leonid Brezhnev's arrival in Belgrade for a meeting with President Tito. The correspondent had flown in from Paris and framed the airport scene like every other diplomatic and presidential airport arrival scene ever broadcast. Nothing was revealed.
The retired correspondent Alexander Kendrick maintains that this conventionaliza-
tion of foreign coverage is a consequence of satellite technology: the network can
get a same-day report now, and so loses interest in deeper (and more expensive)
on-the-spot coverage of all but the most riveting continuing foreign stories (interview, November 17, 1976). I would say that such technology meets the organization's need to process packaged information quickly and cost-effectively; the technology is developed, promoted, and made to appear inevitable toward that end.

have something on X, but it varies too far from the wire services' accounts, an editor may raise an eyebrow. Meanwhile, a prominent, high-prestige story (like Wehrwein's) generates reactions—especially official reactions—which then continue the story. As it continues, the story becomes a force field drawing in other reporters. A combination of events now hardens into a known quantity, a definite thing that matters in the world, "the X story," or simply "X" ("Vietnam," "student unrest," "civil rights," "the New Right," "cults")—because one of the legitimate purveyors of news has certified it as a story.

So stories spread horizontally, from news organization to news organization, as they spread vertically *within* organizations. Reporters talk to each other in a newsroom, or on a fixed beat, or in the course of covering a new, "breaking" story; editors read the competition; network news staff watch the other networks' versions—the mechanisms of emulation are simple, direct, and everyday.[35] A critical mass of attention heaps up; then it "cannot be ignored." If the story has been generated by certified news sources—especially federal agencies and officials—the news organizations are especially likely to recertify it. The sources then have the chance to perform their repertories for attention-getting—press conferences, on- and off-the-record briefings, press releases—to satisfy the newsgatherers' thirst for "new developments," to keep the story circulating as a "developing story." And once the story has been published widely, by definition it is now of wide interest—until, of course, editors decide it is "old news" and "we've run enough on X."

The logic is circular, though it proceeds from the commonly cited—and serviceably vague—editorial motive of *reporting on stories that affect, or might interest, the largest number of readers.* Of course, "affect" and "interest" may conflict, may even be likely to conflict, in any given case. And even the relevant readership may be subject to a variety of changing market calculations, as a newspaper shifts its attentions, say, from working-class inner-city readers toward the more stylish suburbanites whose "upscale" incomes are more attractive to advertisers. But criteria for news-

35. Although local TV stations often broadcast network news at the same time, the networks "feed" their news shows directly to each other's newsrooms. In November 1976, at least, CBS News staff paid less than avid attention to the other networks' news; and in any event, by the time they saw an NBC News piece it would be much too late to take account of it for that evening's news—though not too late to affect the next day's assignments.

worthiness that refer to "effect," "interest," "readership," or even man-biting dogs are all *serviceably* vague: they permit the news organizations both flexibility and stability. That is, they grant the media latitude to gather a wide range of information, and thus allow peripheral groups access to a certain public world while guaranteeing elites surveillance of the new; at the same time, they leave untouched the core hegemonic principles that regularize definition of the real and institutionalize it in regular bureaus and beats, and in dependence on routine sources. In the end, a story is a continuing national story because it has been made a continuing national story.

But the nature of a story is not self-evident. Whether the story has been identified as the Vietnam war, or anti-draft activity, or Katzenbach's attack on SDS, it can be pitched in different ways. And just as there are structured pressures working toward homogeneity, there are counterpressures toward a certain diversity in journalism as a whole. For one, market forces may select somewhat different stories and somewhat different frames; the newspaper that seeks the younger, "upscale" readership of theatregoing, quiche-tasting professionals will be interested in different stories (and approach the same stories differently) than the paper appealing to the older, more settled working class. For another, different generations of reporters and editors may come to see the same story differently.[36] And occasionally individual reporters (like Fred Powledge) do develop strong and discrepant points of view. But in the fall of 1965, if reporters diverged from the middle-thinking administration point of view about antiwar opposition, they seem to have diverged mostly toward the Right. Reporters still began their inquiries with the World War II premise that draft resistance was outrageous and the Cold War premise that Communism was more or less monolithically menacing. With all the routine processes and premises at work, the *Times* seems to have

36. I am using *generation* not just chronologically but socially, to refer to an age group whose common experience in its youth endows its members, in the words of Karl Mannheim, "with a common location in the historical dimension of the social process," limiting them "to a specific range of potential experience, predisposing them for a certain characteristic mode of thought and experience, and a characteristic type of historically relevant action." See Mannheim's formative "The Problem of Generations," in his *Essays on the Sociology of Knowledge,* ed. Paul Kecskemeti (New York: Oxford University Press, 1952), pp. 290–291, and the careful and persuasive application of the concept of political generations by Maurice Zeitlin in *Revolutionary Politics and the Cuban Working Class* (Princeton, N.J.: Princeton University Press, 1967), chap. 9.

helped provoke the administration into denouncing the antiwar movement.

On Tuesday, October 19, the lead story on page 1 of the *Times* was headlined: "JOHNSON DECRIES DRAFT PROTESTS—PRESSES INQUIRY / He Fears Enemy Will Doubt Nation's Resolve and Fight Harder, Prolonging War / CONGRESS ALSO CRITICAL / Mansfield Asserts Marchers are Irresponsible and Hurt Vietnam Peace Efforts." This Washington dispatch quoted not only Johnson's attack and his call for an investigation of anti-draft activity, but compatible decclamations by Senators Mansfield, Dirksen, Kuchel ("dirty and contemptible," "vile and venomous"), Russell, Saltonstall, and Lausche. There was no balancing statement from the Left.

Instead, Austin C. Wehrwein had filed another front-page story from Chicago: "ANTIDRAFT GROUP MAPS NEW EFFORT." Wehrwein now homed in on the announced SDS program—or, to use his words, "master plan," again connoting a conspiratorial "instigation"—and situated the "master plan" in its physical surrounding. Wehrwein described the SDS office accurately as "a warren of dank second-floor offices, badly lighted and in wretched repair, on 63rd Street, in a Negro slum area. . . ." The actual slumminess of the SDS office was becoming a central component of the media frame. *Not that such descriptions were invented*: "it *was* a disgusting office," as Paul Booth remembers.[37] But slumminess was by itself ambiguous; just how was a reader to interpret it? Slumminess could have connotated a *disreputable* SDS: a lowlife group that failed to play the game of making news amidst respectable and reasonably prosperous vinyl (if not leather), in rented hotel suites and institutional conference rooms. Or in a different context, it could equally well have connotated a *sloppily self-sacrificing* SDS: middle-class kids having left homes of middle-class comfort to do good works. If read deeply, it could evoke both. But Wehrwein went on to create a context establishing the physical office as proof of something at first glance pathetic, at second glance sinister:

Civil rights and Left-wing posters adorn the walls along with some modern paintings. One of the posters, designed by Picasso, has a Communist hammer and sickle; it is signed by the Italian Communist Party.

37. Paul Booth, letter to the author, September 16, 1977. When I interviewed Stanhope Gould in 1976, Gould also spontaneously brought up the way the building shook and conversation ceased when the El train roared by just outside the window.

Was the poster there? Yes, along with others Wehrwein refrained from describing in detail. By leaving his description at this point, Wehrwein was elaborating the anti-Communist frame he had brought to the fore in reporting the Katzenbach press conference. If he had specified the great policy differences between the Italian Communist Party and the Soviets, he would have suggested SDS's politics with far greater accuracy. In fact, the SDS leadership had no sympathy for the Soviet Union. For SDS, hanging the Italian Picasso poster meant, in large part, expressing solidarity with the dissidence boiling up within world Communism. But Wehrwein did not grasp, or at least did not report, the poster's symbolic meaning from SDS's side. In the dominant code shared by Wehrwein and most *Times* readers, Communism was an undifferentiated menace, and Wehrwein assimilated SDS into bad company.[38]

Immediately he returned to the "instigation" theme that he had established as a salient issue:

The group's program is based on the theory that student demonstrations are not enough. The group supported the rash of protests this weekend without taking credit for instigating them.

The unpleasant connotations of a "rash" of protests were compounded by the renewed implication that SDS was ducking its responsibility for the "instigation." A "master plan" conjured up in "a warren of dank, second-floor offices, badly lighted and in wretched repair," under the sign of the hammer and sickle, by a group that had just supported a "rash of protests"—evasively at that—and whose politics were unclear except for their "theory that student demonstrations are not enough"—what could an uninformed reader already mobilized against Communism make of such a group and such a "master plan"?

And Wehrwein's frame was not unique. Richard Flacks visited the SDS office during those days and heard other reporters ask "'Have-you-stopped-beating-your-wife' kind of questions."[39] Booth continued to try (as on the next day, October 20) to redefine the central issue as the wrongness of the war—"'There is a growing antiwar movement that thinks the war is corrupt—bankrupt is a better word,' the 22-year-old Mr. Booth said"—only to have such remarks reframed and weakened. Wehrwein again:

38. Compare CBS's earlier, respectful treatment of the SDS premises, in Chapter 2, above.

39. Interview, Richard Flacks, January 9, 1977.

Mr. Booth, who is 1-A in the draft but claiming deferment as a conscientious objector with Draft Board 2 in Washington, was undisturbed about a possible prison sentence.

This same article repeated Under Secretary of State George W. Ball's characterization of the October 15-16 protests as "'beat the draft' demonstrations."

"BUILD, NOT BURN"

Booth's struggle half-succeeded, half-failed. Doggedly he went on trying to change the terms of coverage. Later in the same wild week, he and Oglesby flew to Washington to take some initiative by holding a press conference. What came to be known as the "Build, Not Burn" position was drawn up the night before by Booth with the help of SDS members Arthur Waskow and Paul Cowan. Booth had rented nothing less than the Grand Ballroom of the National Press Club, and it was jammed. Booth's statement had the flavor of a positive challenge to the administration, and, at the same time, a defense against the draft-dodging charge. The essence was this:

Let us see what happens if service to democracy is made grounds for exemption from the military draft. I predict that almost every member of my generation would choose to build, not to burn; to teach, not to torture; to help, not to kill. . . . We are not afraid to risk our lives—we have been risking our lives in Mississippi and Alabama, and some of us died there. But we will not bomb the people—the women, the children—of another country.[40]

Booth's judo tactic succeeded in impressing both media and officialdom. Defending "Build, Not Burn" to the SDS membership a couple of months later, Booth wrote:

The content of the statement got across in some cases—the wire services and a lot of papers carried lengthy quotes comparing what we want to do with what the government was forcing us to do in Vietnam. The *Chicago Tribune* headline was "Oglesby Tells Johnson Protesters' Terms."[41]

Booth's statement got a few seconds on the CBS Evening News. True, the *Times* was less impressed: the Administration got the front page the next day ("SHOW OF SUPPORT ON VIETNAM GAINS

40. Virtually the complete text can be found in Sale, *SDS*, pp. 233–234.
41. Paul Booth, "National Secretary's Report," mimeographed, n.d. [December 1965]; author's file.

STRENGTH IN U.S."), while the SDS gambit ran in distinctly second position as an inside ("jump") page continuation under the sub-head "Exemptions are Sought." But on the whole, Booth was right when he wrote: "The proof of the pudding is in the proverbial eating," and "I think the statement had an excellent overall effect." It was distributed with rhetorical force on a number of campuses; it helped in recruitment; and not least—from Booth's strategic point of view—it was a powerful political tactic in the immediate situation:

In Washington, among faculty, liberal lawyers, and a lot of others, it bolstered our allies and compounded the embarrassment of the Katzenbachs (the Justice Department now says it isn't investigating us).

For all this, outlying SDS groups were furious with both the statement and the way it had come about. Several of the more radical chapters protested that the statement was "liberal" in its zeal to dissociate SDS from draft resistance, and hundreds of individual members complained too that, far from attacking the draft as inequitable and undemocractic, "Build, Not Burn" simply proposed extending and legitimizing it. There was much feeling that Booth had usurped the right to make any policy statement at all. An unprecedented telegram arrived from the new Regional Office in San Francisco:

Western Region SDS dismayed at recent statement on the draft and build not burn. Series of decisions undemocratically arrived at. 1. Small vote and narrow majority hardly amount to democratic mandate. 2. In any case, statement falsely indicates the draft program dropped for all SDS and implies local autonomy nonexistent. 3. NO cannot establish national policy. 4. Build not burn and freedom draft imposed without discussion. 5. Tone of statement deplorable. Mention of draft dodgers, etc., reads like cop out to Katzenbach. NAC and Booth overstepped proper functions. Need indicated to reexamine role of national apparatus. Participatory democracy begins at home. Cordially. Above statement adopted unanimously at meeting of 50 members including representatives of regional office, Berkeley, Davis, Los Angeles, Reed, Sacramento, San Francisco, San Jose, and Stanford. Ken McEldowney, SDS.[42]

Greg Calvert, a leading exemplar of Prairie Power at the 1966 convention and subsequently Booth's successor as National Secretary, wrote later that "Build, Not Burn" was "the greatest formula ever

42. SDS Work List Mailing, No. 28, November 30, 1965.

devised for selling out the radical movement and playing into the cooptive hands of the establishment."[43]

Booth later protested that "Build, Not Burn" had been a tactic of the moment, albeit a tactic consonant with "underlying SDS political views"; he had come to it in the heat of a political battle that had been forced upon him. He insisted that he had not announced any actual program: "the telegram to Johnson asking him to give draft exemption for 'service to democracy' was a *dramatic* gesture, not backed up with the intention to mount—or even advocate mounting—a campaign for national alternative service."[44] When you play under the big proscenium, Booth was saying, you play by the stage rules which the audience understands. In 1965, SDS had a limited repertory of gestures.

Plainly there was an authentic political dispute within the organization; but Booth was more sensitive than his critics to the structure, the timing, and the momentum of the immediate political situation. He was learning the hard way how the media operated, what they noticed, what they didn't. For the reporters, the "story" was draft evasion, not SDS's view of the war. In his report to the membership, Booth acknowledged that "Build, Not Burn" "departed from the set policy of the week of talking about Vietnam" because that policy had largely failed to affect press coverage; "the draft question was the most interesting one to the press and public, and especially at a Washington press conference it couldn't be ignored. . . ."[45] In other words, it was the structure of media choices—and not only Booth's own political inclinations—that had pressed him toward the tactic of a "liberal turn." If SDS was going to get itself off the hook, it would have to pull back from the damning positions the media had imputed to it.

What was the practical alternative? No one proposed one at the time. Twelve years later, after much reflection and much experience with Left politics and the media, Booth speculates that the *politics* of the liberal turn could have been wedded to the *tactics* of a defiant turn:

Suppose [Booth writes] I had demanded a Put-Up or Shut-Up meeting with Katzenbach. That would have been the lead—then the antiwar and draft stuff would be secondary. I could have marched over to Justice and sat-in

43. *New Left Notes*, February 13, 1967, p. 2. This quotation and some of the previous facts were gathered by Sale, *SDS*, pp. 234–235.
44. Booth, "National Secretary's Report" (emphasis in the original).
45. Ibid.

there. Or something. Part of the reason for choosing the liberal turn was my (and Waskow's) failure of nerve. The left-wing [of SDS] was ashamed of what they saw as chickening-out—which was real important because their politics was 80% moral posture, 20% content.[46]

An inventive idea: SDS could have retaken the political initiative while satisfying the SDS militants stylistically. But Booth did not think of it in 1965. Meanwhile, the critics were not proposing any other practical way to cope with the spotlight. What Booth now calls a "failure of nerve" was partly a result of being stampeded by media routines. But Booth under pressure realized, as his critics did not, that SDS had no choice about *whether* to stay in the spotlight, it had only a choice about *how*. If at any point SDS had refused to comment, the refusal would have been treated as comment of a particular type: as evasion. So Booth went on trying to establish just what SDS *was* thinking and doing, while media treatments oscillated between images of *dangerous* SDS and *ineffectual* SDS: in either case, SDS as the deviant other. Demonic or quixotic, SDS was to be seen as a mote in the audience eye.

Over the following weeks, the membership finally voted on the notorious anti-draft program, and coverage was typically anticlimactic. When Evans and Novak had first exposed the provisional program, the spectacle had been front-page news. But follow-up stories are conventionally downplayed; the rare retractions and corrections are almost always tiny items at the bottom of inside pages. The "story" is more newsworthy when it is fresh and false than when it is "old" and true. As it happened, by the middle of November the small proportion of the SDS membership that voted had voted against the program. Paul Booth's Work List report of media reactions takes the story from there:

The press got wind of the defeat of the draft program referendum last night [November 16], and AP called. A series of on-the-spot administrative decisions were made by me . . . predicated on the notion that we should maintain fairly decent press relations, and that the mandate of the membership was clear. . . . We didn't want to close the vote off—they are still trickling in. But when AP called to say they had heard it was losing, I quickly decided to "spill the beans" insted of say "no comment." We had been holding off queries on the subject for 3 weeks.[47]

46. Booth, letter to the author, September 16, 1977.
47. SDS Work List Mailing, No. 27, November 17, 1965.

Booth was defensive, of course, because he had caught flak for monopolizing and misusing media contact during "Build, Not Burn." But he shared with his Left opposition a considerable naivete. Virtually everyone in SDS—from Booth to the West Coast dissidents—had assumed that reporters could be handled, that symbols could be relayed, that the struggle for the media frame could be won if only the right things were said. Even now, Booth went on explaining to reporters that SDS was internally democratic, that it respected its chapters' autonomy, that the vote was a matter of tactics, not principle, and that SDS was still "looking for a way of saying not only that we don't want to fight in Vietnam, but that we want to carry out a program of social change at home, to which we are ready to commit our 'youthful energies.'"[48]

Booth had learned to be scrupulous about the nuances of SDS procedure. But the media were not interested in details. For the most part, SDS appeared to be backing down, acknowledging in public that the program from which it was "backing down" (a program it had never endorsed!) had, indeed, been illegitimate. Presumably, in this logic, the administration had been justified in denouncing SDS, and the media had been right to blow the whistle. In this Catch-22 situation, it is hard to see how SDS could have salvaged its dignity. Booth did summon up suggestions to the SDS activist core:

Local adverse coverage can be offset, if you act quickly. First, if they make it sound like we're backing off in the line of fire, issue a steaming blast at the war policy and tie it around an announcement of your buses to the [November 27] March or some other visible evidence of continued activity. If you have been working on the draft, and don't want to appear undercut by the press, re-announce your program emphasizing the local autonomy. If they run the story as if the members in the referendum have squelched your local program, tell the papers they can get a quote from Booth that the national backs your continuation of local program if they call here.

Booth's punctilious judo move did influence the *New York Times*'s November 19 treatment, "Antidraft Program Dropped," which did make clear that the referendum vote was tactical, not strategic. And the *Times* did itemize some of the substitute proposals for antiwar activity circulating through SDS. But this piece ran on page 5, as an appendix to the jump of a more prominent story. And

48. Ibid.

in other published stories, as Booth wrote on November 17, "it looks like the press is selecting the parts it wants to run, and omitting the others."

DEVELOPING THEMES, I: THE MOVEMENT DIVIDED

As the antiwar movement mobilized throughout the fall, and the administration countermobilized, the media were no longer framing antiwar students as campus scamperers, with their "beards and blue jeans mixed with ivy tweeds and an occasional clerical collar" out for a "holiday from exams" in "warm spring sunshine." The antiwar movement was plainly growing, and part of it, plainly, was militant. Its opposition to the war was just as plainly becoming more vehement. Actual growth and actual militance were not so easily represented as trivial.

So the dominant framing themes shifted, partly as reality shifted, and partly as the major media sorted out their approach toward the war. Throughout the fall of 1965, the liberal national media devoted considerable space to covering intra-movement conflict, the drama within the drama. Where outspokenly right-wing papers like the *New York Daily News* and the *Chicago Tribune* tarred the antiwar movement with the reputation of its most pro-Communist elements, the *New York Times* and CBS News tended first to distinguish between legitimate and illegitimate forms of protest, then to show that the latter was penetrating and contaminating the former. This approach at once *preserved* the image of a rational, sober antiwar protest and *discredited* it. It was, in short, a formula for ambivalence.

A structured ambivalence this was, but at the same time the media did not invent intra-movement conflict. Far from it. While the media are not flat mirrors of reality, neither are they abstract paintings of the imaginary. They are, again, more like fun house mirrors, narrowing and widening, lengthening and shortening, distorting and neglecting what is already there—somewhere. The media versions interpret events by plausibly representing a world that publics already recognize as a real world; and it is a rare story indeed that circulates an utter untruth. Unquestionably there were divisions within the antiwar movement. Indeed, there were probably more of them during the fall of 1965 than there had been in the spring: the Marxist-Leninist cadre of the Progressive Labor Movement (later Party) first organized their own May 2nd Movement to

support the National Liberation Front of South Vietnam, then began moving into SDS; at the same time, liberals were organizing
moderate alternatives. Because there was more movement, there
was more movement for diverse factions to fight over. But it is also
true that, because of their own dominant code, the media now paid
disproportionate attention to internal differences and arguments.
These issues were legitimately newsworthy; but reporters were not
reporting corresponding conflicts within the pro-war mobilization
or the administration. Indeed, the administration was routinely
deceiving the media about its own conflicts on war policy. For their
own reasons, for example, U.S. Ambassador to Saigon Maxwell
Taylor and the Air Force opposed changing the Marines' mission to
offense in April 1965; throughout this period, according to Daniel
Ellsberg, "We [in the government] were lying about how much
controversy there was inside." [49] And for the most part the media
were taking the carefully cultivated appearance of official unity at
face value. *But by virtue of being open to investigation, the antiwar
movement was more vulnerable to the less flattering frames.*

In the *Times* of October 23, for example, all of page 2 but the ads
was devoted to M. S. Handler's story under the four-column headline, "Marxists Join Antiwar Drive but Deny Inspiring It." The
story relayed the views of "the fragmented Marxist parties, searching for a new lease on life"—Spartacists, Socialist Workers Party,
Progressive Labor, Communist Party, all of them claiming they had
negligible influence on the "so-called New Left." Two days later,
a briefer and less prominent article, "NEW GROUP OPENS PROTEST
ON ASIA," carried news of a thirty-campus teach-in including, as
speakers, Norman Cousins, John K. Fairbank, Michael Harrington,
and Norman Thomas. The leaders of the "new campaign," according to John Sibley's page 6 article, "pledged to demonstrate 'not
by civil disobedience but by education.'" John C. Bennett of the
Union Theological Seminary was quoted as saying that pickets and
draft-card burners (of whom, note, there had been *one* by this date)
"may have reached the point of defeating their own purpose; they
are hardening the opposition." [50]

49. Interviews, Daniel Ellsberg, March 2, 1977, and March 17, 1979. When an
insider like Ellsberg goes outside, of course, hitherto secret internal disputes go
public with him.

50. The theme of intra-movement conflict came up again on November 4, with
a page 3 story: "END-WAR GROUP IN N.Y. DISBANDS," recounting a tactical split between SDS and the Socialist Workers Party.

Sibley's relatively delicate accent on intra-movement polarization was attended by a brief sub-story headlined, in small type, "Seeger Critical in Moscow":

Moscow, Oct. 24—An American folk singer, Pete Seeger, sang a Vietnam protest ballad today before an auditorium filled with Moscow University students.

"I wanted to show students here the kind of songs we're singing on college campuses in the United States," Mr. Seeger said afterward. "It would be wrong to leave this one out."

Mr. Seeger, who is completing a private three-week concert tour of the Soviet Union, shrugged off suggestions that he might be criticized for his action. . . .

Such "suggestions" probably came—as they normally do—from American reporters sustaining the dominant code. The issue of propriety was underscored by the attending photo of Seeger, captioned: "PERFORMS IN MOSCOW: Pete Seeger, folksinger, sang ballad protesting war in South Vietnam yesterday at Moscow University." By virtue of its placement next to the "NEW GROUP OPENS PROTEST ON ASIA" headline, the Seeger piece *perforce* showed just what sort of illegitimate antiwar action the moderates were distinguishing themselves from.

Meanwhile, in the back of the Sunday, October 24, news section, a long feature by Edith Evans Asbury appeared under the headline, "David Miller and the Catholic Workers: A Study in Pacifism." Asbury's story was strong on human interest and sympathetic biographical detail. Features about the old-line pacifist Left were normally sympathetic, in fact. Later that fall, the *Times* reflected on the self-immolation of the Quaker Norman Morrison at the Pentagon in a sensitive, sad-toned piece, seeking to understand, in the terms of personal experience, "why he did it." Roger LaPorte's self-immolation a few days later was covered the same way: as an aberrant—though not monstrous—individual act by a decent person, to be understood by a tour through his personal motives. Stopping short of framing these acts of moral witness as signs of insanity, these feature stories proposed to comprehend the actions within the context of the individual biography—or, in the case of Asbury's story, the biography of one small political cluster. The effect was to render the pacifist actions at once commendable and inimitable, since the biographical accounts, in their very sympathy, imparted auras of saintliness. Sometimes genuinely admir-

ing and sometimes patronizing, these accounts customarily treated the pacifist actions outside their political context: the Vietnam
war. At times they directly counterposed pacifists to radicals, as in
Tom Buckley's November 10 account of the self-immolation of Roger LaPorte: "Then, at 5 A.M., the tall slender blond youth, who
looked nothing like the stereotype of the long-haired 'Vietnik' or
peace demonstrator, lit himself on fire." (Buckley did *not* reflect on
the source of the long-haired stereotype.) The *Times*'s use of very
different frames for the Marxist sects, the New Left, the liberals,
and the pacifists contributed, in short, to an overall effect of tangle,
contradiction, and disarray on the antiwar Left.

There was one major exception, though: an accurate and respectful *New York Times Magazine* cover story, by freelance writer
Thomas R. Brooks, appearing on November 7, suggesting that differences within SDS were at most tactical and strategic within a
common spirit of opposition to the war and a more general radicalism. In April, Brooks had written a piece for the *Magazine* on Mao-
ist sects, and shortly afterward articles editor Harvey Shapiro had
asked him to work on a piece for the fall about the new campus
radicalism.[51] With the mid-October draft crisis, another *Magazine*
editor, Kirkpatrick Sale (later author of the first comprehensive
chronicle of SDS), suggested that the piece focus on SDS. Sale
knew that Brooks was on the board of SDS's parent organization,
the League for Industrial Democracy, and therefore surmised that
Brooks would be knowledgeable about SDS. (He did not then
know of the great tension between the two organizations.)[52] In
any event, Brooks got the assignment formally on October 20, just
after the anti-draft flap had made SDS front-page news. Drawing as usual on the daily paper for their story ideas, the *Magazine*
editors wanted a quick background on SDS; Shapiro asked for delivery within eight days. And although Brooks ended up adding a
few lines in response to editorial requests, the story that ran on
November 7 was essentially his original submission.[53]

51. Thomas R. Brooks, letter to the author, March 26, 1979.
52. Telephone interview, Kirkpatrick Sale, March 17, 1979.
53. Brooks, letter to the author, February 26, 1979. The text of Shapiro's telegram, as Brooks has kindly relayed it to me, shows plainly that intra-movement
conflict had a *subordinate* position in the assignment: "Please proceed 3,500 word
story SDS as student wing of peace movement. Twould be done against background whole movement but body of piece would use narrative and dialogue to
describe how and why SDS took on this job. What the arguments among the group
are, characterization of the leaders and rank-and-file, vivid picture of SDS working

Brooks took SDS's political values at face value and articulated them fairly. His capsule biographies of key SDS people presented them, accurately, as all-Americans with roots in mainstream American life; and as competent Americans at that—skilled, decent, intelligent people. The top editors, however, chose for the cover a photo of a National Office staff member standing next to an antiwar poster showing a napalmed Vietnamese child. With plenty of staff portraits to choose from, including several of apple-pie respectability, why did the top editors single out the portrait of a long-haired, droopy-mustached office printer, glaring out of the page with challenge in his eyes? Photos of five other, less hairy staff members appeared safely inside, illustrating the body of the article. Printer Don Yost's long hair was not typical among the office staff. True, none of the other photos printed showed the antiwar poster, and it is no longer possible to know about photos taken but not printed; perhaps none of them contained the antiwar poster, which the top *Magazine* editors liked as a pictorial sign of SDS's politics. And true, the Prairie Power people, many of whom did sport long hair, *were* on the move in SDS, if not in the National Office. The former Sunday editor of the *Times*, who was the major person in charge of choosing *Magazine* covers, does not recollect this particular choice; he recalls, though, that when he sorted through the week's available photos, he generally tried to pick for the cover something that "would attract the reader's eye." [54] Another former *Magazine* editor also supposes that this photo "was chosen because it was more arresting." It should go without saying that a cover story about the Chase Manhattan Bank, the Department of Energy, or a City Hall or State legislature, would not feature the office printer, even if he or she were available for the staff photographer. In any event, such deviant framing made an impression on SDS. One former staff member recalls that the cover photo "really freaked out a lot of people in the organization. Because he was so hairy. [C. Clark] Kissinger did not like that at all. This was not the image they wanted to project at that time." [55] The *Magazine* had solicited a respectful article about SDS and superimposed a frame of hairy deviance over it.

---

among the students and student reaction to SDS preachments. Delivery here October 28." In other words, Brooks's thoroughness and fairness were precisely what his editor ordered.

54. Telephone interview, Daniel Schwartz, April 21, 1979.
55. Interview, James Russell, January 19, 1977.

Still, superimposed-upon as it was, a respectful article on the movement was unusual for the *Times*. Evidently there was no clear-cut ideological line on SDS. The organizationally independent Sunday *Magazine* had more leeway than the daily paper, although it drew its topics from the daily. There was internal conflict over the antiwar movement as there was over the war, and this was how the editors wanted it. "I didn't want a homogenized product," in the words of Sunday editor Schwartz.[56] Over the years to come, articles appeared within a variety of frames. But the editors always feared that an article would go too far toward sympathy with a New Left point of view, and that an antiwar position would blur into support for the Vietnamese Communists. One way to shore up their journalistic version of fairness was to emphasize disarray and disagreement on the Left.

DEVELOPING THEMES, II: THE MOVEMENT CONFRONTED

The *Times* conveyed no impression of disarray and dissension when it covered pro-war forces. They were not, indeed, subjected to very close scrutiny at all. Their internal workings were not investigated. They were taken for granted, as if they were natural forces.

And when the *Times* emphasized divisions between the Left and the pro-war Right, as it so often did, these reports quietly, normally, tilted toward the Right. Time and again, articles overlooked violence that the Right had precipitated, or muffled its origins. As we have seen, the *Times* had for some time played up Left-Right violence during antiwar events, constructing a line of argument to the effect that antiwar events "resulted in" violence. (The violence was then traced to the antiwar *event*, rather than to the attackers.) On other occasions, a bit of understatement could convey the sense that the blame for popular violence was shared. One front-page article, for example, on October 28, was headlined: "STUDENTS CLASH ON SAIGON POLICY AFTER MANHATTAN COLLEGE RALLY." The lead: "Students supporting United States policy in Vietnam and others opposing it clashed briefly yesterday. . . ." The evenhanded lead was belied, belatedly, by the actual account of the origins of the fighting, which came only in the twelfth paragraph, on the jump page: ". . . at the rally's end, some students

56. Telephone interview, April 21, 1979.

turned to the pacifist group shouting, 'Burn those signs.'" It was the Right that had inaugurated the "clash." But the headline and lead magisterially apportioned responsibility with even hands.

Another form of pro-war tilt emerged in the *Times*'s October 30, page 2 announcement of a pro-war mobilization: "50,000 EXPECTED TO PARADE HERE TODAY TO BACK VIETNAM POLICY," by Douglas Robinson. When one compares this piece with the *Times*'s treatment of the October 15 antiwar mobilization, three differences are striking:

1. The *Times* gave no advance notice of the nationally coordinated October 15-16 demonstrations. On October 13, in fact, it reported "A Vietnam Protest Dies in Planning Stage," writing about a single, local, insignificant project. On the day of the first demonstrations, it reported on the Vietnam Day Committee ("Vietnam War Foes to Defy Oakland") and on a meeting of right-wing student government officers organizing against the mildly antiwar National Student Association. As a national story, in other words, the October 15 demonstrations seemed to burst out of nowhere. By contrast, the October 30 pro-war *advance* story got five columns on page 2. Part of the difference conceivably might have flowed from the fact that the pro-war march was a *New York* story, and thus perhaps eligible for space that the metropolitan editor would lobby for;[57] but how much of the discrepancy could be explained by the *Times*'s way of allocating space to its fiefdoms, and by the vagaries of assignment alone? Later, an advance story on the day of the moderates' antiwar march in Washington, November 27, got *one* column on page 12.

2. The October 30 story listed instructions for demonstrators and informed them where various pro-war groups would be assembling for their march that morning. Not once had any such logistical information been supplied for antiwar demonstrations. (The code later proved more flexible—at least when more legiti-

---

57. Leon Sigal (*Reporters and Officials*, p. 31) discovered that, in 1970, "whatever the variation in world events and news flow . . . the front pages of the *New York Times* and the *Washington Post* had a tendency to contain an equal number of stories from the national, foreign, and metropolitan desks." As Sigal points out (p. 30): "On the assumption that the substance of newsworthy stories varies randomly, probability could account for a balance among the three desks over time, but it could hardly explain a tendency toward equal distribution day after day." The explanation must have to do with organizational politics in the newspapers. I am suggesting that similar politics might account for comparable horse-trading on other pages of the *Times*, not only page 1.

mate antiwar groups lobbied tenaciously and skillfully enough. The November 27 advance story did give information on times and places for antiwar assembly.)

3. The event was not distanced, denatured, or marginalized with quotation marks. Whereas antiwar demonstrations had been referred to as "peace marches," the October 30 story called the pro-war event a march or a parade, without quotation marks to make the type stand out as something in need of explanation. The march, or parade, was the kind of traditional event that could be assimilated to the taken-for-granted category without the special trouble, the cognitive novelty, the faint disreputability connoted by quotation marks. After writing straightforwardly about this known happening, the pro-war march, Robinson turned to antiwar actions and insulated himself by enclosing "silent vigil" in protective quotation marks.[58]

DEVELOPING THEMES, III:
THE MOVEMENT LEGITIMATE AND ILLEGITIMATE

Throughout the rest of 1965, the *Times* continued to promote the theme of movement extremism. The emphasis on violence and the emphasis on pro-Communism were aspects of the same framing: extremism of tactics was joined to extremism of program. Even where no violence was occurring, the threat of it, the intimation of it, could become the story. One minor example: a November 20 story from Berkeley, by Wallace Turner, "Oakland Marchers Urged to Use Picket Sign Poles as Protection." The smaller subhead read: "But Critics of Vietnam War Score Advice in Leaflets for Today's Protest." The lead: "A left-wing activist group called the Sparticists [*sic*] handed out leaflets at the University of California today urging that picket sign poles be used for defense 'in case of attack' in tomorrow's anti–Vietnam War demonstration." Where he had been at pains in an earlier piece to discover and denigrate the size of an antiwar crowd (see above), Turner here did not even raise the issue of the size of the Spartacist group. (In fact it was, as always, miniscule.) On the eve of the second VDC march into Oakland, this advance piece was illustrated with a photo of the Communist historian Herbert Aptheker, who happened to be giving a speech at the

58. See Gaye Tuchman's discussion of "the judicious use of quotation marks" in her *Making News: A Study in the Construction of Reality* (New York: The Free Press, 1978), pp. 95–97.

University of California denouncing the McCarran Act. The word *meantime* was the sole connection between Turner's account of official preparations for the march and the Aptheker addendum. Although Aptheker's talk, by Turner's own account, ignored the Vietnam demonstration, Turner cited it as if Aptheker's very presence on the campus spoke for itself and was an important fact about the antiwar movement.

By November, the antiwar moderates around the Committee for a Sane Nuclear Policy (SANE) had taken steps to demarcate themselves from the Left. In organizing their November 27 march in Washington, they had assiduously refrained from calling for the withdrawal of American troops from Vietnam; indeed, they had tried to ban pro-withdrawal signs from the line of march. SANE Executive Secretary Sanford Gottlieb, Norman Thomas, Dr. Benjamin Spock, and Mrs. Martin Luther King, Jr. had met beforehand in the White House with Chester Cooper, an aide to McGeorge Bundy in the National Security Council; Cooper had persuaded them to wire Ho Chi Minh, telling him not to take their demonstration as support, to signal that they were opposed impartially to both North Vietnamese and American policy.[59] So deliberately had the SANE leaders worked to present a reasoning, reasonable, moderate face to both government and press. (Meanwhile, under pressure from actively antiwar chapters, SDS had endorsed the march and acquired a place on the speakers' platform for its president, Carl Oglesby: SDS sent out its own call.) But national media this time seized upon intra-movement conflict in order to discredit the entire demonstration. However hard Sanford Gottlieb, Norman Thomas, and the other SANE leaders had worked to organize *their* impeccably well-tailored and reform-tempered march, they remained vulnerable.

True, the image of moderation seemed to prevail in news frames. In its report on the Saturday march itself, the *Times* did not even mention that one of the rally speakers—in fact, the one most enthusiastically received—was the last speaker, Oglesby, who marked a major ideological turn for the movement with what was to become a famous radical critique of the war as the product of corporate liberalism. (As in April, the *Times*'s lapse can be partly—but only partly—explained by the early Saturday deadline for Sun-

59. Chester Cooper, *The Lost Crusade: America in Vietnam* (New York: Dodd, Mead, 1970), pp. 289–290.

day editions.) As the SANE organizers had wished and worked for, *Times* coverage of the march emphasized the moderate tone and the respectable, "decorous" throng. Typically, one background story bore the headline: "Typical Marcher: Middle-Class Adult." There were, in Max Frankel's phrasing, "more babies than beatniks, more family groups than folk-song quartets." But two days earlier, the *Times* had amplified something less decorous.

That Friday, November 26, the pre-march story on page 4 had carried the six-column headline: "Vietcong Flags Are Sold in Washington as Groups Arrive for March." Directly beneath the headline there appeared a three-column UPI photograph of a Saigon soldier holding a National Liberation Front flag, with the caption: "This is a Vietcong flag. It was captured in August south of the U.S. air base at Danang." The article, by Fred P. Graham,[60] reported that the flags were being sold to delegates arriving for a National Coordinating Committee to End the War in Vietnam conference, distributed from a booth "operated by the United States Committee to Aid the National Liberation Front of South Vietnam." Graham went on to report that the march coordinator and monitors planned to ask the bearers of Vietcong flags to remove them, but had decided "in case of refusal there's really nothing we can do but to allow them to march." Graham did *not* report the size of the United States Committee to Aid the National Liberation Front of South Vietnam. A reader of this article would have had no way of knowing that this was a tiny committee. Its head, Walter Teague, III, of New York City, successfully hyped the media for years. Reporters who were routinely at pains to mention the size of SDS and the size of this or that demonstration never reported on the size of the "United States Committee to Aid the National Liberation Front of South Vietnam." Max Frankel's report on the actual march, by contrast, did minimize the importance of the NLF flags: "There were small clusters of fired-up youths in the crowd, some of whom carried the flags of the Vietcong." But, as Walter Teague had hoped, the image of the "Viet Cong" flag had succeeded in contaminating the project of the march organizers: with a tiny investment of initiative, he had cracked the journalistic code and turned it to advantage. And despite Frankel's grant of respectability to the march, his front-page report ran under a common headline with

60. In 1972, Graham moved to CBS News.

a Hong Kong dispatch sub-headlined: "Asian Communists Sure Public Opinion in U.S. Will Force War's End." This piece reported:

Demonstrators in the United States opposing the war were commended by the Communist Vietcong and Peking for joining in the common struggle against what were described as imperialist policies of the Johnson Administration.

All in all, by amplifying the few NLF flags and the "Communist Vietcong and Peking" response, the *Times* had helped undercut the same "responsible" wing of the antiwar movement which in its editorial of November 27 it was praising with faint damns:

The sponsors of today's March on Washington for Peace in Vietnam have clearly tried to make their demonstration a responsible expression of their belief that intensified efforts are needed to achieve a negotiated end of the Vietnamese conflict. Unfortunately, hope that the march will genuinely contribute to reasoned debate on this subject is in danger of destruction by an influx of extemists who insist on parading under the Vietcong flag and otherwise doing their utmost to outrage millions of Americans.

With a choice of photograph that can only be called sensationalist, the *Times* had done its share to outrage those millions. *The journalistic premium on clash and theatrics was wrestling with the paper's political interest in moderation.* Trapped in its conventions and their self-contradictions, the *Times* had encouraged the same "extremists" it deplored.

Meanwhile, CBS's coverage produced another variety of denigration.[61] A few days before the march, Washington correspondent Bruce Morton broadcast a "situationer," a relatively long piece (close to three minutes) establishing and framing the story in advance. It opened with Morton standing before the White House fence, noting that marchers would be assembling here for their demonstration. The fence, Morton said, had been "newly reinforced." The demonstration was going to call for a cease-fire and other steps toward negotiation. One component of the frame announced itself with a flourish: the march would be moderate, but

61. In the CBS Newsfilm Archive, the only piece of film that survives on the November 27 march is the "situationer" narrated by Bruce Morton. CBS News's other coverage was either done on videotape (and, if indeed it has been kept, is prohibitively expensive for the researcher), or, if done on film, has been lost. So I cannot claim that the Morton piece was entirely typical. But it *was* one of only two or three pieces that CBS ran on the march.

the reinforcement of the fence demonstrated that antiwar violence was possible.

Morton's opening was a single camera shot—in effect, the first "paragraph" of his story. Now the camera showed American Nazis marching with signs that proclaimed "Peace Creeps Go Home" and "Smash Communism," as Morton explained that last April's march of 20,000 had brought such counterdemonstrators: "And no one will be surprised if they show up again." Berkeley's American Legion Post said it was hiring a skywriter to inscribe "SHAME ON YOU" in the sky. There had already been one counterdemonstration: a Syracuse University pro-war petition with 3,000 signatures (with footage of the petition being turned in). The opening "paragraph," on demonstrations, unfolding the essential story of the forthcoming march, lasted twenty-seven seconds. The second, counterpoint "paragraph," on counterdemonstrations, took twenty-three seconds. Balance had been achieved.

Now Morton moved to what would be the essence of his frame. "All in all there've been so many demonstrations," he explained on November 26, 1965, "it's unlikely one more can have much effect." The President would be in Texas anyway. Now that Morton had defined effectiveness as the lead issue, the orienting theme of his report, he could broach countercomment that disputed his ineffectiveness claim *without having to change the frame.* Thus Morton went on: "March Coordinator Sanford Gottlieb disagrees: 'It's common knowledge the President is a political person,'" Gottlieb said on camera, arguing that the President responds to pressure; perhaps his response is not what we want, Gottlieb went on, but we have to demonstrate anyway. Morton now recapitulated his governing theme by asking Gottlieb: "Isn't there a danger that the public is simply getting tired of what has been a long series of demonstrations about Vietnam?" He had framed the issue with something of a leading question, so that Gottlieb was pushed to distinguish the November march from the others. Gottlieb could have done this by calling attention to the seven months that had elapsed since the last big antiwar demonstration in Washington; or he could have underscored the political distinctions. He chose the latter course. The other demonstrations had been protest demonstrations, Gottlieb said; "ours makes specific proposals: to end the bombing and to improve the climate for negotiations." Morton had structured the situation so that, whatever Gottlieb's intentions, the strongest move available to him was to broadcast and magnify conflict on the Left.

And having constructed a framework which effectively restricted Gottlieb, Morton now counterbalanced him with the administration. Back at the White House fence, symbol of the frontier dividing war-makers and war opponents, Morton relayed the administration position: "Secretary of State Rusk has defended the demonstrators' right to dissent, but he has warned they may mislead the Communists." Morton now substantiated Rusk's claim by quoting from a *Peking People's Daily* article encouraging the antiwar "masses."

Having established, in other words, that the demonstration was perhaps dangerous, definitely redundant, and at any rate implicated in Chinese propaganda, and having extracted from an interview with a spokesperson a single sentence about the demonstration's point of view (and this in such a way as to accentuate intra-movement conflict), Morton returned to the futility theme for his summing-up: "Most people have doubts that U.S. foreign policy can be changed on the streets." Most likely, he continued, demonstrating will succeed only in producing traffic jams. Nonetheless, Morton concluded, "police expect a busy but routine day."

Spotlighting tactics and consigning goals to the shadows, Morton asked the viewer to assess the demonstration as a tactical problem severed from purpose. Its substance was to be viewed along the dimensions of legitimacy and potency: it had no raison d'être, only a surface. Having defined the issue this way, Morton disparaged the tactic of demonstrating by predicting its impotence. But within this cognitive framework only different forms of disparagement were possible. If potent, the demonstration would be dangerous: so said the fence, Rusk, and the Chinese. If impotent, the demonstration would be wearisome, or a routine and laughable traffic problem, but in any case no more than an annoyance. In either case, in the eyes of any pro-war or uncertain audience this demonstration was not going to look auspicious.

Morton's frame was conventional. Purposes are not photogenic, tactics may be; at least—so the argument goes—they leave palpable signs like fences and traffic problems. Even more important, events are conventionally understood *as* tactics, and the emphasis on intra-movement divergences was a by-product of that convention. Older, more thoughtful TV reporters like Alexander

Kendrick might use a takeout to talk about political goals, but most reporters of "hard news" would stay away from that tricky territory. To focus on tactics was a way of ensuring that the reporter would "play it straight down the middle"; it also placed the burden of justification on the demonstrators. The conventions of everyday reporting were ideological in two broad senses: (1) through pictures, they embraced what was taken to be the audience preference for visual props and action;[62] and (2) through formal balance, they secured the news organization from the possible economic and political consequences of appearing biased. The conventions also had the effect of sustaining and relaying the world view of a war administration.

SANE should have been less vulnerable than SDS to the force of media framing. The SANE membership and leadership were older, collectively more compact and more practiced in the ways of demonstrations and the ways of the media. SANE's organization was distinctly pyramidal, and the leadership and membership were stable. Sanford Gottlieb and Norman Thomas each had long, continuous experience with reporters; as much as anyone in and around the peace movement, they knew what to say and what not to say to whom, and when. Compared to SDS and other New Left antiwar aggregations, SANE had a clear self-image; it was not rent with semipublic disputes about its identity and its vision. And not least important, SANE's politics were considerably more palatable to the media elites.

These facts measure the minimum force of the framing process. *For all SANE's advantages, it remained vulnerable to the workings of media distortion, not less than SDS.* The SANE "story" had been established, in its main contours, before the March took place. The administration's commitment to the war went essentially unchallenged in high places. The media elite had accommodated to the main lines of the war policy. And the routine norms of journalism (*cover the event, not the condition; the conflict, not the consensus; the fact*

62. The prevailing modes of perception are culturally specific in ways just beginning to be understood. John Adair and Sol Worth have shown, for example, that Navajo filmmakers adopt different conventions than those of Hollywood. (One difference: the Navajos tend to show people walking considerable distances, instead of cutting from the beginning to the end of the long walk and leaving out the middle that most American audiences would experience as boring.) See their *Through Navajo Eyes* (Bloomington: Indiana University Press, 1971).

that "advances the story," not the one that explains it) converged with
the media's political predispositions: acquiescence to the war and
suspicion of mass movements. The frame imposed on SANE was
therefore only another side of the one imposed on SDS. SANE
faced the *minimum* media pressure; how much more vulnerable
SDS was to the full force of the framing process.[63]

63. Carol S. Wolman showed me this point.

II Media in the Making and Unmaking of the Movement

4 Organizational Crisis, 1965

The meanings embedded in media coverage were one thing: their consequences were another. In October 1965, media treatment helped polarize the society, mobilizing a repressive Right and a controlling administration against a caricatured New Left. What impact did the spotlight have on SDS and the rest of the New Left, on their internal life and development, from then on?

Without question, the media spotlight was implicated in the major changes taking place in SDS during 1965—and after. A new generation of members moved into the organization, along with a new generation of leaders. There were structural strains. All these processes accumulated into an organizational crisis, then an attempted resolution, then the failure of that resolution. In the process, the organization was transformed. The analytic difficulty, of course, arises in separating out the impact of the media within the whole spectacular, mass-mediated culture, the impact of the major media among the totality of media, and the impact of media representation within the whole complex of social processes in which SDS was enmeshed. To say that media were deeply *implicated* in the movement's history is accurate—and deliberately loose. It covers a multitude of possibilities—and puzzles.

Plainly the spotlight mattered; the coverage had unintended consequences; it opened certain doors and closed others. But it is not possible to find a simple answer to the question: What was the effect of the media on the New Left? We cannot reprise the sixties with everything else held constant but the existence of mass media, or with experimentallly varied *New York Times* or CBS coverage. The consequences that interest me in Part II are more subtle and elusive; this is why I shall speak of "significance" and "consequences" rather than of "effects," and why I shall speculate rather freely on the consequences of the movement-media *system.* Again, *I am not arguing that the mass media system in general, or its particular ways of covering the New Left, were responsible for the destruction of the movement.* The movement arose in a specific social situation: it emerged from a limited professional-managerial class base, it was socially and politically isolated, and at the same time it was committed to the vast and complex political ambition of organizing the radical transformation of the entire society. Not only that, it hurled itself against an enormously destructive war. Its class narrowness, its deformities and misapprehensions, and the power of the State all weighed on its fate and threw it back on its self-contradictions: all this will be discussed in Part II. The important point is that the movement paid a high price for the publicity it claimed and needed. It entered into an unequal contest with the media: although it affected coverage, the movement was always the petitioner; the movement was more vulnerable, the media more determining. But the movement was never powerless, never without choices, never without responsibility within the limits of the media-movement system as a whole.

To paraphrase Marx: media treatments shape movements, but not in conditions of their own making. Part II will show that the media impact on the New Left depended heavily on the political situation as a whole, on the institutional world that the media inhabit, and on the social and ideological nature of the movement. For convenience's sake at the outset, I can stake out my argument too schematically, and before the necessary qualifications and complications, by saying that the media pressed on SDS and antiwar activity in these ways:[1] (1) generating a membership surge and, consequently, generational and geographical strain among both

---

1. A certain cautionary note is both banal and obligatory. It is only for analytic convenience, which requires sequence, that I construct categories and discuss them one at a time. Analytic categories are mutually exclusive where history is continuing, multi-stranded, borderless, and messy. In what follows, a distinct category for grasping and investigating a phenomenon should not be mistaken for the single factor, the isolated "variable," that is neatly produced and separately measured for effects in a controlled experiment. Moreover, the continuing consequences of media coverage which I discuss in Chapters 5 to 9 were already at work in 1965, so no hard-and-fast chronological divisions are justified.

rank-and-file members and leaders (Chapter 4); (2) certifying leaders and converting leadership to celebrity (Chapter 5); (3) inflating rhetoric and militancy (Chapter 6); (4) elevating a moderate alternative (Chapter 7); (5) contracting the movement's experience of time, and helping encapsulate it (Chapter 8); and finally, (6) amplifying and containing the movement's messages at the same time (Chapter 9).

When SDS went public in 1965 and the media amplified its image, SDS was flooded with new members. A new generation formed its own identity in the organization and brought in new leadership. The Old Guard was displaced, and SDS was soon transformed in a crisis of discontinuity. But what were the political consequences of this transition, and why was SDS vulnerable to this new wave?

THE MEMBERSHIP SURGE AND PRAIRIE POWER

I have already cited the numbers: there is no doubt that SDS was overwhelmed with new members in 1965. They came in two clumps: the first beginning after the April march, and continuing into the early summer as the event-centered publicity was followed by more general reports on SDS in *Newsweek*, the *Saturday Evening Post*, the *New Republic*, the *Nation*, and the *Reporter*; and then a second wave in the fall, especially after the draft crisis of October.

The spring influx was obviously a consequence both of the march itself (including the organizing for it) and of the attendant publicity. National Secretary C. Clark Kissinger had been pushing SDS to organize new chapters on campuses, and the April 17 march had been proposed in December 1964 with that end, among others, in mind. Though a minority of the staff were queasy about the thrust toward a large, "unreal" organization, they were quiet about their reluctance and proposed no alternative. Old Guard members and others involved with them in ERAP projects were reluctant to see SDS turn its energies so vigorously toward the universities, but they were defeated. Kissinger's idea was that SDS would recruit new campus support by organizing a national antiwar action; no one thought of relying on the refractions of the media. After the march, of course, publicity unexpectedly amplified SDS's reputation, transmitting news of a new entity in the world to areas of the country where SDS had been weak or unknown. But the march was proposed first of all as a political action and a re-cruiting opportunity, not as what was later to be called a media event.

To everyone but participants, the march and its publicity aura were a single event, and the upshot of that event was that, after April 17, SDS was engulfed by new members. There were, first of all, those interested specifically in an antiwar movement. Helen Garvy, Assistant National Secretary in 1964–65, remembers spend-ing a lot of time on the phone with new chapter leaders and mem-bers, "trying to figure out how to communicate that SDS was more than a march to all the people who had joined because of the march."[2] Media coverage treated SDS as an antiwar organization and nothing more. Especially in outlying areas, where no other in-formation about SDS was accessible, this sort of image of SDS as an antiwar single-issue group was then passed hand to hand, face to face. Among the letters which poured into the National Office by the thousands during the summer, many sounded these notes: "I saw an article on you and I wondered if you'd send me more infor-mation," and "I heard from a friend what kind of things you're doing and I'd like to join."[3] Demonstration, personal networks, publicity—the flows of signification and attraction (as well as re-pulsion) crisscrossed, intertwined, amplified, and at times correct-ed each other.

Many of these new members were from the hinterlands, and they shifted the organization's center of gravity—at least sym-bolically. They were new recruits from the South and the Great Plains, and they were, in the retrospective view of one staff mem-ber from Oklahoma, "more natively radical. Their radicalism came from almost a nihilism, a root and branch rejection of the society. A profounder kind of alienation than people in the East."[4] Even those of this cohort who came from the Northeast, especially New York City, accepted the prairie identification as a symbolic badge of Americanness and populism. (It was three of these New Yorkers—Bob Gottlieb, Gerry Tenney, and Dave Gilbert—who in early 1967 proposed that the New Left was the vanguard of "the new work-ing class," in a long paper they called, with brash self-conscious reference to SDS's founding document, "The Port Authority State-

2. Interview, Helen Garvy, March 25, 1977.
3. Kirkpatrick Sale, *SDS* (New York: Random House, 1973), p. 216.
4. Interview, James Russell, January 19, 1977. On this "new breed" as it looked at the 1965 convention, see Sale, *SDS*, pp. 204–207.

ment.") Whether or not they came from an actual prairie, these Prairie Power people wore their hair longer and seemed looser in style, less formal and mannerly than the Old Guard generation. They were more likely than the Old Guard to call themselves anarchists; when they formulated a political position at the 1966 convention, it went by the name of student syndicalism. Within SDS they stood for campus organizing and against the centralized National Office; many were students themselves, in fact, when most of the Old Guard had left the campus. In style they were proto-hippies; the Texas chapter organized a "Gentle Thursday" on campus early in 1967. They may not have been the first SDS members to smoke marijuana, but their surroundings guaranteed that they would be the first (at Oklahoma University) to be arrested for it.[5] In the provinces, gestures of revolt that would be less noticeable in the North and East took on an inflamed meaning; greeted with hostility from parents, authorities, and peers, these gestures and probes tended to coalesce into a more distinctive oppositional subculture.

But Prairie Power solidified also because the Old Guard failed to integrate the new recruits. Since 1960, as Bob Ross has argued, the Old Guard had enlarged itself gradually by co-opting new members, bringing them one by one into the circle of personal warmth and political style which embodied SDS ideology. But now the Old Guard was dispersed in ERAP projects, divided between campuses and urban ghettoes, uncertain—and flooded by new recruits. There were too many of them for easy transition, and they were too far-flung to be assimilated into friendship clumps.[6] The Prairie Power people did not mix easily with the more intellec-

5. When the Oklahoma bust took place in 1966, there were some in the national organization who thought the dope-smokers should be censured, and a larger group, perhaps equally puritanical, who thought marijuana was legally defensible but still a political distraction and a tactical stupidity not to be defended by the national organization. See SDS NICNAC (National Interim Committee/National Administrative Committee) minutes, January 18, 1966, quoting an AP dispatch from Norman, Oklahoma, January 10, printed in the *New York Post.* Author's file.

6. Three of Ross's hypotheses are particularly apt: (1) "If new members are not integrated into preexisting primary groups, but stay within the organization nevertheless, they are more likely to be a change element in the organization." (2) "When new members form their own networks of primary group attachments, and are conscious of their new member commonality, they will have the appearance of a new 'movement generation.'" (3) "The more rapid recruitment to an organization, the more dependent it is on old-hand cliques to maintain orderly decision-making." Robert J. Ross, "Primary Groups in Social Movements: A Memoir and Interpretation," *Journal of Voluntary Action Research* 6 (July–October 1977): 139–152.

tualized Old Guard, who were Eastern and Midwestern, included large numbers of Jews (though still a minority), and were more likely middle- or upper-middle-class in origin. Some of the Old Guard ended up welcoming the "new blood," partly because it was seen as representing deeper, "more American" roots for the organization, and partly because its ascendancy would permit the Old Guard to withdraw from burdensome leadership commitments.[7] Others, Alan Haber for one, were aware of the strain imposed by the new recruits: "People came in independently of their connection with the organizational network. Up until that time, pretty much, people were recruited [directly]. . . . And now people began coming to SDS because it was the place to come, like the Travelers Aid Society. And we were not equipped to absorb people that came because they were electrified. [An apt word for the media "zap"!] . . . Now all of a sudden we were overloaded."[8] Haber is quick to add, though, that the overload was unavoidable, since the big demonstrations and publicity were necessary as long as SDS was committed to opposing the war.

The Old Guard's malaise was evident; new leaders were emerging "out of nowhere," and this was occasion for rejoicing mixed with uneasiness. The elite's uneasiness was clearly registered in an astute letter written later in 1965 by Robb Burlage, an early member of the Old Guard. Burlage was himself a Texan, and attuned to the spirit of Prairie People; as a marginal man in SDS, he was well situated to watch the new tension:

Everyone strikes me as very tense and not-at-home with the Big National Thing we are suddenly part-of. We doubt the sincerity of the constituency and we feel unsure about how great a contribution to history will be made by our continuing to go the way of "blocks" on the one hand [a reference to ERAP localism] and "NAC's" [a reference to the National Administrative Committee and national structures in general] on the other. [X], although having good ideas about direction, impressed me as particularly uncomfortable with our population-exploded extended movement family. . . . The news that [Y] wants to get together the old gang (perhaps what [Z] really wants too) is both *moving*, because we do need to help each other, us old guys, figure out what to do now, and *ahistorical*, because there is so much plunging to do to catch up with the young-uns.[9]

7. This mixture of feelings is evident in Paul Booth's letter, quoted above in Chapter 3.
8. Interview, Alan Haber, December 9, 1976.
9. Robb Burlage to Todd Gitlin, December 9, 1965 (emphasis in the original).

As it turned out, the Old Guard could plunge all it liked; as long as it failed to generate a convincing organizational agenda, it would still—by wish, by default, and finally by defeat—have to yield its authority.

WHO WILL SPEAK INTO THE MICROPHONE?
THE OBSOLESCENCE OF THE OLD GUARD

The Old Guard and the organizational structure of SDS had arisen together and were vulnerable together. With the membership surge and the attention paid to external image, the old organization structures—predicated on a tiny staff in New York directly in touch with a small, compact membership—started to break down. The National Office had long maintained a Membership Secretary, charged with keeping in touch with the chapters and answering routine mail. Mail contact worked when twenty letters arrived each day, when there were twenty active chapters and a single campus traveler; it could not cope with hundreds of letters a day, hundreds of chapters coast to coast, a dozen community projects indirectly attached to SDS, and regional offices in San Francisco, Boston, and New York. Compelled to face outward—by the demands of the media and the exigencies of the war—SDS hadn't the resources, day to day, to tend to its internal democratic life.

Prairie Power followed partly from the breakdown of the Old Guard's entrenched and unitary position in the organization. Even before the triumph of the new generation, segments of the Old Guard had developed their own interests opposed to that of the National Office. First the ERAP organizers had left the campus and the national organization altogether, for all practical purposes. Then others had moved to San Francisco and founded the first SDS outpost on the West Coast. Founded only in July 1965, out of range of informal contacts, the San Francisco Regional Office (RO) was especially prone to resent the media-centered activities of the NO. Ken McEldowney, the first of the Old Guard to move to the West Coast, co-founding the RO, recalls his concern with "the integrity of the organization":

During the whole fall, there was virtually no communication from the National Office. The newsletter didn't come out. There were no pamphlets. Nothing happened. For all intents and purposes, we functioned with a monthly newsletter that we printed.[10]

10. Interview, Ken McEldowney, December 26, 1976.

Suddenly, a freshly founded office, largely ignorant of whatever national policy there was, and without long-standing roots in a region far from the organization's center, was being called upon to represent a national SDS which was saddled with an instantly media-made reputation. Who was going to define the regional organization? The nationally circulating images of SDS clashed with the RO's program: "We were trying very hard," McEldowney remembers, "to not just be an antiwar group. We were doing stuff with farm workers, a lot of stuff on the campuses." [11] The problem for McEldowney and others was not just the frame of the nationally originated coverage but the bulk and pervasiveness of it.

McEldowney made his complaints to the NO: if SDS's rudimentary communication system could do nothing else, at least it could convey internal dissonance. A number of McEldowney's broadsides were dutifully circulated to the Work List, among them the plausible charge that the Work List mailings were overstuffed with trivial news. (The habit of mimeographed gossip descended from the days, not so long gone, when SDS was a tighter-knit, face-to-face network.) But McEldowney's major themes were the breakdown in internal communications and the contest over power to control the SDS image. "During the [October draft] crisis," McEldowney wrote in November, "our only constant source of information was the press, so that we had to guess at the thinking that went behind one press release or the other, or one action or another." [12] West Coast resentment swelled especially when the NO answered the Katzenbach and Johnson charges with Booth's widely publicized—and to the SDS Left, "liberal" and "defensive"—"Build, Not Burn" statement. I have already cited (in Chapter 3, above) the protesting telegram sent to Booth from San Francisco.

Factional feeling had been growing for some time, but now it had a firm raison d'être. Evidently the very word *faction* had first been used at the September 1964 National Council meeting. In a letter just afterward, I had written of

unsettling stomach feelings that organization cohesion was now under fire by strong, if indecipherable, conflicts. I say indecipherable because it doesn't seem as if the aggregate of political feelings and personal preferences involved accounts for the strong language and disintegrative caucus-

11. Ibid.
12. SDS Work List Mailing, No. 27, November 17, 1965.

ing. There is something more fundamentally wrong, having a lot to do with size and eclipsing of the friendship base of the "original" SDS.[13]

SDS National Council meetings had ritually supported proposals for leadership training institutes and new post-student organizations, both designed to ease the Old Guard out of a student movement they had outgrown and to transfer authority smoothly to a new movement generation. But the institutes and new organizations never materialized, for the Old Guard was ambivalent about leadership as such, and its ambivalence sabotaged the measures it passed.

The Old Guard had, in fact, shambled along for quite some time, uneasy and impatient with the existing organizational forms but unable to break with them. Without knowing it, the Old Guard was trapped between its new *values* and its old *forms*.[14] On the one hand, it was inclined toward values of community and participatory democracy, values anchored in its own strong personal bonds; on the other, it consisted of what someone called "junior achiever" types, articulate and competitive, adept in the society's standard organizational methods and rules of order.[15] Tacitly acknowledging the conflict between values and organizational forms, SDS held onto the old forms but disdained them as "bourgeois"; thus SDS's Constitution, with its elaborate bylaws and formal provisions for representation and decision-making, was considered something of a joke. Some of the Old Guard were able to keep informal influence without formal accountability; they were in demand as speechmakers but were free of the intricate demands of committee work. Administrative work had low status (thus some of Booth's political isolation). All this meant that the Old Guard as a whole did not take the organizational crisis seriously. Indeed, it was not functioning as a unitary elite: it was split between the administrative and the localist, between the campus and the community based. It could not handle the new pressures or agree on a new identity. As SDS became a political force in the outer world, factions crystallized, rooted in geography, in political difference,

13. Todd Gitlin to Robb and Dorothy Burlage, September 12, 1964. Author's file.
14. See Norm Fruchter, "SDS: In and Out of Context," *Liberation* 16 (February 1972): 19–32, where this argument is extended, and the discussion in Chapter 5, below.
15. Many of the Old Guard had been involved in campus political parties (including VOICE, the SDS chapter at the University of Michigan), student governments, and the National Student Association.

and not least in the tension between movement generations. These fissures were now superimposed. *The Prairie Power pressure and the fight between Booth and West Coast SDS both revealed and deepened an undeniable, irreversible process: the new political identity and the claims of the media spotlight were helping to decompose the old face-to-face community.*

In its disarray, the Old Guard could muster only one specific proposal for reconstructing SDS: it agreed to hold a conference on political ideas, to try to renew a political consensus. The December conference of 1965 was the Old Guard's last chance to reconstruct the organization in its image. It failed, but in its moment of failure it saw clearly into the nature of SDS's crisis.

FROM COMMUNITY TO MASS MOVEMENT

The late-December conference in Urbana, Illinois, only displayed more baldly the organization's incoherence; its failure ended up clearing the way for a new generation of leaders. Working papers commissioned by the Old Guard organizers did not get written. Chapters were so deeply involved in antiwar work that, earlier in the fall, one campus-traveling organizer proposed postponing the conference into the next spring. But some of the SDS leaders did take the hint and put their ideas on paper for the first time in many months. Several were lucidly aware of the spotlight and its pressures. *The fact that these papers left little trace on SDS's choices was a measure of both the shift in organizational identity and the power of the spotlight.* As it turned out, perspicacity was not enough.

It was Paul Booth who had found himself exposed in the center of the beam and had borne the brunt of resentment from the hinterland; now he saw what was at stake. Booth understood that the strain in SDS was at bottom a conflict of purposes. The issue raised in San Francisco of how to deal with the media was one manifestation of a deeper issue: just what was SDS's political identity? Booth began:

The most elementary problem of Students for a Democratic Society is that it straddles two social functions; it serves as the most powerful and important organized expression of the Left in America, and it serves as a radical educational organization for students.[16]

16. Paul Booth, "National Secretary's Report," mimeographed, n.d. [December 1965]; author's file.

The war in Vietnam, Booth went on, had called SDS onto a political stage defined and dominated by the administration, the Vietnamese, and the Right. Booth wanted SDS to haul itself directly into that political theatre:

Politicians and journalists take us seriously—we should do no less. But to take ourselves seriously as a political factor would mean that we would not repeat our last three NC meetings at which program discussion has been lackadaisical at best.

But SDS, caught in its old casualness, had left itself open to Evans and Novak, and hence to the publicity barrage that followed:

No one contemplated the type of reaction from the public that we received. For that reason, the program was discussed in a loose and undisciplined fashion, all kind of wild proposals were bandied about with no thought to the fact that people from the press would then quote them at will.

Booth moved on to defend "Build, Not Burn." After Evans and Novak, SDS had wrested control of the publicity, only to lose it again when

the Berkeley draft-dodging leaflet was published, and a draft card was burned, and all hell broke loose. It became impossible to use the public interest around the draft program as a means of talking about the war; the tables were turned, and even more turned when Johnson had Katzenbach imply that there were Communists in SDS leadership. We were on the defensive, and tried to talk about the war when asked about the draft, with only limited success.

"Build, Not Burn," he argued, was a tactic tailored to the media, a tactic designed to win back SDS's control of its image. He had learned that in order to intervene directly in real-time political events, SDS would have to cope with the spotlight; that the spotlight imposed its own rules, its own timetables; and that because a political SDS would have to respond to the imperatives of the spotlight, *whatever its politics*, it would experience a pressure toward centralized authority that could crack a decentralized, heterogeneous organization.

SDS had been free to take vague positions and to operate casually because it had been unified by its founders' *esprit*, warmth, and solidarity, not by its external image. Now the media would press it to look definite. The chapters might bask in the Barnum effect—"I don't care what they say about me as long as they spell the name right"—but the national leadership would lose its ability to define the organization to its own members. So SDS would have to compensate for its porous, indefinite external boundary by granting more power to its executive. It followed, as Booth argued, that if SDS was going to play in the spotlit arena and remain democratic, it also urgently needed a mechanism to make its spokespersons accountable. It was indeed, as Booth said,

amazing . . . that the organization refuses to admit the fact that it plays an important role in American politics, and as a consequence refuses to create responsible mechanisms for making its decisions from week to week.

Booth was not the only one of the Old Guard to appreciate that this was a critical moment for SDS. For former National Secretary Lee Webb, the new outward-facing SDS was failing to assimilate the new recruits into SDS's reflective political sensibility. Webb lamented that "SDS does not have a rich internal intellectual life," that "SDS influences its membership to become more militant rather than more radical," that "we are opening to the Left and closing to the Right," and finally, futilely, for neither the first nor the last time, that "SDS does not have an adult organization." Webb concluded that "we must broaden the base instead of escalating the tactics and militance." [17]

But the December conference was the Old Guard's last hurrah. The conference seemed paralyzed, even by the participants' enthusiasm for SDS's new importance. Debates were desultory and inconclusive: plainly, much of the new membership was indifferent to the terms and intuitions with which the Old Guard approached the world. Bob Ross of the Old Guard remembers attending a workshop in ideology; the fifteen participants' views ranged from "free market anarchism to technocratic planning." None but Ross "had read SDS's strategic 1963 document, *America and the New Era*, and none had read C. Wright Mills' 'Letter to the New Young Left,' a piece with wide currency among the old guard." [18] Women called an unprecedented workshop to discuss their position in SDS, and ended up closing the doors to men in order to free their speech; this first feminist event prefigured the upwellings of the late sixties and early seventies, of course, and also revealed, in effect, that the Old Guard's ideology and *esprit* had lost their cementing power: a power built, in part, on the subordination of women. At the Na-

17. Lee Webb, "Conference Working Paper, and Suggested Priorities for the N.O.," mimeographed paper, December 1965; author's file.
18. Ross, "Primary Groups," p. 144.

tional Council meeting that followed, the only concrete achievement was the decision to publish a weekly membership newspaper, *New Left Notes*.

By the convention of June 1966, the Prairie Power leaders had come into office; and it was specifically Lee Webb's cautious, coalitionist approach that was defeated by youth-centered "student syndicalism" when Nick Egleson defeated him for the presidency.[19] Egleson had actually been organized into national SDS by Webb in 1963; he was younger than the original Old Guard and was able to serve as something of a bridge between the two generations. But the center of energy was now in the National Office, with Prairie Power leaders Greg Calvert (from Iowa) and Carl Davidson (from Nebraska). Every member of the National Council except one was identified with Prairie Power.[20]

Years later, one member of the Old Guard assesses the new leaders positively:

It's obvious that a new creativity was brought in. We never thought of a mass student movement until they came along. These were people who didn't come from intellectual backgrounds or politicized frameworks.[21]

Yet, ten years later, both groups regret the rupture between movement generations.[22] It was as much a fracture as a transition. Federated, the two generations of leadership could have combined compatible levels of political knowledge, emphasis, and experience. Hindsight sees that each generation was in its distinct way well suited to each phase of organization, and especially to each mode of recruitment, the face-to-face and the mass-mediated. The talents and skills associated with face-to-face leadership were obsolescent in the mass setting. No one in SDS anticipated the fact that the stage was now set for celebrity.

19. Because the Prairie Power group put fewer of its ideas on paper than the Old Guard had done, I cannot easily quote them to articulate what they stood for. Probably their most substantial piece of work was Carl Davidson's pamphlet, "A Student Syndicalist Movement: University Reform Revisited," mimeographed for the 1966 convention, then published in *New Left Notes*, September 9, 1966, and reprinted by SDS that fall.

20. Ross, "Primary Groups," p. 144, citing Sale, *SDS*, pp. 272 and 283–285.

21. Interview, Richard Flacks, January 9, 1977. In fact, several of the Prairie Power leaders of 1966 did come from working-class families; fewer of the Old Guard did.

22. I gather this from interviews and from general informal talk at the SDS reunion held in Michigan in August 1977.

POLITICAL CONSEQUENCES OF THE EARLY COVERAGE, AND SOURCES OF SDS'S VULNERABILITY

How did the early coverage affect the way the movement was seen by its actual and potential friends and antagonists, recruits and allies? We are left to make inferences without much information. No systematic observations were recorded, no systematic inventory of audiences made, no before-and-after surveys or experiments pursued either in the laboratory or in the social field. Still, the standard social-psychological literature, for all its limits, is agreed that mass communications are most influential with respect to new issues, to issues on which opinions have not already formed, and to issues which are ambiguous and/or highly charged emotionally.[23] Since the vast majority of the American public had no independent experience of an antiwar movement in 1965, and since the war was a relatively new fact, it may be inferred that the early coverage was particularly influential—though not, of course, in an ideological vacuum—in defining issues and terms, in framing the movement and structuring later responses toward it. By selecting and emphasizing certain facts for framing, and by framing them so as to marginalize and disparage the antiwar movement, the media established a baseline story which catered to the administration's view of the world. Later events and later reporting altered the original terms, but they had to proceed from the earliest definitions of what the New Left and antiwar activity amounted to. It seems plausible that by surrounding their account of the movement with a distracting frame (frivolity, violence, Viet Cong flags), and by minimizing their account of the movement's rational *arguments* against the war, the media might have helped insulate the growing movement from its potential liberal allies.[24] Meanwhile, activist antiwar liberals gradually learned to use the media to amplify their moderate positions, their demands that the U.S. stop the bombing of North (but not South) Vietnam and negotiate (but

23. Joseph T. Klapper, *The Effects of Mass Communication* (New York: The Free Press, 1960), pp. 53–60.

24. According to Daniel Ellsberg, the Johnson administration viewed the early antiwar movement as misinformed and unreasonable. In part this belief was self-serving, since the administration was keeping secret much of the information which would allow outsiders to enter government debates. But one may also see how media accounts of the movement, which played up its drama and played down its arguments, helped maintain this image of the movement, and thus had the effect of helping seal administration liberals into their hermetic isolation. Interview, Daniel Ellsberg, March 2, 1977.

not withdraw) unconditionally. (Amplification of the moderate position after the Tet offensive of early 1968 is a story I reserve for Chapter 7.)

Earlier studies confirm that media coverage of insurgent activity can impress itself upon public consciousness in just these ways. In their pioneering book, James D. Halloran, Philip Elliott, and Graham Murdock showed conclusively that news treatment of a 1968 anti–Vietnam War demonstration in London was dominated for weeks in advance by the framing issue: Will this demonstration prove violent?[25] After establishing that the media covered the demonstration itself in terms of the frame they had themselves clamped onto it in the preceding weeks, Halloran, Elliott, and Murdock inquired into the impact of this coverage. They surveyed sample groups of demonstrators, police, and nonparticipants, and although their samples were not random, "there were clear indications that these members of the audience . . . defined and interpreted the event from within the framework provided by the news coverage."[26] Summarizing the literature, Graham Murdock concludes:

The evidence now beginning to accumulate strongly suggests that the news media do provide many people with the framework of definitions and explanations with which they approach situations. Further, this process is self-perpetuating. Thus, the fact that particular images and definitions are known to have wide popular currency makes them more likely to be selected by news organizations as a framework within which to present novel or ambiguous situations. This in turn serves to amplify these images and to keep them circulating as part of the common pool of available stereotypes.

But while media framing almost certainly helps shape public consciousness, it does not follow that the media by themselves de-

25. James D. Halloran, Philip Elliott, and Graham Murdock, *Demonstrations and Communication: A Case Study* (Harmondsworth, England: Penguin Books, 1970).

26. This quotation and the next are from Graham Murdock, "Political Deviance: The Press Presentation of a Militant Mass Demonstration," in Stanley Cohen and Jock Young, eds., *The Manufacture of News* (Beverly Hills, Calif.: Sage Publications, 1973), p. 172. The nonparticipants watched the television reports collectively, and Murdock does not explore the question of the possible effects of this setting on cognitive frameworks. Murdock also refers to the fine study by Paul Hartmann and Charles Husband of changing attitudes toward non-whites of white teenagers who had no direct experience of non-whites but were exposed to media accounts of them. See Hartmann and Husband, "The Mass Media and Racial Conflict," in Cohen and Young, *Manufacture of News*, pp. 270–283, and Hartmann and Husband, *Racism and the Mass Media* (London: Davis-Poynter, 1974).

termine the *intensity* or the *duration* of the frame left in the public mind. This is, of course, one of the most difficult issues to study empirically. We have to assume that the deepest impact of media coverage is unconscious, especially when the coverage is relatively consistent and repeated over a long time; but how can traces of a repeated frame be excavated? Interviewing several public samples on the subject of British youth gangs in the early sixties, Stanley Cohen compared public attitudes with press versions and discovered a sort of popular resistance:

For most dimensions of this comparison, the mass media responses to the Mods and Rockers were more extreme and stereotypical than any of the samples of public opinion surveyed. This is not to say that the mass media images were not absorbed and were not the dominant ones to shape the reaction, but rather that the public coded these images in such a way as to tone down their more extreme implications. In this sense, the public could be said to be better informed about the phenomenon than the media or the moral entrepreneurs [local vigilante types] whom the media quoted.[27]

Publics retain the power to tone down the more extreme implications of media frames, or even to reject them. But to the extent that media agree on a frame, and to the extent that the issue lies outside the direct experience of the audience, the media keep the power to push forward their frames as the salient ones, the ones that condition and limit public discussion. The power of the media frame to identify the issue in the first place preserves for the framers an important power over the very terms of public life.

Frames propose and public groups dispose; different audiences may dispose differently, but in any case within limits established by the posing. It is entirely possible, for example, that in 1965 and afterward the media treatment of SDS *attracted* certain populations (in the main, students already primed to be antiwar) at the same time that it was *repelling* older and more conservative audiences. There may well have been a Barnum effect: the media may have stoked up interest in the movement simply by reporting it, virtually regardless of the frame. It is at least conceivable that in 1965 the media were, in effect, helping to *polarize* the public by broadcasting provocative symbols toward which audiences could hardly maintain neutrality. To pursue this idea further, one would ideally

27. Stanley Cohen, *Folk Devils and Moral Panics* (London: MacGibbon and Kee, 1972), p. 201.

want to know how more and less informed, more and less edu-
cated, more and less concerned, and more and less ideologically
primed audiences respond to repeated news images.

Finally, we can grasp the interplay of the movement and media
only within a larger sociology, a live sense of the wider social world
of the sixties. The dominant media in 1965 were committed to political stability within the dominant, largely unquestioned, ideological order. As relayers of news, they worked within a political consensus led by the Johnson administration, a consensus that had
not yet cracked open. With all the later emphasis—both academic
and popular—on the inner social and psychological features of the
student movement, both scholars and the media have overlooked
the dimensions of the liberal default. An agreeable haze of social
amnesia and retroactive liberal self-congratulation spreads over the
histories of the time. One easily forgets how muted were the "respectable" doubts about the war; "respectable" opinion forgets
that only *two* senators, Morse of Oregon and Gruening of Alaska,
opposed the fateful Tonkin Resolution in 1964, and that Gruening's
major Senate speech justifying his vote was not even reported
in the *New York Times* or the *Washington Post*.[28] Critiques of New
Left extravagance easily overlook the fact that generational politics
takes two generations to play. Writing about this period, Thomas
Powers recalls:

Everywhere, those who might have led were silent or discreet. The
churches said nothing, the unions were firmly anti-communist, and even
many leading spokesmen for peace and disarmament were more inclined
to talk about a vague world peace in the future than the war at hand. At the
end of February [1965] the Center for the Study of Democratic Institutions
held a huge meeting at the United Nations to discuss Pope John XXIII's
encyclical, *Pacem in Terris*. More than 2,500 statesmen and scholars spent
three days discussing peace, but they did not formally recognize the war in
Vietnam.[29]

The largely liberal media elite, sympathetic to the purposes if not
the strategies of two Democratic administrations in Vietnam, man-

28. James Aronson, *Deadline for the Media* (Indianapolis: Bobbs-Merrill, 1972),
pp. 74–75. I wrote these lines before my telephone conversation with Max Frankel
of the *Times* (see p. 205, below); Frankel misremembered Gruening as a senator who
only later, with Fulbright, opposed the war.

29. Thomas Powers, *The War at Home: Vietnam and the American People 1964–68*
(New York: Grossman, 1973), p. 50.

aged and sustained the frames which systematically disparaged the antiwar movement. Political commitments and media frames were inseparable.

Here was one deep and unseen root of SDS's organizational crisis. With the Old Left pulverized by McCarthyism as well as by its own ideological poverty, and the liberals largely integrated into the welfare-warfare state, the New Left was forced to try to give birth to itself. Trying at one and the same time to create a new ideological foundation for radicalism and to stoke up an antiwar movement without any substantial elder political authority for guidance, SDS was easily overwhelmed by its tasks, and especially vulnerable to media routines.[30] SDS wanted to be both a communitarian movement, organized face to face, and a mass political movement with a necessarily mediated relation to large publics. In 1965, SDS found itself amidst the transition from one to the other, with no "parental" guidance. The media entered a vacuum as unacknowledged arbiters, surrogate sources of legitimacy.[31]

Political and historical isolation, organizational structure, the leadership's ambivalence, ideology, inexperience—all these, intersecting, contributed to SDS's vulnerability. Devoted to the primacy of unmediated personal relations, SDS was not suave, not disposed to approach the mass media with the professional distance, diplomacy, and slickness that the media expected. Poor in resources, scanty in staff, rather indifferent to the schedules and news criteria of reporters, SDS was from the first uninterested in the standard techniques of public relations. This ramshackle, improvisatory SDS managed well enough when it was small and unknown. But in 1965, the notion of cultivating careful press relations would have seemed impossibly bureaucratic and "businesslike" to a suddenly newsworthy SDS. Coming up with media "angles,"

30. Christopher Lasch and others have stressed the importance of "the missing generation" on the Left, a casualty of McCarthyism as well as of the welfare-warfare state. The New Left knew it was inhabiting an eery hollow in history: that it carried the burden as well as the honor of being "New." See Lasch's *The Agony of the American Left* (New York: Random House, 1969), chap. 5.

31. Michael Paul Rogin pointed out to me that the ideologically "fatherless" New Left was drawn to alternate authorities, and the media were dragooned, unconsciously, into service. The media were symbolically more maternal (nurturing) than paternal (commanding), but they were nonetheless a surrogate in the transition from private (family-community) to public (practical) sphere. The force of this "cathexis" had nothing to do with the *personal* narcissism of New Left activists, however; it was a normal displacement that any individuals would have made in these circumstances, as well as a rational choice. See Chapter 9, below.

observing media timetables and interests, dividing labor and putting staff to work dealing with reporters—all this takes time and effort, but first of all a commitment to the task. Having decided in 1965 to work on a large political scale, SDS still wanted to hold on to the casualness of its communitarian origins. So it gave its scorned and reluctant bureaucrats, like Booth, conflicting mandates: act for us on the political stage, but don't follow the conventional stage directions; speak for us, but don't you *dare* speak for us.

This newly embattled and ambitious SDS was now especially vulnerable to the sectarian mentality. So it happened that the year that SDS went public, 1965, was the year that Leninist factions began to make headway inside the organization: SDS loomed up as a fertile recruiting ground, especially for the Maoists of the Progressive Labor Party. The Old Guard had lost sway and the transition to Prairie Power was both incomplete and unsettling; SDS's identity was now blurred. New members troubled by the ambiguity of the new situation could draw some comfort from the clear lines drawn by the sects; in particular, where Prairie Power placed students at the heart of revolutionary possibility, Progressive Labor saw students primarily as members of the vanguard that would lead the *real* revolutionary class, industrial workers. Over the next few years, pseudo-analytical excess engendered excess, line spawned counter-line: at the end, the Weathermen mobilized a self-destructive politics of guilt and terror to counter what they saw as PL's refusal to join the world revolution in progress. In 1969, the Weathermen and PL between them ended up tearing apart the mass organization on which their chances for vitality and political substance depended.

5 Certifying Leaders and Converting Leadership to Celebrity

THE MANUFACTURE OF CELEBRITY

Faced with the lures and pressures of a world of instant fame, the movement lost control of its ability to certify and control its own leaders. Celebrity as a political resource for the movement, as a means toward political ends, lapsed into a personal resource to be invested, hoarded, and fought over—or abandoned. The movement's leaders, ambivalent from the first about leading, had trouble keeping track of the sources of their authority and the obligations it entailed. The rank and file wanted their leaders to lead, but were uneasy with them at the same time; the mixed messages they sent made the leaders' situation as untenable as it was tempting. The cultural apparatus's structured need for celebrity harmonized with, and selected for, the ambitions of movement leaders.

From the media point of view, news consists of events which can be recognized and interpreted as drama; and for the most part, news is what is made by individuals who are certifiably newsworthy. Once an individual has been certified as newsworthy, he or she has been empowered, within limits, to make news. In the mass-mediated version of reality, organizations, bureaucracies, movements—in fact, all larger and more enduring social formations—are reduced to personifications. Not that this is new: personalizing has been at the heart of news-reporting since at least the onset of the mass commercial press in the 1830s.[1] In the age of mass com-

1. See Michael Schudson, *Discovering the News: A Social History of American Newspapers* (New York: Basic Books, 1978), chap. 1; Helen MacGill Hughes, *News and*

mercial readership, "human interest" attracts audiences and delivers their attention to advertisers. Nowadays, journalism's search for "human interest" has been intensified with news photographs' representation of the human face, with radio's representation of the human voice, and with television's relentless quest for face and voice in dramatic context. The drama most easily packaged for everyday consumption seems to be the drama of *recognizable* individuals: that is to say, of regulars, of celebrities, of stars who embody that mysterious quality we call glamor. As Francesco Alberoni writes, "the stars are proclaimed as such by the collectivity,"[2] and the more recognizable the individual, the more easily he or she may be cathected with the residues of infantile feelings. The modern person, lacking either roots in tradition or a powerfully present God, longs for contact with an idealized parent and identification with an idealized self. But in a society formally committed to egalitarian values, he or she also wants to bring the idealized parent back down to human scale, to the scale of the *admirable*: that being slightly larger than life, slightly smaller than divinity. These desired images, once introjected, are now systematically projected onto the modern social screen. With the rise of the bourgeoisie and of democratic values, and with the decline of the aristocracy and the royal court, political power separates out from glamor. The court loses its monopoly of the celebrated graces, and the star system emerges alongside the system of power. Stars, or celebrities, in the strict sense are precisely famous people without institutional positions of power.[3]

So throughout the last two centuries, the cultural system—of which the news system is part—routinely has needed, and produced, celebrities. In the mass-consuming phase of capitalism, the process accelerates. Newsworthiness is one central element in converting a celebrity's name into a household phrase. After a point, celebrity can be parlayed—by celebrity and by media—into more celebrity: it is like money or a credit rating. Newsworthiness means

the *Human Interest Story* (Chicago: University of Chicago Press, 1940); Robert E. Park, "The Natural History of the Newspaper," *American Journal of Sociology* 22 (November 1923): 273–289; and Robert E. Park, "News as a Form of Knowledge," *American Journal of Sociology* 45 (March 1940): 669–689.

2. Francesco Alberoni, "The Powerless 'Elite': Theory and Sociological Research on the Phenomenon of the Stars," in Denis McQuail, ed., *Sociology of Mass Communications* (Harmondsworth, England: Penguin Books, 1972), p. 93.

3. Ibid., pp. 75–76.

recognition, and recognition leads to and requires talk show appearances, gossip column citations, campus tours, big book contracts, and the rest. C. Wright Mills pointed out the curiously *contentless* quality of celebrity:

The professional celebrity, male and female, is the crowning result of the star system of a society that makes a fetish of competition. In America, this system is carried to the point where a man who can knock a small white ball into a series of holes in the ground wth more efficiency and skill than anyone else thereby gains social access to the President of the United States. It is carried to the point where a chattering radio and television entertainer becomes the hunting chum of leading industrial executives, cabinet members, and the higher military. It does not seem to matter what the man is the very best at; so long as he has won out in competition over all others, he is celebrated. Then, a second feature of the star system begins to work: all the stars of any other sphere of endeavor or position are drawn toward the new star and he toward them. The success, the champion, accordingly, is one who mingles freely with other champions to populate the world of the celebrity.[4]

Behind the celebrity process stands not only competition but the possibility of upward mobility; for the follower or the fan, there is the chance that one might achieve what the star has achieved. That chance, however remote, brings forth admiration, not merely envy.[5] The celebrity world also thrives in a certain vacuum of social principle, in the absence of clear values beyond private attainment. In a society of great social inequality, of impersonal, commodified relationships and mass manipulation, it becomes possible for celebrities to arise who stand for little more than their own celebrity. Their relation to mass audiences is not charismatic in the sense Max Weber intended; celebrities do not incarnate consistent new values. Instead of leadership there is popularity. As William Kornhauser writes: "The decline of authoritative standards and leadership creates anxiety and insecurity; feelings of aimlessness and lack of social direction become widespread. Such a state of anomie generates the quest for new authority and heightens receptivity to pseudo-authority."[6] Charisma can now be *fabricated* as a myste-

---

4. C. Wright Mills, *The Power Elite* (New York: Oxford University Press, 1957), p. 74.
    5. Alberoni, "Powerless 'Elite,'" p. 78.
    6. William Kornhauser, "Mass Society," in the *International Encyclopedia of the Social Sciences* (New York: Macmillan and The Free Press, 1968), Vol. 10, p. 63.

rious aura, as "star quality," in the relation between celebrities and audiences that is incarnated through the mass media.

Wherever he or she starts, the celebrity comes to embody *celebrity*, and to invoke it, and have it evoked, as authority. "Hype" accumulates; who is putting whom on? The audience may save itself from wild, promiscuous credulity with a prevailing and corrosive cynicism. Or credulity and cynicism may, oddly, coexist. But what is being undermined is the possibility of authentic authority based on excellence of character, experience, knowledge, and skill. Instead, we get pseudo-authority "whenever the claim to authority is based substantially on the manipulation of symbols rather than on the invoking of standards."[7] Pseudo-leadership can be conferred by reputation-makers in the absence of the tests which experience rigorously imposes on real authority. If this process is typically absurd, for opposition leaders it is also, as we shall see, disastrous. In the sixties, a movement leader could become a star by being, or appearing to be (what was the difference to the media eye?), a champion radical. Once a celebrity, always a celebrity. Jerry Rubin discovered that he could stay famous, after a point, for being "Jerry Rubin."[8]

How is leadership converted to celebrity in the news media? Partly by the news system's centuries-old search for the dramatically personal. But more specifically, the code of objectivity and balance decrees a search for "spokesmen"—or, in these more enlightened days, and hesitantly, "spokespersons." A new rationale gets superimposed over the traditional preference for "human interest" material. From this process flows the exaggerated argument, not uncommon in both media and political circles, that the media *invented* movement stars. One of the top CBS Evening News producers told me that during the civil rights period "we got suck-

---

7. Ibid. "Pseudo-authority" and "pseudo-leadership" share an affinity for Jeremiah F. Wolpert's concept of "pseudo-charisma," which Wolpert also distinguishes from Weber's original notion: "The pseudo-charisma of our time belies its earlier character by the way in which it can be fabricated through the manipulation of techniques of mass persuasion" (Jeremiah F. Wolpert, "Toward a Sociology of Authority," in Alvin W. Gouldner, ed., *Studies in Leadership* [New York: Harper and Brothers, 1956], p. 681).

8. "Fame is an asset. I can call up practically anyone on the phone and get through. People respect famous people—they are automatically interested in what I have to say. Nobody knows exactly what I have done, but they know I'm *famous*" (Jerry Rubin, *Growing (Up) at 37* [New York: M. Evans, 1976], p. 93, emphasis in the original).

ered" by articulate-sounding, self-nominated spokesmen. By his account, the network thought that because someone *said* he was a spokesman, he *was* one. "You started looking for spokesmen, but only later did you find out that they didn't represent anything. Slick-talkers," he calls some of them, "and *we* gave them their bona fides."[9] This is one lesson the chastened media chiefs have learned from the sixties.

To take another example, from the white radical movement: during the renowned Columbia University student uprising in the spring of 1968, the media singled out Mark Rudd as the single leader-celebrity. Since New York was the media capital of the world, Mark Rudd the head of the Columbia SDS chapter became instantly and lastingly Mark Rudd the national celebrity. Rudd had been elected head of the Columbia chapter just before the uprising, but the chapter had a variety of articulate and politically diverse leaders, none of whom achieved or were granted any standing in the spotlight. Kirkpatrick Sale, then one of the editors of the *New York Times Magazine* and the one most sympathetic toward SDS, recalls that during the Columbia strike "two or three reasonably pro-student stories on Columbia came in over the transom," but the *Magazine* rejected them in favor of trying to find a piece on Rudd alone. Sale argued for a piece about SDS as a whole, or about Columbia and its military connections, but lost.[10]

Michael Klare, an antiwar researcher deeply involved in the Columbia strike, remembers that Columbia SDS included

a reservoir of talented people with different skills who worked with each other and sometimes fought each other, but the live media wanted a leader and Rudd got selected and they would always come looking for him.

By Klare's account, one *New York Times* reporter was "a little more sophisticated" and "did make an effort to understand" (as we shall see below, he was overridden); but television coverage and the images that clustered in its wake were enough to make Mark Rudd the household name and his rhetoric the standard by which the movement was judged. And because the movement was itself vulnerable to the media's definitions, Rudd's rhetoric was also the standard by which the movement judged itself.[11] Rudd himself admitted, later in 1968:

9. Interview, Ron Bonn, November 19, 1976.
10. Telephone interview, Kirkpatrick Sale, March 17, 1979.
11. Interview, Michael Klare, January 2, 1977.

One great failing on my part (of which there were many) was the fact that I allowed this role as spokesman to be converted into that of symbol. To some extent, though, this was inevitable, since the press by nature has to point to one man to exemplify and personify an entire movement. Ideologically, however, the press is not equipped to see that the strike is a mass movement, that we had developed forms of democracy in which each person could and did participate in decision-making, that the strike came out of the failings and problems in our society, not the plottings of a well-organized cabal.[12]

In a later account, written for a movement audience, Rudd repeated that his becoming "leader/symbol/star" was a "bad error," but he insisted that it still "has had some advantages (ability to use my name to draw large audiences, make money, etc.)."[13]

Rudd made the most of these advantages, and there were many SDS chapter leaders who, in the militant mood of 1968 and 1969, were eager to make use of his image and drawing power. When Rudd arrived on the scene of SDS struggles such as the strike at San Francisco State College, he promoted himself as a speaker and was welcomed by SDS militants—themselves trying to shore up their own militancy under pressure from the Progressive Labor (PL) Party faction within SDS—as a "resource" and a "draw." After months of celebrity—via media and public speeches—and involvement in factional organizing against PL, Rudd ran for National Secretary on the Weatherman ticket at SDS's last, fatal convention in 1969, and won within that faction when the organization split in two. Before the vote, he argued that "the Movement needs leadership, the Movement needs symbols, and my name exists as a symbol."[14] At that point, Rudd was not the only SDS activist confused about the difference between leadership and symbolism; such confusion runs rampant not only through the Left, but throughout the politics and the popular hungers of a media-saturated society.

Rudd's name still had a symbolic currency into the late seventies. When he surfaced and turned himself in to New York police in September 1977, after seven years with the Weather Underground, over seventy reporters turned out to record his no-comments. The

12. Mark Rudd, "Symbols of the Revolution," pp. 295–296, in Jerry L. Avorn et al., *Up Against the Ivy Wall: A History of the Columbia Crisis* (New York: Atheneum, 1968).

13. Mark Rudd, "Notes on Columbia," *The Movement*, March 1969, p. 10.

14. Quoted in *The Guardian*, June 28, 1969, as cited in Kirkpatrick Sale, *SDS* (New York: Random House, 1973), p. 577.

Mark Rudd who had been singled out as a national radical leader by national media was still a national symbol, but now of a contrite Jewish boy, "apparently ready," as the *New York Daily News* put it, "to fight for political change within the establishment." [15] Walter Cronkite chuckled as if to say he'd known it all along, as he quoted Rudd's father saying that, at the age of thirty, Mark was now "too old to be a revolutionary." Rudd's actual motives, in 1977 as in 1968, were mostly beside the point, since a role had to be cast both times.

In any event, the argument that the media *invent* movement leaders is only a static half-truth; it misses the much more powerfully absorbing process which Rudd inadvertently hinted at in his defense. Mediated spokespersons are not conjured out of thin air. True, celebrated black leaders like Stokely Carmichael and H. Rap Brown did not formally "represent" majority opinion in black communities, any more than Mark Rudd directly and formally "represented" a majority of Columbia students. But the media *routinely* present performers who are deviant—that is, unrepresentative of the values, opinions, passions, and practices of the larger society. Deviance constitutes their very "news value"—unless they are legitimate authorities, of course, in which case precisely the opposite rule applies, and their official status is what makes them newsworthy. One key to the antiwar leaders' claim to be celebrities was that they did bring with them certain radical credentials; it was their relation not to diffuse *communities* but to *movements* that gave them a plausible claim to newsworthiness by the media's own lights. The SNCC leaders, Carmichael and Brown, who stood for Black Power and draft resistance ("Hell no, we won't go!"); the Black Panthers, Huey Newton, Bobby Seale, and Eldridge Cleaver, who stood for armed self-defense; the organizers of the Chicago demonstrations in 1968, most visibly Tom Hayden, Rennie Davis, and Dave Dellinger of the National Mobilization Committee to End the War in Vietnam; and in a different spirit, Jerry Rubin and Abbie Hoffman of the Yippies—all were long experienced in real movements, in organizations of organizers. They articulated spirits of revolt and resistance which were alive in black communities and on campuses across the country; it would be an error of hindsight to say they came out of nowhere and represented nothing. The point is that

15. Quoted in Kirkpatrick Sale, "Mark Rudd and the Radical Movement," *San Francisco Chronicle*, September 24, 1977.

the media promoted them *selectively,* and thereby conferred on them "bona fides" extending far beyond the borders of the movement. Those leaders elevated to celebrity were flamboyant, or knew how to impersonate flamboyance, and this is the second key to their ascendancy: they knew what the media would define as news, what rhetoric they would amplify. They were already *leaders* in some sense, or the media would not have noticed them; the media made them *celebrities.*

The all-permeating spectacular culture insisted that the movement be identified through its celebrities; naturally it attracted personalities who enjoyed performance, who knew how to flaunt some symbolic attribute, who spoke quotably. It was easiest for exhibitionistic personalities to become enamored of their images and roles, and thus to hold on to the celebrity that media had granted them. For example: "I don't think Mark Rudd ever saw himself [as a spokesman or a celebrity] originally," his antagonistic informant grants,

but he very rapidly got into it. He of course would say that he was using it for political purposes, but it also was obvious to everyone that he got into that role of being the press spokesperson and made himself available for that. . . . As far as I could tell, he did not attempt to combat the phenomenon. He did not say, "This is a collective leadership," and play the role down.[16]

But the phenomenon of celebrity was above all a social phenomenon; personality by itself was a lesser force. On the whole, movement leaders were not especially narcissistic by American standards. It is revealing that although dozens of national SDS meetings took place from 1960 through 1969, my thorough search has turned up only a single photograph of any of the national meetings before 1967. Not a single photograph was taken at the Port Huron convention of 1962. The desire to make history cannot be reduced to the drive for personal fame, glory, or exhibitionism; it is the prevailing individualism of American culture that clamors for just that reduction.

The media system acquired celebrities more regularly and more insistently than most leaders campaigned to be acquired. When a leader-spokesman tried to back out of the spotlight, media practices pushed him or her back in. One CBS News cameraman who

16. Interview, Michael Klare, January 2, 1977.

covered Bay Area political events for four years watched Dan Siegal, a leader of the People's Park movement, try to resist his celebrity:

He really fought against it, . . . he tried to share the leadership. They tried to rotate speakers and that kind of stuff, and I think they dealt with the media as well as they could. They asked that other people be interviewed and all that stuff. But when it came right down to it, the media was either gonna interview Dan Siegal or nobody, and so he would go along with it. . . . And I think a lot of people got put in that position, that it was either you allow them to make certain people stars or you don't get your message out over the air.[17]

Short of abdicating outright (see below), there was little a leader-celebrity could do to shake the spotlight; and abdicating personally could not address the general issue, the media's relentless hunger for stars.

The movement elevated many leaders; the media selected for celebrity those among them who most closely matched prefabricated images of what an opposition leader should look and sound like: articulate, theatrical, bombastic, and knowing and inventive in the ways of packaging messages for their mediability. Usually it was the flamboyant leader who seized media attention: a personality adept at manipulating symbolic devices like the inflammatory slogan (Stokely Carmichael's "Black power!" in 1966), the outrageous promise-that-could-be-framed-as-threat (Rennie Davis's "We're going to shut down Washington" in the Mayday antiwar action of 1971), the flagrant costume (Jerry Rubin's war paint and toy machine gun in 1968). Less often, dissident media workers succeeded in packaging the outspokenly and convincingly *moderate* leader as good copy: Paul Booth, say, during the SDS anti-draft crisis of 1965,[18] or Sam Brown during the Fall 1969 Moratorium campaign (see Chapter 7, below). Late in the sixties, as a centrist peace movement arose, moderate leaders stood a better chance of becoming more newsworthy as an alternative to the flamboyants.

But whether extravagant or moderate, movement leaders could get certified as celebrity-leaders although they were not accountable to a movement base. They floated in a kind of artificial space,

---

17. Interview, Stephen Lighthill, June 16, 1977.
18. See Chapter 3, above. The CBS News field producer, Stanhope Gould, recalls that he "sold" the idea of a story about Paul Booth to his superiors in New York by impressing upon them the fact that Booth was intelligent and articulate. (Interview, Stanhope Gould, November 8, 1976.)

surrounded by haloes of processed personality; the media became their constituency. Tom Hayden, who went through this process, has written self-critically of the surreal feeling of getting appointed to celebrity, and of some of the personal consequences:

The Movement did not choose us [the Chicago defendants] to be its symbols; the press and government did. The entire process by which known leaders become known is almost fatally corrupting. Only males with driving egos have been able to "rise" in the Movement or the rock culture and be accepted by the media and dealt with seriously by the Establishment. (There are a few isolated women who as exceptions prove the rule: Bernardine Dohrn and Bernadette Devlin are seen as revolutionary sex objects, Janis Joplin and Grace Slick as musical ones, Joan Baez and Judy Collins as "beautiful and pure.")

The first step in this power syndrome is to become a "personality." You begin to monopolize contacts and contracts. You begin making $1000 per speech. With few real friends and no real organization, you become dependent on the mass media and travel in orbit only with similar "stars." [19]

Staughton Lynd has written this step-by-step account of his own anointment as a "peace movement leader":

The week Johnson began bombing North Vietnam in February 1965 Yale students who had worked with me in the southern civil rights movement asked me to speak at a university protest meeting. This led to an invitation (no doubt because an anti-government Yale professor was a man-bites-dog phenomenon) to chair a protest meeting at Carnegie Hall in New York. Then on the eve of the SDS-sponsored protest march in April 1965 the SDS national secretary (who already knew me) called me and asked that I chair that gathering too. [The invitation was actually decided upon collectively by the SDS leadership.—T. G.] In August several of us, who were besplattered with red paint as the Assembly of Unrepresented People approached the Capitol grounds, were prominently depicted in *Life* magazine. Finally, in September A. J. Muste phoned to ask me to join "a few of us" in a small discussion prior to an anti-war movement conference. I had arrived at the center of peace movement decision-making by co-option rather than election, through a politics of friendship, and a search for leaders by the media. When in December of that year the *New York Times* informed me that I was a "peace movement leader" the process was complete. [20]

---

19. Tom Hayden, *Trial* (New York: Rinehart and Winston, 1970), p. 109. Once certified, always certified. In the September 12, 1977 issue of *People*, one reads that the August SDS reunion was a failure because "only two" of the Chicago 7 attended. (Only four had been invited.)

20. Staughton Lynd, "The Prospects of the New Left," in John H. M. Laslett and Seymour Martin Lipset, eds., *Failure of a Dream? Essays in the History of American Socialism* (Garden City, N.Y.: Doubleday, 1974), p. 725.

Jerry Rubin and Abbie Hoffman were the two most famous celebrity-leaders; it comes as little surprise that they were the least attached to any organizational base and the least ambivalent about their star status. They used media to invent an "organization" out of high spirits and whole cloth, and formulated the theory of organizing *through* media.

THE VULNERABILITY OF AMBIVALENT LEADERS

Movement leaders could not have become stars so easily unless the movement's structure permitted it; in turn, the cults of personality administered by the mass media increased the movement's vulnerability. For if leaders could rise to glory as spokesmen without being held accountable to a movement base, the movement could never quite develop internal controls and lines of advancement for prospective leaders. While in other countries New Left movements succeeded in developing institutions of post-student radicalism, notably political parties which established adult roles for New Left leaders, the American New Left failed to develop those sustaining institutions and roles;[21] and this failure was both a condition and a consequence of the rise of the isolated, individualist movement star-celebrity. The situation was conducive to the rise of unaccountable leaders. Celebrity became a substitute for a continuing radical role.

Other sources of the movement's vulnerability to the celebrity syndrome were also embedded deeply in the movement's social identity. The New Left elite, and the rank and file as well, had always been ambivalent about formal leadership.[22] The fragility of the movement's own organizational forms—of SDS, in particular—served the contradictory needs of the organization's founders. The Old Guard had set up what Norm Fruchter rightly calls an

21. Robert Laufer, "Radicals and the Life Cycle: A Comparative Analysis of the 1960's Activists in the Netherlands and America," paper delivered to the American Sociological Association meeting, San Francisco, August 1975.

22. Kate Millett catches the same ambivalence in the feminist movement: "All the while the movement is sending double signals: you absolutely must preach at our panel, star at our conference—implying, fink if you don't . . . and at the same time laying down a wonderfully uptight line about elitism. Why can't we stick by what we knew was right to start with—no bloody leaders? Of course the whole world is convinced this is impracticable. They may even be right. But I agree with anti-elitism. Despite the countless sermons against elitism I've observed to come from dogmatic adolescents or envious females, each spinning in her own righteous circle, tripping on ambition, making herself famous in her own little pond for her superior insights." For Millett too, identifying the double bind fell far short of breaking it. See Kate Millett, *Flying* (New York: Alfred A. Knopf, 1974), pp. 92–93.

"ambiguous structure": "a traditional formal organizational structure co-existed with an operating style which stressed consensus and mutual respect." [23] SDS's values stressed the primacy of personal experience and informal relations, yet the organization was endowed by its creators with rather traditional representative and parliamentary structures. The elite dominated indirectly and often informally, refusing to give up either their adherence to the official forms or their commitment to new values and styles.

They used their values and styles, in fact, to sabotage the formal organizational structure. After the early years, most of the Old Guard chose to leave the universities altogether, to work in the ERAP community organizing projects—with their rhetoric of "no leaders"—while they went on dominating national decision-making meetings informally. Fruchter is brilliantly accurate in making plain some of the roots and consequences of the elite's ambivalence about formal leadership, so I quote him at length:

From the beginning, the ambiguity of SDS's formal structure was underlined by the ambivalence with which much of the leadership defined its organizational responsibility. There was a pervasive refusal to take on national office, especially the more administrative roles. The preferred role definitions were leadership activity at each leader's local scene and corresponding influence on the direction of the organization through participation in National Council meetings and conventions. Often this refusal to play responsible roles at the center of the organization was based on . . . genuine humility, the fear of authoritarian roles and the perpetuation of hierarchy. . . . But just as often it was based on a sense that such roles would alter the necessary balance between political work and personal experience, a balance intuited as crucial to the new life styles being developed. The responsible political work necessary to the organization's growth was defined as *too serious* and too intense [I would say *too boring, too cramped, too routine.*—T. G.]—the leadership's commitment to SDS could not be expressed on such a level. Thus, the national office, and its constant malfunctions, began as a joke and ended as a horror. The few national officers and staff who took their political responsibilities as seriously as they could were looked upon with a mixture of respect and contempt by the leadership, but never as exemplars.

The contradiction between SDS's articulated values and SDS's traditional organizational structures thus reflected and perpetuated ambivalences within the SDS leadership itself. Deeply committed, gifted, dy-

23. The following pages perform variations on themes from three important essays by Norm Fruchter, especially "SDS: In and Out of Context," *Liberation* 16 (February 1972):19–32. The quotation is from p. 27.

namic men and women, they were energized into political definition and activity by the eruption of civil rights agitation in the South. But they were also the successful conquerors of the electorates of their childhood and they dominated the parliamentary forms of their high schools and colleges. . . . Without either historical analysis or historical self-consciousness, the initial SDS leadership could not even pay sufficient attention to what was unique about their own forms of association and relationship. *They were unable to be responsible to the national structure they had initiated because it did not correspond to the actual forms of their own work and relationships.*[24]

Members of the Old Guard were perched in a contradiction: they occupied a locus of conflicting class positions and statuses, acting *in behalf of* an underclass and then *in behalf of* less elite students precisely with the strength and confidence *and the special vantage* that came from their experience as an elite. Organizational fragility and unofficial elitism followed directly from the built-in ambiguity of the elite's social station. Unaware of the social constraints inherent in their origins, the elite perceived these strains as issues for voluntary (if any) solution, for moral choice. They did not want to face the fact of their own leadership; nor did they know how to face the social limits determined by their identity as elite students. (Later, they and their successors in SDS and its factions would cast about for ways of addressing these limits: some would decide that students had to become workers, others that SDS had to bring revolutionary consciousness to workers—the traditional Leninist solution—and still others that revolutionary youth as a whole were now a virtual revolutionary class. See Chapter 8.) Moreover, the makeup of the SDS membership, even of local leadership, changed regularly, as students regularly graduated from their age-limited status as students: this still further disrupted continuous relations between leaders and members. No wonder SDS never established enduring patterns of accountability, and its leaders remained vulnerable to the seductions of mediated celebrity.

And all the more so—decisively, I am inclined to think—because of the unremitting pressure of the Vietnam war. The need to oppose this increasingly outrageous war imposed its own logic on the movement's course, for it placed a premium on getting detectable, material results, i.e., dampening the war, if not ending it. In order to feel effective, antiwar leaders made inordinate predictions and claims about the efficacy of each major antiwar action so as to

24. Ibid., p. 28 (my emphasis).

attract an antiwar mass and keep the pressure on Washington. When President Johnson decided not to run for another term, and then again when the Chicago demonstrations seized the media spotlight and showed that the Democratic Party could not proceed with its war business as usual, antiwar leaders felt euphoric: one more dramatic mass action, and then one more, one more, one more . . . might really stop the war, might really convince the more rational bloc of the foreign policy elite that the political costs of continuing the war were simply too high to bear. But this euphoria could not be sustained.

For however much it appeared to be militant revolt, each action actually amounted to a form of *petitioning*: large numbers of people were required to locate their bodies on a given spot and get counted.[25] Many in the movement, half-recognizing this fact and doubting that their petitions were getting anywhere, were driven toward despair. The feeling of powerlessness in the movement fueled its revolutionary turn and inflated its rhetoric; if the demand for immediate withdrawal seemed futile, why not go further, "to the root," and chant "Smash imperialism," "Smash the State," "Kick the ass of the ruling class"? And all the more so when, after 1968, the Nixon administration stood fast behind its deceptive war policy. If the imperialist system really didn't *need* to annihilate Vietnam, as liberals claimed, why didn't the war end? It was hard, and becoming harder, for organizers to present—or even to understand—their demonstrations, however militant, as plausibly effective petitions to power. Leaders now were inclined toward claiming too much, while many of the rank and file and many middle-level cadre, measuring the demonstrations against these same claims, slipped toward disillusion. Given the war, leaders became dependent on mass media; yet as Norm Fruchter argued to no avail in 1971, their very practical—and therefore tragic—dependency helped undermine not only their standing as leaders but the entire movement's credibility:

The organizers of the various mass actions we have attempted during the past six years have rarely, if ever, defined each action as a different form of petitioning. Instead, they have recruited for each action by raising apocalyptic goals to the level of speculative possibility. But the cost, to the anti-war movement, of using wildly speculative hypotheses as the bait for

25. Fruchter, "Protest, Power and the People," *Liberation* 15 (February–March–April 1971): 67–70.

organizing participation in mass actions, is severe. New people who are turned on and energized by what is held out as the possibility of actually ending the war often come to feel used and manipulated. Once the hypothetical balloon is deflated and the actual situation is re-inhabited, a feeling of powerlessness, cynicism, even despair, can succeed the inflated confidence generated by a scenario based on little real possibility. The leadership which consistently indulges in such historical gambling tends to expose itself as charlatans incapable of concrete analysis of the realities of power and decision-making in this country. *And because the leadership tends to define the movement to the nation through the mass media, the discrediting of that leadership tends to discredit the entire movement.*[26]

Given the political context—a student movement had committed itself to lead the fight against the long Vietnam massacre—the media spotlight was centrally implicated in the spiral of disillusion and the movement's self-mystified turn toward revolution. As leaders failed to produce the results they had led their constituents to expect, they tended either to burn out, or to abdicate, or to bounce back with still more extravagant claims: this action will *really* put the administration on the spot; *this time* we will shut down Washington. As followers failed to see any material results from repeatedly "putting their bodies on the line," they wearied of antiwar activity and grew embittered toward leaders whom they felt were guilty of false advertising—leaders whom, to close the circle of irony, they knew mostly through mass-mediated images.

This process was rooted, as we have seen, in the movement's internal structure; in the discrepancy between its values ("no leaders") and its organization; ultimately in its social nature and limits as a largely middle-class student organization unable to define legitimate authority for itself. But it was the actual political situation that converted these vulnerabilities into pitfalls. In the end it was the movement's commitment to effective antiwar action that coaxed it irreversibly into the realm of the spectacle, where what counted was numbers; it was that specific political objective that drove its leaders to seek the celebrity which the media were also seeking for their own reasons; it was the war that counterbalanced its halting search for decentral authority structures and processes, and that rationalized the destructive performances of movement stars. Just as movement values had come into conflict with movement structures, so did the movement's decentralized, dispersed

26. Ibid., p. 69 (my emphasis).

collectives now clash with national, mass-mediated, antiwar structures and the leaders who packaged and represented them. Fruchter, who worked with many of the groups and leaders involved, put it this way:

The political definition and style of work defined as necessary for the national action, as exemplified by the national organizers, runs counter to the concrete politics and non-instrumental style of work increasingly central to movement organizations. Add a consideration of the public dimensions of the role of national organizers of mass actions: the need to publicize the event through the mass media; the need to build suspense by creating a series of smaller events and confrontations; the need to be constantly visible by speaking, travelling, meeting, etc., and the need to build a staff organization to handle the multiplicity of details of contact and arrangement—all these needs which develop naturally out of the commitment to organizing mass actions inevitably transforms the organizers into elitist media stars and makes them, and us, victims of the society's cult of personality.[27]

But the celebrity-making process in movement politics outlasted the war; in a society saturated by mass media, the spectacle always threatens to engulf opposition as soon as opposition turns toward the media for amplification. Black leaders like Stokely Carmichael, who had rooted himself in the local territory of Lowndes County, Alabama, before becoming chairman of SNCC in 1966, entered the same whirlpool when they decided to promote the national mood and rhetoric of black power. In horrific detail, Kate Millett has described the nausea of being a feminist star on a roller coaster of publicity. Black and white, all these leaders found themselves living in an artificial world of jet-plane schedules, press conferences, talk shows, and fancy restaurants; they developed a stake in their celebrity. With the media imprimatur they might be listened to more closely at meetings (though they might also be trashed); they might score as sexual objects or, better, as sexual subjects; they could experience the sweet fusion of glamor and importance. Narcissistic motives, once negligible or contained, inevitably flourished, fattened by rewards, while more cooperative impulses withered. The celebrities lost much of whatever active, reciprocal relations they had sustained with their constituency; this loss hurled them back into the world of the spectacle. But it is those densely lived back-and-forth relations which keep political strat-

27. Ibid., p. 70.

egy alive to actual social possibilities. Sealed off from the possibility of experienced social observation, the celebrities became inferior strategists. Reduced to roles in the spectacle, celebrated radicals became radical celebrities: four-star attractions in the carnival of distracting and entertaining national and international symbols.

Because the media were always searching for prominent personalities, attractive and articulate by media standards, and then, having made them prominent, continued to cover them *because* they were prominent, celebrity piled up for some leaders and eluded others. Media attention was a resource for the movement as a whole, but the sum of it was limited, and therefore individuals were thrown into competition for something intrinsically scarce. And because the movement elite understood the spotlight as a resource, leaders not chosen often resented the chosen ones. Sometimes resentment leaked out into expression; more often it was covert and unacknowledged, rubbing against the formal egalitarianism of movement values. The result was intensified rivalry, infighting, backbiting, malicious gossip, and even recriminations. That the envy was secret did not make it any more manageable; probably less. As Richard Flacks says:

The media select leaders and the people believe them. . . . The internal effect was the stimulation of competition and envy within the movement. That was one of the most destructive elements within the movement. Everyone secretly wanted the attention, and everyone could see that the people getting the attention were really no better qualified than anyone else. What an asshole X was, and how *he* should be the one to speak for the movement. Terrible.[28]

The celebrity-leaders were squeezed into a situation of contradictory logics as they tried to serve the media and their constituencies at once. At any given moment, one or the other had to be sacrificed.

Within the student-based civil rights movement, SNCC also experienced tensions over its leaders' use of media, tensions at once about differential access to the spotlight and about the political rhetoric that prevailed there. Locally rooted SNCC staff throughout the South reacted uneasily to the notoriety of Black Power. They had elected Stokely Carmichael (in 1966) and then Rap Brown (in 1967) as chairmen, but they were not comfortable to find their

28. Interview, Richard Flacks, January 9, 1977.

leaders identified nationally with a rhetoric that was not theirs. One former SNCC field secretary, Maria Varela, recalls that "there was a division. There were people who were from the South, who said, 'You don't have to tell us, we *know* what it means to be black. That's not the issue. . . . There were local black staff that . . . weren't saying this out loud, but quietly they were just not buying it. 'Black power, that's O.K. but then what?' " [29] Local SNCC organizers were already somewhat resentful of leaders who had become minor celebrities as campus speakers (on tours undertaken partly to raise money); resentment flourished as the spotlight switched on and made celebrity national, even international. Thus Stokely Carmichael had already run into major tensions with SNCC even before the media enlarged his image and the slogan "Black Power" into national symbols:

The organization would criticize Stokely for going on the campuses and saying such and such [something "kind of incendiary"], which then got reported. And Stokely would come back and say either, "I didn't say it," or "Yeah, I said it, but tell me what I should say and what I should do." And the Executive Committee would just continue to bitch at him about the things he had done or had not done. I distinctly remember an Executive Committee meeting where he said to them, "You tell me what I should do, as the executive of this organization, and I will do it. If you don't tell me what I should do, then I'm going to do what I think I should. I have to protect my ass, you know, and I will say what I have to." And they didn't tell him.

The staff didn't tell him, again, because they had been stunned by their sudden conversion into a national symbol. They were a working staff; they were not organized to produce national policy statements at all. Maria Varela, who had worked in SDS as well as SNCC, remembers that SNCC in 1966, like SDS in the fall of 1965, was overwhelmed:

We had been sort of thrust into the national picture and . . . we weren't ready for it. We didn't have a philosophy or a strategy for working nationally. . . . And we were winging it. We were divided. There were some of us who wanted to work in the communities still. There were others who thought it was more important to move nationally and raise consciousness and influence. And there were others of us who were saying that that doesn't get you anywhere. But we were really new at a lot of this stuff. [30]

29. Interview, Maria Varela, July 1, 1976.
30. Ibid.

The New Left had reacted against what it saw as the top-heavy, overdisciplined structure and the heavy-handed, uptight, dogmatic style of the Old Left; thus it had identified itself more by a style of work, a voluntarism based on shared values and informal networks, than by any coherent political program or formal rules of accountability. But this hang-loose ideology, far from keeping leaders responsible to their base, enabled leaders to base their legitimacy outside it. The SNCC leaders, like their white radical counterparts, were drawn into symbiotic relations with the media. They could not help becoming "good copy." As Maria Varela says:

You only have so much energy. And if you have a lot of campus speeches to make, and the press is calling you, and somebody wants to know what your reaction is to such-and-such that happened, and you don't have an organization that's there with prepared principles, you just wing it. You just say what you feel like.[31]

By 1968, with the great campus upsurge, with the spotlit Chicago demonstrations and police riot, with the assassination of Martin Luther King and the black uprisings that followed, and with all the attendant publicity, it was possible for white radical leaders to enjoy reputations and ways of life and incomes largely drawn from the world of the spectacle, and only loosely tied to organizational positions. The underground press, circulating in hundreds of thousands of copies in scores of cities and regions, joined the mainstream media in celebrating further the already celebrated "heavies." SDS was hardening rapidly into a battle zone between proclaimedly revolutionary factions outbidding each other in Leninist and/or Stalinist extravagance; and SDS's fratricide and demise, already looming in 1968 though not completed until the fatal rupture of June 1969, only isolated the celebrities further: with left organizations discrediting themselves, the very idea of accountability became wholly abstract in their eyes. The unattached celebrities were impelled to find and occupy personal outposts within the spectacle—to occupy them and then to fortify them against the movement's overt and covert resentment of its alienated heroes. Still other celebrities helped form the Weatherman faction that, ironically, helped fuel "base-building" Progressive Labor as an alternative within SDS. After the Weatherman faction broke away from the PL-dominated husk of SDS in 1969, leaving most mem-

31. Ibid.

bers in the lurch, and even more strongly after the New York City townhouse explosion of March 1970, when the Weatherman group went underground as a network of revolutionary cells, the Weatherer celebrities became a sort of bad revolutionary conscience, helping reduce militants throughout the movement to cheering sections for—or against—"the Revolution."[32]

At the same time, the new feminism was surfacing in 1968 and 1969, partly as a response to media-encouraged *machismo* among the movement's "male heavies." Now feminism elaborated and focused the earlier currents of movement anti-elitist ideology and solidified new grounds for movement hostility to media-anointed stars. (Of course, these tensions were not confined to male-dominated movements; soon, in the women's movement too, leaders were routinely "trashed" for taking the spotlight and transgressing the movement's own ambiguous norms.[33]) In this bitter, desperate, and overheated atmosphere, without coherent procedures for reaching political positions, without legitimate forms of institutionalized leadership, movement celebrities were estranged, step by step, from large constituencies and from peers. They could try to play it straight, to use media instrumentally, to participate only selectively in the spectacle; and some did, doggedly representing antiwar and radical positions as the media tried to convert them to personalities. This was the strategy of Julian Bond, for example, striving to remain a leader against the pressure to become a celebrity. But playing it straight was a difficult strategy to pursue, and

32. On the rise of PL, the Weathermen (later Weather Underground), and other sects, and the collapse of SDS, see Sale, *SDS*, pp. 455–650, and the articles in Harold Jacobs, ed., *Weatherman* (Berkeley, Calif.: Ramparts Press, 1970).

33. On the trashing of feminist leaders, see Millett, *Flying*, passim, and Joreen, "Trashing: The Dark Side of Sisterhood," *Ms.*, April 1976, p. 49. This syndrome outlasted the organized phase of the New Left. Edie Goldenberg (*Making the Papers: The Access of Resource-Poor Groups to the Metropolitan Press* [Lexington, Mass.: Lexington Books, 1975], p. 21) mentions the more muted conflict that erupted in a Boston community organization founded by SDS veterans: "The leaders of The People First (TPF) shied away from the press for a long time. Members of TPF rejected the notion of leadership and hierarchical organization. To be quoted as a TPF leader caused considerable friction, as one TPF leader learned. In a number of news stories, one member was quoted as the TPF leader. Other TPF members complained that he began 'assuming a leadership position.' Informal pressure was brought to bear on him by other group members, and he subsequently assumed a more subdued position in TPF and stopped approaching the press." In this case, the leader in question was able to mobilize publicity because the press had years earlier covered him as an SDS leader in its coverage of campus demonstrations. Once a celebrity, always a celebrity.

an uncommon one, all the more so as the movement swung to revolutionism of one faction or another and relinquished its ability to think out and transmit appealing messages to large publics. The media represented a surer constituency for revolutionism—for invoking a spurious model of revolution—than any real, rooted base. A movement hell-bent on militant action, and a rock-and-rolling, star-worshiping, media-dependent youth culture alongside it, glared at their celebrated leaders without clear criteria for criticism or coherent principles for selective participation in the spectacle: neither celebrities nor constituents could help the other.

CELEBRITY AS RESOURCE: PYRAMIDING

Thus vulnerable, the leader-celebrities developed two polar types of response. They could *pyramid* celebrity or *flee* it. Pyramiding and flight, seemingly alternatives, were oddly equivalent strategies for coping with the pressures of the spotlight and the concurrent loss of working constituency; but neither could address the structural and political weaknesses that had launched the celebrity syndrome in the first place.

By choosing to pyramid their celebrity, "investing" media recognition to accumulate more of the same, the stars could go on believing that they were turning the celebrity role to political advantage—using the media as megaphone for a political position and a strategy; simultaneously, they could turn their celebrity into a career in itself. Abbie Hoffman (who was more expert?) said it: "The celebrity bag is another form of careerism." [34] Again, this was not necessarily because movement leaders were particularly careerist people, certainly not by prevailing social standards; it was more a response, an active response, to the absence of reasonably well-defined, reasonably enduring and accountable work identities for adult radicals as radicals. Staughton Lynd and Tom Hayden described the rush of this trajectory, the lure and pace of it, in the passages I have already cited above. Jerry Rubin and Abbie Hoffman were the grandest exemplars of this choice, and the Yippie style the ideology that came to justify it. (On Jerry Rubin, see be-

---

34. Abbie Hoffman [Free], *Revolution for the Hell of It* (New York: Dial Press, 1968), p. 64. Norm Fruchter has shown that the other major response to the void in radical adult identities was the efflorescence of the underground press, which could not sustain post-student radicalism. See Fruchter, "Movement Propaganda and the Culture of the Spectacle," *Liberation* 16 (May 1971): 4–17.

low.) Tom Hayden and Rennie Davis, more subtle and thoughtful leaders, were also catapulted into the celebrity role, first as organizers of the 1968 Chicago demonstrations, then as defendants selected by the government's own act of apotheosis, the Conspiracy indictments of 1969. Tom Hayden later was able to turn his movement-celebrity notoriety, and Jane Fonda's even greater fame, into the fulcrum of a Senate primary campaign, a new political turn: celebrity itself, as Ronald Reagan, Jerry Rubin, Henry Kissinger, and Eldridge Cleaver have in their different ways discovered, is transferable.[35]

Rennie Davis's famous conversion to the world-saving enterprise of the Guru Maharaj Ji in 1972 was, more than slightly, a logical consequence and continuation of years spent in New Left politics "organizing with mirrors": this apt phrase for the process of making a project real by creating a reputation for it when it is less than real was Rennie's own. In early 1964, Rennie and a staff he personally recruited and inspired brought into being ten or twelve community organizing projects under the auspices of SDS's Economic Research and Action Project. Some of the projects had roots in existing local organizations; some were the hypothetical or wishful projects of would-be organizers; ERAP linked them all with an articulate strategy for "an interracial movement of the poor."[36] Within five months after the SDS National Council had given the go-ahead, Rennie had breathed life into ERAP's reputation for reality—enough to staff the projects with over a hundred summer volunteers and to move ERAP to the fore of discussion on the Left. Half ironically and half in pride and awe of the power of the well-disseminated word, Rennie spoke of organizing ERAP "with mir-

35. In this light, or spotlight, note that politics *generally* and celebrity have converged in America since World War II. One tiny sign: according to a study of gossip columns in Philadelphia newspapers, the percentage of individuals mentioned in gossip columns who were entertainers fell from 70 percent in 1954–55 to slightly more than 50 percent in 1974–75, while the percentage who were politicians ("holders of political office, political candidates, or individuals well known for their political views") rose from 2 percent in 1954–55 and 1964–65 to 10 percent in 1974–75 (Jack Levin and Allan J. Kimmel, "Gossip Columns: Media Small Talk," *Journal of Communication* 27 [Winter 1977]:169–175). Other signs: the political celebrity of Ronald Reagan, S. I. Hayakawa, Jack Kemp, and Bill Bradley, among others; and the prominence of politicians in the new celebrity magazines, *People and Us,* and their television equivalents.

36. On the history of ERAP, the best source is Sale, *SDS,* pp. 95–150. The phrase "interracial movement of the poor" comes from the title of a 1964 working paper by Tom Hayden and Carl Wittman.

rors"—that is, with recruitment speeches, innumerable meetings, conferences (three in the spring of 1964 alone), impressive batches of working papers,[37] foundation prospectuses, a training institute, and the great whirl of word-of-mouth. The mirrors were not yet the mirrors of mass media.

But eventually Rennie, too, was swept up in the tide of localism; the national ERAP office in Ann Arbor was disbanded, and in May 1965 he moved to Chicago with most of the ERAP staff, joining the staff of the JOIN Community Union project in the poor white Uptown neighborhood. Here he worked in a quiet way on a smaller scale, though he still tended to overestimate the value of dramatic events, and triumphed victories as if a deep community base existed to consolidate them. He paid for his enthusiasms too, bearing the brunt of resentment from both organizers and community people.[38] In 1966, JOIN under Rennie's leadership won two rent strikes, forcing the slum landlords to sign contracts guaranteeing repairs; these were the first such contracts signed in Chicago since at least the thirties. But it was one thing to win a contract and quite another to enforce it and turn it to organizational advantage. The tenants were transient, even uncommitted to staying in the city which was their place of exile from "back home" in Appalachia. JOIN and the fragile tenants' unions it spawned could not secure these evanescent triumphs of militancy and short-lived solidarity. Rennie came to know the political limits of a single community organization in a single neighborhood (and the only culturally distinct poor white one at that) of a single city. After two years of fragmentary, inconclusive, inconspicuous success and not enough momentum, Rennie in 1967 left isolated JOIN in isolated Uptown to try organizing a city-wide coalition of poor people's organizations (in which JOIN would be the only poor white group) and a school for organizers. Audacious attempts both, especially in their interracialism, they were before, or behind, their time. They were stillborn.

It was only, in other words, after his—and the rest of ERAP's— failure in dogged, patient organizing that Rennie was ready to

37. Several of the papers from 1964 ERAP conferences were reprinted in Mitchell Cohen and Dennis Hale, eds., *The New Student Left* (Boston: Beacon Press, 1966). Some hold up remarkably well. Mirrors are not necessarily phantoms.

38. For an account of one organizing episode in Uptown, see "Peacemakers, Goodfellows, and the Police," pp. 375–397, in Todd Gitlin and Nanci Hollander, *Uptown: Poor Whites in Chicago* (New York: Harper and Row, 1970).

work more visibly on a larger political terrain. Before, he had kept his distance from SDS's antiwar activities; now the war became more real to him as SDS's political alternative to antiwar work disintegrated. In September 1967, he was one of the American activists who attended an antiwar conference with Vietnamese revolutionaries in Bratislava, Czechoslovakia, and later that fall he went to work with Tom Hayden to plan demonstrations at the Chicago Democratic Convention. It was only then that Rennie began to gather a media reputation. The project demanded "organizing with mirrors" in the grand style, creating the reputation for the event in advance; and Rennie could work before the cameras to suit. In the end, the movement did not flock to the Chicago streets in large numbers, partly in fear of the armament that Chicago police, the National Guard, and the Army mobilized. There were probably not more than 5,000 demonstrators in Chicago. It was the guardians of order who flocked to the streets;[39] the demonstrations and head-beatings that the world watched took place largely because the Daley regime took earlier media reports at face value and rioted against what was actually a small, confused, and intimidated radical presence. But organizing with mirrors was a tactic freighted with irony from the start. Inflating the opposition through the deliberate manipulation of mirrors entailed mobilizing the Right, aiming to polarize the society and thereby end the war by convincing the powers that be that the war was undermining American order. To some extent this strategy had already helped ease Lyndon Johnson out of office. The antiwar movement could trigger the paranoia of authorities, causing them to trip over their own feet and to create chaos that would disrupt the war consensus. As early as May 1967, another organizer articulated the strategy as "awakening the sleeping dogs on the Right." In times of political instability, the media are suited to this sort of politics, because, as Ben Bagdikian points out, they relay news to elites and protesters, rulers and ruled, all at once.[40]

Already in 1965, Rennie would joke about being a hundred years old. Time was foreshortened for him even before he proceeded to put in years at the thankless task that Norm Fruchter has described, mobilizing masses of antiwar demonstrators to put their

39. And many of them were infiltrators. See Chapter 6, pp. 188–189, below.
40. Ben H. Bagdikian, *The Information Machines* (New York: Harper and Row, 1971), p. 1.

bodies on the line one more time, and then again one more time—
to travel to Washington for the counter-inauguration in January
1969, to go back for the giant antiwar Mobilization in November,
and then during the Cambodia invasion in May 1970, and then
again on Mayday, 1971. Each time, Rennie made extravagant predictions about the next demonstration's impact on the war. And
this cycle of claims and mobilizations coincided with wild and de-
moralizing sectarianism in the residues of the New Left. SDS fragmented in 1969 and no organization ever replaced it. Rennie knew
he had lost any practical relation to a living movement. But as the
movement eroded, police surveillance and harassment did not; we
have almost certainly not discovered the full scope of it yet.

So Rennie's 1972 embracing of God in the form of the teenaged
Guru Maharaj Ji, so hard for his embittered followers to grasp at
the time, can be understood as an odd, transcendentalized conclusion to years of leaping after an effective agency for urgently
needed social transformation. For years, Rennie had put himself
on the line for a succession of impossibilities: for an interracial
movement of the poor (1964), for an insurgent coalition to transform Chicago (1967), for stopping the Democratic Convention
(1968), and for shutting down the United States government (1971).
Each time, his terrain of action was enlarged; each time, bridges
were burned; each time, the stakes went up; each time—*in the nature of the case*—his relation to constituents became more manipu-
lative. Maharaj Ji was an heir as he was a negation of the political demiurge. Rennie's conversion was not simply the betrayal it
seemed; it was both an *extension* of the New Left's utopian vision
and an *abdication* conceived and misconceived as a higher calling.
Unintentionally, it preserved Rennie's acquired status as leader-celebrity while changing its terms; this time he would have a captive
audience. Outside the consciousness of either the convert leader or
his outraged former followers, Rennie's conversion was his spir-
itualized attempt to overcome an untenable position in a disin-
tegrating movement: from a movement that had overstated its real
political possibilities, to the mysterious power of a teenaged god
incarnate, was not so great a leap. The organizer-with-mirrors got
trapped behind the looking glass.

CELEBRITY AS CAREER: PERFORMING

The career of Jerry Rubin personifies another course, another
variant of pyramiding and a greater, typically American success:

the slide toward inflated rhetoric that followed from the celebrity conferred by the mass media. Rubin had been involved in the Free Speech Movement of 1964 and had headed the Vietnam Day Committee of 1965; each had been made to appear both trivial and outlandish by the media. So when Rubin was subpoenaed by the House Un-American Activities Committee (HUAC) in the summer of 1966, he was inventive enough to try to devise a stratagem which would permit him to make a political critique of HUAC despite the interference of the image-transmitting process. He thus situated himself in the avant-garde artistic tradition of straining for effect.

R. G. Davis, then the director of the San Francisco Mime Troupe (and no relation to Rennie), remembers talking with Rubin in the Café Mediterraneum in Berkeley about tactics for his impending appearance before HUAC: "What image was good for him? We talked about the variable of what you could dress like. And we talked about it a lot. I suggested that he come up in an American Revolutionary costume. . . . It seemed to me that *they might not report what he had to say, but they would take a picture of him*. It was unlikely that the press would have listened to his statement."[41]

Experienced activists had learned that they could not determine which of their words, if any, would end up on the air. A twenty-minute interview or speech might be recorded, and a fifteen-second clip would end up on the evening news. So R. G. Davis and Rubin applied themselves to the judo tack: turning the unavoidable spotlight to some political advantage. Davis goes on:

I think there was general agreement that if you had a long statement and you answered questions, they still would distort. . . . I don't know how we got there, but I remember firmly saying, "The American Revolution was an easy [image] to get, and it would be a great statement about freedom of speech." Here was a solid image that everyone would recognize as a real contradiction. A House Committee that is investigating what people think and say! And the contradiction would be obvious if you could get it across that way. It felt to me like the dollar, you know, the straight image of America. He thought that was a good idea. He said he was going to do it.

Rubin did wear the American Revolutionary costume before HUAC, and his image was broadcast far and wide. Rubin's act of devout derision helped discredit the Committee on campuses.[42]

41. Interview, R. G. Davis, December 3, 1976 (my emphasis).
42. One can successfully *épater les bourgeois* when these *bourgeois* are already

On top of the small fame of the Vietnam Day demonstrations of 1965, Rubin's appearance gave him a national reputation not only within the movement but outside it; it launched his career as a purveyor of conspicuous symbols. *Because of the media's procedures for identifying and confirming leaders, and his skill in manipulating them, and because of the weakness of the movement's organizations,* he was able to operate for years as a freelance broadcaster of symbols, outside any sizable organization, speaking for "youth," for "the movement," and for any action he thought represented his shadow Yippie group.

This made him a celebrity if not a leader; after he left Berkeley to organize the March on the Pentagon in 1967, he had no organized base. Many of his peers disliked what they saw as his egotism, and many resented him as a usurper of the spotlight; this resentment probably drove him still further toward flamboyance and unaccountability. His own desire for the spotlight, undoubtedly the product of several political and personal purposes, matched the media's need for quotable, eccentric, engagingly wacky personalities. Again, though, the issue is not simply personality but the structure of movement assumptions, tolerances, and vulnerabilities. One of Rubin's co-workers in the Berkeley antiwar movement, Michael P. Lerner, recalls a widespread feeling in the movement there that Rubin's "ego was so offensive they had to smash it." Lerner argues that this antagonism explains "not only why Jerry left Berkeley, but . . . why Jerry then moved toward the politics which he didn't really believe in. And he moved toward it for opportunistic reasons."[43] By Lerner's account, only a few months before Jerry helped found the Youth International Party in 1967, "Jerry wasn't a Yippie":

His reaction at first to the hip phenomenon was curiosity, interest, but not identification. So what was happening was that as the more straight-line political people were giving him less and less place to be a political person, presumably because of his great sin of wanting to have his name in the paper, or his face on TV, . . . he began to move more and more to trying to

---

losing nerve and power. HUAC had already lost some of its aura of frightfulness when Dagmar Wilson of Women Strike for Peace testified without the customary rituals of deference in 1964. By 1966, HUAC's old-fashioned, small-town anti-Communism was vulnerable to ridicule, as well as civil libertarian criticism. Thus Rubin's theatrics helped clarify and accelerate an existing mood, and depended on it. HUAC was finally overthrown by the House, but only when more efficient and less theatrical and vulnerable forms of repression had been perfected.

43. Interview, Michael P. Lerner, December 7, 1976.

find a politics that would give him a space for . . . getting some kind of personal recognition and allowing for him to be who he was.

Deprived by resentful constituents of the chance to use the media *legitimately* as political amplification, but still committed to that use of both media and themselves, Rubin and other such leaders were isolated. As Lerner puts it, "they were driven to the media as their base when their own base abandoned them."

But sustained media performance requires a recognizable persona, an objectified quasi-identity like a newscaster's or a comedian's. Lerner's theory draws support from a notion proposed by the old Berkeley movement hand Michael Rossman: that Rubin's Yippie show was a willed fusion of hippie and politico styles for media consumption. In an open letter of March 1968, Rossman— himself an anti-leader partial to the styles and projects that for shorthand can be called "hippie"—wrote to Rubin: "Years ago I asked one of my students what she thought of Leary and his League of Spiritual Discovery, traveling pitchman selling the Way. 'Leary,' she said, 'is a Harvard professor who dropped acid.' Don't become known as a politico who dropped acid, Jerry."[44]

Rubin acquired a *following* instead of a face-to-face political base. His following was organized precisely as a mass media audience: atomized, far-flung, episodic, not alive politically except when mobilized in behalf of centralized symbols of revolt. Among all the movement leader-celebrities of the late sixties, Rubin enjoyed the quintessential notoriety, moving from the leadership of one improvised, occasional organization to another: from the Berkeley mayoral race of April 1966 to the San Francisco Be-In of January 1967, to the March on the Pentagon in October 1967, to Yippie and the Chicago demonstrations of August 1968. By then, he and the rest of the Yippie handful were almost automatically news. He learned that he could make news by playing the role "Jerry Rubin." With Abbie Hoffman, Paul Krassner, and occasional others, he could call press conferences and infuse the Youth International Party with a solid reputation for size and significance. As Michael Rossman wrote to him, "In our developing theology of organizing, you're into the Leadership Heresy; Yippie is a hippy bureaucracy that decrees."[45] Although his media-summoned constituency failed to descend on Chicago for the demonstrations in 1968, Ru-

44. Michael Rossman, "Letter to Jerry Rubin," in *The Wedding within the War* (Garden City, N.Y.: Anchor Books, 1971), p. 270.
45. Ibid., p. 267.

bin's celebrity status remained untouched, for the Chicago city government, the police, and the national apparatus of repression took his media reputation at face value and thereby ratified it. In the fall of 1968, he dressed up again for the cameras in a confused uniform of Indian war paint, hippie beads, Vietnamese sandals, and a toy machine gun—a living emblem of the confusion of iconographic realms in the late days of the New Left, and of the counterculture's insensitive, mechanical appropriation of the insignia of oppressed peoples. The underground papers, themselves severed from day-to-day political life and growing wild with revolutionism, joined the national media in amplifying this mishmash.[46]

And then the Chicago Conspiracy trial of 1969–70, which Rubin construed as a sort of reward for his rebellion and revelry, provided him an almost daily stage for his continuing show. Stanhope Gould, the field producer who supervised much of CBS's coverage of the trial, remembers accompanying Rubin and Abbie Hoffman with a camera crew on their speaking engagements. Why Rubin and Hoffman rather than, say, Rennie Davis, Tom Hayden, or Dave Dellinger? I asked Gould. "Because they were the most colorful and symbolic of the [Chicago] Seven," Gould said. By contrast, Gould had earlier produced and edited a takeout on Rennie Davis when Rennie had been subpoenaed by HUAC before the Nixon inauguration ("in-hog-uration") protest of January 1969. Replete with "lots of long-lens, artsy-craftsy stuff," by Gould's account, this "mood piece" of five or six minutes meant to explain how Rennie Davis, the son of one of President Truman's Council of Economic Advisors, had grown into a radical leader; and thus Gould intentionally omitted a balancing spokesman of the HUAC type. Because the piece wasn't balanced, Gould's superior, Russ Bensley, the top CBS News producer in charge of takeouts, canceled it. Over the ten years that Gould worked for the Cronkite News, this was one of the very few pieces he completed that was not aired; he had violated an outer limit which had not been drawn clearly until after the fact. But the standard that ruled out a respectful investigation of Rennie Davis's political evolution permitted coverage of more "colorful and symbolic"—and more easily dismissible—movement celebrities.[47] Yippie avant-garde defiance

46. See Fruchter, "Movement Propaganda," pp. 4–17.
47. Interview, Stanhope Gould, November 13, 1976.

was permissible as entertainment; sympathetic treatment of a would-be organizer of communities was not.

Rubin's performances were not devoid of method or strategy; rather, they were justified by an explicit theory of revolution. Rubin believed that his self-dramatizations, and the spectacular events they accompanied, mobilized oppositional consciousness and revolutionary action. His concept of mass organization mirrored the mass media's theory of itself. The mass media try to turn the audience into replicas of the ideal consumer; Jerry Rubin believed he could turn part of his audience, youth, into replicas of himself, and inspire them to reproduce the symbolic events he and the media could define as revolutionary actions. Ché Guevara had called for "two, three . . . many Vietnams" throughout the Third World; in the spring of 1968, Tom Hayden had called for "two, three . . . many Columbias." If "two, three . . . many Columbias," why not two, three . . . many Chicagos, Yippies, Rubins? In January 1970, on a day off from the Conspiracy trial in Chicago, R. G. Davis taped a discussion with Rubin in which Rubin articulated his theory of media effect:

The year after Chicago, there were more demonstrations on college and high school campuses than any other year. And I would say it was directly and psychologically related to Chicago, the memory and myth of Chicago. People sang, "I miss Chicago." There was a riot in Berkeley the week after Chicago. Chicago reached people through the media. It became a myth in their own heads, it became exaggerated way out of proportion. And they tried to act it out in their own situation thanks to Chicago.

Rubin went on to argue that "FSM [the Free Speech Movement] created Columbia, thanks to the media." Davis objected: "But Columbia was so many years after FSM." Rubin responded:

But dig this: the kids who watched FSM were ten, eleven years old. Five years later, campuses were up all over the country. And it wasn't through traditional political organizing—reading books, and getting leaflets and hearing arguments. It was through being turned on by something they saw on television.[48]

Rubin argued that mobilization through media "doesn't negate the micro" level of local organizing; "we were just on a macro level." But his contempt for the written word spoke more loudly. Rubin's confusion between image and reality was shared by much of

48. Discussion taped by R. G. Davis, Chicago, January 8, 1970.

his youthful audience, raised on television as it had been; Rubin's genius was to transpose that confusion into a theory of revolutionary mobilization. In his conception, the revolutionary mass was just that: a *mass*, to be "turned on" by media buttons. Since in this view the revolutionary task reduced itself to mobilizing that passive mass for a specific action—an assumption similar to conventional marketing assumptions—the problem of the mobilizer was simply instrumental: not whether or why to mobilize for a newsworthy action, but *how?*

Of course, Rubin could only have thrived as a celebrity if the media reported him. That he was "colorful and symbolic" *even when he explicitly violated approaches more legitimate in the movement* was the basis of his success as a celebrity. *It was precisely the isolated leader-celebrities, attached indirectly to unorganized constituencies reached only through mass media, unaccountable to rooted working groups, who were drawn toward extravagant, "incidental," expressive actions— actions which made "good copy" because they generated sensational pictures rich in symbolism.* They were repelled by the movement and attracted by the media at the same time. This logic of symbiosis was to reach one culmination, appropriately enough, in the Symbionese Liberation Army of 1973: a tiny group with no actual political base kidnapped a newspaper heiress and hijacked the spotlight with a memorable hydra-headed logo, some extravagant rhetoric ("Death to the fascist insect!"), and a political program that, only a few years later, no one remembers.

CELEBRITY AS TRAP: ABDICATING

One distinct alternative to the pyramiding process in the movement was to refuse leadership altogether. A leader abdicated if he or she was no longer willing or able to withstand the conflicting demands of the media world and the movement base, and was unwilling to step up the tension (double or nothing) by leaping further into the glittering, envy-provoking, fickle world of celebrity. Since the movement was not clear about the difference between legitimate leadership and authoritarianism, leaders were reluctant to lead; and at the same time, internal criticism veered into ad hominem attacks. The resulting binds stepped up the pressure on leaders who were already deeply unsure of the basis of their authority. And so abdication was a strikingly common way out. Staughton Lynd was one of the better-known leaders who chose that route;

Mario Savio of the Berkeley Free Speech Movement was another; a third was Robert Moses of the Student Nonviolent Coordinating Committee.

Moses was perhaps the most inspiring of the early SNCC leaders, one of the first to organize in dangerous Mississippi, a man whose courage, clarity, and stature in the movement were extraordinary. But especially as SNCC formalized its structure, Bob Moses could not believe in the authority he exercised. At a tumultuous meeting of the SNCC staff in February 1965, Moses renounced not only his leadership but his very name. One SNCC worker wrote this account at the time:

Bob Moses came in Monday night after the structure and the elections were done, drunk. He had been fighting all weekend, fairly or unfairly, rightly or wrongly, for the voice of the silent people—the Negroes in Mississippi, the quiet bewildered staff. He had been saying that "if you want to have slaves, you had better give them the vote and call them free men, because that's the only way the world will let you do it." So now he was drunk. First he shared cheese, bread, and an empty bottle of wine. Then he spoke. . . . First he announced that he had changed his name—he was no longer Robert Parris Moses, but Robert Parris [his mother's name]. He didn't want to be, and he wasn't the myth we had created. He wanted to be a person again. No one had shouted him down in the past few days, because he was Robert Moses. Now he would be Robert Parris.[49]

Bob Moses soon left SNCC altogether, worked in early antiwar projects, and then abandoned the United States for over a decade in Africa.

Mario Savio, the most visible FSM leader, also rejected his own leadership in the course of criticizing the movement's "excessively undemocratic character." His parting words were strikingly close to Bob Moses's: "If the action isn't organized by you," he told a noon rally on the steps of Sproul Hall, April 26, 1965, "it's not worth being organized." "Lest I feel deserving of the charge of 'Bonapartism' which even I sometimes have made against myself, I'd like to wish you good luck and goodbye."[50] Not only did the media assign Savio a power that his own political base did not;[51] to

49. Nancy Stoller, "The Ins and Outs of SNCC," *Studies in Brandeis Sociology*, Brandeis University, n.d., p. 18, quoting her own 1965 letter.
50. "Mario Resigns FSM Leadership," *Daily Californian* (Berkeley), April 27, 1965, p. 1.
51. Interview, Michael P. Lerner, December 7, 1976.

make matters worse, the same media which granted him celebrity also flayed him unmercifully. The status conferred by the media was an ambiguous gift—and for a sensitive person, wrenching.

Indeed, all the celebrated movement leaders suffered from an enormous breach between the status conferred by the media and the support they could not muster from co-leaders and constituents. Breach easily became tension, and the tension could be devastating. The abdicators refused to be the victims of the conflicting demands made upon them; to save themselves from the dissociation of the looking glass, they removed themselves from leadership altogether. And then the movement suffered from the loss of its more sensitive leaders: the field was left to those less vulnerable to peer criticism, less accountable to base.

ALTERNATIVES FOR LEADERSHIP

Between abdication and the pyramiding of celebrity, there remained one slender choice: to try to use the media straightforwardly to broadcast ideas, without getting trapped in celebrity's routines. Many counted this the ideal choice; most spotlit leaders believed this was, in fact, what they were doing, and often they were making the attempt. But resisting the temptation of converting celebrity to outright stardom—playing court jester on the campus circuit or on talk shows, trying to slip one's few sentences about racism or war between commercials and Hollywood gossip—took enormous self-discipline. Experience was not sufficient guide. The inconsistent anti-authoritarianism of the white radical movement worked havoc on Paul Booth, on Rennie Davis, on Mario Savio, and on a good number of others.

The question arises then: in what circumstances could movements succeed in holding their leaders accountable, keep them from departing into the world of celebrity, and encourage them instead to use the media for political ends while minimizing damage to leaders and movement both? For one thing, a youth movement in a culture that celebrates youth is probably especially prone to the pressures and consequences of celebrity. Its leaders, lacking the adult rewards of career and family, are more dependent on the media for esteem; youth amidst the mass culture market feels entitled to fame, whether as rock star, athlete, or activist. Each way, the personal importance of access to media gets inflated. But more, a movement that could agree on goals and positions would permit its leaders less discretion to create policy in front of the cameras.

The New Left, again, refused the self-discipline of explicit programmatic statement until too late—until, that is, the Marxist-Leninist sects filled the vacuum with dogmas, with clarity on the cheap. And finally, a movement organization could agree on formal procedures to review a leader's mass-mediated presentations. The movement would struggle to align its leaders with its policies, while leaders and constituents would agree on the prerogatives and obligations of each role. The issue, at bottom, is whether a movement can develop clear standards for what it expects from leaders, standards which do not jam its leaders into double binds; and whether leaders can avert celebrity's traps without abandoning leadership altogether.

The New Left met none of these conditions; thus its peculiar vulnerability to the spotlight. The pressure of political events intensified the strain on its structural weaknesses. And so it was difficult for any leader to maintain a plain, consistent, utilitarian approach to the media: to use the spotlight without getting burned up. Even more so because on the seemingly revolutionary wave of the late sixties, it seemed more and more that the way to be assured of access to that spotlight was to look and sound ever more extravagant.

6 Inflating Rhetoric and Militancy

The link between celebrity and militancy was made possible and creditable in the movement by the undeniable war. Vietnam bled every day; and by most available signs (all but the self-serving claims of the National Liberation Front, in fact), it certainly seemed that the rational teach-ins and decorous picket lines and draft resistance and electoral campaigns were failing to dampen the American military onslaught. What Lyndon B. Johnson thought of antiwar "nervous nellies," and later what Richard Nixon and Spiro T. Agnew thought of "nattering nabobs of negativism," was all too plain; but to what degree the antiwar movement was actually retarding the escalation of the war was a closely guarded secret and remains a difficult matter to establish. One interesting fact reported by David Halberstam in *The Best and the Brightest* is that the military in late 1966 were urging President Johnson to bomb Hanoi and Haiphong, blocking the harbor and, in Halberstam's words, "taking apart the industrial capacity of both cities." They had programmed a computer, they told Johnson, to determine how many American lives had been saved in 1945 when the atomic bombing of Hiroshima and Nagasaki had averted the need for an invasion of Japan. Johnson asked to meet the programers, and said to them: "I have one more problem for your computer—will you feed into it how long it will take five hundred thousand angry Americans to climb that White House wall out there and lynch their President if he does something like that?" "Which ended for a time," Halberstam writes, "the plan to bomb Hanoi and Haiphong." [1]

1. David Halberstam, *The Best and The Brightest* (New York: Random House, 1972), p. 641.

But the movement usually felt ineffectual. When Richard Nixon let it be known that he would be blithely watching the football game on television as hundreds of thousands demonstrated during the huge Mobilization against the war, November 15, 1969, the movement took him at his word. Daniel Ellsberg has argued since[2] that the antiwar movement was actually at that moment retarding the administration's plan to escalate the war dramatically—invading Cambodia and Laos, mining Haiphong and other ports, the B-52 bombing of North Vietnamese cities (all this actually done later, but piecemeal), bombing the Red River dikes and the connecting rail lines to China, and *possibly* landing Marines in southern North Vietnam *and* dropping nuclear weapons in the north (using airbursts to maximize deaths). But the movement had no inkling of its veto power. The juxtaposition of unstoppable war with apparently failing tactics was the greatest force pushing the antiwar movement toward heightened militancy. Or rather: first toward heightened militancy, and later away from activity altogether. Desperation and passivity were linked moments in the movement's response to its sense of ineffectuality.

During the years 1965 through 1970, the movement was also being radicalized. The longer the war went on, the less it looked like an accident, the more like a symptom. The argument that the war was one consequence of American imperialism gained more and more repute, more and more credence after Carl Oglesby first enunciated it in his speech to the November 1965 March on Washington. At the same time, many in the movement concluded that opposing the war required expressing solidarity with the National Liberation Front of South Vietnam and with North Vietnam. The Vietnamese were no longer represented as napalmed victims; now they were heroic fighters, women bearing rifles on their backs, a patient Ho Chi Minh. Underground papers as well as the mass media relayed these images. NLF flags were more common now at rallies; a number of movement leaders visited Hanoi. Other images of militancy accompanied images of the Vietnamese: posters of Malcolm X and Ché Guevara, among others, adorned many a wall; so did posters endorsing armed struggles against imperialism throughout the Third World. By 1969, images of white radicals training in the use of firearms were circulating throughout the movement, though the imagery was considerably more widespread than the practice.

2. In a speech at the Institute for Socio-Cultural Studies in Berkeley, July 1976.

But even militancy is not necessarily flamboyance, not necessarily an outrage to the sensibility of the majority. Flamboyant
acts like flag-burning and trashing expressed the pointed anger of
militants; they also, most likely, isolated the movement from many
potential allies. The media apparatus (including the *underground*
press), and the part of the movement that knew how to manipulate
the media, together linked militancy with flamboyant gestures,
and set new standards for New Left activity. It was the movement's
enfants terribles who deciphered the media code and exploited it,
but everyone in the movement had to acknowledge the rising
threshold for coverage. For it was obvious from within the movement that the media were giving lurid prominence to the wild-
est and most cacophonous rhetoric, and broadcasting the most
militant, violent, bizarre, and discordant actions, and, within the
boundaries of any action, the most violent segments. The managing editor of the *New York Times*, Clifton Daniel, told a Public
Broadcast Laboratory interviewer that the *Times* gave light coverage to the January 15, 1968 Jeanette Rankin Brigade (the first wom-
en's antiwar action) for two reasons: because of its size *and because
there was not expected to be violence.*[3] Where a picket line might have
been news in 1965, it took tear gas and bloodied heads to make
headlines in 1968. If the last demonstration was counted at 100,000,
the next would have to number 200,000; otherwise it would be
downplayed or framed as a sign of the movement's waning. The
most outrageous, most discordant, most "colorful" symbols were
the surest to be broadcast—"Viet Cong" flags, burning draft cards
and (later) flags and (still later) ROTC buildings. The result was
that newsmaking power was passing into the hands of the more
theatrical leaders and militant activists, *agents provocateurs*, and the
police. As it had turned leaders into celebrities, the media system
enticed them toward greater and greater flamboyance—and eventually, dialectically, it also inspired a moderate alternative. In the
process, the media helped generate one of the central political par-
adoxes of the decade: as the antiwar movement grew in numbers
throughout the late sixties, and as polls showed the population

3. Public Broadcast Laboratory, "Journalism—Mirror, Mirror on the World?"
(1968). I am centering on national media, but a sociologist who studied local news
operations in 1971–74 reports the same selectivity: "While covering a demonstration
at a local university, I asked the cameraman what was the most newsworthy thing.
He replied, 'You mean, out of the whole thing? The flag coming down. The other
stuff, I wouldn't have bothered . . .'" (David L. Altheide, *Creating Reality: How TV
News Distorts Events* [Beverly Hills, Calif.: Sage Publications, 1976], p. 75).

turning steadily against the war,[4] the central organization of the New Left isolated itself and disintegrated.

"THE NEW LEFT TURNS TO MOOD OF VIOLENCE"

Bit by bit the movement was surrounded by a firebreak of discrediting images, images partly but *only* partly of its own making. The specter of violence hovered over media representations before it became popular in the movement itself. But the media, with their agenda-setting power, are not simply prophetic; their images can be, in important measure, self-fulfilling. In Part I, we saw early examples of the violence-on-the-Left frame; as time went by, this frame became more conspicuous. One case will show how the *New York Times* applied the full weight of its credibility to containment-through-innuendo: a containment that was to be self-fulfilling. On Sunday, May 7, 1967, the *Times* ran a Page One article by Paul Hofmann, headlined: "The New Left Turns to Mood of Violence in Place of Protest." Here is the lead:

> "We are working to build a guerrilla force in an urban environment," said the national secretary of the left-wing Students for a Democratic Society, Gregory Calvert, one day recently.
> "We are actively organizing sedition," he said.
> Mr. Calvert, a 29-year-old former history teacher, spoke pleasantly about revolution in his dingy office on Chicago's Skid Row. The threat of violence in his words characterizes the current radicalization of the New Left.

The article then jumped to a back page and went on for seventy-eight more column-inches under the headline: "Today's New Left, Amid Frustration and Factionalism, Turns Toward Radicalism and Direct Action." The caption to a small photograph of Calvert said he "aims at building guerrilla force." Calvert was quoted further as saying: "Che's message is applicable to urban America as far as the psychology of guerrilla action goes. . . . Che sure lives in our hearts." The first four subheads were "'Che Lives in Our Hearts'" "'I'm No Pacifist'" (a quotation from another SDS organizer), "'Calls Violence Necessary'" (ditto) and "Action Above Ideology." The article made perfunctory mention of "a vaguely defined 'participatory democracy'": it lumped together radicalism, direct action, and violence; it said about Staughton Lynd, an undeviating

---

4. Gallup Polls registering antiwar feeling from August 1965 through October 1968 are given in Jerome Skolnick, *The Politics of Protest* (New York: Ballantine Books, 1969), p. 44.

advocate of nonviolence, that "he appeared to distinguish between active violence and civil disobedience . . ." (implying that civil disobedience was somehow passive violence). If this were not glaring enough, in the column next to the Hofmann article the *Times* ran a story with this headline: "RIFLE CLUB SEES GUNS AS RIOT CURB: Says Armed Citizens Could Be Vital for Dealing With Actions by Urban Mobs." Perhaps a curious coincidence; or perhaps an editor's act of grouping and framing, composing a common theme, as if to say: there is violent polarization going on, left and right, and they are functionally equivalent acts of extremism to be deplored by all law-abiding citizens. In any case, the next day's *Times* continued the new framing with a reaction story: "Trends of the New Left Alarm Intellectuals of 'Old Left' at Conference Here." This was the sign and embodiment of a major reworking of the mass-media frame on the movement.

SDS President Nick Egleson responded in *New Left Notes* with a letter of rebuttal that the *Times* did not print. Calvert reported to the SDS membership that he had been quoted out of context. "Clearly," Calvert wrote in *New Left Notes*, the *Times*'s "intention was to raise the spectre of violence on the part of the 'radical' movement in order to advance the 'liberal' cause." Here is Calvert's version of his encounter with Paul Hofmann:

The question of "guerrilla" forces was raised in my office when I walked in one afternoon to find Paul Hofman [*sic*] talking with SDS assistant national secretary Dee Jacobsen. Hofman explained that he was traveling around the country gathering material for a major article on the New Left. Conversation quickly moved to topics beyond the frontiers of the U.S. Hofman talked at length about his experiences in Cuba when he was the *Times* Havana correspondent. I asked him about Che Guevara. He talked for several minutes about Che, describing his last public appearance in Havana. Che was, apparently, very tired and quite discouraged, especially by what he had observed in the Soviet Union. . . . Hofman expressed his belief that Che was dead—a belief based on what he called "circumstantial evidence". . . . I replied with the often repeated phrase: "Even if Che is dead, he still lives in the hearts of the people."

Hofman asked whether I could be called a "Guevaraite." I said "No"—that I did not believe such a term would mean much to people. I added, however, that I felt that young Americans who worked for the radical transformation of this society were similar in many respects to guerrilla organizers in the Third World. They both work against tremendous odds and with severely limited resources; their effectiveness depends on winning the respect and support of their constituencies; their enemy is the same, whether in the ghetto, the university, or in a peasant society—aggressive, expansive American capitalism which uses human and material resources of the earth for exploitive rather than creative ends. [Evidently this was the sequence that gave Hofman his lead.—T.G.]

We talked for a while about the decentralist and radically democratic faith of the New Left with its slogan of "participatory democracy." Hofman said, "you should like my Spanish anarchist friends, always insisting on workers control," and went on to describe what he knew of the Spanish freedom movement.[5]

The Hofmann article had large repercussions. Several of SDS's wealthy benefactors were dismayed. And as Paul Booth had discovered in October of 1965, public political statements by national secretaries, whether "liberal" or "extremist," were disruptive forces within the organization. At the 1967 SDS convention, Calvert was forced to admit to alarmed and nonviolent delegates that submitting to Hofmann's interview had been "a stupid thing, a trap." Calvert tried to convince his interlocutors that the problem was structural, that national officers of a political organization could not avoid becoming political spokespersons.[6] But the bulk of the movement's base was more temperate than its leaders, and now the media amplification process helped sever the two, leaving leaders saddled with a reputation for militancy. "Organizing with mirrors" looked like good strategy, for if the process of selective and distorted amplification were this strong, why not try to capitalize on it?

The process of increasing militancy was thus partly rooted in the media practice of presenting selected features of the movement *itself*, or a sequence of events labeled "the movement," as the social problem requiring solution. This practice in turn was a result of one of the media's hegemonic routines: the convention of *describing* an exceptional event rather than *explaining* its sources in normal, everyday social life. The responsible agent of an event then tends to become the issue, especially when the events protested—a war, an investment—are taking place elsewhere, outside the reporter's purview and therefore outside "the story." The media practice of defining the movement as an issue in itself also coincided with the rise of a revolutionist position within the movement itself: a posi-

5. Greg Calvert, "Response to the Sensationalist Press: Divide and Rule," *New Left Notes*, May 22, 1967, p. 2.

6. Kirkpatrick Sale, *SDS* (New York: Random House, 1973), pp. 359–360, quoting from minutes of the convention.

tion itself parasitic on mass media and justifying itself as if in self-caricature. When Abbie Hoffman proclaimed about the 1968 Chicago demonstrations, "We were an advertisement for revolution,"[7] he articulated a wider mood in the movement: a forced giddiness bound to a core of despair. Aspiring to revolution but lacking any real agency, the movement was bound to seal itself off. Organizing with mirrors meant deluding oneself about what was real, though it might take years to discover, or accept, that one was suspended in social space with nowhere to go. It was a serviceable gambit for a movement that refused to face the nature—and the limits—of its social identity. Different Leninist factions strained to become the vanguards of the classical proletariat or some surrogate (the "new working class," or the Third World, or youth); they all disregarded the actual finitude of the movement. Swept along by high political winds—always the war, then the Eugene McCarthy campaign, then Johnson's abdication, then the assassinations of Martin Luther King and Bobby Kennedy—the movement came unglued.

The movement had started, after all, from the isolation of an elite university social base. For years, fitfully, inconsistently, doggedly, it had tried to work its way outward to the rest of the society. Organizing with mirrors required less patience, less sacrifice, less tedium, less time; and it seemed to stand a chance of turning out effective. But with an inconsistent strategy and a drastic misunderstanding of itself, the movement ended up quarantined. "The students," "the radicals," "the revolutionaries" became predictable and therefore containable characters in a tedious play that outwore its ostensible audience. Increasingly outrageous action led to increased media coverage and selective amplification, and to police suppression, which in turn fueled the movement's anger and paranoia, inspiring still more police reaction and still more stereotypic coverage of outrageous symbols.

The climax came in Chicago in 1968. Movement organizers pro-

7. Abbie Hoffman [Free], *Revolution for the Hell of It* (New York: Dial Press, 1968), p. 134. Interestingly, two of the Yippies' forebears in this sort of thinking were Zinoviev, the head of the Comintern, and Bela Kun, the failed Hungarian revolutionary, who in 1921 encouraged a doomed Communist uprising in central Germany, during an ebb-tide period for revolution in Western Europe; they believed this desperate venture might "electrify" (their word!) the dormant German working class. See Isaac Deutscher, *The Prophet Unarmed: Trotsky 1921–1929* (New York: Oxford University Press, 1959), pp. 3–4.

claimed their intent to force the Democratic convention to confront the war in Vietnam. Mayor Daley and federal officials dutifully turned the city into an armed camp. Some convention week activities were media events tailor-made to crack any lingering image of politics as usual: one group of demonstrators, for example, let themselves be filmed in Lincoln Park practicing the Japanese snake dance as a tactic for minimizing their vulnerability to police violence. As a logistical operation this rehearsal was sheer bravado; Japanese students had devised the tactic to fill the space of *narrow* streets in order to keep police at a distance; the snake dance had no use on the broad boulevards of Chicago's Loop. But as a media event, intersecting with Mayor Daley's own counter-events, it worked wonders. The media amplified such images of polarization and preparation, bluff and bravado; Mayor Daley seized on such reports as pretexts to justify police overkill; and crucially, the media relayed the results to the world. Demonstrators therefore felt vindicated when the National Guard first rolled its barbed-wire troop carriers down Michigan Avenue on Tuesday night of convention week; their conviction that behind the bland civics-book rationale of the political system lay the sheer might of the State, their prediction that the convention would be possible only at the point of the bayonet, had come to pass—and in the cold light of the networks. Across Michigan Avenue from the Conrad Hilton Hotel, as floodlit demonstrators took up the rousing chant, "The whole world is watching! The whole world is watching!" in front of the cameras, police clubs swung, blood flowed, cameras ground, image became reality, reality was doubled back as image, and accusation became self-fulfilling prophecy. It was this cycle that the Nixon administration eventually seized upon and furthered to justify repression—including repression of the press itself for amplifying the bad news—and its own paranoia.

The President and Vice-President of the United States understood this process well, and tried to turn the spotlight to their own advantage. Five days before the mid-term election of 1970, President Nixon gave a speech at San José Civic Auditorium. Demonstrators had gathered, and the police barricades had let them approach unusually close to the President's motorcade route. Afterward, Nixon stood on his limousine to taunt them. "That's what they hate to see!" he said, raising his hands in the sign of a V. Objects were thrown at him. The President's entourage were "jubilant."[8] The media relayed the message that the President had been attacked, though no one was arrested for attacking him. CBS News, for example, interviewed Senator George Murphy ("The fact that the President of the United States and the Governor of California . . . plus a United States Senator had their lives and safety endangered by a howling mob of radical terrorists numbering well over a thousand I find not only unbelievable but completely unacceptable") and Nixon's press secretary, Ron Ziegler ("This was no outburst of a single individual; this was the action of an unruly mob that represents the worst in America. . . . President Nixon feels that the time has come to take the gloves off and speak to this kind of behavior in a forthright way. Freedom of speech, freedom of assembly cannot exist when people who peacefully attend rallies are attacked with flying rocks"). The report contained no statements from any demonstrators; the principle of balance, scrupulously applied to the opposition, is usually not accorded to the statements of officials, least of all one year after the Agnew-Nixon barrage against network television.[9]

I have been told by a student who was present on the scene that night that the handful of stone-throwers were strangers unknown in San José's antiwar circles before or afterward. No matter. The President also knew how to manipulate symbols, not least the movement's own kit bag. He had come to power, as presidents must, as a manufacturer of images; by manipulating the movement and *its* images, he could effectively isolate it, containing its spread and influence. The Nixon administration's interest in destroying the movement interlocked with the media's interest in extravagant stories; the government strategy for destroying the movement most likely included a strategy for swelling the movement's reputation for violence. And doubtless such a strategy did not start from zero when Richard Nixon entered the White House. We know too little of the actions of *agents provocateurs* under both Johnson and Nixon; but if we begin to extrapolate from the evidence that has trickled to light in a few researches of recent years, we are jarred by some extraordinary facts.[10] Ten years after the fact, CBS

8. This incident is described lucidly in Jonathan Schell's *The Time of Illusion* (New York: Alfred A. Knopf, 1976), p. 130.

9. CBS Evening News, report by Hal Walker from San José, October 30, 1970; in CBS Newsfilm Archive. *New York Times* coverage was not balanced either; see Leon V. Sigal, *Reporters and Officials: The Organization and Politics of Newsmaking* (Lexington, Mass.: D. C. Heath, 1973), pp. 93–95.

10. On the general modus operandi of *agents provocateurs*, see Paul Cowan, Nick

News attributed to Army sources the claim that in Chicago during 1968's convention week *"about one demonstrator in six was an undercover agent."* In the movement crowd that blocked traffic and got attacked by police along Michigan Avenue that Wednesday, according to CBS, *at least two hundred were undercover agents.*[11] The questions come thick and fast even if these figures are exaggerated by a factor of five or ten. Just who wanted blood to flow in Chicago, and why? We know now that Jerry Rubin's Chicago bodyguard, who was dressed as a longhaired biker and who pulled down an American flag in Grant Park, was a Chicago policeman. We know that an SDS campus traveler in upstate New York, with a penchant for violence, was on the government payroll. What further provocations were mounted, and what do they imply about the entire course of the movement in the late sixties? We await the disclosure of information that intelligence agencies obviously do not want to disclose and may indeed have destroyed.

But provocateurs by themselves cannot explain everything; provocateurs must move in a movement that tolerates their wild talk and wild action.[12] The movement's own incendiaries, rhetorical and actual, colluded in a self-defeating system of rising rhetoric, rising militancy and theatrics, rising publicity, rising government repression, and presumably rising provocation. Beginning with sensational coverage of the Columbia strike of April–May 1968,[13] SDS became big national news—and remained so, as a public bugaboo, symbolizing campus protest and uproar, throughout that fall and the following spring.[14] A new generation of SDS

Egleson, and Nat Hentoff, with Barbara Herbert and Robert Wall, *State Secrets: Police Surveillance in America* (New York: Holt, Rinehart and Winston, 1974); Gary T. Marx, "Thoughts on a Neglected Category of Social Movement Participant: The Agent Provocateur and the Informant," *American Journal of Sociology* 80 (1974): 402–442; and Morton H. Halperin et al., *The Lawless State: The Crimes of the U.S. Intelligence Agencies* (New York: Penguin Books, 1976). To my knowledge, no evidence has yet come to light—but who is looking and where?—about the sources of the San José incident.

11. CBS News Special, "1968," broadcast on August 25, 1978: transcript, pp. 28, 31. © 1978 CBS Inc. All rights reserved.

12. Todd Gitlin, "Casting the First Stone," *San Francisco Express Times*, Vol. 1, No. 36 (September 25, 1968), p. 2.

13. On media skewing of the Columbia uprising, playing up the unruliness of the demonstrators and playing down Columbia's role in war research and neighborhood domination, see Jerry L. Avorn et al., *Up Against the Ivy Wall: A History of the Columbia Crisis* (New York: Atheneum, 1968); Sale, *SDS*, pp. 441–443; and Jack Newfield, *The Dutton Review*, No. 1 (1970).

14. Sale, *SDS*, pp. 479–480.

leaders rose to power and prominence on their ability to ride the waves: they were inclined to believe their own press notices. This ritual dance of image and ambition proceeded through the militant demonstrations of the spring of 1969, which were, as Kirkpatrick Sale writes,

hystericized, the media salivating over the few violent demonstrations and ignoring the peaceful, somehow picturing the beaten and bloodied students as the aggressors, turning that photograph of armed blacks at Cornell into the suggestion of gun-shooting killers on the loose in academia without conveying that the students had armed themselves in self-defense, that they were leaving a building after a negotiated settlement, and that the guns were not even loaded.[15]

It was hard to tell whose interest was best served with that much-photographed Cornell rifle, or with any of the scores of extravagant images that the media selectively amplified that spring. Some in the movement were delighted; they had already begun to flaunt a gun-toting image. This was the "revolution as theatre" excoriated by liberal and even radical critics. But the critics usually missed the irony as well as the selective amplification: the revolutionists were impaled on the point of their own provocations.

Amid all this hysteria [Sale wrote], SDS as an organization collapsed, in June of 1969, and one of the many reasons had to do with the effect of this press coverage, or rather the reaction to this press coverage by students and SDSers. On the one hand, many students shied away from an SDS increasingly made to seem violent and mindless, resulting in a decline in membership and effect during the 1968–69 school year; on the other hand, much of the SDS leadership accepted the overblown image of SDS presented by the media and began to see themselves as a serious revolutionary force whose importance was to be measured, as the press did, by the amount of violence it created, resulting in a rush to revolution that left much of the student constituency behind and led, ultimately, to the Weathermen.[16]

Or as Flacks sums it up:

The result of [the broadcast tone of flamboyance, hate, challenge, and outrage] is that it alienates people who should at least be neutralized; it sets a tone for the event which allows it to be distorted. It creates the basis for police intervention. And it sets the wrong political basis for the movement, by giving the people the wrong basis for joining and so attracting the

15. Kirkpatrick Sale, "Myths as Eternal Truths," *More* 3 (June 1973): 4.
16. Ibid.

wrong people. When I moved out here [Santa Barbara], I discovered that the average student thinks that radical equals violent. If you stop violence or oppose violence, you are not radical. You have sold out if you used to riot and you don't any more.[17]

The Weathermen were indeed, as Sale says, the dead end of the process of rhetorical inflation; but even more than he indicates, they internalized their own projected image and devised a rhetoric and practice of ferocity. They aimed to disrupt normal conventions; instead they enrolled in an older one, taking the devil's part in a predictable national mythology pitting forces of order against forces of chaos. When the Weathermen ran wild through the Chicago streets, trashing cars in front of the cameras in their "Days of Rage" in October 1969, they played out the demonic role which had been cast, in effect, by Nixon's counterrevolution, and which served to justify it.

Had Nixon been more adept at wooing the Eastern media elites, he might have built a lasting political base from the prevailing hostility to the revolutionaries. But Nixon had his own famous paranoia about the press, and politically he was committed to the newer money and the outsider elite networks of the Southern rim. Meanwhile, a good many reporters had turned more sympathetic to the New Left in Chicago, while, after the January 1968 Tet offensive, the media elites, along with much of the rest of the Eastern Establishment, had tilted toward a liberal position on the war: if they remained hostile toward the student Left, by the fall of 1969 they were more friendly to the antiwar moderates, amplifying them (as Chapter 7 tells, below) as a legitimate alternative. The strategy of the administration, in turn, was to honor no such distinction; Nixon was at least as bothered by the Moratorium as by the Weathermen, since the moderates of the Moratorium were potentially a *majority* antiwar force and could not so well be singled out to justify repression. Just so, he was as offended by Daniel Schorr as by Rennie Davis, since the media refused to be sufficiently enthusiastic about his version of the war. Even after Tet, media criticism of the war was dampened and practical: the war was a failure or a mistake, not the consequence of a coherent world policy. The media showed the futility and the self-punishment entailed in the American policy, but not a great deal of the consequences for Vietnam; the secret but known carpet bombing of

17. Interview, Richard Flacks, January 9, 1977.

Cambodia, for example, went almost entirely uncovered. And their coverage of the antiwar movement, while more sympathetic to *legitimate* opposition after Tet, was careful not to offend the administration too far; thus the networks decided not to give live coverage to the November 1969 Mobilization and Moratorium. As early as October 1967, the networks had considered—and rejected—live coverage of the giant demonstration at the Pentagon. According to a CBS informant, CBS News refused, early in 1971, to broadcast film that it had already shot of the Winter Soldier Investigation, in which antiwar Vietnam veterans said they had committed atrocities or had watched other American troops commit them.[18] In the end, the media chiefs kept what seemed to them an even keel. It was only when the administration pushed them and the rest of the Eastern Establishment too far—with the Agnew barrage, the enemies list, the prior restraint against the newspapers publishing the Pentagon Papers, the Fielding break-in, and the Watergate burglary—that the media ended up sympathetic to the legitimate political system's revolt against Nixon's transgressions. The movement and the President each melted in the spotlight glare. With Watergate the cycle was complete: above the battle, only the spotlight remained intact, with the media assuring the country that, in the end, the system had worked.

REVOLUTIONARY WILL AND ACTION NEWS

Throughout the late sixties, the flamboyant movement *celebrity* ascended to prominence alongside a distinct style of movement *politics*: the episodic uprising that mobilized "revolutionary" countercultural youth identity. "Youth will make the revolution," one poster had it. In some versions, youth would do it alone (Yippie, Revolutionary Youth Movement); in others, they would be the allies, agents, or vanguard of larger forces. In either case they would do it "in the road." The premium was on street-fighting, on "moving in the streets," and, later, on trashing. Throughout 1968, many movement people came to admire "bikers" and "greasers" and to study karate as their hatred and fear of the "pig" police grew.

---

18. The public Winter Soldier testimony took place from January 31 to February 2, 1971. According to my anonymous informant, the veterans' charges were not broadcast because they were "not confirmable." Maybe they were not confirmable in principle (because all other witnesses were dead, say); more likely they were not confirmable because the network's version of "news" does not go in much for independent investigation. Most important of all, antiwar veterans were not legitimate sources of jarring news.

By October 1969, the Weathermen were affirming "Kick ass!" and "Fight the people"—the American people, after all, were colluding in imperialism—while they denounced the earlier cohorts of "movement creeps" for being "wimpy."

The sequence of events at Columbia in April–May 1968 is illuminating and illustrative. Mark Rudd was one of the "action faction" in the Columbia SDS who had wrested control of the chapter from the more intellectual, more theoretical-minded "praxis axis." With a boost from the media, as we have seen, Rudd came to personify the style of the "action freak." (Even at that, the media exaggerated Rudd's militancy, as if the role of "wild student militant" existed to be cast before and despite the fact.)[19] Michael Klare, who had coordinated the research that revealed Columbia's ties with the Pentagon through the Institute for Defense Analysis (IDA), resents the attention that the media paid to Rudd:

The people who tended to become noticed were people who were the most activist and . . . flamboyant, the ones who called for action, the ones whose rhetoric was "Tear down the walls," "Seize buildings." That was what the cameramen liked to hear. They weren't interested in what I had to say about Columbia's ties with IDA, for instance.[20]

Of course not: *action* was what was defined as news. Whereas the site of the Columbia gymnasium, SDS's other major issue, could at least be photographed, there were no pictures to be taken of an IDA installation on campus. So Klare does not remember once having the chance to tell a television audience about the IDA's work in weapons research. By the normal workings of commercial journalism, the building occupations and the police bust were routinely *decontextualized*, abstracted from the political situation that provoked them.

How did this process affect the Columbia SDS chapter? Klare argues, plausibly I think, that the media attention to decontextualized action lured the chapter into a self-defeating spiral of activism:

Up until then, Columbia had been strong as a movement because so much work had gone into education and teach-ins, dorm meetings—they were very good about that. And I think it broke down after . . . the spring uprising.

19. For examples of Rudd's tactical moderation during the Columbia uprising, see Avorn et al., *Up Against the Ivy Wall*, pp. 46, 50, 61, 63n., and 69.
20. Interview, Michael Klare, January 2, 1977.

Not that the spotlight was the only factor: the "praxis axis" which believed in organizing dorm meetings had already lost the initiative to Rudd. "All these effects were cumulative," as Klare says. But the media played a part there too, as a resource which Rudd and the "action faction" could command in the chapter's internal maneuvers. In Klare's view:

The most destructive element of the 1968 uprising in the media was the sense of messianic power that the SDS chapter had: that it could skip intermediate steps; that because of its name and its prestige and its charisma, it could bring down the university. And several disastrous events happened afterwards because of that miscalculation, in which SDS crumpled. Some people carried to the extreme of Weatherman. Mark Rudd was very much involved in that. This media imagery was very much a part of the calculation with which he entered Weatherman, and other people got involved in it too.

After "Columbia"—the name of an event now, not a situation and a process—the image spread; the popular slogan, "two, three, many Columbias" affirmed the virtues of decontextualized actions. The movement's own internal media promoted the same slogan. Other SDS chapters would come to know the Columbia events as a series of mythic media images: in the spirit of the image, they would try to replicate it, as they would try to replicate "Chicago," "San Francisco State," "Harvard," and so on in the next year and a half. (This, we saw, was also Jerry Rubin's political strategy; Rudd was no Yippie, but the structure of the temptation was the same.) Columbia's SDS would even see its image reflected back to it via the uprising in Paris, for a few weeks after the first occupation of buildings at Columbia came the great and galvanizing uprising at the Sorbonne. Klare recalls:

We were able to watch [the Sorbonne occupation] on television. There were TVs in common TV rooms, and in people's apartments. The Sorbonne thing, the thing about that that hadn't gone on at Columbia the first time [in April], and had a visual impact, were the barricades, fighting back against tear gas. The French police used immense amounts of tear gas and there were pictures on the screen of students with face masks, picking up the tear gas and throwing it back to the police. This had not happened in the first Columbia bust. People blockaded buildings, but, to my recollection, there was no fighting back against the police. People got hurt, but there was no collective sense of "us fighting the pigs." Between the first and second Columbia things, the Sorbonne had an impact. Because the second Columbia bust was very different. First of all, people built blockades and locked off the campus from the police. . . . It was obvious that those blockades were not going to keep out the police. It was more symbolical than anything else. Also you saw people wearing face masks and helmets and there was also throwing things at the police.[21]

The surge toward street-fighting and symbolic barricades accelerated through the year. In the absence of revolutionary conditions, revolutionary will spilled forth to take up the slack. Régis Debray was widely quoted: "The duty of the revolutionary is to make the revolution." Debray's book about Latin American guerrillas was held applicable to the United States. Mark Rudd wrote that the Paris Commune of 1871 "has long been a symbol of revolutionary will, dedication, and struggle,"[22] neglecting to say that it had been first of all a symbol of a mobilized revolutionary *class*. The goal of radicalization obscured, and compensated for, the facts of social and political isolation. The political context was dominated by the failure, the literal assassination, of electoral liberalism (Bobby Kennedy) and active nonviolence (Martin Luther King, Jr.). A critical mass of the movement's activists lost their residual faith in the ability of liberal authorities, with their norms of civility, to accomplish political change "through the system." Revolutionism was the magnetic field shaping the new rhetoric and the new symbols.[23]

The media transmitted images of the turn toward revolution-

21. Ibid. The account in Avorn et al., *Up Against the Ivy Wall*, confirms Klare's description. Actually, during the first occupation of Hamilton Hall, in April, the black students voted explicitly *not* to barricade the building (p. 61). Klare adds that the TV lights themselves inflamed actions, just as the Kerner Commission and the Right asserted: "The TV itself became the event. The *New York Times* sitting down and talking to someone, didn't have any drama to it. When the TV camera came on campus, it always attracted a crowd itself. And then if Mark Rudd got in front of the cameras, then more people would come, and so he would warm up and he would have a ready-made crowd. And a lot of this happened at night when the lights added to the whole atmosphere. And at the Sorbonne a lot of this stuff took place at night too, flares and that whole World War II atmosphere. And that's what Columbia became too, the electric light things and the . . . lights for photos. And whenever there was Mark Rudd up there with a bullhorn, there would be the TV cameras and the lights going like crazy and the people went berserk" (interview, January 2, 1977).

22. Mark Rudd, "Symbols of the Revolution," in Avorn et al., *Up Against the Ivy Wall*, p. 294.

23. As hopes and expectations shattered, there was also an active upwelling of rage rooted in primitive experience and need. But Christopher Lasch's important analysis of the common narcissistic personality structure (*New York Review of Books* 23 [September 30, 1976]: 5–13) is too broad and general to be helpful in explaining the historical specificity of this upwelling in the New Left. See also Chap. 9, below.

ism as they transmitted images of one of its central rationales: the growing brutality of the police. Together, these images helped render the street-fighting style legitimate *within* the movement as they helped render it anathema for the audience *outside*. By diffusing highly charged symbols that could be "read off" with diametrically opposed valuations and emphases, according to social interests and experience, the media unintentionally helped polarize the society between revolutionism and embattled reaction. Right-wing critics of television news during this period overlook the fact that, for example, CBS broadcast a three-part feature about police "getting tough" on demonstrators and blacks across the country in mid-August 1968. Narrated by John Laurence, who also covered many of the movement's demonstrations that year, it treated with sympathy the rising police fury against demonstrators, and showed police carrying illegal but officially tolerated weapons. Ten days later, of course, came the famous live coverage of the Chicago police riot.

Viewers drew wildly different conclusions from the Chicago coverage: antiwar and movement sympathizers were everlastingly horrified by police violence, while the Right accused the networks of bias and rallied to the side of the police. Right-wing congressmen called for investigations, the networks' *bête noire*. CBS News President Richard Salant soon was promising retrenchment: "If the set of circumstances that occurred in Chicago ever occurs again, I think we'll report it somewhat differently." [24] The network found itself occupying a shrinking center: Walter Cronkite at first condemned police tactics, then later in the week thought better of this breach of neutrality and apologized to Mayor Daley. The CBS News Producer Ron Bonn remembers "learning an awful lot about journalism, about television," that week. "What I didn't expect," he says with some vehemence, was to get gassed on the street and then to come into CBS headquarters "to find a stack of telegrams from a thousand miles away . . . telling me I didn't know what was going on in the streets of Chicago." "You tend to think of your audience as objective," Bonn told me in a tone of lost innocence. "Instead, they have prejudices." [25] Indeed, polarized audiences interpreted what they saw on the screen in polar ways.

24. Quoted from a Public Broadcasting Laboratory interview, "After Chicago, What?" *TV Guide*, March 1, 1969. There was, in fact, far less live coverage of the demonstrations at the 1972 Republican Convention in Miami Beach, though those demonstrations were numerically larger than the Chicago events.

25. Interview, Ron Bonn, November 19, 1976.

THE AESTHETICIZING OF VIOLENCE IN FILMS

America lost its balls in the frontier and since then there have been no mighty myths and now we hunt for them in lonely balconies, watching *Bonnie and Clyde*.

—Abbie Hoffman[26]

This is a study in the power of news media above all, but the subject of mass-mediated militancy requires a few words about some films of the late sixties. Despite the triumph of television, films were central to the imagery of the time. And especially for the youth market: critics, at least, credited *Bonnie and Clyde*—and the blander *The Graduate*—with bringing the college-educated young back to the movies. Beginning with *Bonnie and Clyde* in 1967, Hollywood made a sequence of youth-culture films for the big, increasingly sophisticated, and increasingly estranged youth audience; each film treated violence as romantic and shocking at the same time—violence decontextualized, violence aestheticized, violence the camera reveled in, violence that did not even need to plead its reasons. These films were both emblems and reinforcers of the new mood.

Arthur Penn's *Bonnie and Clyde* was the most skilled, the most provocative, and probably the most popular; it launched not only new fashions but a hero cult; it stylized violence in living color. Though Penn's heroes lived during the Depression and started robbing banks to help out (or make a gesture toward helping out) dispossessed farmers, they were not the creatures of economic ruin. Unlike the characters in 1937 and 1949 movies based on the same real-life Bonnie Parker and Clyde Barrow, Penn's characters were freestanding angels, children of the sixties set three decades back.[27] Their doomed life of crime began as a lark, an escapade of sexualized bravado up against boredom and impotence. And though Bonnie and Clyde went through a brief phase of "serving the people," most of their crimes in the film were *chosen* actions, more willed than compelled. Bonnie and Clyde were on the run, finally, because they were on the run, because that was the way to live. Penn muted the context, the situation: there were references to the poverty of the time, but they were stylized and distanced,

26. *Revolution for the Hell of It*, p. 85.
27. For a detailed comparison of these films, see Pauline Kael, "Bonnie and Clyde," in her *Kiss Kiss Bang Bang* (New York: Bantam Books, 1969), pp. 59–79 (first published in *The New Yorker*, October 21, 1967).

like the fading FDR posters on the walls of dusty towns, serving only vaguely to motivate the glamorous recklessness of Bonnie and Clyde. Penn filmed Bonnie's family in softened pastel light and slow motion, displaying family roots as both beautiful and unreal, the occasion for a brief nostalgia only. What Penn moved to the foreground was *will*, the will to be young and free and potent: will as excitement, the drive to overcome impotence in a flat world. When Bonnie fondled Clyde's pistol, she was naming the game: before the first robbery, before any social rationale, this was an act so touching in its gaucherie that it established the two of them as cherubic rebels. Outlaw rebellion was the only living energy within reach. Though there were a few intimations of kinky sex, it was Penn's genius to keep them no more than intimations, to keep sexual as well as class motives firmly in the background.[28]

At the end, when the relentless, robotic policeman Frank Hamer and his reinforcements tore Bonnie and Clyde apart with machine-gun fire, the lover-outlaws were crucified in the air; they were made to die for us, the young and innocent. Their deaths, like those of their victims, were aestheticized; the camera savored their destruction. Gangster movies had stylized death for decades, often by "shooting" death scenes at a distance; but Penn indulged close up in the shock of bodily damage. He shot the scene with four cameras, each at a different speed and with a different lens, he said in an interview, "so that I could cut to get the shock and at the same time the ballet of death. There's a moment in death when the body no longer functions, when it becomes an object and has a certain kind of detached ugly beauty. It was that aspect that I was trying to get. . . . [W]e were trying to change the character of death, to make their deaths more legendary than real."[29] But all along, Penn had been manipulating emotions with alacrity, working hard to bring the audience to identify with his star-crossed lovers. As he reconstructed his shifts in tone from the innocent to the shocking, Penn started from the fact that his characters were "relatively shallow, rather empty people" without "a moral dilemma which would

28. John Cawelti matched the finished film against the shooting script by David Newman and Robert Benton and showed that Penn dampened the script's far more explicit three-way sexuality connecting Bonnie, Clyde, and their moronic sidekick C. W. Moss. See John Cawelti, ed., *Focus on Bonnie and Clyde* (Englewood Cliffs, N.J.: Prentice-Hall, 1973), pp. 139–140.

29. "Bonnie and Clyde: An Interview with Arthur Penn," by Jean-Louis Comolli and André S. Labarthe, in Cawelti, *Focus on Bonnie and Clyde*, pp. 16, 17 (first published in *Evergreen Review* 12 [June 1968]).

help us to understand what the characters are going through in their interior lives. Consequently, we had to deal more at the level of the outer side, like the cartoon. . . . I thought in terms of cartoons—each frame changing. Here we laugh, here we cry, here we laugh again, and so we cut the film like that and the images were made up like that instead of long, fluid ones." His interviewers asked if it didn't "seem dangerous to you to be able to manipulate at will the reactions of the public which, being less interested in the characters, is only responsive to your manipulation?" "Yes," Penn acknowledged, "it seems to me a little dangerous, but it seemed to be the best way to tell this story."[30]

At the Hollywood premiere, I heard, someone in the audience stood up at the end and yelled, "Fucking cops!" He got the point. The spirit of Bonnie and Clyde was everywhere in the movement— and in the larger youth culture surrounding it—in the summer and fall of 1967 and on into 1968. Pauline Kael wrote in the *New Yorker* that the film had "put the sting back in death."[31] Peter Collier in *Ramparts* quoted a friend of his: "*Bonnie and Clyde* belongs to young people today in a way no other film has since the Beatles' movies. It speaks to them. It is about their life, about the cops beating on their heads and the inertia they have to wade through."[32] The caricaturist David Levine had a different inspiration about the nature of criminality: in the *New York Review of Books*, he drew Lyndon Johnson as Clyde and Secretary of State Dean Rusk as Bonnie. But Levine's grasp of this deep convergence was rare. The film reviewer in the left-wing *Guardian*, Gerald Long, was more in tune with hip sympathies: he linked Bonnie and Clyde in all seriousness with Ché Guevara and the NLF hero Nguyen Van Troi. As Peter Collier wrote early in 1968, a bad year for cautions, "if it is true that *Bonnie and Clyde* belongs to 'us,' perhaps we should be all the more careful about what it says."

Bonnie and Clyde uncovered a new market, and other films went on to merchandise the spirit of stylized violence, violence as act of will rather than consequence. I went to see American International's low-budget *Wild in the Streets* in the spring of 1968 on the recommendation of one movement leader; he chortled as he told me the story of the movie's rock-and-rolling youth leaders, who lock

30. Ibid., p. 18.
31. Kael, *Kiss Kiss Bang Bang*, p. 79.
32. Peter Collier, review of *Bonnie and Clyde*, in Cawelti, *Focus on Bonnie and Clyde*, pp. 29–30 (first published in *Ramparts* 6 [May 1968]).

all the country's adults (the proverbial over-thirties) into concentration camps and keep them whacked out on LSD. The revolutionary strategy of *Wild*'s vanguard cadre had its explanations—parental suffocation, police violence—but they were relatively feeble and perfunctory, as if the filmmakers knew they had to go through the motions of justification but no more. Again, "revolution" was decontextualized: "revolution for the hell of it." In the bloody spring of 1968, it was easy to lose a sense of the real. Increasingly the cultural artifacts, like the movement itself, were taking for granted a context of political extremity.

Then, in the spring of 1969, Lindsay Anderson's popular *If . . .* traced the eruption of rage from English public-school alienation to murderous freak-out. Mick (Malcolm MacDowell) was a disaffected student who at the outset was papering his wall with grisly news-photographs: his violent imagination was no creature of context. He was attractive compared to his acquiescent schoolmates, so from the beginning the film belonged to him. In love with death, unable to love humans, Mick was the avenger who scorned all context. He and a waitress snarled at each other, "went ape," before making love. The petty but incessant violence and absurdity of the school routines confirmed Mick's estrangement; the school was a closed political universe. Dramatically it seemed right when Mick began recruiting a commando cadre without going through the motions of explaining his project. On graduation day, they started shooting at random into a crowd of parents and school authorities; the first to die was the school's one decent teacher. In San Francisco, *If . . .* was advertised with the blurb, "REVOLUTION!! Which Side Are You On?"—which in itself, of course, says nothing about how audiences respond. But in my experience, two different San Francisco audiences took it as allegory for the actual political situation. What the distributor called "revolution" was nothing but an eruption of preexisting rage somehow inserted into an institutional setting. It was violence proud not to need, not to dwell on, its alibis—violence akin to the opening-fire-in-the-streets stunt that André Breton had commended as "the ultimate surrealist act."[33] *If . . .* was attacked by some radicals for its "counterrevolutionary adventurist ending," but this partial critique missed the point. Anderson had tilted the whole film toward precisely that ending and

33. André Breton, *Second Manifeste du Surréalisme* (Paris: Éditions Kra, 1930), p. 69.

no other. The film's logic justified Mick and his friends' assault, and San Francisco audiences got the point: during the time of People's Park and the National Guard occupation of Berkeley in May 1969, they cheered when the movie rebels opened fire on the stuffy parents and the fuddy-duddy headmaster.

And in just this spirit, Stew Albert, one of the founding Yippies, wrote in the *Berkeley Tribe* in the fall of 1969 that Sam Peckinpah's *The Wild Bunch* was "a revolutionary film" because "it shows you have to pick up the gun." Whatever Peckinpah's intentions, his aesthetics of violence matched the hardening mood. His blown-apart blood-spurting bodies pretended to be nothing other than what they were; they insisted on violence as a life-and-death struggle of its own, a lust of the blood. True, the film threw in, as if in afterthought, a bit of oppression as justification for retaliatory violence. But there was none of the innocence of *Bonnie and Clyde*; by 1969, movie violence needed not even Bonnie and Clyde's thin motivations. Militancy had been severed from strategy and value. *But of course it was by no means only the Left that indulged in the aestheticizing of violence.* Peckinpah's vision curiously resembled the television vision of the Vietnam war, a steady exposition of bloodshed severed from meaning, purpose, or reasonable cause. This was the living-room image of Vietnam, rendering the war at once vile, normal, and incomprehensible, and conceivably helping to bring about, over the years, a certain war-weariness.[34] Aestheticized, the image of violence outside reason or context was coming to dominate American popular culture.

The climax of this bloody series was *Easy Rider*, released in the fall of 1969. In a countryside symbolizing limitlessness, Peter Fonda and Dennis Hopper celebrated the risky freedom of two freaks with motorcycles, the frontier idyll turned back on itself, our anti-heroes moving eastward this time: a Southeast Passage to paranoia. Women were props to testify to the glories of the restless and inarticulate. (All these films were deeply sexist, in fact, and all were set in open space, where violence is a shocking assault on nature and the peaceful "feminine." The same was true for another popular film of the same season: the more genial *Butch Cassidy and the Sundance Kid*.) *Easy Rider* indulged in portents of apocalypse; it

34. Todd Gitlin, "Sixteen Notes on Television and the Movement," in George Abbott White and Charles Newman, eds., *Literature in Revolution* (New York: Holt, Rinehart and Winston, 1972), pp. 358–359.

was a lyric in behalf of paranoia, saying to the counterculture: yes, you'd *better* fear those ignorant Southern fascist hard-hats. The lasting image was of a counterculture better off contained in its California ghetto, or in the media *image* of its California ghetto. The media had for a long time purveyed a succession of stereotypes of "California culture," stereotypes that were never quite false. From Nathanael West's anomic drifters to Peter Fonda's dopers was not so far a trek; nor was it so far from Horace Greeley's westward-going young men to the media-lured hippies of 1967's Summer of Love. Now, in *Easy Rider*, the frontier was finally sealed after two centuries; California was the end of the blacktop. The paths of glory led but to the wrong end of the shotgun. *Easy Rider* was no celebration of violence, but a tantalizing warning about the consequences of transporting deviance out of its ghetto. Countercultural audiences were transfixed by the image of their demons as they watched this cautionary tale. Stay weird in L.A. was the moral, where there *is* no context, where the road is never ending. Otherwise violence comes down out of the blue.

MILITANCY AND THE MOVEMENT

These films were part of an edgy, apocalyptic popular culture whose fuller and more intricate analysis awaits another occasion. In pop music, Bob Dylan's nightmare surrealism, the Rolling Stones' pulsations, Jim Morrison's "Break On Through to the Other Side," the Jefferson Airplane's "got a revolution"; in European films, Gillo Pontecorvo's easily oversimplified *The Battle of Algiers* (1966; released in the U.S. in 1967); later Hollywood films with libertarian notes and authoritarian overtones, like the popular *Billy Jack* (1971); and not least, the flamboyant images of the underground press—all these and many more items of popular culture thrived in *and reproduced* an apocalyptic, polarized political mood. None of this invented tear gas or nightsticks, napalm or Ho Chi Minh, SDS or the Yippies or the Chicago police, or the new taste for street-blocking confrontation or building-seizing militant nonviolence; but *in ensemble* they shaped a symbolic environment that was conducive to revolutionism out of context, to the inflation of rhetoric and militancy out of proportion to the possible.

Of course, the politics of confrontation was not simply an expression of theatrical tactics out of context, not simply an effusion of surrealism. It was at the same time strategic in intent: it aimed to stop a war. In the next chapter, I shall take up the argument that it *did* help stop the war, or retard it, by forcing the foreign policy elite to choose between further escalation in Vietnam and restoring political stability at home. But if the rising tide of militancy did help convince the elite that continuing the war would rip the country apart, the movement's inflated rhetoric and militancy, its theatrics and bravado, also did great damage to the movement's ability to survive, to grow, to mature, and to adapt to a more repressive political climate. Again, the movement was both actor and acted-upon in a complex political tangle. The media inflated the sense that there was an extremist movement; parts of the movement pursued confrontation for both strategic and expressive reasons; and the State escalated repression. Let me summarize provisionally some consequences of this entire process *for the movement*:

First, *the movement was isolated—and isolated itself—politically,* just at a time when antiwar sentiment was growing fast and, if unified, could have multiplied its political weight.

Second, *face-to-face organizing dried up.* By the time of the Newark and Detroit ghetto uprisings of 1967, most of the ERAP projects had reached their limits; some of the organized community people moved toward autonomy, wanting to get free of the student organizers.[35] The staffs had been attracted anyway by the antiwar movement; now they had more than one reason to move to antiwar work. One SDS proposal called for anti-draft organizing in working-class communities, thus marrying the style of community organizing with antiwar content; but for the most part it never got off paper.[36] Because of the glare of the media spotlight, the temptations of celebrity, and—not least—the urgency of the war, it was

35. See, for example, Todd Gitlin and Nanci Hollander, *Uptown: Poor Whites in Chicago* (New York: Harper and Row, 1970), pp. 375–397. As Maria Varela told me (interview, July 1, 1976), local organizing also dried up for SNCC as the organization became identified with its spokesmen, Stokely Carmichael and H. Rap Brown. See also Richard Flacks, *Youth and Social Change* (Chicago: Markham, 1971), p. 134.

36. One organizing project that did materialize in the late sixties was the Boston Draft Resistance Group, which organized quite deliberately outside the media spotlight. Barrie Thorne has written about the distinct stylistic and strategic approaches that separated the BDRG from its rival, the New England Resistance, which worked to create a succession of media events. See Barrie Thorne, "Resisting the Draft: An Ethnography of the Draft Resistance Movement," unpublished Ph.D. dissertation, Brandeis University, 1971; and her "Protest and the Problem of Credibility: Uses of Knowledge and Risk-Taking in the Draft Resistance Movement of the 1960's," *Social Problems* 23 (December 1975): 111–123.

hard for leaders to commit themselves to the unrewarding, tedious work of grass-roots politics. As Mark Rudd said contemptuously to me at a meeting just after the Chicago demonstrations of 1968: "Organizing is just another word for going slow."

And third, *there arose—with no small assist from the media—a moderate alternative to the movement.*

7 Elevating Moderate Alternatives: The Moment of Reform

THE TET CRISIS AND AMERICAN ELITES

We were part of the change. As protest moved from left groups, anti-war groups, into the pulpits, into the Senate—with Fulbright, Gruening, and others—as it became a majority opinion, it naturally picked up coverage. And then naturally the tone of the coverage changed. Because we're an Establishment institution, and whenever your natural community changes its opinion, then naturally you will too.

—Max Frankel, *New York Times* Editorial Page Editor[1]

The Tet offensive of January–February 1968 derailed the conventional assumption in Washington that the war, however wise or foolish in the first place, was in any event on its way to being won. The coordinated NLF assault had immediate and decisive repercussions throughout American politics, throughout the media, and at every level of the society. In retrospect, Tet marked a major turning point in the self-image of America in the world. The battles and their interpretations electrified the media as they did Washington and Wall Street; Tet reverberated everywhere. The routine workings of news gathering portrayed the Tet offensive—had to

---

1. Telephone interview, Max Frankel, March 23, 1979. In fact, Senator Ernest Gruening of Alaska was one of the earliest opponents of the war, and one of the *two* senators (the other was Wayne Morse of Oregon) to vote against the Tonkin Resolution of 1964, which Lyndon Johnson then took as *carte blanche* for his escalations. Senator Fulbright began to criticize the war in 1965, though not to call for withdrawal until later. Frankel in 1968 was a top *New York Times* Washington correspondent.

portray it—as a shattering blow to the conventional American military assumptions, goals, and claims—those same assumptions that the media had for years been relaying and, occasionally, calling into question. Now the news relayed images of NLF troops infiltrating the American Embassy compound in Saigon, with bloody fighting throughout the cities of South Vietnam. The administration had been "guardedly optimistic," in the jargon of the time; suddenly the enemy was quite visibly within the gates. Whether or not the news exaggerated the military success of the NLF, as has been argued (and disputed), the NLF's *political* victory—especially as measured by the incapacity of the Saigon regime, and the disruption of "pacification" in the countryside—was evident.[2]

Tet was not only big on-the-spot news, but it provoked some unusual reconsiderations within the media. James Reston of the *New York Times* asked on February 7: "What is the end that justifies this slaughter? How will we save Vietnam if we destroy it in the battle?"[3] Walter Cronkite flew to Vietnam for the second time, then returned and summed up his new view in a half-hour special report on February 27:

To say that we are closer to victory today is to believe, in the face of the evidence, the optimists who have been wrong in the past. To suggest we are on the edge of defeat is to yield to unreasonable pessimism. To say that we are mired in stalemate seems the only realistic, if unsatisfactory, conclusion. But it is increasingly clear to this reporter that the only rational way out then will be to negotiate not as victors, but as an honorable people who lived up to their pledge to defend democracy and did the best they could.[4]

2. My account of the Tet crisis and the political responses in Washington and New York is indebted to Herbert Y. Schandler's extremely thorough *The Unmaking of a President: Lyndon Johnson and Vietnam* (Princeton, N.J.: Princeton University Press, 1977), and also to Godfrey Hodgson's *America in Our Time* (Garden City, N.Y.: Doubleday, 1976), pp. 353–361. See also Schandler's voluminous bibliography. In *Big Story: How the American Press and Television Reported and Interpreted the Crisis of Tet 1968 in Vietnam and Washington* (Boulder, Colo.: Westview Press, 1977; abridged edition, Garden City, N.Y.: Anchor Books, 1978), the reporter Peter Braestrup argues that the American media effectively exaggerated the success of the NLF offensive; but see also the critical reviews by Peter Arnett, *Columbia Journalism Review*, January–February 1978, pp. 44–47, and Noam Chomsky, "10 Years After Tet: The Big Story That Got Away; Widely Hailed Book on Vietnam Reporting Asks Wrong Questions, Gets Wrong Answers," *More* 8 (June 1978): 16–23.

3. Reston, "Washington: The Flies That Captured the Flypaper," quoted in Schandler, *Unmaking of a President*, p. 198.

4. As quoted in CBS Transcript for CBS News Special, "1968," August 25, 1978, p. 3. © 1968 CBS Inc. All rights reserved.

Cronkite was disputing the war's efficacy, not its goals ("to defend democracy"); but since the Johnson administration had staked its defense of the war precisely on its efficacy, Cronkite's remarks (and similar ones from the other networks and from *Time* and *Newsweek* and the *Wall Street Journal*)[5] amounted to an effective critique of Johnson's war strategy. Presidential Press Secretary George Christian later told CBS News Washington Bureau Chief William Small that when Cronkite delivered this report, "the shock waves rolled through government."[6]

If so, they rolled through a government that was ready for them. In order to understand the subsequent shifts in media frames, we have to consider the political-economic crisis in its entirety, at least briefly. Now that the going war strategy had evidently failed by its own lights, inside government opinion began to polarize. The war would have to be accelerated greatly or negotiated to an end; the middle ground had vanished. Moderates and pillars of the Establishment within and near the administration now began to feel, like Walter Cronkite, that this war, whose objectives they still endorsed, was unwinnable. A new consensus of the foreign policy elite was forming. Clark Clifford, the influential Washington corporate lawyer, former top adviser to President Harry Truman, and now Johnson's incoming Secretary of Defense, was the decisive agent who lost faith in the war effort and set out to mobilize influential opposition within the highest political-economic circles of Washington and New York. While Clifford and his allies maneuvered in the wake of Tet, Chairman of the Joint Chiefs of Staff Earle G. Wheeler requested 206,000 new troops for Vietnam. The inner debate was joined. Some Pentagon and State Department officials, working with Clifford, opposed this request. News of the policy debate within the government got to *New York Times* reporters Hedrick Smith and Neil Sheehan, and the *Times* editors ran their piece as the lead, Sunday, March 10, under the three-column headline: "WESTMORELAND REQUESTS 206,000 MORE MEN/STIRRING DEBATE IN ADMINISTRATION; FORCE NOW 510,000/ SOME IN DEFENSE & STATE DEPARTMENTS OPPOSE INCREASE." News of still another major troop request reverberated throughout the press and provoked intense debate in Congress and elsewhere.

5. Summarized in Schandler, *Unmaking of a President*, pp. 198–199.
6. Quoted in William Small, *To Kill a Messenger: Television News and the Real World* (New York: Hastings House, 1974), p. 123.

Clifford, convinced of impending disaster if Johnson continued to escalate, persuaded the President to consult with the informal advisory group later known as the Wise Men, a Who's Who of the financial and foreign policy elite of the Truman, Eisenhower, Kennedy, and Johnson administrations: Dean Acheson, George Ball, McGeorge Bundy, C. Douglas Dillon, Cyrus Vance, Arthur Dean, John McCloy, Gen. Omar Bradley, Gen. Matthew Ridgeway, Gen. Maxwell Taylor, Robert Murphy, Henry Cabot Lodge, Abe Fortas, and Arthur Goldberg.

Just the previous November, the Wise Men had told Johnson that they were satisfied with the conduct and the military success of the war. But in the interim, Senator Eugene McCarthy had decided to make a run for the Democratic presidential nomination. The country was enmeshed in an economic and political crisis whose dimensions expanded with every week. During the first half of March, the economic bill for the war came due. Inflation showed up because Johnson was deficit-financing the war without daring to increase taxes or to cut domestic spending. The balance of payments turned against the United States, resulting in a fourth-quarter deficit in 1967. After Tet, and after reports of a possible rise in military expenditures, the dollar dramatically lost its stability in the international market, and speculators drained American gold reserves. On March 12, Senator McCarthy came within a few hundred votes of winning the New Hampshire primary. The London gold market was closed on March 16 to cut off the gold drain. The same day, Senator Robert Kennedy formally entered the race for the Democratic presidential nomination.

It was in this critical situation, on March 25, 1968, that Pentagon chief Clifford convened the Wise Men. Clifford, with his close ties to the top financial interests, was able to stand up to Johnson and to mobilize the powerful group capable of telling him off. As Herbert Schandler writes after prolonged discussions with all the living principals, "alone among the presidential advisors, [Clifford] dealt with Johnson as an equal. Clifford manifested his personal fealty to the president by telling him the way he saw it, rather than by protecting his own cherished government position by telling the president what the president wanted to hear. Also, *he was able to go outside the bureaucracy, to consult with friends in Congress and in the business and economic community.*" [7] Clifford, as Schandler writes,

7. Quoted in Schandler, *Unmaking of a President*, p. 342 (emphasis added).

"had talked to many of his friends in the business community and sensed the doubts that had also developed in their attitude toward the war." Clifford told Schandler in 1972: "I had the feeling that we were at a crucial stage in the decision-making process. I thought it was going to take something very substantial to shift the president's attitude. I needed some stiff medicine to bring home to the president what was happening to the country."[8] That stiff medicine would be the concerted opinions of the Wise Men. These fourteen men—corporate lawyers, ex-Cabinet officers, ex-ambassadors, and ex-generals—were briefed by the sitting foreign policy makers and military chiefs; they deliberated; and then they sat down with President Johnson and told him that in political and economic terms the war was too costly and that, at the very least, "an increase in American forces would be unthinkable."[9] Cyrus Vance, later Secretary of State, said: "We were weighing not only what was happening in Vietnam, but the social and political effects in the United States, the impact on the U.S. economy, the attitude of other nations. The divisiveness in the country was growing with such acuteness that it was threatening to tear the United States apart."[10] "The meeting with the Wise Men served the purpose that I hoped it would," Clifford exulted later. "It really shook the president."[11] Three days later, Johnson announced four decisions in a nationally televised speech: (1) there would be only a token increase in the number of American troops in South Vietnam, but nothing like the 206,000 requested by General Wheeler; (2) the South Vietnamese armed forces would be expanded; (3) the U.S. would cease bombing North Vietnam north of the 20th parallel; and (4) he would not run for a second full term as President of the United States.

As the war lost legitimacy and popularity, antiwar activity became respectable. Within the general shift in political momentum, the media now helped frame the respectable opposition as an explicit alternative to the radical, confrontational Left. The slogan was "Clean for Gene," and the well-publicized students who

8. Quoted in ibid., pp. 254–255.
9. Ibid., p. 264. My account of the meeting of the Wise Men relies mostly on ibid., pp. 259–265.
10. Quoted in Townsend Hoopes, *The Limits to Intervention* (New York: David McKay, 1969), pp. 215–216.
11. Quoted in ibid., p. 264.

shaved their faces and dragged their suits out of the closet to slog through the New Hampshire snow were vivid, visible alternatives to the scruffy, bearded, draft-card burning Viet Cong-flag carriers. Having defined the latter as the movement archetype, the media could now introduce the "Clean for Gene" movement as something genuinely new, something different. Especially after Tet and the New Hampshire primary, their propensity to see the "Clean" movement as news followed not only from the conventional news code but from reporters and editors turning against the war themselves, growing more sympathetic toward a legitimate opposition. At the same time, the McCarthy and Kennedy campaigners were claiming the mantle of a safe alternative. There was, in short, a tacit alliance of interests between the liberal movement and the media. This implicit alliance deepened throughout 1968 and 1969. Just as Lyndon Johnson became convinced by the political-economic elite that the war was economically and politically insupportable, so did many reporters and some (though not all) of the media elite become convinced that the war was dangerously threatening the social order. The events of 1968 made the media interest in a moderate antiwar alternative even more intense. Especially after the Chicago convention, as a staff member of the 1969 antiwar Moratorium put it to me, "some folks in the press wanted to find some clean-cut kids who were opposing the war but doing it in a clean way." [12] The celebrated Moratorium of October and November 1969 tried to capitalize on this interest. What was going to be brought out by the media—as a chemical stain brings out certain features of cells and leaves others in the vague background— was *conflict* between moderates and radicals. The moderates were undoubtedly on the move and undoubtedly had a vast popular base and high-level political support in Congress; it was the media, though, that in this setting did a good deal to present them as an *alternative* to the rest of the antiwar movement.

MEDIA ON A TIGHTROPE:
EXTRAORDINARY MEASURES TO SECURE MODERATING FRAMES

The frame of moderation-as-alternative-to-militancy was now brought into play, and more deliberately so over time. All the normal rules of selectivity succeeded in polarizing the images of respectable and unrespectable movements. As I shall argue in Part

12. Interview, Susan Werbe, November 15, 1976.

III, the routine (or hegemonic) news-gathering and framing procedures are the ones that operate night after night to govern the content of news. But occasionally the ordinary rules have to be secured or changed by extraordinary measures. When mass movements mobilize, the routine procedures work, in a sense, too well; by amplifying unpalatable, destabilizing news, they arouse political opposition in high places and threaten the networks' political position. Those are the moments when the media managers intervene for political purposes, *precisely to change the standard frame.* Outside political authorities may themselves intervene to force the change if it is not forthcoming spontaneously. Such moments kept cropping up in unstable 1968: Tet, the riots after Dr. King's assassination, Chicago, Nixon's election. Media managers did intervene then to impose the new frames from above, to change the rules—at times over the heads of recalcitrant reporters.

Examples of explicit corporate intervention to change a news angle are rare, by all accounts. Blair Clark, who was general manager and vice-president of CBS News from 1961 through 1964, knows of no occasion during his tenure when CBS Board Chairman Paley or President Stanton intervened directly to change or direct a specific news story.[13] Other reporters, managers, and producers generally agree. (This is not to speak of the weight of general policy directives, or of the prevailing atmosphere, the force of the taken-for-granted, or of self-censorship, all routine.) On the other hand, Edward Jay Epstein reports that NBC News, at least, was more vulnerable to directives from superiors at the network. In the early sixties, NBC President Robert Kintner, by his own testimony, "wrote up to '35 memos . . . in a two-day period' to the head of his news division, asking why the network carried specific news stories, or otherwise commenting on the news."[14] CBS News, occupying its own building far across town from network headquarters, claims greater insulation from network (and therefore political) pressures. (NBC News is ensconced, with the rest of NBC, in the RCA Building in Rockefeller Center.) Perhaps CBS News's physical separateness is more than symbolic; several CBS News people insist that News President Richard Salant insulated them from both network and outside pressures (even includ-

13. Interview, Blair Clark, November 12, 1976.
14. Edward Jay Epstein, *News from Nowhere: Television and the News* (New York: Vintage Books, 1974), p. 74, quoting from Robert E. Kintner, "Broadcasting and the News," *Harper's Magazine* (April 1965), p. 52.

ing routine complaint mail). The other side of this insulation, of course, is that any directives that did come down *to* Salant would be unknown to lower-level employees; the grapevine does not seem to reach down very far. It remains true, of course, even at CBS, that, as Epstein says in his thorough investigation of the workings of television news in 1968–69, "although news executives claim to have some 'autonomy' over news decisions, they are still responsible to network executives for the overall performance." [15] At CBS at least, whatever moments of executive intervention do happen are hard to unearth. But I hasten to say in advance, before unearthing one or two, that instances of direct intervention in news operations are interesting mostly not as proofs of conspiratorial management but as indices of the weight of routine framing, the institution's commitment to it, and the force of the norm of reportorial independence—a force great enough that it will only occasionally be violated by extraordinary commands. If the frame is important enough, its "normality" will be reinforced precisely by the abnormal order. The exception proves the rule.

At the networks, the 1968 moderation frame seems to have been imposed in stages. It is my impression—though only that—that it was clamped onto the black movement first; more research is needed to confirm or deny that the moderate-militant split became a standard component of reporting about the black movement, especially after the assassination of Martin Luther King and the riots of April. In any event, network executives were aware that their spotlight was also a magnifier of street rhetoric and demonstrative or violent militancy. Already in 1967, CBS President Frank Stanton had said: "There seems to be a tendency on the part of persons who are setting up demonstrations to accomodate the networks to reap the most publicity and exposure." [16] Epstein reports that Johnson administration pressures had already become more explicit after the hot summer of 1967. After the Newark and Detroit riots, the Justice Department convened a conference for news executives, with Federal Communications Commission representatives "sitting in," in Poughkeepsie, New York. The conference centered "on the need for 'guidelines' in covering racial disturbances and, in general, the ways that television could help ameliorate

15. Epstein, *News from Nowhere*, p. 74.
16. Quoted in William S. Paley's memoir, *As It Happened* (Garden City, N.Y.: Doubleday, 1979), p. 304.

or 'cool down' the tensions in the ghettos by 'better news treatment.'" NBC News President Reuven Frank later wrote to Roger Wilkins, the Justice Department official who had helped organize the conference, protesting that "the discussion was asking a medium of journalism to act as an instrument of social control. We must never accept such a request. . . . It is not for us to cooperate with government in establishing guidelines." But within the year —after the King assassination and Chicago—all three networks had adopted their own guidelines for covering riots, more or less matching the government's suggestions.[17] CBS instructed its news staff that "the best coverage is not necessarily the one with the best pictures and most dramatic action."[18] And at the same time, militant leaders were to be censored. Epstein reports that in late 1968 or early 1969,

NBC producers agreed [at whose behest?—T. G.] that stories which showed black militant leaders threatening violent acts against society were not desirable, and earlier two black militants, Stokely Carmichael and H. Rap Brown, had been "banned" from NBC, according to the executive producer.[19]

Evidently at NBC, at least, the rise of moderation was to be accomplished by the deliberate eclipse of militancy.

Clearly, the networks were jarred by the public outcry against their coverage of the Chicago convention. Congressmen threatened investigations, and by the time President Nixon was elected in November, the networks were battening down the hatches. NBC News President Frank said on Public Television on December 22:

There are already controls of a very insidious nature, an atmosphere is building up that concerns me a great deal, that news people, acting according to their best lights, keep feeling that their almost conditioned actions and decisions may be subject to review. And I am afraid of a process of self-censorship developing.[20]

17. Epstein, News from Nowhere, p. 75. Interestingly, Roger Wilkins is at this writing an editor of the New York Times, and according to Daniel Schorr it was Wilkins who, in 1975, wrote the Times editorial (headlined "Selling Secrets") punctiliously denouncing Schorr for having published the secret House Select Intelligence Committee report in The Village Voice. Daniel Schorr, Clearing the Air (Boston: Houghton Mifflin, 1977), pp. 208–209.
18. Paley, As It Happened, p. 304.
19. Epstein, News from Nowhere, p. 192.
20. Ibid., p. 76, quoting from the transcript of the Public Broadcast Laboratory's "The Whole World's Watching," December 22, 1968, p. 68.

Frank's words are revealing. Those "best lights" were the routine ("almost conditioned") news procedures, the standard code, now maybe "subject to review" at higher levels—levels higher than Frank's, that is to say; levels above the news operation as a whole. But self-censorship was not sufficiently reliable to mute the reporting of militancy. According to Epstein, by January 1969, the time of the Nixon inauguration, full-fledged censorship was in force at NBC. Epstein writes that the movement's "counterinauguration" was simply ignored:

NBC gave strict orders that there was to be no live or film coverage of the "counterinauguration," which was being held by antiwar dissidents; and NBC News relayed orders to its field producers, editors, correspondents and camera crews not to cover or film any of these protests unless they actually disrupted official ceremonies. The demonstrations, and the few violent incidents that did occur, were thus not shown on the NBC network.[21]

I know of no such explicit instructions at CBS News. But at whatever level these matters were decided, and with whatever degree of self-censorship, CBS News framed its scanty coverage of the disruptions by apologizing to viewers for having to bring the bad tidings.[22]

During that winter, in fact, there is evidence of more than one instance of political pressure effectively applied to the CBS network to see that the prevailing frame was managed in the interest of political moderation. Late in 1968, CBS News decided to film an explanatory takeout on the long strike for black and Third World demands at San Francisco State College. According to the producer:

That came about because [CBS News President] Dick Salant asked the right question. Every day or two, the L.A. bureau would give us a minute of headbeating. So finally Salant asked: "What is *wrong* out there?" I was sent out to split off [the correspondent] from daily headbeating coverage, and to find out what was wrong.[23]

The correspondent and the producer worked on the piece for two weeks, interviewing all the principals. After all this and much discussion, they jointly located the root of the problem in the racial inequities of the California Master Plan for Higher Education, just as the strike leadership had done. They filmed a sequence showing

21. Ibid.
22. Hodgson, *America in Our Time*, p. 376.
23. Interview, Ron Bonn, November 19, 1976.

the correspondent explaining the Master Plan—a lecture complete with blackboard inside "one of hundreds of empty classrooms at San Francisco State." (The Hayakawa administration at the college had been denying that the strike was effective.) "What's behind the turmoil" was racial stratification, he told the camera. CBS News ended up with an unusually long piece, over fifteen minutes of film, to be broadcast in two parts, on two successive nights. On January 23, 1969, the first segment, including the lecture on the Master Plan, was aired on the Cronkite News.

The political flak was instant and thick. In a letter to the author just afterward, a CBS employee in a position to know reflected:

This organization is extremely sensitive to criticism, particularly when it is put in the form of a specific critique and coupled with a demand for equal time. The Trustees (Dumke, Luckman) were furious. Reagan was speechless. Hayakawa scornful.[24]

The second half of the piece was not aired on January 24 as planned. Instead, the correspondent was sent back to San Francisco State to report evenhandedly that "the revolutionary left" and "the angry, conservative trustees" were equivalently obstructionist and mutually reinforcing. His new, revised emphasis came down in behalf of "what has been called the silent majority, the uncommitted students who would settle for a peaceful campus and an opportunity to pick up normal college life."[25] The new ending, labeled as "an important lesson . . . for many students all across America now trying to make up their own minds about the issues at San Francisco State," was a homily addressed to the nation using the standardized truth-lies-somewhere-in-between formula:

The middle ground, that silent majority of students, has not been heard through most of this conflct, so that silent moderates at other schools may now be concerned that unless they find their own voice, unless they develop their own leaders and find new ways of promoting reform, then America's higher education may be faced with destruction in the kind of death struggle between left and right now going on at San Francisco State.

One of the cameramen on the story remembers: "All of a sudden we were shooting stuff that we hadn't been shooting before. [The correspondent] was obviously getting flak over it. . . . I remember

24. Letter to the author, February 10, 1969.
25. This quotation and the next two are from pp. 15 and 16 of a transcript of the CBS Evening News of January 28, 1969. © 1969 CBS Inc. All rights reserved.

feeling that he was watering the thing down, that he was backing and filling a lot, that he was trying to be all things to all people."[26] Five days after the first installment, the revised second half was aired. The aforementioned CBS employee wrote soon thereafter: "All the outside forces may have conspired to change the thrust of the report, but they should not have been allowed to distort the facts."[27]

The television news elite, under the network chiefs' guiding spirit, had resolved not to let themselves be vulnerable again as they had been in Chicago. At the same time, they were in the thick of reconsidering American policy in Vietnam after Tet. By accenting the difference between legitimate and illegitimate movements, by elevating the former and disparaging and/or withdrawing attention from the latter, they could work to restabilize American politics around a new moderate antiwar consensus, while remaining responsive to the administration's definition of the situation both in Vietnam and at home. Many months before Vice-President Agnew was unleashed against the media, the networks were working—most likely informally and undeliberately—to regulate themselves along these lines. At CBS as elsewhere, correspondents would learn that the limits of the permissible were being redrawn. If the grapevine did not inform them, they would learn simply by watching the news;[28] they would not repeat the mistake made in the first installment on San Francisco State. That November, Vice-President Agnew would ask the rhetorical question, "How many marches and demonstrations would we have if the marchers did not know that the ever-faithful TV cameras would be there to record their antics for the next news show?" In his textbook on network news, CBS Senior Vice-President and News Director William Small did not ask how many vice-presidential speeches we would have without the cameras. Instead, Small assured his readers, "as time went on, television reporters as others made careful measure of these [movement] efforts and bent over backwards at times to have balance."[29] One way to "bend over backwards" was to scant militancy, to stress moderation, and to

26. Interview, Stephen Lighthill, June 16, 1977.
27. Letter to the author, February 10, 1969.
28. Jeremy Tunstall's point about newspapers is transferable to television: "The function [of transmitting policy to journalists] is . . . performed in the columns of the paper itself" (Tunstall, *Journalists at Work* [London: Constable, 1971], p. 46).
29. Small, *To Kill a Messenger*, p. 132. Small is the CBS official who fired Daniel Schorr for releasing the Pike Committee report.

play one against the other. A fine balancing act indeed, to satisfy influential liberals on the one hand and Nixonian censors—who were not given to fine distinctions among "enemies"—on the other.

MORATORIUM AND MOBILIZATION

From elevating the silent majority to elevating the moderate, respectable, "responsible" minority was not a great distance. The moderate antiwar movement went on growing under Nixon, and soon imposed a new set of choices on the media. In the spring of 1969, for example, David Hawk, who had worked in the McCarthy campaign and who was himself a draft resister, helped organize a draft-resistance protest on the part of student government leaders. The media coverage, Hawk remembers, was favorable, like that of the "McCarthy kids," but likewise canted in a stereotypic way: "To the consternation of many of those students, there was a distinction being made [by the media] between them and the freaks and hippies."[30]

Over the summer, Hawk and Sam Brown conceived the idea of the Moratorium: for one day in October, two days in November, and so on as long as possible, they would organize a range of decentralized no-business-as-usual antiwar actions around the country. Hawk and Brown started with the spring draft-resisting student government people; this gave them a campus base. Then, as Hawk tells the story, they began holding briefing sessions for sympathetic reporters whom they knew from the McCarthy campaign. Because of their involvement with McCarthy, they were considered "credible." By telling reporters, "This is what students are going to do in the fall," they got some articles written. Hawk and Brown made photocopies and sent them around to campuses with the message: "See, this is what's going to be happening in the fall." "It made us seem sort of real," Hawk says. In language strikingly like Rennie Davis's, he says this strategy was "sort of like building with mirrors." "It was very calculating," Hawk reflects, "and it worked."

Another Moratorium organizer also remembers that the press treated them as "very cute" and "acceptable"—especially when compared with "the radicals."[31] It was no small help that liberal

30. This and the following quotations are from my interview with David Hawk, November 12, 1976.
31. Interview, Susan Werbe, November 15, 1976.

Democrats and Republicans, including senators and other elected officials, were flocking to the antiwar standard, lending their legitimacy to preparations for the October Moratorium. Brown and the other Moratorium organizers were able to provide reporters with regular bursts of news, as respectables like John V. Lindsay, Averell Harriman, and Senator Charles Goodell announced their support. One CBS News staff member who covered many of the Washington press conferences that fall confirms the importance of these names:

I could tell what was news. If they said, "We have 75 union leaders who've signed a petition, including a guy who's head of the municipal workers, . . . Jerry Wurf," sure. But six kids who have the power to call a news conference because it's close to a march, no.[32]

The Moratorium press conferences were a distinct contrast to the press conferences of the more radical Mobilization coalition: the Mobilization had no celebrities to offer, and reporters tended to see their many spokespersons as slingers of unnewsworthy rhetoric:

The news conferences that the Trots [Socialist Workers Party] used to have, where they would stand up there and talk about—what's the phrase they used to use?—talk about "the trade union movement." . . . They would all start with their little raps: "The working class this and that." They didn't know a working person from their elbow.

Reporters, thinking "there was a major story breaking," spent a goodly amount of time with Sam Brown and David Hawk of the Moratorium. It was no small factor that the reporters assigned to the Moratorium were, or seemed to Hawk to be, especially sympathetic. "By that time, the press corps was pretty dovish," Hawk says, partly because of the shock of Tet, partly because the Republican administration was less effectively solicitous of their good will than the Democrats who had previously administered the war, and partly because of personal sympathies. Even at ABC, traditionally the most conservative network, by 1970 most of the correspondents and news executives personally opposed the war.[33] By the time of the Cambodia invasion in the spring of 1970, the three networks brought to public hearing a total of eight doves and no hawks.[34] (All the administration had speaking in its behalf was the

32. This quotation and the next are from my interview with a CBS employee who wishes to remain anonymous.
33. Interview, former ABC News writer Carolyn Craven, October 27, 1976.
34. Robert Cirino, *Power to Persuade* (New York: Bantam Books, 1974), p. 195.

fait accompli of the invasion.) One content analysis of war coverage argues that certainly by 1972 network news was tilted definitively against the war.[35] Without question, dovishness—even the most Establishment-minded sort which television was partial to—tipped over into sympathy for the Moratorium. In 1969, CBS had just begun using pictorial logos, visual tags, to label continuing stories, and their symbol for the antiwar "story" was a dove looking very much like the Moratorium's symbol. Before the first big Moratorium day, October 15, 1969, newspapers began to publicize the upcoming demonstrations, giving the dates and schedules of the varied events. (As we saw in Part I, above, they did not do so for the SDS antiwar march of April 1965.) The media were amplifying the moderate alternative to militancy, willy-nilly.

In the process, of course, they were far from inventing the distinction between moderates and militants (or radicals). Both segments of the antiwar movement had their own reasons for polarizing. The Moratorium drew attention quite deliberately to its relative moderation. "We were frightened of the militancy of the student strikes," David Hawk says, "and we wanted to communicate that that was not the character of the Moratorium. And that worked." The Moratorium "came across constructive and gentle."[36] Coverage before and during the Moratorium events emphasized the range of activities, the size of crowds, and the wide range and respectability of supporters, though it was also at pains to relay (skeptically) President Nixon's mild, politic disdain ("whistling in the dark", CBS's Dan Rather called it) and the insistence of Republicans that the President wanted peace too and that demonstrators of good will were being used by Hanoi and other Communist regimes. On October 13, NBC Nightly News led with a 2½-minute introduction, asserting that the Moratorium had spread "through a broad representation of nearly all elements of American society." They read the President's letter which insisted that he would not

35. Ernest Lefever, *TV and National Defense: An Analysis of CBS News 1972–1973* (Boston, Va.: Institute for American Strategy, 1974), cited by Michael J. Robinson, "American Political Legitimacy in an Era of Electronic Journalism: Reflections on the Evening News," in Douglass Cater and Richard Adler, eds., *Television as a Social Force: New Approaches to TV Criticism* (New York: Praeger, 1975), p. 138. The nature of television coverage of the Vietnam war, much commented on and not so much studied systematically, is being investigated by Professor Lawrence Lichty of the Department of Communication at the University of Wisconsin, Madison, and by Dan Hallin of the Political Science Department at the University of California, Berkeley.

36. Interview, David Hawk, November 12, 1976.

be influenced, but they pointed out that Nixon was in fact responding by issuing the letter and what they accurately called "other public relations devices."[37] The Moratorium was being legitimated.

CBS News coverage bulked large: the Moratorium and reactions to it took up most of the Evening News on both October 14 and 15.[38] One recurrent theme threading through CBS's coverage was one of those verbal oppositions that TV news prefers: spokesmen of the Right professed concern that well-intentioned marchers were being used by Communist manipulators, while the demonstrators denied the relevance of the distinctions and said they smelled red herrings. On the Cronkite news of October 14, for example, Agnew's distinction-making from the White House—"The leaders and sponsors of tomorrow's Moratorium, public officials and others leading these demonstrations, should openly repudiate the support of a totalitarian government which has on its hands the blood of 40,000 Americans"—was followed immediately by Roger Mudd's wrap-up: "Tonight the Moratorium headquarters here accused the Nixon administration of trying to discredit the patriotism of millions of Americans who sincerely desire peace." In Chicago, U.S. Attorney Thomas Foran was quoted as accusing the Chicago 7 defendants of "trying to turn the Moratorium into a violent rampage":

It is a situation like last week when some of these defendants participated in activities with the Weatherman group of SDS, who announced that their protest was the war in Vietnam. These men who offered to support that group now intend to corrupt what may well be a sincere effort of many American citizens to protest the war.

Foran was then answered by defendant Tom Hayden:

All he could say was that these people . . . somehow are involved with Weatherman and they want to be cut loose so that they can destroy the Moratorium. This is what he said last year. Well, I think this is the threadbare politics of the Johnson administration, now picked up by the Nixon administration and put forward by their puppet, Foran, over and over simply as a means to avoid the fact that this country is just coming to a stop over the war in Vietnam.

---

37. NBC Nightly News, October 13, 1969, as reported in notes taken by Dan Hallin.

38. The following quotations are all taken from transcripts of the CBS Evening News for October 14, 15, and 16, 1969. © 1969 CBS Inc. All rights reserved. I am indebted to Dan Hallin's notes from his own viewings of these broadcasts.

On October 15 itself, Walter Cronkite introduced the Moratorium as "dramatic" and "historic in its scope." He pointed out that it sought immediate withdrawal from Vietnam, and he stressed its large numbers but observed that the total size of its support was unknown. "With scattered exceptions," Cronkite said, "the Moratorium was a dignified, responsible protest, in its sponsors' words, and appealed to the conscience of the American people"; he also cited examples of contrasting irresponsibility by antiwar extremists. In one of the film reports that followed, a soldier at Fort Benning, where the headquarters building had been painted overnight with peace symbols, was interviewed: "My personal opinion is that dissent and demonstration in a democratic society, if it's constructive and positive, is a good thing. On the other hand, I don't have any sympathy with professional agitators or violence merchants." In another film report, the correspondent said: "SDS had its origins on this campus, but today's Michigan protest was different, peaceful, within the law, not confined to a radical minority." (It was true that SDS had its origins in Ann Arbor, but not that its origins had been anything other than peaceful.)

ABC News, meanwhile, framed the Moratorium as vague first and large second. Anchorman Howard K. Smith began his introduction:

The word "Moratorium," applied to war debts after World War I and bank deposits during the Depression, means an agreement to postpone payment. It has never been clear how it applies to Vietnam. However, today it covered such a wide range of expressions of dislike for the war that its very vagueness seemed proper.

Smith noted that Senator Edward Kennedy's antiwar proposal was like Nixon's policy, and noted: "If they're not careful they may blunder into agreement." Only later on did he get to the theme of representativeness, which had dominated the other network reports: "The word 'protestor' generally evokes an image of long hair and love beads. But today the crowds that marched and chanted and cheered looked more like a cross-section picked by the census bureau." [39] ABC covered most fully (though CBS and NBC did not ignore) the pro-Nixon and pro-war demonstrations and speeches around the country. Overall, the boost to the Moratorium from so many reports from so many places was enormous. Even where the

39. ABC Nightly News, October 15, 1969, as reported in notes taken by Dan Hallin.

news treatment was less than flattering, the Barnum effect was operating.

But in one sense Howard K. Smith was right: after October 15 the Moratorium was in danger of losing whatever sharp definition it had achieved. Its approach was under siege from two directions: from the Left, and from the White House. Independently, the co-alition known as the Mobilization, or "Mobe"—a continuation of the coalition that had sponsored the 1967 Pentagon and 1968 Chicago actions—had been working since the summer for a large Washington demonstration on November 15. Especially after Nixon's November 3 "Vietnamization" speech made plain that his "secret plan" for ending the war was to continue it more quietly, the Moratorium organizers realized their grass-roots supporters would want to get to Washington for the Mobe demonstration. So the Moratorium joined in, submerging its localist strategy for the moment and taking major responsibility for the march.

Now the line of moderate-versus-militant demarcation began to shift. Gradually over the next month, the major media found themselves less interested in the boundary between Mobe and Moratorium than in the relation of both to a third force: a Justice Department demonstration being organized separately by Abbie Hoffman and others of the Chicago 7. The preeminent theme was now: Is there going to be violence on November 15? Thus, Bruce Morton's CBS News report on October 16 stated the Moratorium-Mobe dichotomy and then directed it quietly into a more forbidding nonviolent-violent dichotomy. Observe the flow of his report:

The Moratorium won't be the only demonstration, though. A group with a somewhat more rigid ideology, the New Mobilization to End the War, is planning a mass march on Washington November 15th. A Student Mobilization Committee plans a campus strike to precede that march. All these groups have their national offices in one building, and all say they are co-operating with each other and will keep cooperating. But the possibility of splits in the protest movement is there. The Moratorium's leaders were pleased most by two things—the size of their turnout, and the peace which prevailed. But already some more radical groups are forecasting more violent tactics if the war continues.

The White House, meanwhile, was working to tar the *entire* demonstration with the "more violent" brush. The typical *New York Times* story of the week preceding November 15 preserved this distinction. For example, on the front page of the previous Sunday edition there appeared the following statement:

The Justice Department announced last week that it had intelligence information showing that a number of militant, though generally unidentified groups, were planning to create confrontations with authorities during the demonstrations. Leaders of the mobilization, however, contend that they are making every effort to keep the activities peaceful.[40]

But according to a member of the Mobe steering committee, "a lot of [the Moratorium people] in fact believed what was being said in the newspapers, that we were going to become violent."[41]

For their part, many antiwar militants in SDS and other groups had been just as interested in distinguishing themselves from moderates as moderates had been in distinguishing themselves from militants. From 1968 through the Moratorium and after, radicals commonly felt that the mobilizing moderates were Johnny-come-latelies who were "blunting the radical cutting edge" of the antiwar movement. In Chicago during convention week, New Left approaches to "the McCarthy kids" were mixed, with early and late SDS generations dividing sharply; former SDS president Carl Oglesby wrote a densely argued and widely circulated appeal, taking seriously the antiwar feelings of liberals and attempting to turn them against the Cold War as a whole; while the incumbent National Secretary Mike Klonsky made a denunciatory, liberal-baiting speech in Grant Park just after McCarthy supporters had been mauled by the same Chicago police who had been beating radicals. The wall poster published by the unofficial but influential SDS Movement Center said: "Those of us who have been in the streets for the past five days didn't give a flying fuck whether McCarthy would win or lose; and now that he's lost, still don't."[42] As SDS hardened, so did its view of liberals. Mark Rudd wrote in *The Movement* that the Columbia rebellion of 1968 had answered "the McCarthy threat."[43] In the same spirit, when the Moratorium operation started up, a majority of the Mobe steering committee saw the Moratorium "more as a threat than as an addition to the anti-war movement." Like the SDS bitter-enders, they feared los-

40. *New York Times,* November 9, 1969, p. 1.
41. Interview, Douglas Dowd, June 23, 1977.
42. Quoted in Kirkpatrick Sale, *SDS* (New York: Random House, 1973), p. 475.
43. Mark Rudd, "Notes on Columbia," *The Movement,* March 1969, p. 7.

ing the only base they could halfway claim, the aroused antiwar campuses. But through the fall, the bitter-end position weakened. Within the Mobilization, according to steering committee member Douglas Dowd, "the anti-Moratorium was initially a majority position and it ended up as being a very small minority." [44]

During the November 15 Mobilization itself, the strategy of dissident militants was to capitalize on the publicity attending the Mobe by creating events off to the side of the main events. Expressing their anger by trashing at the Saigon embassy or throwing rocks at the Justice Department, they would try to claim the spotlight and fill it with images of sweeping "revolutionary" militancy. Distrusted by the Mobe, they wanted to display their anger. What they performed was, in fact, high theatre. When Martha Mitchell said that one teargassed demonstration near her Watergate apartment reminded her of the Bolshevik Revolution, she was honoring the success of a theatrical event, not a political tactic. In promoting these spin-off operations, the militants were playing their appointed roles in what they did not know was the strategy of the Nixon White House.

It is abundantly clear now that *the White House was the only one of the protagonists which consistently wanted the lines blurred between moderates and militants*. It was not only in Nixon's *imputed* interest to blur the line, to implicate antiwar moderates in the most provocative tactics of the militants; it was deliberate strategy. If the White House could discredit the moderates, it might win back the disgruntled centrist forces—men like Senator Jacob Javits, for example, who had supported the October 15 Moratorium. Nixon's November 3 "Vietnamization" speech was the carrot in the "game plan"; Spiro Agnew's November 13 Des Moines speech against the media was the stick. Good cop, bad cop: the roles were divided up all fall, sometimes sharing speechwriters, as the White House consistently refused to disavow Agnew. Thanks to Jeb Magruder's post-Watergate memoir, we know something of the secret tactics. Here is a passage from White House Appointment Secretary Dwight Chapin's memo to H. R. Haldeman, "The 'Peace' Movement and November 15," written October 16, the day after the first Moratorium:

44. The last two quotations are from my interview with Douglas Dowd, June 23, 1977.

Following our discussion in the car tonight, the objective is to isolate the radical leaders of the "moratorium" event and the leaders of the "Mobilization" committee. *They are one and the same* and their true purpose should be exposed. At the same time, those people who are loyal to the country and who have been disillusioned by the war should be pulled back into the fold of national consciousness.

Chapin's memo went on to propose a week-by-week "Action Timetable," including "a full-fledged drive . . . against the media" and an orchestration of high-level activity against the November 15 Mobilization committee, including:

October 17 to 20. . . . 1. Congressmen and Senators who endorsed the October 15 activity are approached by moderates within their parties—told not to rush off on the November 15 thing—it is different. . . .[45]

3. The Cabinet, agency heads and other appropriate officials should be given some facts about the November 15 mobilization groups—they should start talking it down in private situations. . . .

October 20-26. . . . A representative of the Justice Department and a spokesman for the FBI should hold a press conference on Monday, October 20. They would brief the press with documented information on the leaders of the two movements [i.e., the Mobe and the Moratorium].[46]

This memo also proposed that the President busy himself with football on November 15. Magruder tells us: "The President largely followed Chapin's game plan."[47]

So the Nixon administration had set out to blur liberal-radical lines in order to condemn the whole antiwar movement and to mobilize a "silent majority" against it. Agnew's neologism "radiclib" was the name for that fused opposition. In the main, meanwhile, the big media were trying to keep the lines distinct, in effect defying the White House strategy. The clash of frames could be rather blatant, as witness this exchange between CBS's Bruce Morton and Vice-President Agnew on the CBS Evening News, October 22:

45. Presumably some of the "difference" had to do with the prospect of violence, i.e., the stone-throwing that was to materialize at the Justice Department building. The Moratorium would be tarred with the brush of the Mobilization and the Chicago defendants.

46. Quoted in Jeb Stuart Magruder, *An American Life: One Man's Road to Watergate* (New York: Atheneum, 1974), p. 81.

47. But where Chapin had urged Nixon to attend a game in person, Nixon instead let it be known that he was watching a game on television. No doubt inadvertently, Nixon was symbolically confirming that the televised version of a game is functionally "as good" as the "real" thing.

MORTON: Sir, you did, I think, characterize the leaders of the Moratorium as dissidents and anarchists. These are mostly people out of the McCarthy campaign. Is that your view of that wing of politics in this country?

AGNEW: Well, I think that some of the leaders are clearly anarchistic. For example, the New Mobilization Committee has a member of the Communist Party on its—among its leadership. The young students are dissident, yes. I wouldn't call them anarchistic. I think they're very poorly led, although well motivated.[48]

On November 13 and 14, the first two days of antiwar events in Washington, CBS went on treating Mobilization and Moratorium events as well-mannered and nonviolent, which by all accounts they were. On November 13, after a report on the March Against Death (from Arlington National Cemetery to the White House) to remember the war dead, the main CBS report was on a parade marshal's training school. The correspondent's lead-in was clear: "Lesson for the day: we are here for peace, we do not seek violence, we do not want it, but if it happens we will try to cool it." There followed an unusually long "take" of the instructor's lesson in nonviolence.[49] On the 14th, Harry Reasoner, sitting in for Walter Cronkite, opened with: "The nationwide protest against the war, now in its second day, has been distinguished so far by nonviolence." The March Against Death was again the lead and longest component. Then Bruce Morton reported that three hundred paratroopers had been moved into the Justice Department building because "it was at Justice that the closest thing to trouble came, a demonstration sponsored by the Yippies, not the Mobilization, directed not against the war but against the Chicago trial of seven radical leaders." From New York, Robert Schakne reported on a Central Park rally:

It was, surely, a different kind of antiwar protest. The principal symbol: black balloons, to represent American soldiers who had died this year in Vietnam. American flags, quite deliberately, were conspicuous by their presence, to make the point that those who oppose the war are as patriotic

48. Transcript, CBS Evening News, October 22, 1969. © 1969 CBS Inc. All rights reserved. White House correspondent Robert Pierpoint went on to say that "Agnew is emerging as the Nixon Administration's hatchet man," and that Nixon was "enjoying the political benefits of both worlds," of both Agnew's and "softer voices." As Agnew was defining a seamless Left, Pierpoint was defining a seamless White House.

49. Ibid., November 13, 1969. © 1969 CBS Inc. All rights reserved.

as those who support it. The crowd was overwhelmingly but not exclusively young, the sponsors many of those who had worked in the McCarthy and Kennedy campaigns. . . .[50]

But the media's own routine processes—always the stress on conflict!—blurred the clear boundary. On the CBS Evening News of November 15, the rowdy Justice Department demonstration was the news-tail that wagged the dog. Though only a tiny percentage of the half million antiwar demonstrators in Washington went to the Justice Department, where a minority of a minority threw projectiles and broke windows and hurled back police tear gas, this peripheral demonstration was CBS's lead story—over the objections of many CBS people, including the anchorman, Roger Mudd. According to a CBS staff member who was in the newsroom that night, the lead was explained by the fact that "there were terrific pictures and sometimes—sometimes and not very often—that does determine what's on." [51] My source for this tale asks: "What's more important, that a bunch of scruffy people charge the Justice Department, or that that many people [the 500,000 of the main body of the demonstration] were in one place at the same time to sing?" Frames were in conflict, and the scruffiness-and-violence frame overcame the clean-cut image. For David Hawk, this coverage was "mixed" and "muddied": "It just came out mushy." [52]

This muddied product had the effect of satisfying the White House's script; so did the fact that this coverage of the largest demonstrations in American history was on film, not live. Moratorium leaders had expected it to be live, as might be expected. So too had CBS reporters. Indeed, when I got to New York City seven years later to research this book with CBS News staff, I called one contact and told him I was looking at the way CBS handled antiwar activity in the sixties. Before I had a chance to say another word, he exclaimed: "If you're asking me why CBS didn't cover the Moratorium live in 1969, I can't tell you." Another source, former CBS correspondent Daniel Schorr, told me that in the CBS News Washington bureau it had been "a normal assumption" that the Moratorium would be covered live: "Clearly everybody knew that not

50. Ibid., November 14, 1969. © 1969 CBS Inc. All rights reserved.

51. Interview with a CBS employee who wishes to remain anonymous. Unfortunately, CBS News does not have transcripts of the November 15 (Saturday) broadcast.

52. Interview, David Hawk, November 12, 1976.

covering that live was a command decision."[53] Others in CBS have confirmed this assumption.

If, in the judgment of reporters on the scene, the November Moratorium warranted live coverage, why did CBS News make a decision counter to the prevailing news judgment? For one thing, live news coverage is expensive in commercials lost from regular programs. But it was not only live coverage that the network avoided; the bulk and scope of filmed coverage shrank. Late on the night of October 15, CBS had broadcast a special half-hour report of the Moratorium; they did not do so on the night of November 15. What had changed since October? For one thing, TV news subjects itself to what Stanhope Gould calls the "we've done it" syndrome; the network news people are loath to repeat themselves.[54] But whether the "story" had changed or not since October 15 was a matter of interpretation; war news was reported incessantly although "we've done it." The Moratorium and Mobilization had worked together despite tensions to pull off the largest demonstration in American history. As we have seen, this prospect was immensely displeasing to the administration. The other thing that had changed was the administration's strategy toward (or as the Chapin memo put it, "against") the media. On November 4, the new FCC chairman, Dean Burch, had called up the heads of

53. Interview, Daniel Schorr, May 3, 1977.—This may not have been the first time such a "command decision" was made at CBS. The late Bill Greeley of *Variety*, the entertainment industry's trade journal, reported that unnamed officials of CBS "called the other networks to kill off any live or special coverage of the peace march on the Pentagon" in October 1967 ("Progress in Viet War Coverage [Airing Once-Nixed Film A Sign of the 'Times']," *Variety*, June 28, 1972, pp. 1, 61). Greeley mentioned other acts of censorship against antimilitarist probing during the Johnson years, including CBS's killing of "producer Jay McMullen's proposal for a telementary on corruption in Saigon after months of research" and turning "a telementary launched by producer Gene De Poris on the military-industrial complex into a primer on rocketry." (The former quote is consistent with Alexander Kendrick's statement to me [November 17, 1976] that he was prevented from reporting in any depth on political and economic factors in Saigon in 1966: the cameramen wanted only "blood and guts," and the producers in New York were only interested in graft scandals involving Vietnamese generals.)

Greeley suggested that these "aborted projects" could be laid at the door of the network's "close ties with President Lyndon B. Johnson." Those ties were indeed real and, in the Johnson style, personal. (See below, p. 276.) But since self-censorship in war and antiwar coverage continued under Nixon, who lacked such intimate relations with media chiefs, we must conclude that personal relations are only one method by which the White House may maintain media compliance when the normal, hegemonic routines do not suffice; intimidation is a functional equivalent. For more on these matters, see Part III.

54. Interview, Stanhope Gould, November 13, 1976.

the three networks and asked them personally for transcripts of the previous day's "instant analyses" following Nixon's speech. It was utterly unprecedented for the FCC to intrude upon the networks so directly. Then, on November 13, Spiro T. Agnew gave the first of his speeches against the Eastern media. It stretches credulity to believe that these events had no bearing on the CBS decision not to cover the November 15 march live and not to give it extra coverage that night. The Nixonian crusade against the media might also have some bearing on the unusual circumstance that, *despite the anchorman's protest*, the Justice Department demonstration, with its clouds of tear gas immensely pleasing to Haldeman & Co., ran as the lead story on CBS News that night.

The *New York Times* of November 16, meanwhile, ran a three-tier banner headline on page one upholding the moderate-militant boundary: "250,000 PROTESTERS STAGE PEACEFUL RALLY IN WASHINGTON: MILITANTS STIR CLASHES LATER." Max Frankel's separate interpretive story on the front page, "Parade Marshals Keep It Cool," underscored the distinction with an explicit contrast between the daylight Mobe marchers ("all smiles") and the nighttime militants ("the radical minority that has been spoiling for a fight"). "The mean or just plain rowdy here this weekend," Frankel wrote, "have been flotsam on a sea of serene people who frown upon all violence, in Vietnam or Washington." Photography produced a discordant image: a four-column photo showing two NLF flags (no longer "Viet Cong" flags by 1969) prominently and much larger than scale in the foreground, captioned: "Demonstrators at foot of the Washington Monument. Some wave flag of National Liberation Front of South Vietnam." Still, for the most part, the *Times* maintained the essential distinction, as witness two other front-page headlines: "TEAR GAS REPELS RADICALS' ATTACK," on the one hand, and "More Than 100,000 on Coast Demonstrate in Moderate Vein," on the other.[55]

Interestingly, this same polarization between peaceful marchers and violent militants also framed British TV and newspaper coverage of the giant anti–Vietnam War demonstration in London in October 1968. The British media almost universally construed the situation just as the American media did in 1969, speculating in advance about whether violence would take place, then playing up

55. Note the similarity between the *Times*'s coverage of the 1969 Mobilization and its coverage of the SANE antiwar march of 1965 (pp. 117–119, above).

the "violent" side march against a U.S. government building (the U.S. Embassy, in this case), and setting it against the peaceful and much larger main demonstration.[56] This framing prevailed in both ITV and BBC news, suggesting that direct commercial considerations cannot account for these emphases. We shall have to look further, to the media's *political* functions and constraints in the managing of opposition within liberal capitalist societies.

ROUTINES AND STEREOTYPES

Direct and deliberate political news management to achieve a particular political result has its importance; I have not dwelled on episodes of heavy-handedness in order to dismiss their significance. In Part III, I shall look more carefully and generally at the relation between extraordinary interventions and routine practices in determining the news. But I want to close this discussion by stressing again the force of the *routine* news frames and their consequences for the New Left. It seems probable that the impression and then the actuality of polarization between militants and moderates was deepened by media treatment. This for technical, structural, and political reasons. *Technically*, for one thing, the spotlight is a resource essentially limited in quantity. There are only so many minutes of news time on the Evening News; and although the *New York Times* or any other paper can add pages for late or important news, there are only so many column inches on the front page. To the extent that moderation took the spotlight, militants lost it, and felt the loss. The loss gave them another incentive to intensify their militancy: to keep or to get back the spotlight. There was, in other words, a rivalry built into the scarcity of the media attention defined as necessary by antiwar activists.

And brevity leads to stereotyping. The media oversimplify reality in order to make it easily digestible. The actual brevity of television news—an entire Cronkite News broadcast, if set in type, would take up about a column and a half in the *New York Times*—is superimposed upon producers' and reporters' prevailing conception of their audience as weary, impatient, and uneducated. What results is the construction of simplistic packages around events. This happened today; it is this type of phenomenon (a "peaceful" demonstration, "encouraging" statistics, "useful" negotiations), not that

56. See James D. Halloran, Philip Elliott, and Graham Murdock, *Demonstrations and Communication: A Case Study* (Harmondsworth, England: Penguin Books, 1970).

("violent," "discouraging," "failed"); it is good, says X; it is bad, says Y; it will mean thus-and-such—all this in ninety seconds or so. By the *structure* of its format and assumptions alone, television emerges with cartoonlike stick-figure representations. The subtleties of situations and processes go under.[57] Correspondents are often new to the story, since there are so few correspondents, so few camera crews, and so many potential stories. Furthermore, the correspondents are often chosen for their star quality, not their knowledge or talent. Moderate versus militant was a convenient peg for a reporter in a hurry.

And, moreover, the chain of political interventions we have detailed, over and above all the normal factors, had the effect of making demonstration violence a central theme of the coverage; probably this increased the salience of the moderate-militant divisions, especially in the eyes of uncommitted audiences without independent information about actual differences on the Left. For this compound of reasons, a simple opposition of moderate versus militant—as if these were two timeless categories with little content and less history—was the most convenient packaging. That oversimplified dichotomizing *coincided with, and reinforced, the sloganizing and polarization of a frustrated and contained opposition movement.*

We spiral back to the movement's own failure. The movement was *doubly* contained: partly by the conventionalized definition —packaged, stereotyped, and mass-distributed by the media—of militancy as an alternative to moderation; and partly by its own insistence on revolutionism. As opposition to the war became more widespread and legitimate, as moderates came to speak of unilateral Amercian withdrawal from Vietnam, much of the radical movement that had tried to articulate and focus that opposition found itself curiously stranded and desperate, frantically summoning up extravagant political world views about a coming revolution to explain and justify that feeling to themselves. Lacking a sufficient political base, the flamboyant sects resorted to the engine of revolutionary will—which gave them no political base, no political resonance, but a disproportionate access to the media. Other sects stood more stolidly (and Stalinistically) for the revolutionary need to organize the working class, and were not eager for the spotlight;

57. On stereotyping in television news generally, see Todd Gitlin, "Spotlights and Shadows: Television and the Culture of Politics," *College English* 38 (April 1977): 789–801.

they were taking refuge in quasi-Bolshevist fantasies about the prospect for a revolutionary working class in the United States. As the media oversimplified the texture of the Left, the complexity of its identity and its ideas, so did many activists strive to strip away their own complexity. Irony upon irony: amidst growing antiwar feeling, amidst active (if often amorphous) social disaffection in the Army, in high schools, among women and minorities, the core of the late New Left was effectively contained, protesting all the while that its revolutionary credentials were in order.

8 Contracting Time and Eclipsing Context

ON DISCONTINUITY AND
THE DECONTEXTUALIZATION OF EXPERIENCE

Television did not invent radical movements or demonstrations. Neither did the daily press. The French Revolution preceded all the forms of modern communication and propaganda, even daily newspapers. The Russian and Chinese Revolutions took place without broadcasting. But the system of mass communication was and is important in helping to shape a specific environment for movements of opposition: the media belong to, shape, and are shaped by a modern society that generates a new order of experience. One thing that is modern, Marx and Baudelaire both recognized in their own ways, is a new sense of time, a new velocity of experience, a new vertigo.[1] When T. S. Eliot wrote, "We had the experience but we missed the meaning," he was speaking partly of the loss of traditional concepts of time and, conjointly, the mass availability of synthetic meanings. The synthetic timetables and images of the modern world suffuse and throw into question our knowledge of the real. The mass media routinize this "missing" and then not only propound meanings for experience but actually help constitute it. One of the most striking effects of the whole media system on the texture of modern life lies in its reconstruction of the experience of time.

For the New Left, of course, an eery and delusory contraction of

1. See Marshall Berman, "'All That Is Solid Melts into Air': Marxism, Modernism, Modernization," *Dissent* 25 (Winter 1978): 54–73.

time followed directly from the momentum of the war and the repression, and from the hermetic quality of movement experience. Inside the movement, one had the sense of being hurled through a time-tunnel, of hurtling from event to event without the time to learn from experience. Even outside the movement, people everywhere defended against the dizzying sense of onrushing time, the bombardment of incomprehensible events, by straining after a simplified political universe; "Smiling through the Apocalypse," *Esquire* entitled a collection of essays. Within the movement, one felt one was living several lifetimes, sometimes simultaneously, sometimes end to end, within a few years. Mark Rudd's "Organizing is just another name for going slow" was the ultimate insult, and Rudd was not alone in thinking it. The media could also agree that gradual change was irrelevant to the larger rhythms of history.

Movement events conditioned the experience of time: one marked one's life experience by "Chicago," which signified *this*, by "People's Park," which signified *that*. Life came to seem a sequence of tenuously linked exclamation points. But what were the sentences between? This "event time," as Barrie Thorne calls it, entailed an experience of discontinuity and a loss of a sense of political reality, a loss of context. In this late-sixties rush, the mythic and real decontextualized violence which I've written about could flourish; almost everyone in the movement was losing track of what was politically actual and what was impossible. Not only was the war a constant spur to direct action, but the media, which the movement depended on to amplify opposition, were always hungry for novelty: hungry, precisely, for new events, new trends, new actions. The movement and the media were joined symbiotically in their quest for the novel. Stanhope Gould, speaking of network news producers' "we've done it" syndrome, remembers CBS News staff complaining in the early sixties: "Oh shit, we've got to lead with civil rights again."[2] The news's low tolerance for continuity might indeed, in some times and some places, effectively black out a movement event or diminish its coverage. If a movement were committed to publicity—and how could an antiwar movement not be committed to publicity?—it could not afford to take the chance of being overlooked. In the sixties, then, the media's "we've done it" syndrome, against the background of the war and the movement's attempt to end it, would itself have sufficed to

2. Interviews, Stanhope Gould, November 8 and 13, 1976.

force the movement to rush ahead conjuring up new and unprecedented events, one after another after another. The movement's "event time," in short, was coupled with the media's.

This weird symbiosis had immediate effects on the movement. Dependent on the spotlight, an organization like SDS or the anti-draft Resistance was artificially accelerated and, finally, stifled by the constant, wearing search for *something new*. The media's low tolerance for "staleness" helped rev up the movement pace, as Barrie Thorne contends in this account of the New England Resistance:

The effort to stay newsworthy also contributed to the fast-moving quality of Resistance events. After the first few draft card turn-ins, the form lost its novelty, not only to Resistance participants (who had gradually come to routinize the risk and had figured out what to expect) and to the government (which had worked out a mode of response), but also to the media. . . . [S]anctuaries, like draft card turn-ins, gradually lost their appeal. In March, 1969, a resister pointed to the way the media had lost interest in the draft resistance movement.

"Even if the Resistance doesn't affect the draft, some still hold that the act of resisting affects other people, this in itself being worthwhile. When I turned my draft card in on October 16, 1967, and when the first trials of Resistance members began, our acts received wide attention by the media (our acts being essentially media-oriented). But now card turn-ins, induction refusals, and trials have lost their dynamism and novelty. They are stuck in the 5-line blurb on page 39 of the paper or put between the weather and the sports on the evening newscast—if covered at all. Thus, the audience for our actions reverts back to the same sympathetic people we always talk to."[3]

As this resister concluded, one result of the "we've done it" syndrome, coupled with the movement's dependency on the media, was self-containment. Movement people started thinking like promoters, specialists in headlines. Was this project succeeding? Failing? What was real? There was no clear way to tell. The movement was desperate for concrete results in Vietnam, but it was up against a deceptive administration. It came to want "revolution," but it had no clear theory to tell it what that was, where it would come from, or how to recognize approaches to it or retreats from it. The pace of events, the rush of mass-mediated, distanced, and dis-

3. Barrie Thorne, "Resisting the Draft: An Ethnography of the Draft Resistance Movement" (unpublished Ph.D. dissertation, Brandeis University, 1971), pp. 341–342.

torted experience, helped disorient the movement, deprive it of a sense of political context. All one could measure clearly was the number of minutes one "got" on the Evening News. And finally: exhaustion. Not knowing what was real, the movement kept pushing nevertheless. In 1968, 1969, and 1970, the New Left was like the character in the Roadrunner cartoons who in his fervor and ignorance speeds over a cliff but keeps running, running, running—until he looks down and sees he is running on air. Then he crashes.

In all these ways the New Left entered into an intense, condensed version of the discontinuity of experience and the dissociation from reality which have characterized life in the modern West. Certainly the experience of discontinuity long predates television; but the mass media in general and television in particular deepen it. The historical process of modernization *is*, among other things, the development of a discontinuous public time-space. The city itself as a social and political entity is a discontinuity, a discordance. A walk down the main street of a major city in the nineteenth century was already a jarring—or enlivening—experience of social discontinuity. As Georg Simmel wrote: "The psychological foundation, upon which the metropolitan individuality is erected, is the intensification of emotional life due to the swift and continuous shift of external and internal stimuli."[4] Experience, once bound to regular rhythms of work and ritual, becomes abrupt: becomes, paradoxically, *regularly* abrupt. And all the more so over the last century and a half, as the regular, cyclical, nature-bound rhythms have been dislodged almost everywhere in the West and replaced by synthetic time and an irruption of images.

News participates centrally in this process; the experience of reading the newspaper or watching television in this sense resembles the experience of walking down a busy city street. The stimulations of the city are now extended into the private dwelling place. The pace and plausibility of news increased with the mass-circulation daily commercial press, aided by the telegraph, in the 1830s; then with news photographs in the 1890s; then with motion pictures and glamorous mass advertising from the 1890s on; then with radio and television. Television now boosts the quantity of bombardment into quality. Just as the physical building and re-

4. Simmel, "The Metropolis and Mental Life," trans. Edward Shils, in Donald N. Levine, ed., *Georg Simmel: On Individuality and Social Forms* (Chicago: University of Chicago Press, 1971), p. 325. (First published in 1903.)

building of the city has become normal, so has the "revolution," the turning over, of commodities and fashions and "lifestyles"— and news—to suit. Probably there has never been an historical period without rapid change; but capitalist production and its extension into the realm of images has made the experience of on-rushing change a constant. In the economy, changes of fashion and planned obsolescence become the underpinnings of the productive system; in the individual psyche, perpetual adaptation (or the simulation of it) becomes a *sine qua non* of comfort and status. Up to the present and through it, the express-train pace of goods development and advertising dovetails with the helter-skelter development of new technologies—which accompanies and feeds the accumulation of capital. Not only the forms of mass culture but the forms of art are subject to what Harold Rosenberg called "the tradition of the new." This is one built-in irony of the capitalist economy and the development of the forms of news within it: *the stability of the system is predicated on the institutionalization of change and speed.* Technological change, fashion change, lifestyle change—the rhythms of experience reproduce the rhythms of production. The standardized rhythm is that which both accelerates the pace of life—increased productivity on the assembly line, in the office, or in school—and at the same time domesticates it into interchangeable units of time (the hour-long classroom period, the three-minute rock record, the sixty-minute TV show). Commercial television, with its rapid cuts, its routine use of montage, its jagged "flow" from program to commercial to station break to program, is thus a socialization into discontinuity of experience, velocity, and hunger for jolts of change. And by making possible near-instantaneous transmission of information about events, the broadcasting system makes possible sped-up social reactions to events, and thus sped-up spirals of activity and counteractivity.[5]

The hurried-up movement in the late sixties was *conditioned* by the mass media to a decontextualization of its own experience which was fatal to its own political balance and continuity. Hard pressed by the Vietnam war, the movement became accustomed to rapid-fire emulation: it developed a "two, three, many" syndrome

5. On the acceleration of social change in a modern news system, see Ben H. Bagdikian, *The Information Machines* (New York: Harper and Row, 1971), p. 14. On the regularization of schedules and formulas in television entertainment, see Todd Gitlin, "Prime Time Ideology: The Hegemonic Process in Television Entertainment," *Social Problems* 26 (February 1979): 251–266.

of reproducing events outside their original contexts. The *instantaneity* of the spotlight had the effect of contracting the lived time, the *durée*, of the movement, and kept encouraging an already immature, class-isolated movement to misunderstand its political situation, to decontextualize its activity. In haste, constantly off balance, the movement was especially prone to lose its grasp of actual political possibilities. Acting, producing mediated images, reacting hastily to the unanticipated consequences of those images, the movement entered a feedback loop without correcting errors. Political tactics based on mass-media images of faraway tactics in other circumstances—like the Columbia movement's imitation of Parisian barricades in 1968 (see Chapter 6, above)—were precisely what the routine media code emphasized. The movement furthered this process by circulating tokens of its own decontextualized revolutionary symbol world: posters, buttons, flags, slogans, even oversimplified theories. This mislearning system peculiarly recapitulated the decontextualized "learning system" that is mass advertising. From the association of Salem cigarettes with the blue-sky clear-water countryside, to the association of a nineteenth-century military tactic with a twentieth-century student uprising, the dissociation of action from context is a central and continuing feature of modern capitalist society. For a movement that intends to transform society, not to enter into its stabilizing rituals, such a dissociation is murderous. And in general: the New Left's complicated but always intense relation to the mass culture helped further deprive it of anchorage—in tradition, in previous generations (themselves disrupted), in actual community, and in direct relations with political constituencies. A mass market culture, even with Bob Dylan records and *The Battle of Algiers*, is simply not a sustaining basis for oppositional political culture. A strategically minded political movement cannot afford to substitute the commodity process of news, fashion, and image for a grasp of its own situation, a suitable organizational form, and a working knowledge of social conditions, structures, and interests.[6]

6. The big iceberg under the water in the last two sentences is this question: Among American political movements, was the New Left unique in its intimate relation to mainstream culture? Or were there similar symbioses in the relations between Populist and Popular Front movements, to name two important ones, and the mass culture of their times? This needs a great deal of research and thought.

THE VULNERABILITY OF A STUDENT MOVEMENT

To be more specific about the particular impact of the mass media on the tempo of events in the sixties, we need another background as well: we have to look briefly at the tension locked into the mainspring of a student movement *as such*. A radical student movement is, of its nature, unstable. Because of its narrow social base, it is naturally prone to hubris when it confronts a world resistant to its hopes. The number of public college and university students in the United States doubled between 1950 and 1960, and then again between 1960 and 1966, so that the U.S. became the first society in the history of the world with more college students than farmers and farm workers combined. But at the same time, four-year college students were still a small and class-specific minority of the population. *A radical student movement's volatility follows directly from the conflict between the enormous scope of its ambition—to transform the whole society, root and branch—and the narrowness of its social and cultural base.* That narrowness, in turn, is conditioned by the absence of a radical tradition with a formative culture and by the lack of social institutions of leftist continuity. In these circumstances, a student movement feels, at times, as great hopers have felt from Rousseau to Marx and Bakunin, that it is nothing and that it wants to be everything; and then, during intoxicated moments, that its potential strength knows no bounds. In the first mood, it needs a proletariat, or a functionally equivalent substitute proletariat, to realize its radical vision. But because the radical intelligentsia constitutes a social group in itself, it develops versions of its own interest; and because it has been shaped for various forms of domination, for collaboration in the established order of power and privilege, it wants to maintain what domination it can manage. Activity in the service of an actual or surrogate proletariat, or *politics for others*, is one "moment" of a student movement's history. The quest for a political identity of its own, or *politics for selves*, is another. That quest may lead to inflated images of the movement's actual significance and potential: ideas of "youth as a class," for example, which had some currency in the late sixties. At its most inventive and persuasive, a student movement is able to serve both itself *and* others, uniting the two "moments": for example, organizing against military research at a university *both* because that research contributes to destruction in Vietnam *and* because it cripples the university as a center of independent, critical, and ethical learning.

The uniting of the for-others and for-selves themes in a single project is the movement's most fruitful approach to overcoming its isolation without denying its own identity: this is the basis of a political realism that is also radical. But a reconciliation of these polar themes is itself often provisional and fragile. False solutions offer themselves. It is tempting, for example, to ignore one's social identity altogether, or to work to efface it by strokes of the will: the children of professionals going to work in a factory, say. The déclassé impulse among small but recurring groups of revolutionary intellectuals flows from their reluctance to put up with their own social location, since it seems to limit their universalist hopes. Another probe toward a solution is to accept one's identity and, in turn, to brandish it, to universalize it: thus the "new working class" theory, in which students are the vanguard of an emergent global class, an "expanded proletariat" of all those who do not own the means of production, which has socialism instilled in its needs. This is not the place to consider these arguments critically: I am concerned here, rather, with their functions in helping to resolve socially determined dilemmas. In this light, the most ingenious solution to the built-in dilemma of the radical student movement is Marxism-Leninism, which offers students a way of *preserving* their dominion over the working class by transfiguring it into the Party. As Lenin propounded it, the working class by itself is capable of nothing higher than "trade union consciousness"; at a stroke, intellectuals became indispensable to getting the proletarian "class in itself" to shape up into the "class for itself" that makes the revolution. Since the Party is the *sine qua non* of revolution, Leninist theory neatly— if disastrously—outfits revolutionary intellectuals with an identity which preserves their self-image as "for others" while entitling them to power "for selves."[7]

Leninism, then, is a strong—though resistible—tendency for isolated radical student movements. The whole theory needs elaboration on another occasion; the question here is: How have the mass media affected a cycle that long preexists them? In nineteenth-century Russia, for example, a much smaller student move-

7. See the earlier version of this argument in Todd Gitlin, "The Dynamics of the New Left," *Motive* 31 (November 1970): 45–48, and the similar argument in Alvin W. Gouldner, *The Future of Intellectuals and the Rise of the New Class* (New York: Seabury Press, 1979).

ment, itself cut off from a generation of elders, was twisted in a similar vise between for-others and for-selves politics: in succession, it exhausted various stages, from the Populism of V Narod! (To the people!) to reformism and terrorism as twin responses to the failure of base-building in the countryside. As the peasantry, the social base of Populism, eroded, the Populist form of politics-for-others obsolesced along with it; and as the working class grew, a few remnants and spiritual heirs of Populism generated Bolshevism as a solution.[8] Whatever sense this made or didn't make in late Czarist Russia, the adoption of Leninism by SDS factions in the United States of 1969 represented a triumph of decontextualization. If Bolshevism had roots in the failures as well as the successes of Populism, the *Americanized* Bolshevism was a weird transplant serving internal needs of the movement without any concrete relation to American history or actual knowledge of the actual working class. But *the contraction of time in a media-saturated society fueled the wishful thinking of a student-based movement.* Reflection and consideration were at a premium. Concrete information took too long to unearth. As the organizer Maria Varela says of SNCC in 1966 (see Chapter 5, above), "we had been sort of thrust into the national picture and . . . we weren't ready for it." From 1965, too, SDS was thrust, and thrust itself, into a whirlwind of images and a fever of image-making that prevented it from getting a grip on its unavoidable, socially conditioned dilemmas. It was in a hurry to slash through old knots. From the moment it became a go-getting political organization and entered the spotlight, the student movement of the sixties traversed in four years an agonized course from the political-cultural enlightenment of the Port Huron Statement and the populism of ERAP to a compound of Bolshevism and terrorism—a course similar to what took the nineteenth-century Russians decades. Looking for recruits, looking for support, looking to fracture the political consensus and to amplify the possibility of an alternative way of life, the movement had submitted to the spotlight: it got burned, and burned out.

8. For a clear summary of the history of Russian Populism, see Aileen Kelly, "Good for the Populists," *New York Review of Books* 24 (June 23, 1977): 10–15. The comprehensive source is Franco Venturi, *Roots of Revolution* (New York: Grosset and Dunlap, 1966). Among the Populist intellectuals, by the way, Alexander Herzen was most alert to the dangers of living in contracted time, although he was concerned about the revolutionaries' *own* haste. He wrote to Bakunin: "The slowness of history infuriates us: is it permissible to speed the process up?" The answer was No. (Quoted in Kelly, "Good for the Populists," p. 14.)

9 Broadcasting and Containment

I have saved the most obvious consequence of the movement-media history for last. Some of what the movement wanted to broadcast, about the world and about its own purposes and its nature, *got broadcast.*

Opposition movements enter the media spotlight for rational purposes. They want to recruit supporters and sympathizers. They want to challenge the authority of the dominant institutions. They want to attract, or at least to neutralize, third forces.[1] They may want the protection that publicity affords when they vocally and visibly confront a liberal conscience with threats to its values. They want to place issues on local or national political agendas. They may want to intimate new social possibilities by broadcasting images of a counterculture. They may want to redress specific grievances. Toward these ends it is difficult to see how an opposition movement can avoid addressing the mass media at some point in its career.

So the temptation of the radical movement of the sixties into the realm of the spectacle was not simply a result of its organizational and personal frailties. Not only were there powerful rational arguments in behalf of using the spotlight, but publicity did have many of the effects intended. It diffused some of the ideas, some of the concerns, some of the terms of the movement. It diffused them in an oversimplified and often distorted and debased form—in a

1. See Michael Lipsky, "Protest as a Political Resource," *American Political Science Review* 62 (1968): 1151–1153.

diffuse form, one might say—but it did diffuse them. Publicity helped antiwar feeling become a normal fact of American political life. In the South, television brought startling news of civil rights activity to the cabins of illiterate sharecroppers;[2] and it brought images of repression—those unblinkable cattle prods, those police dogs of Birmingham—to the living rooms of Northern liberals, and helped mobilize them into the financial base of the movement and the political base for its achievements (and its limits) in national politics. For isolated civil rights workers in dangerous areas of the Deep South in the early sixties, attention in the national press was a form of protection against local sheriffs.[3] Even SNCC, which distrusted reporters and preferred not to speak with them at all, found it did not dare shirk the spotlight.

Movement workers were deeply ambivalent about publicity, and for good reason. True, participants in almost all movements seek "psychic gratification" in media coverage; the short-lived thrill of getting in the papers or getting on television helps compensate for the arduousness of movement work and the inevitable setbacks.[4] But as I've already argued, movement people were not exceptionally narcissistic men and women; indeed, in their capacity to commit themselves to projects beyond their immediate gratifications, they may well have been less narcissistic than the norm. More to the point is the fact that publicity can be partial compensation for the unrewarding ardors of political work. Harvey Molotch is right to say that movements' concern with publicity flows not only from "activists' own knowledge that media are the means for organizational goal attainment" but from "the activists' sense that media coverage means that what they do *matters in the world*."[5] Even framed amidst commercials and the clutter of other bits of "information," even distorted in manifold ways, a single evanescent appearance on the TV evening news permits a semblance of access to an audience many times larger than what one could speak

2. Ben H. Bagdikian, *The Information Machines* (New York: Harper and Row, 1971), pp. 16–18.

3. Interview, Maria Varela, July 1, 1976. After 1965, when black protest moved North and West, the national coverage, too, turned hostile. According to Varela, "There was a certain point when SNCC was covered as 'young valiant kids' and then there was a certain point when SNCC was given coverage as 'these radicals who wanted to destroy a lot of things'" (ibid.).

4. Harvey Molotch, "Media and Movements," unpublished paper, 1977.

5. Ibid., p. 3.

to in a lifetime of nightly community meetings; simultaneously, it sends a message directly to the powers that be. Yet this sort of access can also be delusory, to the extent that media-made reputation is confused with substantive social power over public decisions: in the sixties, the barrage of publicity attending the movement may have raised expectations of quick change among the less experienced rank and file, and the inevitable disappointment of those expectations may have helped drive many of those people out of insurgent politics altogether. Some of the more sophisticated New Left leaders became aware that the spotlight, necessary as it may have been, was also exposing their vulnerabilities, taking the pace of the movement's development out of their hands, and detracting from their ability to define the movement for themselves. They became aware of the problem, but they did not know what to do about it. As the examples of Paul Booth and Dan Siegal show (see Chapters 3 and 5, above), once the spotlight was switched on, whether a leader cooperated with reporters or not did not make a great deal of difference in the nature of the coverage. A more canny and more rooted leader like César Chavez worked for years in obscurity to organize a union before turning to the glare of the mass media.

Precisely what made the mass media valuable instruments for an opposition movement—their capacity for mass exposure—was what made them dangerous. Although in the nature of the case we cannot be terribly certain, it seems plausible that distinct audiences would have interpreted the same media messages in contrary ways, so that the small audience inclined toward militancy had its inclinations reinforced, while the majority audience used the same footage to justify its condemnation of "violent tactics." Polls of public opinion toward police and demonstrators after the 1968 Chicago and 1970 Kent State demonstrations suggest as much, the pro- and anti-demonstrator opinion tilting toward or away from the police on the basis of the same mediated information. The only relevant empirical studies I know of attribute a limited but real impact to media definitions of social and political reality. For example, a survey of the attitudes of British trade union members toward unofficial strikes showed that the electronic media (but not newspapers) made "a small but significant contribution" to rank-and-file opposition to those strikes, though not to opinion on other social issues. But tempering that effect, the media "had not affected the degree of support for the use of legal penalties in counteracting" unofficial strikes.[6] Groups of police and uncommitted night-school students watching British television coverage of the 1968 antiwar demonstration in London tended to accept the media version of the events; demonstrators, however, did not.[7] In other words, *audiences with less direct experience of the situations at issue were more vulnerable to the framings of the mass media.*[8] In 1967, financial supporters of SDS were estranged indubitably and directly by the *New York Times*'s presentation of the Calvert interview (see Chapter 6, above). In the United States, without the sort of traditional loyalties which British trade unions enjoy, the New Left rank and file especially may well have suffered from media definitions of movement events and concerns; and along with the movement's own sectarianism, media images may have backhandedly coaxed them to withdraw from movement politics altogether. The seventies' prevailing myth, reinforced by the media, that the movement accomplished little has helped isolate it historically from succeeding cohorts: why continue a loser?

All these possibilities suggest that the media helped *contain* the movement in the course of difusing images of it. Unfortunately, most studies of "opinion change" inquire into people's reactions only to relatively brief exposures to discrete messages; but newspaper and especially television coverage of routine events succeeds in framing precisely *through repetition.* I suggest that the more attentive audience in the sixties was able to attend more selectively to images of the movement, while the less attentive and less informed bulk of the audience was more vulnerable to the crude elements of the framing. In 1968, according to one survey, 59 percent of the TV audience said that it drew its main picture of the world from television;[9] and even for those who still read newspapers, most of the newspaper coverage of deviant activity did not contradict the television framing. About unconscious impacts of repeated frames we can only surmise: for example, conceivably the repeated

6. Jay G. Blumler and Alison J. Ewbank, "Trade Unionists, the Mass Media and Unofficial Strikes," *British Journal of Industrial Relations* 8 (March 1970): 52.

7. James D. Halloran, Philip Elliott, and Graham Murdock, *Demonstrations and Communication: A Case Study* (Harmondsworth, England: Penguin Books, 1970), p. 307.

8. This extrapolates the findings presented in Joseph T. Klapper, *The Effects of Mass Communication* (New York: The Free Press, 1960), pp. 53–60.

9. The Roper Organization, Inc., "Changing Public Attitudes Toward Television and Other Mass Media, 1959–1976" (New York: Television Information Office, 1977), p. 3.

association of antiwar activity with futility bolstered the White House view that such activity was a waste of time, if not, indeed, an obstruction of peace. The repeated distinction between moderates and militants probably helped harden that division. In his study of British youth gangs, Stanley Cohen argues that the media, by accentuating the opposition between Mods and Rockers, actually helped bring it about:

> Constant repetition of the warring gangs' image . . . had the effect of giving these loose collectivities a structure they never possessed and a mythology with which to justify the structure. . . . Even if these images were not directly absorbed by the actors, they were used to justify control tactics, which . . . still further structured the groups and hardened the barriers between them.
>
> The mass media—and the ideological exploitation of deviance—also reinforced another type of polarization: between the Mods and Rockers on the one hand, and the whole adult community on the other.[10]

So it was with the New Left. The media spotlight brought the incandescent light of social attention and then converted it to the heat of reification and judgment. The spotlight turned out to be a magnifying glass. The State used that glass to help point, and justify, its heavy hand of repression. The isolated, inexperienced movement that came from the shadows caught fire under the glass, illuminated the landscape, and burned out; then, dialectically, so did the administration that pushed repression one or two burglaries too far. All opposition movements to come would inherit this history, all the ambiguity and irony of it.

10. Stanley Cohen, *Folk Devils and Moral Panics* (London: MacGibbon and Kee, 1972), p. 166.

III Hegemony, Crisis, and Opposition

10 Media Routines and Political Crises

THEORIES OF THE NEWS

Where do news frames come from? How are they fixed into the appearance of the stable, the natural, the taken-for-granted? And how, despite this, are the prevailing frames disputed and changed? How are we to understand the systematic denigration of the New Left?

Herbert Gans has recently put forward a list of theories that purport to explain how certain stories are selected as news, a list that will serve as a starting point.[1] First, there are *journalist-centered* theories, which explain the news as a product of professional news judgments. In the extreme form of this viewpoint, journalism is a profession with autonomous criteria for training, recruitment, and promotion, serving the public interest by following its own stated and unstated rules concerning objectivity. Like any other profession, journalism is—or ought to be (there is this tension in thought about the professions generally)—insulated from extrinsic considerations, whether from political pressures, pressures from publishers, news executives, or advertisers, pressures from outside interest groups, or, indeed, conscious or unconscious ideological screens operating within journalists themselves. In less extreme form, such theories are commonly held by journalists, and also by politicians like Nixon and Agnew who hold journalists guilty of a special ideological bias.

---

1. I adapt the following discussion from Herbert Gans, *Deciding What's News* (New York: Pantheon, 1979), pp. 78–80. The typology of theories is essentially Gans's, but I have altered his capsule descriptions considerably.

A second group of theories stresses *the inertia, the sheer habit of news organization*. Some of the organizational theories emphasize commercial imperatives; others, the organizational structure of the news operations themselves.[2] Compatible with these theories, and not sharply demarcated from them, are the more recent *phenomenological* approaches to news as a social construct, which emphasize the human agency of news, the informal rules which journalists adopt to enable them to process vast amounts of information and to select and repackage it in a form that audiences will accept as The News.[3]

The third approach is *event-centered*: it argues that news "mirrors" or "reflects" the actual nature of the world. From this point of view, if media treatment of the New Left changed between 1965 and 1969, it must have been because the movement, and the events it was involved in, changed. The mirror metaphor, as Edward Jay Epstein showed, was common among news executives in the late sixties.[4] Although it has waned in credibility as critics from the first two groups have pointed to the systematic selectivities of news, mirror theory retains a commonsense standing among many journalists and news executives; it is reproduced in Walter Cronkite's nightly closing, "And that's the way it is."

There are also theories which locate the causes of story selection *in institutions or social conditions outside the news organization*: in technological factors, national culture, economics, the audience, the

2. The major organizational studies are Warren Breed, "Social Control in the Newsroom," *Social Forces* 33 (May 1955): 467–477; Edward Jay Epstein, *News from Nowhere: Television and the News* (New York: Random House, 1973); Leon V. Sigal, *Reporters and Officials: The Organization and Politics of Newsmaking* (Lexington, Mass.: D. C. Heath, 1973); Bernard Roshco, *Newsmaking* (Chicago: University of Chicago Press, 1975); and Robert Darnton, "Writing News and Telling Stories," *Daedalus* 104 (Spring 1975): 175–194. Also see the excellent survey of this literature by Philip Elliott, "Media Organizations and Occupations: An Overview," in James Curran, Michael Gurevitch, and Janet Woollacott, eds., *Mass Communication and Society* (London: Edward Arnold, 1977), pp. 142–173, and Elliott's bibliography.

3. The major phenomenological studies are Gaye Tuchman, "Objectivity as Strategic Ritual: An Examination of Newsmen's Notions of Objectivity," *American Journal of Sociology* 77 (1972): 660–679; Tuchman, "Making News by Doing Work: Routinizing the Unexpected," *American Journal of Sociology* 79 (July 1974): 110–131; Tuchman, *Making News* (New York: The Free Press, 1978); Harvey L. Molotch and Marilyn J. Lester, "News as Purposive Behavior: On the Strategic Use of Routine Events, Accidents, and Scandals," *American Sociological Review* 39 (February 1974): 101–112; and Molotch and Lester, "Accidental News: The Great Oil Spill as Local Occurrence and National Event," *American Journal of Sociology* 81 (September 1974): 235–260.

4. Epstein, *News from Nowhere*, pp. 13–18.

most powerful news sources, and/or the ideologies of the dominant social powers. As Gans points out, each of these theories has something to recommend it, and each falls short of completeness. Professional, organizational, directly economic and political and ideological forces *together* constitute, from the traces of events in the world, images of The News which are limited in definite ways and tilted toward the prevailing frames. Gans himself composes a synthesis of these approaches, viewing "news as information which is transmitted from sources to audiences, with journalists—who are both employees of bureaucratic commercial organizations and members of a profession—summarizing, refining, and altering what becomes available to them from sources in order to make the information suitable for their audiences. Because news has consequences, however, journalists are susceptible to pressure from groups and individuals (including sources and audiences) with power to hurt them, their organizations, and their firms. . . . [S]ources, journalists, and audiences coexist in a system, although it is closer to being a tug of war than a functionally interrelated organism." These "tugs of war" are in the end "resolved by power," and news is therefore, among other things, in the words of Philip Schlesinger, "the exercise of power over the interpretation of reality."[5]

Gans is right to look both inside and outside news organizations for explanations of the news, and right to conclude that the production of news is a system of power. These conclusions are irresistible; they help comprehend the framing patterns I have demonstrated in Parts I and II. What I seek here is not so much an *alternative* as a *more ample* theoretical domain within which to understand the framing process and the media-movement relationship. For this purpose I want an approach attuned to the particular procedures of journalism, yet sensitive to the fact that journalism exists alongside—and interlocked with—a range of other professions and institutions with ideological functions within an entire social system. I want an approach which is both structural and historical—that is, which can account for regularities in journalistic procedure and product, yet which at the same time can account for historical changes in both. Such an approach should encompass not only news and its frames, but movements and their identities, goals, and strategies; it should comprehend both news and movements as contending conveyors of ideas and images of what the world is and should be like. As I suggested in the Introduction, the most comprehensive theoretical approach can be found in recent developments of the Gramscian idea of hegemony. After briefly canvassing the Gramscian territory, we can draw together some of this book's themes and explore the specific question of the sources of news frames for the New Left and opposition movements in general.

IDEOLOGICAL HEGEMONY AS A PROCESS

There exists no full-blown theory of hegemony, specifying social-structural and historical conditions for its sources, strengths, and weaknesses.[6] But a certain paradigm has been developing during the seventies, after the collapse of the New Left and the translation of Antonio Gramsci's prison writings,[7] and it is this paradigm—a domain of concerns, sensitivities, and conclusions—that can help situate the history of media-movement relations. Unfortunately, Gramsci, who was the first to specify the concept in a modern Marxist context,[8] wrote ambiguously and in fragments: he was isolated in a Fascist prison, he was at pains to pass censorship, and he was at times gravely ill. Condemned to prison between 1926 and his death in 1937, Gramsci filled notebook after notebook trying to understand, among other things, why the working-class uprising in Northern Italy after World War I had failed; why the working class was not necessarily revolutionary; why most of it could be defeated by Fascism. Without neglecting the role of force in securing State power, Gramsci centered on the limits of working-class consciousness, on the issue of whether and when the

6. The following paragraph is based on p. 251 of my "Prime Time Ideology: The Hegemonic Process in Television Entertainment," *Social Problems* 26 (February 1979): 251–266.

7. Antonio Gramsci, *Selections from the Prison Notebooks*, ed. and trans. Quintin Hoare and Geoffrey Nowell Smith (New York: International Publishers, 1971). There is no single passage in which Gramsci unequivocally defines and applies the concept of hegemony; rather, it is a leitmotif throughout his entire work. But see especially pp. 12, 52, 175–182.

8. But note that his distinction between hegemony and coercion corresponds in some ways to Machiavelli's distinction between force and fraud in the operations of the State. See Sheldon S. Wolin's commentary in *Politics and Vision: Continuity and Innovation in Western Political Thought* (Boston: Little, Brown, 1960), pp. 220–224, and Wolin's references to Machiavelli in notes on p. 470. Gramsci honored his intellectual lineage by writing eighty pages of commentary on Machiavelli's *The Prince* under the heading *The Modern Prince* (pp. 125–205 in the *Prison Notebooks*).

working class could successfully challenge the prevailing bourgeois conception of its place in the world.

Gramsci's concept can be defined this way: hegemony is a ruling class's (or alliance's) domination of subordinate classes and groups through the elaboration and penetration of ideology (ideas and assumptions) into their common sense and everyday practice; it is the systematic (but not necessarily or even usually deliberate) engineering of mass consent to the established order. No hard and fast line can be drawn between the mechanisms of hegemony and the mechanisms of coercion; the hold of hegemony rests on elements of coercion, just as the force of coercion over the dominated both presupposes and reinforces elements of hegemony.[9] In any given society, hegemony and coercion are interwoven. Recently, Raymond Williams[10] and Stuart Hall[11] have elaborated the notion of hegemony and begun to use it in the analysis of popular culture. In Hall's words, drawing on Gramsci's terminology:

"hegemony" exists when a ruling class (or, rather, an alliance of ruling class fractions, a "historical bloc") is able not only to coerce a subordinate class to conform to its interests, but exerts a "total social authority" over those classes and the social formation as a whole. "Hegemony" is in operation when the dominant class fractions not only dominate but *direct*—lead: when they not only possess the power to coerce but actively organize so as to command and win the consent of the subordinated classes to their continuing sway. "Hegemony" thus depends on a combination of force and consent. But—Gramsci argues—in the liberal-capitalist state, consent is normally in the lead, operating behind "the armour of coercion."[12]

Further, hegemony is, in the end, a process that is entered into by both dominators and dominated.[13] Both rulers and ruled derive

9. In an astute essay, Perry Anderson has shown with a close reading of Gramsci's *Prison Notebooks* that various major inconsistencies were built into Gramsci's own original usage of his term: specifically that Gramsci was ambiguous in how he positioned culture and hegemony vis-à-vis the State and force in his diagraming of society. (Perry Anderson, "The Antinomies of Antonio Gramsci," *New Left Review*, No. 100 [November 1976–January 1977], pp. 5–78, especially pp. 12–44.) These issues are not at the center of my current concern, but further development of the theory of ideological hegemony should not overlook the clarifications of Anderson's essay.

10. "Base and Superstructure in Marxist Cultural Theory," *New Left Review*, No. 82 (1973), pp. 3–16; later reworked and extended in *Marxism and Literature* (New York: Oxford University Press, 1977), pp. 108–114.

11. Stuart Hall, "Culture, the Media and the 'Ideological Effect,'" in Curran, Gurevitch, and Woollacott, *Mass Communication and Society*, pp. 315–348.

12. Ibid., p. 332.

13. See, by contrast, Georg Simmel's notion of domination as "a form of interaction" in which the dominant "will draws its satisfaction from the fact that the act-

psychological and material rewards in the course of confirming and reconfirming their inequality. The hegemonic sense of the world seeps into popular "common sense" and gets reproduced there; it may even appear to be generated *by* that common sense.

In liberal capitalist societies, no institution is devoid of hegemonic functions, and none does hegemonic work only. But it is the cultural industry as a whole, along with the educational system, that most coherently specializes in the production, relaying, and regearing of hegemonic ideology. The media of the culture industry are ordinarily controlled by members of top corporate and political elites, and by individuals they attempt (with varying success) to bring into their social and ideological worlds. At the same time, the ruling coalitions of "class fractions" are to a great extent dependent on these ideology-shaping institutions (1) to formulate the terms of their own unity, and (2) to certify the limits within which all competing definitions of reality will contend. They structure the ideological field within which, as Hall says, "subordinate classes 'live' and make sense of their subordination in such a way as to sustain the dominance of those ruling over them." [14] Because at any given moment there is not a unitary functioning "ruling class," but rather an alliance of powerful groups in search of an enduring basis for legitimate authority, the particular hegemonic ideology will not be simple; "the content of dominant ideology will reflect this complex interior formation of the dominant classes." [15]

The hegemonic ideology will be complex for a deeper structural reason as well. The dominant economic class does not, for the most part, produce and disseminate ideology directly. That task is left to writers and journalists, producers and teachers, bureaucrats and artists organized for production within the cultural apparatus as a whole—the schools and mass media as a whole, advertising and show business, and specialized bureaucracies within the State and the corporations. Thus the corporate owners stand, as Alvin W. Gouldner points out, in marked contrast to previous ruling classes:

---

ing or suffering of the other . . . offers itself to the dominator as the product of *his* will" (Simmel, "Domination," trans. Kurt H. Wolff, in Donald N. Levine, ed., *Georg Simmel: On Individuality and Social Forms* [Chicago: University of Chicago Press, 1971], p. 96). In this sense, hegemony differs from domination: in hegemony, dominator and dominated alike believe that the dominated is consenting *freely*. I am grateful to Mark Osiel for calling my attention to Simmel's discussion.

14. Hall, "Culture, the Media and the 'Ideological Effect,'" p. 333.
15. Ibid.

"Unlike the slave-owners of antiquity or the ruling nobility of feu-
dalism, the dominant class under capitalism is actively and routinely engaged in the conduct of economic affairs."[16] By itself it
cannot directly command the political or the administrative or the
cultural apparatus that conditions the consent of the governed,
even should it desire to do so. Rather, distinct strata have emerged
and solidified, charged with specialized responsibilities for the administration of the entire social order. The liberal capitalist political
economy is layered as an economy and a polity which meet and
interpenetrate at many levels but remain organized separately; the
executives and owners of the cultural apparatus—the press, mass
entertainment, sports, and arts—are also interlocked at high levels
with the managers of corporate and political sectors. But these sectors operate according to different principles. What Gouldner writes
about the differentiation of political and economic sectors might
then be extended, *mutatis mutandis*, to the cultural order:

In consequence of these developments, the system of stratification under
capitalism differs profoundly from that of previous societies. . . . With the
growing differentiation between the economic, political, and bureaucratic
orders, and with the growing specialization among different *personnel*, each
of the newly differentiated spheres develops a measure of *autonomy* and,
we might add, of "slippage," from the other. The operating personnel of
the administrative, the political, and the ruling classes, each develop specialized standards and skills for dealing with their own spheres, thereby
making the latter less intelligible and less accessible to the direct supervision of the dominant economic class.[17]

The fact that power and culture in a modern social system are to
some considerable degree segmented and specialized makes ideology essential: ideology comes to the fore as a potentially cohesive
force—especially in a society segmented in all the realms of life experience, ethnically and geographically as well as politically and
occupationally. At the same time, the relative autonomy of the different sectors legitimates the system as a whole. And crucially, as
Gouldner points out, the economic elite now becomes dependent

16. Alvin W. Gouldner, *The Dialectic of Ideology and Technology: The Origin,
Grammar, and Future of Ideology* (New York: Seabury Press, 1976), p. 229. A similar
approach to relations between economic and political structures is contained in Anthony Giddens, *The Class Structure of the Advanced Societies* (New York: Harper and
Row, 1973).
17. Gouldner, *Dialectic of Ideology and Technology*, p. 230 (emphasis in the
original).

on other sectors for securing the allegiance of the whole society. Specifically:

Ideology assumes special importance as a symbolic mechanism through which the interests of these diverse social strata may be integrated; through the sharing of it the several dominant strata are enabled to make compatible responses to changing social conditions.[18]

But the need for unifying ideology is also a vulnerability for the system as a whole:

It is precisely because the hegemonic elite is *separated from* the means of culture, including the production of ideologies, that ideologies developed in capitalist society may often be discomforting to the hegemonic elite, so that they prefer other mechanisms of dominance and integration more fully and routinely accessible to them.[19]

Indeed, the hegemonic ideology of bourgeois culture is extremely complex and absorptive; only by absorbing and domesticating conflicting values, definitions of reality, and demands on it, in fact, does it remain hegemonic.[20] In this way the hegemonic ideology of liberal, democratic capitalism is dramatically different from the ideologies of pre-capitalist societies and from the dominant ideology of authoritarian socialist or Fascist regimes. What permits it to absorb and domesticate criticism is not something accidental to liberal capitalist ideology, but rather its core. The hegemonic ideology of liberal, democratic capitalist society is deeply and essentially conflicted in a number of ways. At the center of liberal capitalist ideology there coils a tension between the affirmation of patriarchal authority—currently enshrined in the national security State—and the affirmation of individual worth and self-determination. Bourgeois ideology in all its incarnations has been from the first a contradiction in terms, affirming the once revolutionary ideals of "life, liberty, and the pursuit of happiness," or "liberty, equality, and fraternity," as if these ideas were compatible, or even mutually dependent, at all times in all places. More recently, the dominant ideology has strained to enfold a second-generation set of contradictory values: liberty versus equality, democracy versus hierarchy, public rights versus property rights, rational claims to truth versus the arroga-

18. Ibid., pp. 230–231.
19. Ibid., p. 232 (emphasis in the original).
20. I have drawn much of this paragraph from my "Prime Time Ideology," pp. 264–265.

tions of power. All opposition movements in bourgeois society—whether for liberation or for domination—wage their battles precisely in terms of liberty, equality, or fraternity (or, recently, sorority)—in behalf of one set of bourgeois values against another. They press on the dominant ideology in its own name.

And, indeed, the economic system routinely generates, encourages, and tolerates ideologies which challenge and alter its own rationale. For example, as corporate capitalism became dependent on an indefinite expansion of consumer goods and consumer credit, it began to commend and diffuse hedonist values which conflicted with the older values of thrift, craft, and productivity. Workers are now told to be self-sacrificing and disciplined for eight hours a day and to relish their pleasurable selves for the next eight: to give themselves over to the production interests of the company or the office during the week and to express their true, questing, consuming selves over the weekend. Inevitably, hedonism and self-affirmation spill over from the realm of consumption into the realm of production, disrupting workplace efficiency and provoking managerial response: this whole process is central to what Daniel Bell rightly calls "the cultural contradictions of capitalism."[21]

But contradictions of this sort operate within a hegemonic framework which bounds and narrows the range of actual and potential contending world views. Hegemony is an historical process in which one picture of the world is systematically preferred over others, usually through practical routines and at times through extraordinary measures. Its internal structures, as Raymond Williams writes, "have continually to be renewed, recreated and defended; and by the same token . . . they can be continually challenged and in certain respects modified."[22] Normally the dominant frames are taken for granted by media practitioners, and reproduced and defended by them for reasons, and via practices, which the practitioners do not conceive to be hegemonic. Hegemony operates effectively—it does deliver the news—yet outside consciousness; it is exercised by self-conceived professionals working with a great deal of autonomy within institutions that proclaim the neutral goal of

21. Daniel Bell, *The Cultural Contradictions of Capitalism* (New York: Basic Books, 1976). On deliberate corporate attempts to define popular happiness as the consumption of mass-produced goods, and to bring workers to identify themselves as consumers, see Stuart Ewen, *Captains of Consciousness: Advertising and the Roots of the Consumer Culture* (New York: McGraw-Hill, 1976).
22. Williams, "Base and Superstructure," p. 8.

informing the public.[23] Yet we have seen in Part I that the news frame applied to the New Left was not neutral; it held reporting within definite limits. Specifically how was this possible? How, more generally, does hegemony take place within journalism as a totality of techniques, assumptions, and choices?

THE WORKINGS OF HEGEMONY IN JOURNALISM

As Ben Bagdikian puts it, news outside regular beats usually results from three stages in selection: (1) an editor decides that a certain scene should be looked at as the site of a newsworthy event; (2) a reporter decides what is worthy of notice on that scene; and (3) editors decide how to treat and place the resulting story.[24] Behind this process stands the institutional structure of the media, and above all the managers who set overall corporate policy, though hardly with utter freedom. (In the argument to come, I shall single out national commercial television, but the argument about print media would not be essentially different.) By socialization, by the bonds of experience and relationships—in other words, by direct corporate and class interest—the owners and managers of the major media are committed to the maintenance of the going system in its main outlines: committed, that is to say, to private property relations which honor the prerogatives of capital; committed to a national security State; committed to reform of selected violations of the moral code through selective action by State agencies; and committed to approving individual success within corporate and bureaucratic structures.

The media elite want to honor the political-economic system as a whole; their very power and prestige deeply presuppose that

23. In a 1971 national survey of over four thousand journalists (including editors), a little over three-quarters said that they had "almost complete freedom in deciding which aspects of a news story should be emphasized"; 60 percent said that they had "almost complete freedom in selecting the stories they work on" (though only 48 percent of editorial employees in the larger organizations, those employing over 100 persons, claimed freedom of selection); and 46 percent said that they made their own story assignments (as opposed to only 36 percent in the larger news organizations). See John W. C. Johnstone, Edward J. Slawski, and William W. Bowman, *The News People: A Sociological Portrait of American Journalists and Their Work* (Urbana: University of Illinois Press, 1976), p. 222. Asked to rank aspects of their jobs in importance, the journalists in this sample placed public service first, followed, in descending order, by autonomy, freedom from supervision, job security, pay, and fringe benefits (p. 229). Such ordering is roughly what sociologists find among the professionals generally, though journalists differ from other professionals in lacking a generally agreed-upon training program and credential (chap. 6).

24. Interview, Ben H. Bagdikian, May 2, 1979.

system. At the same time, they are committed, like members of any other corporate elite, to their own particular economic and political advantage. The networks above all—far more than prestigious newspapers like the *New York Times*—play for high profit stakes. The resulting conflicts—between particular corporate interests and what the networks take to be the interests of the corporate system as a whole—constitute one irreducible source of strain within the system as a whole. Even a news organization's methods for legitimizing the system as a whole, its code of objectivity and balance, pull it in conflicting directions: at one moment toward the institutions of political and economic power, and at another toward alternative and even, at times, oppositional movements, depending on political circumstance. Organized as a distinct pyramid of power, the network develops the strategy of neutralization, incorporating the competing forces in such a way as to maximize its audiences and thus its profits, its legitimacy, and its stature. It claims and earns legitimacy (Harris Polls show TV news to be the most credible of *all* American institutions, though it shares in the general relative decline) in part by sanctioning reliable routines of objectivity; yet those very routines of objectivity sometimes permit —indeed, may insist on—the entry of challenging social movements into the public ideological space. The network's claim to legitimacy, embodied in the professional ideology of objectivity, requires it, in other words, to take a certain risk of undermining the legitimacy of the social system as a whole. The network's strategy for managing this contradiction is to apply the whole apparatus of techniques that we have examined in Part I, precisely to tame, to contain, the opposition that it dares not ignore.

After all, the legitimacy of a news operation rests heavily on the substantial—if bounded—autonomy of its employees. The audience must believe that what they are viewing is not only interesting but true, and the reporters must be permitted to feel that they have professional prerogatives to preserve. To avoid a reputation for having an ax to grind, the top media managers endow their news operations with the appearance, and a considerable actuality, of autonomy; their forms of social control must be indirect, subtle, and not at all necessarily conscious. Their standards flow through the processes of recruitment and promotion, through policy, reward, and the sort of social osmosis that flows overwhelmingly in one direction: downward. The editors and reporters they hire are generally upper-middle-class in origin, and although their personal values may be liberal by the conventional nomenclature of American politics, they tend to share the *core* hegemonic assumptions of their class: that is, of their managers as well as their major sources.[25] Their salaries are handsome (in 1976, CBS News paid its correspondents between $35,000 and $80,000 a year, not counting fringe benefits and perquisites), and they share tastes and vacation spots and circulate at dinner parties with many of their sources. In the essentially impersonal operations of the newsroom, their relatively homogenized outlook ordinarily overwhelms any discordant personal opinions they might harbor, at least when it comes to defining a story and selecting its essential themes. Their common approach to the world infuses their homogenized cadence and tone: the news voice conveys the impression that the world is unruly because of deviations from a normally adequate and well-managed social order.[26]

The network chiefs want to maximize both audience size and prestige: size determines the rates they may charge advertisers, and prestige, desirable for its own sake, also boosts the upper-middle-class audience for whose attention advertisers will pay more. In working to maximize the audience and to report the news "as it is," the networks must operate, of course, under the (ordinarily glazed) eye of the Federal Communications Commission, Congress, and whatever interventions the White House may attempt. The FCC is charged by 1934 law with ensuring that local stations serve "the public interest, convenience, and necessity." Since in practice this empty phrase is interpreted to mean that the local channels must run a certain amount of news and "public affairs" programs, and since it is cheapest and most profitable by far for the affiliates to meet this requirement by broadcasting what the networks have to offer (along with local news), the FCC is in effect constraining not only the local stations but the networks. In effect, through the so-called Fairness Doctrine, the FCC is requiring the networks to provide response time for interests—but not *all* interests—offended by their coverage. (Consider this boundary to the permissible: It is not "the Commission's intention to make time

25. Gans, *Deciding What's News*, p. 209; Johnstone et al., *The News People*, pp. 25–28.

26. There has not been much discussion of the meanings and impact of style and format in television news. See my "Spotlights and Shadows: Television and the Culture of Politics," *College English* 38 (April 1977): 789–801; Tuchman, *Making News*, chap. 6; and Gans, *Deciding What's News*, Part 1.

available to Communists or to the Communist viewpoints.")[27] But how much do the networks actually fear FCC regulation, and how much does their fear explain the timidity of news departments in their habit of imposing "balance" upon each news story? Probably not very much. CBS, at least, wants to repeal the Fairness Doctrine, to "deregulate" broadcasting, arguing that the balance requirement violates their First Amendment rights and that deregulation would permit more aggressive, freewheeling journalism.[28] On the other hand, ABC News, early in 1979, defended the Fairness Doctrine. How unconstrained the networks want their journalism may be doubted. Skepticism comes easily when the FCC has placed only the lightest of hands on programming at large, and no restraint at all on the vast profits in broadcasting. For all the broadcasters' hue and cry, the FCC has never lifted a station license for violations of the Fairness Doctrine, and continued violations have only once played a part in a decision not to renew.[29] The networks' top commands are probably more concerned about the possibility of congressional investigations and constricting laws, about losing profits to cable and satellite systems, about direct protests from offended political powers, and about vaguely anticipated regulation and repression in a hypothetical future. (One top CBS producer exclaimed to me in November 1976, "We're weak as hell. The First Amendment is a frail reed. Look what Mme. Gandhi did in India— she closed down the press just like that.") In any case, the conventions about objectivity, balance, legitimate sources, and the rest are all derived from newspaper journalism: and no Fairness Doctrine applies there.

In the force field of intersecting political pressures—from the White House, the FCC, Congress, and the affiliates—the networks test the boundaries of the permissible; they carve out an ideological sphere in which they are free to move as they please. With documentaries especially, where the total air time and budget are so limited to start with, choices of subject and slant will depend most

27. FCC, "Application of the Fairness Doctrine in the Handling of Controversial Issues of Public Importance," *Federal Register* 29, Part 2 (July 25, 1964): 10416, cited in Epstein, *News from Nowhere*, pp. 64–65.

28. See, for example, William Small, *To Kill a Messenger: Television News and the Real World* (New York: Hastings House, 1970), pp. 267–270. Small was head of CBS News's Washington Bureau, then Senior Vice-President and Director of News of CBS News, and is at this writing a high executive at NBC News.

29. Nicholas Johnson, "Audience Rights," *Columbia Journalism Review* 18 (May–June 1979): 63.

directly on the larger interests (in both the economic and the ideological sense) of the media elites. These interests, in turn, will of course take into account larger ideological currents in the society, and decisions will be made to amplify some and to dampen others. With the network's mass market mentality, "controversial" decisions—that is, decisions to broadcast anything of political substance—are not taken lightly. For example, CBS's "The Selling of the Pentagon" in 1971 capitalized on a rising tide of antimilitarist sentiment, expressed CBS's desire to declare independence from the military propaganda apparatus, and pointed the finger at a strictly limited, isolable sector of Pentagon operations. For all its limits, though, "Selling" drew complaints of bias—and congressional subpoenas for top executives. In a glare of First Amendment publicity, CBS stood fast against releasing outtakes to Congress, but subsequently failed to give the "Selling" producer, Peter Davis, new assignments; nor did it broadcast another documentary critical of the military until mid-1976, when the Vietnam war and the Nixon administration itself had ended. Early in 1977, likewise, CBS broadcast Bill Moyers's dramatic two-hour exposé of CIA-sponsored military actions against Cuba. It is hard to believe that such a broadcast would have been made under an administration that was not moving toward *détente* with Cuba. Yet Moyers shortly thereafter left CBS, saying that there was no room there for serious documentaries; and the top CBS Evening News producer, Ron Bonn, argues that "the most serious damage done to our branch of the free press by Mr. Agnew" was to "make it possible to think the formerly unthinkable—that maybe television *didn't* have [the obligation to provide a steady flow of news and public affairs]—that maybe it should just shut up and run some more game shows. I date the decline of the serious documentary, of tough, controversial television from that time, from that administration, and from that man." [30] One need not rue the loss of a Golden Age of "tough, controversial television" to observe a loss of luster: a decline from the sixties, when network news conventions were fresher and more fluid and had not yet quite hardened into bureaucratically fixed patterns.

But day to day, political and corporate pressures have not changed much: they go on setting unspoken outer limits for the routines that journalists are trained for and believe in. Once hired

30. Ron Bonn, letter to the author, May 1, 1979.

and assigned, reporters customarily form strong bonds with the sources (especially in Washington) on whom they depend for stories. They absorb the world views of the powerful. They may also contest them: when one institutional source disputes another (the General Accounting Office against the White House, say, or the Environmental Protection Agency against the Department of Energy); or when they come to believe that the powerful are violating the going code of conduct;[31] or when they develop, consciously or not, their own interest (as when their spouses and children actively opposed the Vietnam war); or, on occasion, when they resent, and organize to protest, one of their publishers' more outspoken editorial opinions.

But even when there are conflicts of policy between reporters and sources, or reporters and editors, or editors and publishers, these conflicts are played out within a field of terms and premises which does not overstep the hegemonic boundary. Several assumptions about news value serve, for the most part, to secure that boundary: that news involves the novel event, not the underlying, enduring condition; the person, not the group; the visible conflict, not the deep consensus; the fact that "advances the story," not the one that explains or enlarges it.[32] Only where coverage under these rules flies in the face of immediate institutional interest, or might be construed to be at odds with it, or wanders into some neutral zone where interests have not yet been clearly defined, is there ground for conflict between reporters and media elites over the integrity of the news operation. When outside political powers complain, top news executives mediate between them and the reporters; they may ask the staff to document their factual claims, for example. In newspaper rooms, national and foreign editors mediate between the top editors who are their superiors and the reporters who work beneath them.[33] CBS personnel almost universally say that the news executives insulate them from direct

31. Gans, *Deciding What's News,* p. 60.
32. Some of the historical constancies throughout the 150 years of mass commercial newspapers are underscored in Helen M. Hughes, *News and the Human Interest Story* (Chicago: University of Chicago Press, 1940), and Darnton, "Writing News and Telling Stories." The concept of "advancing the story" comes from Cindy Samuels, Assistant Manager of the New York Bureau of CBS News, who defines it qualitatively: "If you have a story, and it gets bigger, then something else happens that moves it forward, you say it moved forward and it got bigger, you don't say it got bigger and it moved forward" (interview, November 13, 1976).
33. Sigal, *Reporters and Officials,* p. 19.

political pressures with great skill and reliability (with the important exception of the censored Watergate takeout; see p. 278, below)—which is not, of course, to deny the *in*direct pressures and understandings that one way or another find their way into the preconscious stuff of news policy.

Finally, there are organizational factors that in a lesser way constrain the news. Budget ceilings, for example, lead to shortages of bureaus, correspondents, and crews, all of which increase television news's dependence on a few big stories, preferably the *dramatic* and the *metropolitan*.[34] For the same reasons, many major newspapers have been shutting down their expensive out-of-town bureaus, especially abroad, and increasing their dependence on the wire services and on the *New York Times* and *Los Angeles Times–Washington Post* services.

The work of hegemony, all in all, consists of imposing standardized assumptions over events and conditions that must be "covered" by the dictates of the prevailing news standards. On television especially, this work is fairly routine. It *is* work: effort is expended on it. But certain conventions make the effort less burdensome to news processors. One such convention is the ritualized news story format. The correspondent identifies the problem; there is a rising curve of narrative which establishes the situation, identifies protagonists, and sets them against one another; whatever complication emerges from this conflict then dissolves as the correspondent wraps up the package as neatly as possible. (The term *wrap-up* is well chosen.) Meanwhile, on the screen, the pictures stereotypically illustrate the package. Despite the industry's rhetoric about the value it places on TV pictures as such, the regular format is actually what one perceptive cameraman calls the "illustrated lecture."[35] The ratio of film (or tape) shot to film used

34. See Epstein, *News from Nowhere*, pp. 105–112, and Gould, "The Trials of Network News," *More* 3 (May 1973): 8–11. For example, in November 1976, the Northeast bureau of CBS News, located in New York and responsible for the territory from Maryland through Maine, had a total of five camera crews.

35. Interview, Stephen Lighthill, June 16, 1977. In a systematic study of British television news, the Glasgow University Media Group makes the same point: "In most newsfilm the shots do not directly relate to one another in the ways we are used to from the feature cinema. Rather they are used to illustrate the audiotext and the rules governing their juxtapositioning come not from the visual but from the audio track—indeed largely from the commentary. . . . It is because the journalistic logic dominates the film logic that common professional opinion of television news journalists as film makers is a low one" (*Bad News* [London: Routledge and Kegan Paul, 1976], p. 29).

is very high, often twenty or thirty to one; the film used must be *selected* to illustrate the verbal story. It is the correspondent's narration that situates the story, identifies its components, and names the point. Television's reputation as a visual medium for news is based disproportionately on some extraordinary pictures (e.g., Jack Ruby shooting Lee Harvey Oswald), on routine disaster coverage, on "shooting bloody" in war; but in the bulk of stories, most actual pictures are decorative and illustrative—shots of coal shovels gouging coal out of a seam, with the "natural sound" of gouging, as the reporter talks about the energy crisis; and so on. If, at times, the words and pictures are slightly discrepant, this discrepancy may be one index of friction in the work of hegemonic superimposition. Aspects of the pictures may imperfectly, inadvertently, or weakly testify to the existence of a discordant reality which the correspondent is working to assimilate into a conventional framework. Battlefield footage in Vietnam, for example, might in its bloodiness fight against the government's we-can-see-the-light-at-the-end-of-the-tunnel frame, which is relayed, however skeptically, by the correspondent's voice-over narrative. The closer to air time the story breaks, the fewer hands and minds may intervene to process the film into the dominant frames. But most of the time discrepancies are flattened out by producers and editors splicing the piece together in New York (or another major bureau). Commonly the lecture is unitary and controlling. The lecture format enables the correspondent and the producer to clamp a rather definite frame onto a minute or two of film—selected from footage which itself has been shot selectively from amidst a complex and contradictory reality.

So stereotyping does result in part—as network people often admit and complain—from their simple shortage of time. The network news runs to some 22½ minutes of reporting every evening: that is what is left after commercials take their bite from the half-hour. But stereotyping also results from the organization's desire for easy ways of transmitting and manipulating bits of information—bits which, moreover, need to be easily interchangeable and easily edited, re-edited, or reorganized at the last minute, usually by producers and editors who have been nowhere near the scene of the story. If the network is to "cover the day's news," it has to simplify stories so that they can be processed and covered in one-and-a-half or two minutes; even a "long" takeout may be only three or four minutes. (Probably on average it is even shorter in the seventi₁ s than in the sixties, though, in 1977, NBC News installed one major takeout each evening as "Segment 3.") The imperative of finding "good pictures" (usually vivid illustrations) adds to the premium on simplification.

But although the length of a day or an hour is fixed, the way in which time pressure is experienced is not a neutral, technologically determined, ineradicable feature of a world of scarcity. What is experienced as time pressure actually flows from a combination of immediate economic imperatives and the more general imperatives of the commercial system as a whole. In the first place, the affiliate makes considerably more money on locally originated programs—where it sells advertising time directly—than it does on network programs; thus the affiliates resisted the networks' move from fifteen to thirty minutes of national news, starting with CBS in 1963, and they have so far successfully resisted the CBS news executives' desire to expand from thirty to forty-five or sixty minutes.[36] The more general imperative is that the network must sell a reliable audience to the sponsors, and a reliable audience is usually (though not always) one that can be counted on to tune in at a given time every day (or, in the case of an entertainment, every week). Although the weekliness of entertainment has broken down, at least temporarily, with the success of "Roots" in early 1977, and although the networks are now liable to cancel series with greater alacrity than ever before, the dailiness of news remains a commercial necessity. And this regularity is not simply concocted by network elites: *it makes good sense to an audience conditioned to a regular existence by regularity in its school schedules and regularity in its working schedules.* A regularly programmed life-world conditions, and is partly reconditioned by, the orderliness of the news and entertainment formats.

The orderly format ends up promoting social stability, which is what much of the audience longs for: a sense that whatever is wrong in the world, it can be put right by authoritative (almost always official) agencies. Even if the story is about disorder, it likely turns to the restoration of order under benign official aegis.[37] Con-

---

36. CBS and NBC News went from fifteen to thirty minutes of evening news in September 1963. According to Godfrey Hodgson, whose theories of the importance of the media in the American sixties overlap mine somewhat, one reason for the expansion was that the networks had forfeited a good deal of legitimacy in the quiz show scandals of 1959–60, and were seeking to make good their losses. See Godfrey Hodgson, *America in Our Time* (Garden City, N.Y.: Doubleday, 1976), pp. 142–145.

37. Gitlin, "Spotlights and Shadows," p. 792; Gans, *Deciding What's News,*

tent that starts out seeming destabilizing and threatening—a mass demonstration, a riot, a new style of political deviance—may thus end up confirming the inherent rightness and necessity of the core hegemonic principles. The same process operates after news of scandal or disaster. After Watergate and Nixon's resignation, the new media frame was: "The system works." Official folk heroes such as Senator Sam Ervin, or Harold Denton of the Nuclear Regulatory Commission after the accident at Three Mile Island, are elevated as new mass-mediated fountainheads of authoritative moral and technical excellence, to replace the fallen gods.

In general, then, stereotyping solves an enormous number of practical problems for journalism. But why should time pressure and the desire of newsworkers and audiences for regular stories, rhythms, and authoritative *dramatis personae* lead to *particular* stereotypes? To process news from the campuses in the sixties, journalists had to reify a category of "student activists"; but why *this* stereotyped version and not *that*? As Harvey Molotch and Marilyn Lester point out, the imperative of building a large audience cannot, by itself, explain any specific frame; in strictly market terms, how could executives be sure in advance that their ratings would suffer from this news treatment rather than that?[38] Reporters hear little from their actual audience, tend to have a low opinion of the audience's knowledge and attention span, and form images of this abstract audience compounded of wish, fact, and indifference. Abstractions of market and audience explain little indeed. Rather, the stereotypes usually derive from editors' and reporters' immediate work and social circles, and from premises that filter through the organizational hierarchy: from sources, peers, and superiors, on occasion from friends and spouses, and from the more prestigious media reports, especially those of the *New York Times* and the wire services.[39] Journalists and executives may justify these images in terms of audience interest ("America is tired of protest," as the *Times* editor said about uncovered demonstrations against nuclear weapons in Colorado; see p. 5 above), but they perceive that audience through a frame, darkly.

---

p. 54. In a study that Gans cites (p. 226), Mark R. Levy concludes that many television news viewers "watched to be reassured that the world both near and far was safe [and] secure, and that . . . it demanded no immediate action on their part" (Levy, "The Audience Experience with Television News," *Journalism Monographs*, No. 55 [April 1978], p. 13).

38. Molotch and Lester, "Accidental News," p. 254.

39. See Gans, *Deciding What's News*, p. 201 and chap. 7.

At the same time, news stereotypes are not frozen. As Harvey Molotch points out, "news" is a rather undefined state of affairs.[40] Anything *could* be news, for news is what news-gatherers working in news-processing organizations say is news. Therefore, it is historical and contestable; all deep social conflicts are in part conflicts over what is news. Despite the widespread claim that objectivity in news is possible, any attempt to exact a general definition of news—a routine, universalizable definition—comes to naught. Ask a reporter what is news and one is likely to elicit vague references to "what is important" or "what is interesting" or "what is new." As one probes these notions, posing examples and counterexamples, the general criteria dissolve. Reporters finally acknowledge that "what is important" depends on who is asking, or on "the situation," or on "news judgment." These notions have to be just clear and specific enough to justify the claim that journalism is a profession, and then to justify the naming of a particular beat that can be relied upon to produce news (the police beat, for example); and just general enough to allow for the "unlikely" story— that is to say, for "news."

The professional insistence that objective journalism is desirable, and that objective determinations of newsworthiness are possible, arose during the nineteenth century, albeit fitfully, as part of the sweeping intellectual movement toward scientific detachment and the culturewide separation of fact from value.[41] From time to time, as in the sixties, the value of objectivity gets questioned; it always returns, virtually by default. "Opinion" will be reserved to editorials, "news" to the news columns; whatever was in the minds of the ideologues of objectivity, generations of journalists have aspired to that value, even enshrined it. And the aspiration does have the effect of insulating reporters greatly—though far from perfectly—from the direct political pressures of specific advertisers, politicans, and interest groups, and even, in the more prestigious news institutions, from the prerogatives of interfering publishers.[42] Journalists are trained to be desensitized to the voices

40. Molotch, "Media and Movements," unpublished paper, 1977.
41. Michael Schudson, *Discovering the News: A Social History of American Newspapers* (New York: Basic Books, 1978).
42. Of course, publishers went on ensuring that their immediate economic interests would be protected. Newspapers do not ordinarily cover antitrust suits against themselves, for example, and their coverage of downtown business developments tilts toward the downtown businesses that are their advertising mainstays. The closer to home the affected interest, the greater the strictures on news coverage.

and life-worlds of working-class and minority people;[43] they are also trained in locating and treating "the news" so that it is "credible" and, by their own lights, "important." "Credibility," "importance," "objectivity"—these elusive categories are neither arbitrary nor fixed. They are flexible enough to shift with the expectations and experience of news executives and high-level sources, yet definite enough to justify journalists' claims to professional status and standards. A top TV producer told Herbert Gans: "They can order me to do something on big or small issues, for after all this is a company and a business, but they rarely exert that influence. *I am as autonomous as I could expect to be.*"[44] I stress the final sentence. Journalists' ideals are fluid enough to protect them from seeing that their autonomy is bounded: that by going about their business in a professional way, they systematically frame the news to be compatible with the main institutional arrangements of the society. Journalists thus sustain the dominant frames through the banal, everyday momentum of their routines. Their autonomy keeps within the boundaries of the hegemonic system.

THE LIMITS OF HEGEMONIC ROUTINE

Still, traditional methods of news-gathering often contradict the demands that interested publics make for "credibility" and "responsiblity" as their needs and expectations develop and shift. As oppositional groups and movements make claims for coverage, reporters may change their images of their audience or even of the world, and, too, their "instincts" about what is "newsworthy," "interesting," or "important." These changes may be more or less subtle, more or less conscious: reporters may be influenced even as they resist overt pressures to report an issue in this or that way. Their vulnerability depends on many things: personal life-experience, specific organizational arrangements, and the shifting boundaries of the ideologically permissible in the wider society as well as within the newsroom. But this vulnerability also begins with the fact that reporters have only sparse contacts with their actual readers and viewers; their everyday sense of audience cannot be strong enough to insulate them against specific, focused pressures. And media managements cannot entirely overcome the symbiosis between reporters and their movement beats, even when

43. Thelma McCormack, "Establishment Media and the Backlash," paper read to meetings of the American Sociological Association, Washington, D.C., 1970, pp. 32–33.
44. Gans, *Deciding What's News*, p. 96 (emphasis added).

they wish to, since the organization's ability to generate the commodity called "news" depends on the reporter's ability to achieve rapport with a client group. Management's worry about reporter-source rapport is suggested, for example, in the *New York Times*'s practice of rotating reporters out of a foreign country every year, on the theory that within a few years familiarity will obstruct their critical distance.[45]

When movements mobilize, then, reporters may be pulled into the magnetic fields generated by their alternative or oppositional world views. Now the routines of objectivity prove somewhat adaptable. For normally, in the course of gathering news, reporters tend to be pulled into the cognitive worlds of their sources. Whatever their particular *opinions*, for example, Pentagon correspondents define military issues as generals, admirals, and Pentagon bureaucrats define them: as a choice between this missile system and that, not as a choice between the arms race and disarmament. When movements become newsworthy, reporters who cover them steadily are subject to a similar pull. Indeed, they may use the rhetoric and practices of objectivity to justify covering the movement sympathetically and to protect their work from editorial dampening.[46] Or further: when opposition is robust and compelling, reporters may even go so far as to jeopardize their mainstream careers. Thus, in 1970, Earl Caldwell of the *New York Times* refused to turn over to a grand jury his notes on the Black Panther Party, arguing that he could only do his job of covering them objectively if the Panthers could trust him. For although the main sources of news are official, the media also need other sources: they must survey the society for signs of instability, they must produce dramatic news, and thus they are vulnerable to the news-making claims of unofficial groups. Because the idea of "objectivity" and the standards of "newsworthiness" are loose, the hegemonic routines of news coverage are vulnerable to the demands of oppositional and deviant groups. *Through the everyday workings of journalism, large-scale social conflict is imported into the news institution and reproduced there: reproduced, however, in terms derived from the dominant ideology.* Discrepant statements about reality are acknowledged—but muffled, softened, blurred, fragmented, *domesticated* at the same time.

That is, the vulnerability of the news system is not neutrality. The news routines are skewed toward representing demands, in-

45. Darnton, "Writing News and Telling Stories."
46. Tuchman, *Making News*, pp. 100 ff.

dividuals, and frames which do not fundamentally contradict *the dominant hegemonic principles: the legitimacy of private control of commodity production; the legitimacy of the national security State; the legitimacy of technocratic experts; the right and ability of authorized agencies to manage conflict and make the necessary reforms; the legitimacy of the social order secured and defined by the dominant elites; and the value of individualism as the measure of social existence.* The news routines do not easily represent demands, movements, and frames which are inchoate, subtle, and most deeply subversive of these core principles. Political news is treated as if it were crime news—what went wrong today, not what goes wrong every day. A demonstration is treated as a potential or actual disruption of legitimate order, not as a statement about the world. These assumptions automatically divert coverage away from critical treatment of the institutional, systemic, and everyday workings of property and the State. (In 1977, for example, the *New York Times* hired its first investigative reporter assigned to business.) And secondly, the needs and values of sources, constituencies, and journalists alike are structured within the dominant ideology as a whole. Journalists and audiences collaborate in preferring media products which ratify the established order of commodity production and State power. Within these real limits, and only within them, the media may work out a limited autonomy from the expressed interests of political and corporate command posts; they may even affect the ways in which the elites understand their own immediate choices.

When the *New York Times* published parts of the Pentagon Papers in 1971, it risked legal penalties for relaying evidence that several administrations had lied about what they were doing in Vietnam. It did not report that the Papers confirmed some of what antiwar activists had been saying about the war for years. Editorial Page Editor Max Frankel told me that he compared the Pentagon Papers and the *Times*'s war coverage, and "discovered we didn't do so badly. If you read the papers carefully, the press didn't do all that badly, given what we knew. Though true, it was hard for the general reader to put it all together."[47] The antiwar movement, researching and writing outside the *Times*'s conventions for objectivity, had presented over the years a range of views that rather successfully "put it all together," amassing a strong case that American policy was systematically neocolonial, racist, and criminally targeted on the civilian population; but the *Times* did not

47. Telephone interview, Max Frankel, March 23, 1979.

cover these revelations and analyses at the time, and it would not have been seemly, in 1971 or since, for the *Times* to endorse the world view of the radical opposition, even retroactively. The solution to these unfortunate matters had to be left in the hands of duly constituted authorities; the *Times* could not criticize its own conventions or comprehend its own blind spots.

A news item like Dan Rather's routine report on FBI lawbreaking (discussed in the Introduction, pp. 5–6, above) illustrates how a certified social problem and a legitimate solution are ordinarily framed together. The FBI has been committing burglaries and illegal wiretaps for forty years, the story says. These illegalities continued through the period of "civil disturbances of the sixties." Thus, by implication, popular movements—responsible for "civil disturbances"—are not to be looked to as ways of keeping the FBI in line. Or, by the same token, a report on the landing of the first two Concordes at Dulles Airport (on both CBS and ABC News, May 24, 1976) becomes (1) a certification that the "controversy" over the plane's noise is legitimate controversy, (2) a certification that noise-detecting machines placed by the Federal Aviation Authority will determine ("objectively") whether the noise is "excessive," and (3) a deprecation of what ABC called "almost unnoticed" demonstrators, who were, in their leaflets and signs, asserting their own right to say what is excessive noise. The complete message is: when there is legitimate ground for "controversy," it will be defined and taken care of by authorities, not by marginal disruptors.[48] And yet, at the same time, those demonstrators lurking in the margins for a few seconds of film may suggest—to viewers primed to receive this alternative layer of the message—a different model of social action. The FBI's and Air France's views of the world do not totally fill the ideological space; but their definitions of problems ("civil disturbance," noise levels whose seriousness can be certified only by officially monitored machines) are preferred and relayed, while conflict between these and alternative views is denatured, managed, and contained.

Thus, in brief: sources are segmented and exist in history; journalists' values are anchored in routines that are at once *steady* enough to sustain hegemonic principles and *flexible* enough to absorb many new facts; and these routines are bounded by perceptions of the audience's common sense and are finally accountable

48. I draw these examples from my "Spotlights and Shadows," pp. 792 and 795, where I discuss them in more detail.

to the world views of top managers and owners. These factors shape the news; even centralized manipulations by the State have to respect these limits. Everyday frames and procedures suffice to sustain the legitimacy of the economic-political system as a whole.

Yet the hegemonic system for regulating conflict through judgments of newsworthiness presupposes a certain minimum of political stability. When political crises erupt in the real world, they call into question whether the hegemonic routines, left to themselves, can go on contributing to social stability. Now some of the opposition movement's claims about reality seem to be verified by what mainstream reporters and editors discover about the world. *Then the hegemonic frame begins to shift.* Thus, in 1968, editors at the *New York Times* and other establishment news organizations turned sympathetic to moderate antiwar activity. The Tet offensive shattered the official rationale that the war should be pursued because it was not only just but winnable. The observed and reported facts of Tet subverted the Johnson administration's own claims—precisely the claims which had structured the media's dominant frame. At the same time, amidst what they experienced as economic and political crisis, the foreign policy elite (the "Wise Men") began to turn against Johnson's war policy. The elite media amplified their critique of the war—a critique itself lodged within the hegemonic assumption that the United States had a right to intervene against revolutions everywhere—just as business and political authorities influenced media executives to shift positions on the war. But the political crisis was not confined to a back-and-forth process between sealed-off elites; the elites experienced political crisis precisely because of the upwelling of opposition—both radical-militant and liberal-moderate—throughout the society. That opposition made its way simultaneously into the newsrooms. Younger reporters had already begun to share in their generation's rejection of the war. And crucially, editors, like other members of their class, worried about their sons' draftability and were influenced by their antiwar children and spouses (wives, mostly). Ben Bagdikian, former national editor of the *Washington Post*, remembers this complaint by Executive Editor Ben Bradlee: "We tell reporters not to march in a demonstration. But what can you do when their wives march in demonstrations?"[49] Reporters wheeling around to see the war differently were obviously more inclined to frame the anti-

49. Interview, Ben Bagdikian, May 2, 1979.

war movement differently. After the Chicago police riot of August 1968, they were still less inclined to assume that the police were the legitimate enforcers of a reasonable social order.

If editors had not shifted away from administration war policy—if elite authorities had not turned against the war—it is hard to know how far the journalists would have been able to stretch their frames for antiwar activity. Frames are in effect negotiated among sources, editors, and reporters; how they will emerge in practice is not preordained. But as the antiwar frame changed, the formulae for denigrating New Left actions remained in force; now they were clamped onto the *illegitimate* movement. As we saw in Chapter 7, the media were now at pains to distinguish acceptable from unacceptable opposition. Respectful treatment of the moderate antiwar activists, including the Moratorium, was clamped within the newly adjusted hegemonic frame: the war is unsuccessful, perhaps wrong; but ending it is the task of responsible authorities, not radical movements.

This adjusted frame presented problems for the media, the State, and the movement alike. The hegemonic routines had been amplifying—and distorting—an opposition movement. Legitimate authorities were not coping smoothly with the economic and political crisis; willy-nilly, they were firing up opposition; they were now widely seen as incompetent managers. At this point, *the normal routines for constructing news and reproducing hegemony became, from the point of view of much of the political elite, unreliable.* Opposition seemed to dominate the news and to contest routine management of the frames for war and antiwar news. Top media managers bridled at the normal results of hegemonic routines; therefore, from 1968 through 1973, and especially (but not only) under pressure from the Nixon White House, they interfered more directly in the news-gathering process. The forms of direct intervention are hard to smoke out. They are singular (by definition they are not routine), they may be idiosyncratic, and news of them is embarrassing: after all, they fly in the face of the hegemonic claim to professional journalistic autonomy. But a few examples of executive intervention have surfaced. During the Columbia University uprising in the spring of 1968, for example, Managing Editor A. M. Rosenthal of the *New York Times*—an organization deeply entangled with the Columbia administration—went to the unprecedented length of filing a front-page story *under his own by-line*, focusing on how brutish the occupying radicals had been in messing up Columbia President Grayson Kirk's office.[50] The *Times* Magazine that spring ran two pieces inspired by the Columbia rebellion: one a general alarm by Harvard neo-conservative James Q. Wilson, the other a critique of militant nonviolence by Supreme Court Justice and Johnson advisor Abe Fortas. Herbert Gans writes that *Newsweek* killed its own reporter's story, which was sympathetic to the radicals, after its top editors saw the *Times* account.[51] In crisis, the normally hegemonic routines threatened to undermine hegemonic ideology; caught in a bind between class loyalties and strict professionalism, executives were now more likely to intervene in the news process in order to sustain their deepest principles.

But precisely because the media have established some independence from the State, top political officials may feel threatened enough by amplified dissidence, however domesticated, to crack down directly. The State can intervene in media operations most subtly by withholding interviews, by preferring competitors, or by feeding false information to reliable reporters. The President can reward compliant editors and writers with prestigious political jobs (thus, for example, Johnson appointed pro-war *Washington Post* editor J. Russell Wiggins to a lame-duck term as Ambassador to the United Nations);[52] or the President and other officials can alternately scold and cajole insufficiently docile media powers, or try to intimidate them directly. In October 1963, John F. Kennedy tried to convince *Times* publisher Arthur Ochs ("Punch") Sulzberger to transfer David Halberstam out of Vietnam.[53] Lyndon Johnson preferred to phone reporters with his complaints; he also liked to go over low-level heads, calling his friends Frank Stanton and Robert Kintner, the presidents of CBS and NBC, respectively, appealing to them in the name of old ties and patriotic duties. Stanton above all had been Johnson's friend and counselor since 1938, when Johnson had acquired CBS affiliate status for his wife's Austin radio station. Former CBS News General Manager and Vice-President Blair Clark told me that while covering the presidential campaign of 1956, he

50. See Gay Talese, *The Kingdom and the Power* (New York: World, 1969), pp. 513–515, and Richard Pollak, "Abe Rosenthal Presents the *New* New York Times," *Penthouse*, September 1977, p. 50. *Times* publisher Sulzberger was a Columbia trustee.

51. Gans, *Deciding What's News*, p. 347, n. 32.

52. David Halberstam, *The Powers That Be* (New York: Alfred A. Knopf, 1979), pp. 545–546.

53. Ibid., pp. 445–446.

had shared a plane ride with Johnson, who had asked him: "How well do you know Frank Stanton?" and then advised: "You better know Frank better. He's one of the finest men in America. Why, he and Ruth were down on the ranch doe-shooting last week." [54] During the mid-sixties, Johnson was regularly infuriated by CBS's war coverage, and Stanton, as chairman of the Board of Trustees of the RAND Corporation, a top military research think tank, was in any event no critic of the main thrust of Cold War and interventionist politics. So Stanton regularly relayed Johnson's anger— in Chairman Paley's presence, no less—at weekly lunches of CBS News executives. At one point in 1964, according to David Halberstam, Johnson complained to Stanton about Dan Rather's work—nothing radical here—and Stanton relayed the complaint to News President Fred Friendly, who, violating the norm (news executives are supposed to insulate reporters from high-level intervention), chewed out Rather for irresponsible reporting. [55]

Johnson's style was mostly person-to-person; he was the master of arm-twisting. But he could go further when pressed: in August 1965, CBS correspondent Morley Safer—a Canadian by birth—covered the U.S. Marines setting fire to Vietnamese huts in the village of Cam Ne. Simply as film, Safer's piece was so strong and so shocking that, as David Halberstam says, the news executives "simply could not fail to use it." They ran the piece. Early the next morning, according to CBS officials whom Halberstam interviewed, Johnson called Stanton and woke him up. "Frank," said the President of the United States, "are you trying to fuck me?" "Who is this?" asked the sleepy Stanton. "Frank, this is your President, and yesterday your boys shat on the American flag." Johnson insisted that Safer must be a Communist, got the Royal Canadian Mounted Police to investigate him, and, when informed later that Safer was not a Communist, only a Canadian, insisted: "Well, I knew he wasn't an American." [56]

But for all this, Johnson kept his fury at CBS behind closed doors. Beginning late in 1969, by contrast, the Nixon Oval Office launched a *public* crusade, a protracted campaign against not only the media but the Wall Street–Council on Foreign Relations establishment as a whole. Johnson had to keep face with Frank Stanton; Nixon owed no such debts. He was blunter and more sweeping; he

54. Interview, Blair Clark, November 10, 1976.
55. Ibid., pp. 432–442.
56. Ibid., pp. 486–492. Quotations from p. 490.

had a Vice-President who specialized in threatening rhetoric; and he orchestrated years of attacks, including, not least, threats to regulate the networks more closely. Only in retrospect are we entitled to say that he paid a price for overstepping; he might have succeeded.

For most of the Nixon years, the media strained to occupy a middle ground between the Nixon White House and the newly legitimized antiwar movement. Nixon had campaigned in 1968 as a "peace" candidate, and the media relayed that frame unskeptically. He had campaigned to "bring us together," and the media shared that objective as well. In fact, at the beginning of Nixon's first term in office, the media processed antiwar coverage into a frame that legitimated his administration as the agency to end the war. With all due respect to Vice-President Agnew and the White House's critique of network "instant analysis," both NBC and ABC had gone so far toward the presidential frame as to have promulgated the policy that the "story" in Vietnam was now the negotiations, not the battles. In March 1969, as Edward Epstein discovered, the executive producer of the ABC Evening News, Av Westin, sent a telex message to the Saigon bureau:

I think the time has come to shift some of our focus from the battlefield, or more specifically American military involvement with the enemy, to themes and stories under the general heading: We Are On Our Way Out of Vietnam. . . .

And as Epstein writes: "Quite predictably, a radical change from combat stories to 'We Are On Our Way Out'–type stories followed in ABC's coverage of the Vietnam war."[57] NBC decided likewise. The air bombardment of Cambodia and Laos was downplayed to the vanishing point. Such decisions admirably suited the purposes of the Nixon administration, which wanted not so much to extricate America from the war as to create an *image* of extrication ("Vietnamization").

Nonetheless, Nixon was unplacated: he found the incoherent, superficial, halting, unreflective media version of the war, and its amplifying of the moderate antiwar movement, an obstacle still. And so came the heavy hand. The new chairman of the FCC, Dean Burch, phoned the three network heads on the morning after Nixon's "Vietnamization" speech of November 3, 1969, asking for

57. Epstein, *News from Nowhere,* pp. 17–18; Hodgson, *America in Our Time,* p. 378.

transcripts of the networks' "instant analyses." After Vice-President Agnew's anti-media speeches of November 13 and 20, the White House mobilized the local affiliates against the networks. Nixon and his staff orchestrated a campaign to manage the news during the Mobilization and Moratorium of November 15. In 1971, Nixon went to court seeking to restrain the *New York Times* and other newspapers from publishing some of the Pentagon Papers. In 1972, Charles Colson of the White House staff called and visited CBS's Paley and Stanton, complaining about the first part of Stanhope Gould's takeout on Watergate; as a result, CBS News President Salant ordered the second installment cut from fifteen to seven minutes.[58] Salant has denied that Colson's intervention was the direct immediate cause,[59] but the overall impact of the Nixon campaign against the media is deniable only at the cost of common sense. Even a top CBS producer acknowledges that Agnew's crusade "made us more cautious," though he is quick to add: "That might not have been a bad thing: where we would have double-checked a fact before, we would triple-check it now."[60] A CBS cameraman remembers considerably more apprehension: "Everybody was running scared. Everybody was being incredibly cautious. And [correspondents] would make jokes about it to us. Like, 'We can't offend Mr. Agnew,' or 'We have to be careful because Agnew's watching.'"[61] A few months later, Walter Cronkite said: "I think the industry as a whole has been intimidated."[62] Everyone I spoke to who was connected with CBS at the time is at pains

58. On Colson's intervention and CBS's response, see Timothy Crouse, *The Boys on the Bus* (New York: Random House, 1973), pp. 174–175; Robert Cirino, *Power to Persuade* (New York: Bantam Books, 1974), p. 35; William S. Paley, *As It Happened* (Garden City, N.Y.: Doubleday, 1979), pp. 318–327; Daniel Schorr, *Clearing the Air* (Boston: Houghton Mifflin, 1977), pp. 52–58; and Halberstam, *Powers That Be*, pp. 651–661. On the Nixon White House and its campaign against the networks generally, see Jeb Stuart Magruder, *An American Life* (New York: Atheneum, 1974), pp. 81 ff. and 105 ff., and my discussion above, pp. 224–229; the extremely thorough account in William J. Porter, *Assault on the Media: The Nixon Years* (Ann Arbor: University of Michigan Press, 1976); Thomas Whiteside, "Shaking the Tree," *The New Yorker*, March 17, 1975, pp. 41–91; and Schorr, *Clearing the Air*, pp. 14–120.

59. Salant twice refused my attempts to interview him about CBS coverage of the New Left, in the fall of 1976 and again in the spring of 1977, claiming that "I have the world's worst memory and can't remember what happened yesterday, let alone the sixties." He did insist, however, that "the way we work here at CBS News, the choices were never mine." (Letter to the author, October 18, 1976.)

60. Interview, Ron Bonn, November 19, 1976. See Bonn's further remark, above, p. 262.

61. Interview, Stephen Lighthill, June 16, 1977.

62. Cronkite was speaking on March 3, 1970, as quoted in James Aronson, *Deadline for the Media* (Indianapolis: Bobbs-Merrill, 1972), p. 9.

to deny there was any direct management interference with reporters after November 1969; but documentaries, news specials,
and "instant analyses" suffered. The Nixonian chill was felt—and
resisted.[63]

Yet the power of *direct* political intervention is still easily exaggerated. In this case, *TV Guide* was announcing on September
27, 1969—fully six weeks before Agnew's opening barrage in Des
Moines—that the networks were going to be retrenching in their
coverage of the Left, that they would be shifting toward "exploring
middle and lower-middle-class Americans."[64] "Middle America"
and the "silent majority" were the new shibboleths. Thus did the
networks strive to maintain a political equilibrium in which their
corporate position was secure. They do not need to be chided in
public to know that their room for maneuver is limited. The low-
background potential threat of the State is a constant. Political crises may disrupt the normal equilibrium of institutions. Yet between
crises and normal situations—between situations requiring extraordinary State or corporate interventions into the news, and situations in which the routine procedures are left to take their
course—there is no hard-and-fast line. Indeed, the late sixties
were a time when political crisis itself became routine—Tet, the antiwar campaigns within the Democratic Party, the intervention of the
Wise Men, the balance-of-payments and gold crises, Johnson's abdication, the King and Kennedy assassinations, black uprisings,
student rebellion, Chicago, the November 1969 Mobilization, and
the killings at Kent State and Jackson State. Extraordinary interventions into news policy became more ordinary.

The media, finally, are corporations of a peculiar type. It is not
only that broadcasters are regulated, directly and not, by the State;
so are many other industries. (In any event, newspapers and news-

---

63. According to Daniel Schorr (interview, May 10, 1977), when Chairman
Paley, in June 1973, discontinued all vestiges of "instant analysis," even the bland
summaries that CBS had instituted in late 1969, correspondents in the Washington
bureau "were all rocked by that; we were all very angry." Several, including Schorr,
wrote a letter of protest to Salant, who acted as if he welcomed it as ammunition
against Paley's decision. And indeed the decision was rescinded in November. See
also Schorr, *Clearing the Air*, pp. 61–64.

64. Cited in Hodgson, *America in Our Time*, pp. 382–383. Hodgson's interesting
discussion of the 1968–69 media retrenchment (pp. 369–377) emphasizes the conservative force of public opinion and the media elite's fear of finding itself too far
ahead of the mass audience. There is no question that the media managers felt this
fear. But their fear of the public reaction was inextricably entangled with their fear
of the potentially regulating State. These were experienced as a single fear.

magazines are not directly regulated, and their framing procedures and the frames that result are not vastly different from those of the networks.) More to the point, the product that the networks sell is the attention of audiences; their primary market is the advertisers themselves. (Newspapers, too, draw the bulk of their income from advertising.) To assemble the largest and richest possible audiences, for whose attention advertisers will pay the highest rates, the media may risk offending particular corporate interests. They see themselves exercising a general steering function for the entire political economy. As CBS President Stanton said in 1960: "Since we are advertiser-supported we must take into account the general objectives and desires of advertisers as a whole."[65] But the networks' profit interests are, in general, perfectly compatible with their journalists' routines for achieving objectivity. The "good story" in traditional journalistic terms is also appealing to a mass audience: "common sense" ratifies the hegemonic frames. The news organization therefore has two reasons to reward the production of "good stories": for the network, good journalism is good business; but more, the media have a general interest in stabilizing the liberal capitalist order as a whole, and it is this interest, played out through all the hegemonic routines, which stands behind the dominant news frames. The whole hegemonic process in journalism operates in a reformist key: it exposes particular business and State violations of the core hegemonic principles. Precisely for that reason, the relations among media, corporations, and the State are intrinsically thick with conflict.[66]

So it is hardly surprising that businessmen regularly complain that the networks are biased against them.[67] In the first issue of a

65. *Television Network Program Procurement: Report of the Committee on Interstate and Foreign Commerce, House of Representatives,* 88th Cong., 1st sess. (Washington, D.C.: Government Printing Office, 1963), p. 335, as quoted in Erik Barnouw, *The Sponsor* (New York: Oxford University Press, 1978), p. 57.

66. See Gans, *Deciding What's News,* pp. 68–69, 203–206, on the muckraking Progressivism of American journalism.

67. Business critiques of the news media are legion. Among the more articulate versions are "Business and the Press—Independent or Interdependent?" a speech by Donald S. MacNaughton, Chairman and Chief Executive Officer, the Prudential Insurance Company of America, November 4, 1975, excerpted in the *New York Times,* Business Section, March 7, 1976, p. 12; "The Values That Can Serve Mankind," Remarks by David Rockefeller, Chairman of the Board, the Chase Manhattan Bank, before the Northern California Region of the National Conference of Christians and Jews, April 7, 1976; and the discussion in Leonard Silk and David Vogel, *Ethics and Profits* (New York: Simon and Schuster, 1976), pp. 104–116, drawing on comments from many executives who are members of the Conference Board. Media

closed-circulation magazine called *Chief Executive*, for example, Walter Cronkite urges businessmen to make themselves more available to reporters in order to respond to charges against corporate practice. Cronkite argues that businesses need a reliable press to satisfy their own intelligence function, and he tries to enlist them in the networks' contest with the State over press freedoms and the First Amendment. He defends the bond between business and the news media as "something known in the biological sciences as symbiosis":

> It's a word that may have been sullied and discredited in your minds by that group of ill-fated young fanatics who called themselves the "Symbionese Liberation Army," but it remains a valid concept.
> Symbiosis is a curious relationship. It is defined as the intimate living together of two kinds of organisms whereby such association is advantageous to each. It seems to me that journalists and business leaders are bound together in just such a relationship.
> Newspapers, broadcasting outlets and networks survive on the advertising revenues that come from business. Journalism can thrive only so long as the business community remains healthy enough to provide these funds. Business, on the other hand, depends upon journalism to foster its own growth—through the dissemination of information through news and advertising.[68]

This is what the "Dean of the World's Broadcast Journalists" (the magazine's blurb) urges upon an audience of top business, government, and other executives. Campaigning for symbiosis, as other top media people have also been doing, Cronkite acknowledges implicitly that it is far from an accomplished fact. On the other hand, the fact that he takes the trouble to spell out the goal reveals that the media elite is defensive. It is media strategy to *accomplish* symbiosis with the corporations as a whole, to guide that sym-

---

responses include "Business and the Press: Who's Doing What to Whom and Why?" Remarks of Arthur R. Taylor, President, CBS Inc., before the Financial Executives Institute, October 21, 1975; and "Businessmen Can Look Better If They Try," by Dan Cordtz, economics editor at ABC, in the *New York Times*, Business Section, July 18, 1976, p. 12. The tone of these latter two articles is strikingly similar to Cronkite's appeal, below, for a symbiotic division of labor: the media have *their* jobs to do, business has *its* job to do, and businessmen should learn how to make more effective use of the existing media system. In other words, the media spokesmen are defending a functional division of labor between economic and cultural-legitimation spheres.

68. *Chief Executive* 1 (July–September 1977): 26. Weirdly enough, the role of the young heiress-terrorist in the film *Network* was played by Walter Cronkite's daughter Kathy.

biosis, and in the process to guide the whole society toward a stable environment in which the media corporations may flourish. Just as the networks must be careful not to offend core interests of the State, so they must take care not to violate the most central premises of the business system as a whole: they must sanction the right of private control over investment and production, just as they sanctify their own right to control the space within which public communication takes place. The business practices exposed in the news—bribes, sudden health hazards, damage to the environment—are precisely the exceptional; and the frames generally cushion the impact of these reports by isolating exceptional corporations, by blaming "the public," by speaking from the angle of consumers and not workers, and by refraining from attempts at general explanation and radical solution. Yet, in this weakly reformist process, the media set terms for discourse which, corporations believe, threaten the legitimacy of the corporate system as a whole. *The media seek symbiosis with the corporate system precisely through the bounded routines of "objective" journalism.* This drive is utopian; it does not cease, though it is always, in the end, unconsummated.

11 Seventies Going on Eighties

IMPLICATIONS FOR MOVEMENTS

Straining to take advantage of the media's interest in "exciting" or "important" news, opposition movements step into this web of conflicting yet interdependent corporate and State powers. One core task of opposition movements is to contest the prevailing definitions of things, the dominant frames. They must "rectify names," they must change the way people construe the world, they must penetrate and unmask what they see as the mystification sustained by the powers that be. In this sense, all insurgent movements must be empirical in their approach to the conventional definitions of objective reality; they must probe to discover *in practice* how far the principles of news "objectivity" can be severed both from the disparaging codes and from the corporate and State interests that sustain and delimit them.

Since the sixties, opposition movements have become still more sensitive to the impact of the media on their messages and their identities. At one extreme, the Symbionese Liberation Army learned how to manage an exercise in total manipulation, commandeering the media for a moment of spurious glory. At the other, the women's liberation movement, recognizing some of the destructive and self-destructive consequences of the spotlight, has learned from the experience of the New Left and worked with *some* success to decentralize leadership and "spokespersonship," avoiding *some* (not all) of the agonies of the single-focused spotlight.[1]

1. On relations between the feminist movement and the media, see Monica B. Morris, "Newspapers and the New Feminists: Blackout as Social Control," *Journal-*

This is after much trial and much error. The results are uneven.

To what extent have the terms of hegemony been renegotiated? Hegemony exists in historical time, and its boundaries are adjustable as the media adjust to new social realities. *The more closely the concerns and values of social movements coincide with the concerns and values of elites in politics and in media, the more likely they are to become incorporated in the prevailing news frames.* Since the sixties, for example, consumer organizations have been elevated to the status of regular news makers; they and their concerns are reported with sympathy, sufficiently so as to inspire corporate complaints and counter-propaganda in the form of paid, issue-centered advertising. Ralph Nader and other public-interest lawyers have become respected celebrities, often interviewed for response statements, photographed in suits and ties and sitting squarely behind desks or in front of bookshelves, embodying solid expertise and mainstream reliability. They have learned to make the journalistic code work for them, while journalists have extended them the privilege of legitimacy. At times, environmentalist groups like the Sierra Club have been adept at using the media to publicize particular issues and to campaign for particular reforms. In the seventies, the prestigious media policymakers have legitimized some political values of their ecologically-minded peers in class and culture. These concerns have been institutionalized in government agencies like the Environmental Protection Agency and the Council on Environmental Quality, which now serve as legitimate news sources. The more radical wings of the environmental movement—those which challenge the raison d'être of centralized mass production and try to join the concerns of labor and environmentalists—are scanted.

Indeed, the very concept of a *movement* has been certified; an *activist*, left or right, is now a stereotyped persona accorded a right to parade quickly through the pageant of the news. Consumer activists, environmentalists, gay activists, feminists, pro- and anti-busing people, as well as anti-abortionists, Jarvis-Gann supporters, Laetrile legalizers, angry loggers, farmers, and truck drivers —many movements which can be presented as working for (or against) concrete assimilable reforms have become regular, recognizable, even stock characters in newspapers and news broadcasts.

ism Quarterly 50 (1973): 37–42; Kate Millett, *Flying* (New York: Alfred A. Knopf, 1974); Jo Freeman, *The Politics of Women's Liberation* (New York: David McKay, 1975), pp. 111–116, 147–150, 228; and Gaye Tuchman, *Making News* (New York: The Free Press, 1978), chap. 7.

The media spread the news that alternative opinions exist on virtually every issue. They create an impression that the society is full of political vitality, that opinions and interests contend freely—that the society, in a word, is pluralist. But in the process, they do extend the reach of movements that agree, at least for working purposes, to accept the same premise—and are willing to pay a price.

It is hard to know in advance what that price will be, hard to generalize about the susceptibilities of movements to the publicity process and its internal consequences. Of internal factors, two seem bound to increase a movement's *dependency* on the mass media: (1) the narrowness of its social base; and (2) its commitment to specific society-wide political goals. And then two other factors, when added onto the first two, seem to produce the most destructive *consequences* of media dependency: (3) the movement's turn toward revolutionary desire and rhetoric in a nonrevolutionary situation; and (4) its unacknowledged political uncertainties, especially about the legitimacy of its own leaders. Thus, in the case of the New Left: (1) It was contained within a relatively narrow social base: students and the young intelligentsia. (2) It had a specific political purpose, to end the war. These two factors in combination were decisive in forcing the movement into dependency on the media, although they did not by themselves generate destructive consequences. Proceeding into national reform politics from its narrow social base, the movement could hope to end the war only by mobilizing wider constituencies. Attempting to affect government policy in a hurry, it was forced to rely upon the mass media to broadcast the simple fact that opposition existed. And then the other factors came into play. (3) The New Left, in its revolutionary moment, allowed itself to believe it was in a revolutionary situation. In this mood, which flowed from (though it also contradicted!) the reformist antiwar moment, much of the New Left determined to muscle its way through to a political transformation so far beyond its means that it hurled itself into a politics of spurious amplification. Now mass-mediated images, and metaphors borrowed from the histories of previous revolutions, were dragooned into the Leninist role of vanguard organization—with consequences predictably ludicrous and self-destructive. And at the same time, (4) the New Left's ambivalence about criteria for leadership, especially when coupled with its inability to engender a coherent political ideology and organization, left all parties damaged: leaders were vulnerable to the temptations of celebrity, while the rank and file were stranded without means of keeping their leaders accountable. On the face of it, the black movement of the sixties and seventies shared these vulnerabilities, and for the same reasons. For the black movement also began with a narrow social base, the black population and students; it campaigned for the specific purpose of ending de jure segregation; it failed to give clear signals to its leaders; and a significant portion ended up committed to a revolutionary project within a nonrevolutionary situation.

But each factor is powerful insofar as it reinforces the previous factor or factors. If the chain can be broken, then the consequences of the previous factors can be minimized. If a movement is committed to working for specific political goals but refuses to devote itself to revolutionary politics, it may avoid the most severe dependency on the media; it is more likely, too, to be able to control the content of its publicity. The United Farm Workers, for example, are entrenched within a narrow social base and are committed to specific goals; but they have an undisputed leader whose media presence is (I am told) heralded with pride rather than envy; and by avoiding revolutionism, they have been able to occupy the media spotlight without subjecting themselves to its most destructive glare.

Reformist movements, then, are less vulnerable to structural deformation in the publicity process than are revolutionary ones. Reformists can achieve media standing by getting *their* experts legitimated; the standard frames are equipped to show them—and their class—to relatively good advantage. Revolutionaries, by contrast, can achieve media standing only as deviants; they become "good copy" as they become susceptible to derogatory framing devices; and past a certain point, precisely what made them "good copy" may make them dangerous to the State and subject, directly or indirectly, to blackout. But to say that reformist movements are less vulnerable to disparagement is not to say that they are immune. They, too, must confront the spotlight's tendency to convert leadership to celebrity, to highlight extravagant rhetoric (if not action), and to help induce transitional crises of generations. Likewise, the standard journalistic frames persist in marginalizing the most radical aspects of movements and setting them against the more moderate. They cover single-issue movements, but frame them in opposition to others: feminists against blacks, blacks against chicanos. *The routine frames that I examined in Part I endure for reformist as well as deeply oppositional movements.* Even reformist movements must work industriously to broadcast their messages without having them discounted, trivialized, fragmented, rendered incoherent. Awareness of the media's routines and frames is no guarantee that a movement will be able to achieve publicity for its analysis and program on its own terms; the frames remain powerful, processing opposition into hegemonic order. But surely ignorance of the media's codes condemns a movement to marginality.

SOME RECENT FRAMES: THE TREATMENT OF MOVEMENTS AGAINST NUCLEAR POWER AND NUCLEAR WEAPONS

I close with recent movements. What has not changed in media framing is more striking than what *has* changed. The movements against nuclear power and nuclear weapons in the late seventies have faced, first of all, the problem of getting over the high threshold for media coverage. In August of 1976, some 177 demonstrators of the Clamshell Alliance in New England were arrested while attempting to block construction of a nuclear reactor at Seabrook, New Hampshire. The *New York Times* reported this fact in two short paragraphs on page 32. The *Washington Post* and the *Los Angeles Times* did not report it at all. But the 1976 resignations of three General Electric reactor-designing engineers were covered far more thoroughly: the defection of experts, with its latent themes of spunky individualism and expertness united, was an unprecedented public event in the history of the nuclear industry. In April–May 1977, the Clamshell Alliance went back to occupy the Seabrook reactor site, and this time, 1,414 persons were arrested. The Clams, as they called themselves, had trained thoroughly in nonviolent action and worked hard to present themselves as gentle and friendly. Indeed, this was the largest nonviolent demonstration of the seventies and one of the largest in American history. Although New Hampshire Governor Meldrim Thomson warned beforehand that the demonstration would turn out to be "a cover for terrorist activity," not a single injury was reported. The *New York Times*'s treatment was respectful and lengthy. Other papers, as well as the television networks, also stressed the Clams' amicable relations with the police, and then, over succeeding days, the state's logistical problems in housing the arrested in an armory. The Clams' case against the reactor was, of course, scanted. A month later, the *Washington Post* described a follow-up demonstration by saying that "the people involved are older, . . . mellower and more inward directed than the antiwar demonstrators of a few years ago." Such comparisons, shared and indeed sought by the movement, were common. Still, on the NBC Nightly News of July 26, 1977, David Brinkley intoned with his customary authoritativeness: "The Seabrook nuclear power plant has been . . . the center of riotous protest."

Yet, predictably, the 1979 disaster at Three Mile Island altered the prevailing frame. Three Mile Island shook the nation's elites; it was the Tet of the nuclear power industry. Reporters now began calling up anti-nuclear-power groups, asking for information about reactor safety. Academically certified experts close to the movement, like Dr. John Gofman of the University of California at Berkeley and the onetime General Electric engineers, became quasi-legitimate sources, and were now cited frequently in the press giving their balancing statements against claims by Metropolitan Edison (the operators of Three Mile Island), Babcock & Wilcox (the builders of the plant), and even, though more rarely, the Nuclear Regulatory Commission (NRC). Reporters felt that they were being lied to by officials and business executives, and were saying or strongly implying so. Walter Cronkite referred one night to "the Harrisburg syndrome." The networks were reporting information leaked from within the NRC, showing how little the official regulatory agency had known about what was happening in Pennsylvania. At the same time, the networks played up the soothing announcements of Harold Denton, the NRC's man in charge on the spot. Denton was now certified—and not only by the media—as the authority who could be trusted to tell the truth and recommend the necessary reforms. Like Senator Sam Ervin and then Gerald Ford in the Watergate crisis, he was an official folk hero.

But while the media were busy confirming the dangers that the movement had warned against for years, they were treating the activities of the movement itself with the customary mixture of undercoverage, trivialization, respect, and disparagement. On April 7, 1979, some 20,000 people rallied at San Francisco's Civic Center against the opening of a nuclear plant at Diablo Canyon, two hundred miles south. Local reports emphasized the cheer of the sunny day, while the *New York Times* buried its brief report about *five* thousand demonstrators (upgraded to seven thousand in the Late City Edition) as a tag to another story, on page 28. The *Times* mentioned only one speaker, Ralph Nader, and two entertainers, Jackson Browne and Bonnie Raitt; it did not mention the famous and unfamous speakers (including Daniel Ellsberg) who denounced the nuclear *weapons* research going on at nearby Livermore, or those who spoke about the mortality rates of Native American uranium miners in the Southwest, or those who spoke about the American nuclear industry's export of reactors to politically hospitable dependencies such as the Philippines. Over one-third of the article was devoted to quotations from a Pacific Gas & Electric spokesman defending the safety of the plant, with a weak answer from duly constituted authority, the U.S. Geological Survey; no movement people were quoted at all. Later in the spring and summer, when Governor Jerry Brown had come out against Diablo Canyon, California media began to frame the movement as a field for Brown's presidential ambitions, an occasion for his personal strategy. But on July 1, CBS News did a long, respectful takeout on the national movement against nuclear power, comparable to Fred Powledge's 1965 discovery piece on the New Left. After Three Mile Island came so close to home, the movement against nuclear power was now on the legitimate map.

Meanwhile, the movement against nuclear *weapons* has received far less national coverage. It is a smaller movement, true, but not as much smaller as its image suggests. Since April 1978, demonstrators have been rallying and sitting on the tracks leading to the factory in Rocky Flats, Colorado, where the plutonium triggers for all American H-bombs are manufactured. Hundreds of demonstrators have been arrested, tried, jailed, and fined, including, most famously, Daniel Ellsberg. Dr. Carl Johnson, the top health officer of Jefferson County (which includes Rocky Flats), has concluded from his study of the area around the plant that plutonium leakage—including two big effusions resulting from massive fires in 1957 and 1969—has caused cancers and will go on causing more. The governor of Colorado and the district's congresswoman have expressed grave concern about the immediate health dangers. Colorado newspapers have covered both the demonstrations and the health study; so, in a scattered, fragmented way, have other papers from time to time around the country. But throughout the year 1978, there was only a single, quite minor network story about any of this, and that on the underwatched weekend news. During the biggest demonstrations, in late April and early May 1978, the *New York Times* ran a small notice on page 14.

The *Washington Post* and the *Los Angeles Times* ran nothing. As I've already noted, a *New York Times* Washington editor explained to one of the arrestees—an old friend of his, as it happened—"America is tired of protest. America is tired of Daniel Ellsberg."

Carl Johnson has not been certified as a national source; the threshold for disputing the factual assurances of the national security State is very high. But at the same time, the *New York Times*, early in 1979, reported on page 1 of its Sunday edition about the revival of enthusiasm for disarmament within American churches: another piece comparable in its respectful tone and broad scope to the Powledge feature on the New Left in March 1965. A few weeks later, CBS's Evening News presented a reasonably balanced five-part takeout series on the arms race, and disclosed that Billy Graham was now horrified by the dangers of nuclear holocaust and had recanted his bellicose support of the Vietnam war. The *Times* and CBS were thus relaying and amplifying the respectable detente position of the Carter administration and the churches, especially as the SALT II treaty neared signing. Shortly thereafter, though, ABC News ran a ten-part series supporting the hard-line Pentagon position that the United States is "falling behind" the Russian military. Between them, CBS and ABC were reproducing the central conflict in high policy circles *predominantly within the frames and terms of the elite factions.* The media were reorganizing frames as they had done after Tet. But this time the policy elite were more fundamentally divided—between supporters of detente and more strenuous militarists, between supporters of deterrence strategy and supporters of counterforce preparation for "limited nuclear war"—and the media were polarizing to suit. But the *movement* against nuclear weapons remained marginal to this narrowly confined debate: when the movement's specific opinions made sense as auxiliary supports to the detente elite, they were reported, but the movement's more deeply oppositional point of view, its critique of the institutional and ideological underpinnings and premises of the arms race, remained outside the spotlight.

To sum up, then: an opposition movement is caught in a fundamental and inescapable dilemma. If it stands outside the dominant realm of discourse, it is liable to be consigned to marginality and political irrelevance; its issues are domesticated, its deeper challenge to the social order sealed off, trivialized, and contained. If, on the other hand, it plays by conventional political rules in order to acquire an image of credibility—if, that is, its leaders are well-mannered, its actions well-ordered, and its slogans specific and "reasonable"—it is liable to be assimilated into the hegemonic political world view; it comes to be identified with narrow (if important) reform issues, and its oppositional edge is blunted. This is the condition of movements in all the institutions of liberal capitalism; one major site of the difficulty lies within the mass media. By framing movements in all the ways I have tried to demonstrate, by excluding and by taming, the media reinforce one of the central rhythms of American political history. Opposition movements emerge, but their radical identities weaken. The political system has so far proved capable of responding with reforms sufficient to absorb and divert much of the movement's energy. Some of the movement's radical imagery endures, but in a denatured form, as a disembodied set of slogans and vague moods. The ghostly aura of a movement lives on to inspire, and haunt, the next generation of reformers, while the most radical content curdles into sectarian isolation. A movement's general spirit and its specific single-issue programs are split apart, to the detriment of each.

But it would be mistaken to think that the established order simply sheds or absorbs radical challenges while remaining the same.[2] The cultural commodity process permits change in the hegemonic ideology, *and may even require it*. The self-contradictions in hegemonic ideology give it the flexibility to shift with circumstance, and even to turn opposition to its own advantage. Once disturbed, the system does not simply return, pendulumlike, to point zero and go on as if nothing has happened. The oppositional spirit is transformed and moves into other channels; it moves, for example, from politics into culture, into political cynicism and hip "lifestyles." The New Left's political spirit, its search for a society of participatory democracy and personal worth, has split apart into discordant cultural and political elements: into fragmented local counter-institutions[3] and impotent national Leninist "parties"; into working-class shop-floor militancy, and into self-protective middle-class privatism and its scatter of "human potential" psychologies and mysticisms; into socialist feminism and into an inter-

2. The following paragraphs benefited from discussions with Paul E. Willis, Jon D. Cruz, and David Wellman.

3. On the limits of counter-institutions and local insurgency, see the provocative, well-coordinated collection of essays edited by John Case and Rosemary C. R. Taylor, *Co-ops, Communes & Collectives: Experiments in Social Change in the 1960s and 1970s* (New York: Pantheon, 1979), and my review in *The Progressive*, June 1979, pp. 55–56.

est-group feminism of limited reform and personal advancement; into the struggles among oppressed nationalities for their shares of shrinking public goods; and into authoritarian religious cults and ideologies of managerial self-actualization.[4] Within the search for spiritual wholeness and political community arises the totalitarian temptation, reaching one sort of culmination in the People's Temple; within the search for authentic personal freedom arises the old bourgeois desire to build a fortress against human bonds: each of these cultural and political projects grows rigid and self-limiting, even dangerous, in the course of excluding critical elements within the others. The radical project for the eighties is to regather the elements of cultural revolt, to form of them a coherent political opposition, and to overcome the centrifugal tendencies of the seventies: tendencies which represented the playing out of the incomplete and self-contradictory revolts of the sixties.

As the mass media have suffused social life, they have become crucial fields for the definition of social meaning—partially contested zones in which the hegemonic ideology meets its partial challenges and then adapts. The cultural industries, including the news organizations, produce self-contradictory artifacts, balancing here, absorbing there, framing and excluding and disparaging, working in complicated ways to manage and contain cultural resistance, to turn it to use as commodity and to tame and isolate intractable movements and ideas. In the process, they may actually magnify and hasten manageable forms of political change. One thing seems certain: the society will go on helplessly manufacturing, and deforming, the opposition it deserves; yet as long as the political economy continues to deliver what the majority define as the essential goods, the legitimacy crisis of the system as a whole will likely remain within bounds. A resistible hegemony is resisted because it cannot satisfy human needs; it cannot be taken entirely for granted; it is hegemony in process.

4. On new managerial ideologies, see Richard Sennett, "The Boss's New Clothes," *New York Review of Books* 26 (February 22, 1979): 42–46.

Appendix on Sources
and Methods

THE MOVEMENT

To speak of "the movement" is already to elude sharp definition. In the 1930s and 1940s, "the movement" meant specifically
the Communist Party and the organizations, projects, and institutions more or less in its orbit. But in the 1960s, "the movement"
was more elusive: defining it moved into the realm of subjectiv-
ities, doubts, and quizzical quotation marks. Who was in, who was
out? It depended on whom you asked, and when. And yet we
must start with the fact that there were several thousand young
people who, in 1963 and 1964, began to casually call themselves
"the movement," to *know* themselves as "the movement," and to
speak of their needs and responsibilities within "the movement."
When they asked questions like "What should the movement do
about the war?" they were speaking of themselves, or of "people
like us," in whatever contested ways that phrase was meant. By
"the movement" some meant specifically the civil rights movement, but the term usually referred to both black and white activists who shared some commitment to the realization of civil rights,
peace, and some sort of radically democratic political-economic
and cultural transformation, and who believed in undertaking
some sort of direct action toward those ends. "New Left" was another self-determined term, first used by SDS in 1963, which deliberately adapted it from the British New Left of the late fifties. "New
Left" meant both New (not Old, that is to say, neither Communist
nor Social-Democratic) and Left (committed to social equality, opposed to militarism and racism, and loosely socialist).

In this movement that was both distinct and, at its boundaries, loosely defined, the two major national organizations were Students for a Democratic Society (SDS) and the Student Nonviolent Coordinating Committee (SNCC). I have written principally of SDS, which was the largest and most energetic national radical student organization throughout the sixties. (SNCC was a staff organization, an organization of organizers; it had many supporters, but no "members.") Insofar as there was an organizational (and spiritual and intellectual) center of the New Left, SDS was it, from 1960 through its dissolution into warring Leninist factions in June 1969. Ever since, SDS remains the major point of reference for analysis and discussion of the New Left.

So I have taken SDS as my major movement protagonist. Its boundaries were sharp: there were identifiable leaders, identifiable members, identifiable generations, and clear organizational procedures; this also makes SDS a convenient object of study. And I was a part of it. My experience in SDS has been first my ally, then my adversary, and finally, I trust, my plain source, impetus, and correction. I was President of SDS from June 1963 to June 1964. In 1964–65, I was an elected member of the SDS National Council, and one of two Coordinators of the SDS Peace Research and Education Project in Ann Arbor; in that capacity I helped organize the Chase Manhattan project (March 1965) and the March on Washington to End the War in Vietnam (April 1965) discussed in Part I. This makes me one of the Old Guard in SDS, though not an original member, since I was in Cambridge, Massachusetts, through June 1963, when SDS was being organized in Ann Arbor. From June 1965 through June 1966, I was one of a half-dozen members of the National Administrative Committee in Chicago, in close touch with National Office business (including the draft crisis of October 1965); I was also one of seventeen members of the National Council which met quarterly to set organizational policy. In later years, I did not maintain direct organizational ties—though I did go on attending National Council meetings and conventions through June 1967, and kept up personal contact with a number of SDS officers. Through 1968 and 1969, I grew steadily more estranged from the direction of the national organization; in opposition, indeed in fascination, I stayed aware of what was being said and done both in the National Office and a number of chapters, and worked to comprehend the drift of things. During most of that period I was an editor of the *San Francisco Express Times* and a freelance writer; I stayed in touch with a range of New Left and antiwar projects.

My own memories served as an indispensable source, then, stretched and tempered by such documentary records as exist. In the course of my research, I studied, assessed, and at times quoted from personal correspondence from that period. I also consulted my nearly complete file of SDS Work List mailings (sent every week or two to key activists from 1963 through 1966), membership bulletins, SDS pamphlets and working papers and press releases, and the weekly *New Left Notes*, which SDS published from 1966 through 1969. I interviewed key participants in the staffs and committees which I discuss. And Kirkpatrick Sale's chronicle, *SDS*, served as a valuable secondary source: his facts are accurate—no mean achievement!—and so is his rendition of the spirit and strategies of SDS leaders (though not necessarily the rank and file, and not SDS women) at various points throughout the sixties. I crosschecked and interrogated all these sources, aware of the risks of retrospective accounts, the temptations of consciously and unconsciously selective memory, including my own. But the only alternative to retrospective accounts is to write nothing: that is, to rely on the versions written at the time. This is not the place to review all the sources; suffice it to say that almost all are remarkably poor— Sale's book is still in a class by itself—and that the historical record should not be left to them by default. Many of the issues that concern me clarified themselves only after the fact; that is the way history happens; that is why historians are needed, not simply archivists. Some of the joys of this work erupted when I refigured: what happened was not what I thought was happening at the time it happened. Critical reflection on one's own experience is one of the sublime pleasures of the sociological imagination.

So SDS is at the center of my account. I have detoured only occasionally, for comparative purposes and where the facts were accessible, to local and regional movements like Berkeley's Free Speech Movement in 1964, the Vietnam Day Committee in 1965, and People's Park in 1969, or time-limited campaigns like the teach-in wave of 1965. I have not analyzed the antiwar movement as a whole, although, in Chapter 7, I have probed the rise of the National Moratorium in 1969, and its relation to the Mobilization Committee to End the War in Vietnam ("Mobe"). These groups, along with the May 2nd Movement, the National Coordinating

Committee to End the War in Vietnam, and The Resistance, were essentially networks of organizers; none of them was a sustained membership organization. Nonetheless, my decidedly unsystematic but strong impression (somewhat confirmed in Part II) is that what I found to be true of the SDS-media relation would hold for the New Left as a whole: the media's framing devices were similar, as was the impact of the process on activists.

As for generalizations about other movements, I have hazarded some here and there in Parts II and III. When I undertook my research, I hoped—first ambitiously, then idly—to study the movement-media process for the black movement, the women's movement, and the environmental movement, as well as for the New Left. But early immersion in SDS sources quickly convinced me that the comparative task was unmanageable for a single researcher lacking co-workers or more lifetimes. I hope to see writers putting similar questions to the histories of SNCC (which I discuss in passing in Part II), the Southern Christian Leadership Council,[1] the Black Panther Party, and other black groups, as well as insurgent movements of other ethnic minorities, feminism, the environmental and consumer movements, pro- and anti-abortion movements, pro- and anti-busing movements, the Jarvis-Gann property tax revolt, and other reform and opposition movements.

THE MEDIA

I wanted to study "the media"; but which forms and which news organizations? Despite the claims of grand theory and of the former Vice-President of the United States, their coverage is not uniform and their significance is not identical.

I intended at first to study at least two television networks: the networks remain unique in their centralized symbolic force, their rise *in the sixties*, and their national reach. Certainly I wanted to study CBS News at least. CBS has been first or second in audience size, and in reputation, since the beginning of television news, averaging about 25 million viewers a night. In 1976, CBS's Evening News was broadcast by 205 local affiliates, NBC's by 195, and ABC's by 154. (ABC has gained since then because of its prime time success.) The CBS and NBC Evening News went from fifteen minutes to thirty in 1963, ABC News only in 1967. Since I wanted to

---

1. A start has been made by David J. Garrow in *Protest at Selma* (New Haven, Conn.: Yale University Press, 1978).

look at the *development* of network news through the sixties, and since ABC could not provide the fixed baseline of a news show constant in length, I eliminated it from the start, at least as my primary network. Between CBS and NBC, institutional policy made my decision for me. CBS would grant outside researchers limited access to their Newsfilm Archive, *which is the only archive even halfway open for news broadcasts made before August 1968* (when Vanderbilt University began videotaping all three networks' nightly news shows). NBC was closed to outsiders. So was ABC. I could not use their news even as secondary objects of comparison.

Deciding to examine CBS alone among the network news operations did not settle as much as I had hoped or had been led to expect. When I got to the CBS Newsfilm Archive in New York City, I found that it was impossible to find and to see—let alone to study—a large proportion of CBS News footage on the movement. Some material had been recorded on videotape, not on film, especially when it had been "fed" into the network from an out-of-town bureau; once the report had been transmitted, the tape had been reused and, in the process, wiped clean. If any copy was left in the world, it was the CBS "aircheck" copy, which CBS would not show. One would have to buy a copy to see it, I was told, and the cost was prohibitive. But more important, much film was simply lost. Some cardfile entries said that a film piece had been borrowed by a CBS News producer, or a documentary unit, or an auxiliary unit like *60 Minutes*, and lost by them, or kept there—in either event, never returned to the archive. Sometimes one day's coverage was there and the next day's was nowhere to be found, not even in the form of the audio track. When I checked with the separate audio tape archive, asking to hear the audio side of certain pieces, I was told: "We can only keep so much, because of space, so obviously somebody decided back then not to save these."

And even when the film existed in the archive, there were obstacles to comprehending it whole. Before 1966, most newsfilm was shot in black-and-white, and in these cases I was shown negative film—not easy to decipher. A further problem was that most newsfilm, whether black-and-white or color, was sent to New York and/or edited there on two (or sometimes three) separate reels, which were then broadcast simultaneously, superimposed on each other to make a complete image. (Usually, but not always, one reel played sound for some seconds while the other played picture; then they traded off.) When the reels were shown to me in the archive viewing room, it was almost always technically impossible to show the two reels simultaneously, as they had been broadcast; seeing them end to end, I probably lost some sense of the sight-and-sound wholes. Moreover, I saw only the film pieces, not the openings and closes supplied by the anchormen; before Vanderbilt University began videotaping network news in August 1968, no one saved those leads and closings. Finally, I was not permitted to see all the footage I succeeded in locating and asked to see. And because I could get an archive clerk assigned to me only briefly, I saw each news piece only once or twice. I took detailed notes, but it would surely have been better if I had been allowed to return to the clips in order to review them. The CBS Newsfilm Archive exists primarily for in-house use, and secondarily for sales to filmmakers. There is only a single viewing room. Evidently there are also union restrictions on the time of the projectionists. For all these reasons, I ended up deciding to study CBS's coverage, as best I could un-cover it, alongside that of the *New York Times*.

But I have not let the irregularity of the CBS data divert me from discussing what there is to discuss. When a subject is impor-tant or intriguing enough, one studies it as best one can, with the best records available. If the data are not systematic, neither can the analysis be; but one still does not let the disappearance of some evidence decree one's historical subjects. In this case, if I could not see all the film I intended to see, I did have the compensatory ad-vantage of reading the daily Editor's Logs for 1965 and subsequent years, which told me the subjects, locations, correspondents, and times for each news show's stories. I was able to get transcripts for *weekday* (not weekend) CBS News shows after March 1967 (when transcripts were first routinely kept), which provided the words but without any description of the pictures. And more important, I spoke at length and often more than once with a number of the CBS personnel involved in producing news reports of the move-ment (and other subjects) in the sixties. I spoke with correspon-dents, researchers, field producers (in charge of particular stories), and high-level producers on the Cronkite News. Thanks to cooper-ative CBS people, I was able to watch the Evening News operation in action, from both newsroom and control room; I also watched the editing process go on in an out-of-town bureau; soon I had a feel for the production process. Of course, I have watched unnum-bered hours of television news, have reflected much upon its pat-terns, and have read the sociological and journalistic accounts recently published on the workings of CBS News and other news operations. Given the fact that the missing material is missing, I feel confident that my conclusions are as conclusive as possible.

As for the *New York Times*, it was the obvious choice for the study of the impact of newspaper coverage on a social movement. The *Times* has the best claim to be called *the* national newspaper and *the* newspaper of record. As a routine channel for governmental leads and the revelations "released" by one agency or another looking for outside support, it plays a variety of key roles in national decision-making.[2] Leon V. Sigal writes: "Because of their extensive readership among the politically influential, the *Times* and [Washington] *Post* function as something akin to house organs for the political elite."[3] The *Times* sets agendas, generating and certifying issues in government, business, intellectual, professional, and academic circles throughout the country.[4] As a syndicator of news and features, it purveys frames directly to many other daily newspapers around the country. But probably more important, journalists throughout the country believe the *Times* and believe *in* it. In 1962, according to one study, about 90 percent of all Washington correspondents read the *Times* and considered it "fair" and "reliable."[5] Thus the *Times* ends up influencing the content of wire service stories, TV and radio news, and newsmagazines.

The *Times* is, in fact, one of the main channels through which network news workers form pictures of the world, what is happening there, and what, within that world, deserves investigating. At CBS News, decision-makers regularly clip the *Times* for leads

2. See Thomas Bethell, "The Myth of an Adversary Press," *Harper's Magazine*, January 1977, pp. 33–40.

3. Leon V. Sigal, *Reporters and Officials: The Organization and Politics of Newsmaking* (Lexington, Mass.: D. C. Heath, 1973), p. 47.

4. Periodically the *Times*'s Sunday Business Section runs full-page ads in which corporation executives testify to the indispensability of the *Times*. For example, note this quotation from Robert E. Kirby, Chairman of the Westinghouse Electric Corporation, on March 28, 1976: "While I sometimes find it difficult to agree with the *Times*, I find it equally difficult to get along without the *Times*. To manage a business—particularly a complicated business—requires information. I, for one, can't afford to pass it up." At the bottom of the page, each ad ends: "*The New York Times*: Makes things happen where affluence and influence meet."

As for elite intellectuals, Charles Kadushin (in *The American Intellectual Elite* [Boston: Little, Brown, 1974], pp. 140–141) points out that "*The New York Times* was read literally by 98 percent of our sample." With regard to Vietnam: "The editorial pages were not as important as the news itself. . . . *The New York Times* had a very important role in aligning intellectuals against the war in Vietnam."

5. William L. Rivers, "The Correspondents after 25 Years," *Columbia Journalism Review* 1 (Spring 1962): 8, cited in Sigal, *Reporters and Officials*, p. 40.

to stories. During a research visit to New York City in November 1976, I noticed that, one night, CBS and NBC News each broadcast a reasonably thorough piece on union organizing drives in the South. When I asked a CBS producer to explain what seemed an odd coincidence, he replied immediately that the *Times* had run a piece on the Southern organizing campaign the previous Sunday, and confirmed that CBS commonly followed the *Times*'s lead. Another informant pointed out that *Times* reporting can certify reality decisively when network news is itself divided on an issue. In the mid-sixties, a CBS researcher "had developed close ties with [District Attorney] Jim Garrison in New Orleans, and had some interesting information [about Garrison's investigation of the Kennedy assassination]. . . . His material was all rejected. Mike Wallace was in New Orleans covering an American Legion convention when the [New Orleans] *Times-Picayune* broke the story about the Garrison information. And so they had talent down there, they had the information, the local paper had written the information, and CBS had a scoop against the other networks. They did a piece and Cronkite wouldn't take it. The next morning, the *New York Times* had it, and then they used it. They had a lack of journalistic self-confidence. Maybe fear of provoking the powers that be."[6] Not doing much original reporting, and without any research staff to speak of, CBS assigns to the *Times*—along with the Associated Press and United Press International—the role of gatekeeper and certifier of new reality.

The networks are hardly alone, of course, in according the *Times* the prestige it courts. The *Times* is unabashed about aiming for greatness; with the country's largest staff of reporters, both at home and abroad, it can come close to making its reputation as "newspaper of record" stick. And of no small importance to this study, the leadership of the New Left took the *Times* quite seriously indeed, and not just in the New York area. In Cambridge, Massachusetts, in the early sixties, and in Ann Arbor, Michigan, in 1963–65, SDS leaders read the paper avidly, studying it for political straws in the wind. Even in the San Francisco Bay Area, late in 1965, two SDS organizers lamented: "On the West Coast, it is said you have to read the *New York Times* to find out what SDS is doing nationally."[7] Their ironic lament contained an indisputable truth.

6. Interview, Michael Nolan, December 28, 1976. Nolan was assistant to the assignment editor at CBS News.

7. Roy Dahlberg and Carolyn Craven, untitled paper for SDS December Conference, n.d. [December 1965]; author's file.

Accordingly, I searched—with the invaluable help of Glenn Hirsch—through microfilm archives of the *Times* for 1965–70, paying deepest attention to stories about SDS in particular, but noting also coverage of other radical and antiwar activity. On occasion, for comparative purposes, I looked at other papers' coverage of events reported in the *Times*. In my historical accounts of movement–media relations, however, especially for 1965, I concentrate on the *New York Times* coverage—partly because of its intrinsic importance in setting national political agendas, partly because of its agenda-setting function for other media, and partly because of its accessibility—or at least the accessibility of its Late City Edition, the one that gets microfilmed. I do think, however, that it would be edifying to scrutinize other major metropolitan dailies (and the wire services and newsmagazines) over the same period. Without further study, not too much should be extrapolated from the example, however powerful, of the *New York Times*. In 1977, a *Los Angeles Times* reporter found that over a five-month period, the *New York Times*, the *Washington Post*, and the *Los Angeles Times* rarely agreed on the most important story of the day. One-fifth of the time there was not a single story that appeared on the front page of all three papers.[8]

Comparing CBS News and the *New York Times* turned out to be revelatory in one way I had not at all expected. I had started out with the assumption that many of the framing mechanisms that concerned me were peculiar to television, in degree if not altogether in kind. It is a commonplace that television compresses and oversimplifies the news, lends itself to symbolic condensations, and turns itself over to good pictures at the cost of narrative complexity. None of this is untrue. But I discovered to my surprise that the *Times*'s and CBS's frames for covering the movement were not so different after all, that roughly the same analytic model could be brought to bear on both television and newspapers, and that, at least with respect to the New Left, CBS had nothing in particular to be ashamed of. Journalists and media executives as well as scholars usually presume that print and TV news are substantially different in tone, techniques, content, and impact; the same factors are trotted out defensively by both newspaper people (there are things we can do that television can't, so we're indispensable) and television people (there are things newspapers can do that we can't, so don't

8. David Shaw, "Page 1 News: Press Rarely in Agreement," *Los Angeles Times*, June 24, 1977.

expect too much of us).[9] On the one side, there is newspapers' "depth," their "investigations," and their greater capacity to relay information; on the other, there is TV's "immediacy," its "credibility" and "emotional impact," and its "accessibility." It may be that the two media are converging as newspapers lose circulation and scramble for a suburbanized audience which is, in turn, conditioned by two decades of television.[10] But it remains important to study variations among media (not only networks and newspapers but, importantly, wire services, radio, and local television) and among distinct institutions within a single medium.

I have tried to be precise about variations as well as similarities in frames and journalistic procedures. But I cannot resist the conclusion that although different news organizations may have employed the various framing devices with greater or lesser frequency, the overall *repertory* of frames was standard and remains standard. The forms of distortion are essentially the same from newspaper to newspaper, and (despite the rivalrous claims of difference made by both sides) between major newspapers and networks. My impression of newsmagazine and wire service coverage is that, by and large, they select from the same repertory.[11] If there *are* differences, the New York Times and CBS News may have differed from other media institutions principally in the *range* of their frames—at times respecting movements, at times trivializing them, at times attributing menace to them—and in the relative contradictoriness and complexity of their stories. Certainly differences in treatment are important, from the CBS network to a local station, from the *New York Times* to the *San Diego Union*, from

9. See Paul Weaver's clear statement about similarities and differences, "Newspaper News and Television News," in Douglass Cater and Richard Adler, eds., *Television as a Social Force: New Approaches to TV Criticism* (New York: Praeger, 1975), pp. 81–94. Perhaps inadvertently, Weaver shows the similarities to be considerably more striking than the differences. Differences that remain salient include (1) the TV anchor's or correspondent's great claim to omniscience because he or she appears "in person," and (2) TV's preference for "good film," other things being equal. But the second difference may be shrinking as newspapers gravitate back to heavier use of photos and sensational reports.

10. An early survey of the new suburbanized metropolitan paper, with its indulgence in "lifestyle," personality, and news "briefs," is Fergus M. Bordewich's "Supermarketing the Newspaper," *Columbia Journalism Review* 16 (September–October 1977): 23–30. The phenomenon is recent enough to have passed without much comment to date.

11. But researchers take note: according to Harvey Molotch and Marilyn Lester ("Accidental News," *American Journal of Sociology* 81 [September 1975]: 240n.), the wire services keep their copy only three years, and do not index it.

the *New York Daily News* to the *Chicago Daily News*. But in large measure these are variations on the same themes, within a hegemonic whole.

ON ANALYZING NEWS

A few notes about the news stories I chose to present in Part I, and how I went about looking at them:

I detailed coverage of the New Left in 1965 because the major frames were set in place then; that was the year in which the "New Left" went on the media agenda. By looking closely at that coverage, we can discover the original frames and watch them hardening into the taken-for-granted conventional wisdom, the hegemonic definitions of how things are.

I decided to exploit the fact that there are few enough recoverable *Times* and CBS News items for that year to permit a readable analysis of all of them, piece by piece. The risk was a certain repetition in the narrative, but I decided that it was more important to give the reader a chance to see the whole framing process unfold in a year of coverage. At least I know that the uncertainties in my analysis are inherent in cultural exegesis itself, not in my sampling procedure.

I also had theoretical reasons for preferring the qualitative, exhaustive approach to news history. I wanted the suppleness of the qualitative "literary" approach to cultural artifacts, whether newspaper articles, TV pieces, comic books, or museum pieces. I wanted to "tease out" those determining but hidden assumptions which in their unique ordering remain opaque to quantitative content analysis. At its best, qualitative analysis is more flexible than the quantitative kind; it aspires to a level of complexity (I do not claim it is bound to achieve it) that remains true to the actual complexity and contradictoriness of media artifacts.

As Stuart Hall points out, both qualitative and quantitative methodologies begin with "a long preliminary soak" in the materials.[12] The question is then whether to identify countable categories and to investigate the patterns of their recurrence, or to use "the preliminary reading to select representative examples which

---

12. My discussion of qualitative methodology is heavily indebted to Stuart Hall's treatment of these matters in his Introduction to *Paper Voices: The Popular Press and Social Change, 1935–1965*, by A. C. H. Smith with Elizabeth Immirzi and Trevor Blackwell (London: Chatto and Windus, 1975), pp. 11–24, especially pp. 14–17. The quotation is from p. 15.

can be more intensively analysed."[13] I chose both methods: to identify key categories of content, and also to analyze examples of news treatment selected for their political significance. What I did *not* do was to count instances of recurrent themes: (a) partly because I could not locate some network pieces; (b) more importantly, because much of the subtlety I find interesting would probably be lost in quantitative sieves; and (c) still more importantly, because I wanted to analyze news coverage especially at crucial— that is to say, atypical—political moments. The criteria for selecting those moments had to be brought to the news material from without, from a larger sense of political process. Again, this is not simply a study of the content of media versions of the New Left to demonstrate distortion, but a study of the political significance of those versions, both as revelations of the politics of media institutions and as influences upon the movement itself.

It needs to be said, I suppose, that the "literary" choice emphatically does not amount to a choice of the intuitive against the objective. Both qualitative and quantitative methodologies rely on preliminary interrogations of the material, interrogations which proceed, at least implicitly, from "intuitive" assumptions about what *matters* in the content, what needs to be either analyzed or counted. The contrasts between the two methodologies in their pure forms are of a different order, as Stuart Hall nicely argues:

> The error is to assume that because content analysis uses precise criteria for coding evidence it is therefore objective in the literal sense of the term: and because literary/linguistic analysis steers clear of code-building it is merely intuitive and unreliable. Literary/linguistic types of analysis also employ evidence: they point, in detail, to the text on which an interpretation of latent meaning is based; they indicate more briefly the fuller supporting or contextual evidence which lies to hand; they take into account material which modifies or disproves the hypotheses which are emerging; and they *should* (they do not always) indicate in detail why one rather than another reading of the material seems to the analyst the most plausible way of understanding it. Content analysis assumes repetition—the pile-up of material under one of the categories—to be the most useful indicator of significance.
>
> Literary/linguistic and stylistic analysis also employs recurrence as one critical dimension of significance, though these recurring patterns may not be expressed in quantifiable terms. . . . These recurring patterns are taken as pointers to latent meanings from which inferences as to the source can

13. Ibid.

be drawn. But the literary/linguistic analyst has another string to his bow: namely, strategies for noting and taking account of emphasis. Position, placing, treatment, tone, stylistic intensification, striking imagery, etc., are all ways of registering emphasis. The really significant item may not be the one which continually recurs, but the one which stands out as an exception from the general pattern—but which is *also* given, in its exceptional context, the greatest weight.[14]

None of which is to say that quantitative techniques have no use in studies of media content. If they are harnessed to the qualitative approach, and if (no mean practical consideration) sufficiently inclusive materials are at hand, quantitative methods could shed some light on the surface content of news. They would not alert the student to, say, the significance of a *New York Times* reporter's mention of "warm spring sunshine" in a story about an antiwar demonstration (see Chapter 2, above), though they could tell us how often this sort of framing takes place in different types of news stories. In any event, it is late in the day for methodological exclusivity; in the act of interpretation and criticism, the proof of the pudding is in the eating.

14. Ibid.

Selected Bibliography

This bibliography encompasses those published books and articles and miscellaneous speeches and papers that I have cited in the text, as well as other major sources I have consulted. It does not include newspaper articles and television news stories and transcripts cited by date in the text, nor the interviews I conducted. Nor does it include the many materials published by SDS—working papers, Work List mailings, *Bulletins*, issues of *New Left Notes*, and pamphlets—nor the correspondence cited in the text. All these are either in my possession (as mentioned in notes to the text) or in the SDS archives at the Wisconsin State Historical Society, Madison.

Adair, John, and Sol Worth. *Through Navajo Eyes.* Bloomington: Indiana University Press, 1971.

Adamson, Walter. "Beyond Reform and Revolution: Notes on Political Education in Gramsci, Habermas and Arendt." *Theory and Society* 6 (November 1978): 429–460.

Alberoni, Francesco. "The Powerless 'Elite': Theory and Sociological Research on the Phenomenon of the Stars." In Denis McQuail, ed., *Sociology of Mass Communications*, pp. 75–98. Harmondsworth, England: Penguin Books, 1972.

Altheide, David L. *Creating Reality: How TV News Distorts Events.* Beverly Hills, Calif.: Sage Publications, 1976.

Anderson, Perry. "The Antinomies of Antonio Gramsci." *New Left Review*, No. 100 (November 1976–January 1977): 5–78.

Arnett, Peter. "Tet Coverage: A Debate Renewed." *Columbia Journalism Review* 16 (January–February 1978): 44–47.

Aronson, James. *Deadline for the Media*. Indianapolis: Bobbs-Merrill, 1972.

Avorn, Jerry L., and members of the staff of the *Columbia Daily Spectator*. *Up Against the Ivy Wall: A History of the Columbia Crisis*. New York: Atheneum, 1968.

Bagdikian, Ben H. *The Information Machines*. New York: Harper and Row, 1971.

———. *The Effete Conspiracy*. New York: Harper and Row, 1972.

Balzac, Honoré de. *Lost Illusions*. Translated by G. Burnham Ives. Philadelphia: George Barrie, 1898.

Barnouw, Erik. *The Image Empire*. Vol. 3, *A History of Broadcasting in the United States*. New York: Oxford University Press, 1970.

———. *Tube of Plenty: The Evolution of American Television*. New York: Oxford University Press, 1975.

———. *The Sponsor: Notes on a Modern Potentate*. New York: Oxford University Press, 1978.

Barthes, Roland. *Mythologies*. Translated by Annette Lavers. New York: Hill and Wang, 1972.

———. *Image—Music—Text*. Translated by Stephen Heath. New York: Farrar, Straus, and Giroux, 1977.

Becker, Lee B., Maxwell E. McCombs, and Jack M. McLeod. "The Development of Political Cognitions." In Steven H. Chaffee, ed., *Political Communication*, pp. 21–63. Beverly Hills, Calif.: Sage Publications, 1975.

Bell, Daniel. *The Cultural Contradictions of Capitalism*. New York: Basic Books, 1976.

Berlet, Chip. "COINTELPRO: What the (Deleted) Was It? Media Op." *The Public Eye* 1 (April 1978): 28–38.

Berman, Marshall. "'All That Is Solid Melts into Air': Marxism, Modernism, Modernization." *Dissent* 25 (Winter 1978): 54–73.

Bethell, Thomas. "The Myth of an Adversary Press." *Harper's Magazine*, January 1977, pp. 33–40.

Blumler, Jay G., and Alison J. Ewbank. "Trade Unionists, the Mass Media and Unofficial Strikes." *British Journal of Industrial Relations* 8 (March 1970): 32–54.

Blumler, Jay G., and Denis McQuail. *Television in Politics: Its Uses and Influence*. London: Faber, 1968.

Bordewich, Fergus M. "Supermarketing the Newspaper." *Columbia Journalism Review* 16 (September–October 1977): 23–30.

Braestrup, Peter. *Big Story: How the American Press and Television Reported and Interpreted the Crisis of Tet 1968 in Vietnam and Wash-*

ington. 2 vols. Boulder, Colo.: Westview Press, 1977. Abridged edition, Garden City, N.Y.: Anchor Books, 1978.

Breed, Warren. "Social Control in the Newsroom: A Functional Analysis." *Social Forces* 33 (May 1955): 467–477.

Breton, André. *Second Manifeste du Surréalisme.* Paris: Éditions Kra, 1930.

Brown, Les. *Television: The Business Behind the Box.* New York: Harcourt Brace Jovanovich, 1971.

Cantor, Muriel G. *The Hollywood TV Producer.* New York: Basic Books, 1971.

Case, John, and Rosemary C. R. Taylor, eds. *Co-ops, Communes and Collectives: Experiments in Social Change in the 1960s and 1970s.* New York: Pantheon, 1979.

Catledge, Turner. *My Life and The Times.* New York: Harper and Row, 1971.

Cawelti, John, ed. *Focus on Bonnie and Clyde.* Englewood Cliffs, N.J.: Prentice-Hall, 1973.

Chaffee, Steven H., ed. *Political Communications.* Beverly Hills, Calif.: Sage Publications, 1975.

Chomsky, Noam. "Ten Years After Tet: The Big Story That Got Away; Widely Hailed Book On Vietnam Reporting Asks Wrong Questions, Gets Wrong Answers." *More* 8 (June 1978): 16–23.

Cirino, Robert. *Power to Persuade.* New York: Bantam Books, 1974.

Cohen, Mitchell, and Dennis Hale, eds. *The New Student Left.* Boston: Beacon Press, 1966.

Cohen, Stanley. *Folk Devils and Moral Panics.* London: MacGibbon and Kee, 1972.

————. "Mods and Rockers: The Inventory as Manufactured News." In Stanley Cohen and Jock Young, eds., *The Manufacture of News: A Reader,* pp. 226–241. London: Constable, 1973; and Beverly Hills, Calif.: Sage Publications, 1973.

Cohen, Stanley, and Jock Young, eds. *The Manufacture of News: A Reader.* London: Constable, 1973; and Beverly Hills, Calif.: Sage Publications, 1973.

Cooper, Chester. *The Lost Crusade: America in Vietnam.* New York: Dodd, Mead, 1970.

Cordtz, Dan. "Businessmen Can Look Better If They Try." *New York Times,* Business Section, July 18, 1976, p. 12.

Cowan, Paul, Nick Egleson, and Nat Hentoff, with Barbara Herbert and Robert Wall. *State Secrets: Police Surveillance in America.* New York: Holt, Rinehart and Winston, 1974.

Cronkite, Walter. "Where Are You, Mr. Chairman?" *Chief Executive* 1 (July–September 1977): 26–28.

Crouse, Timothy. *The Boys on the Bus.* New York: Random House, 1973.

Czitrom, Danny. "Bilko: A Sitcom for All Seasons." *Cultural Correspondence*, No. 4 (Spring 1977), pp. 16–19.

Darnton, Robert. "Writing News and Telling Stories." *Daedalus* 104 (Spring 1975): 175–194.

Deutscher, Isaac. *The Prophet Unarmed: Trotsky 1921–1929.* New York: Oxford University Press, 1959.

Dreher, Carl. *Sarnoff: An American Success.* New York: Quadrangle, 1977.

Elliott, Philip. "Media Organizations and Occupations: An Overview." In James Curran, Michael Gurevitch, and Janet Woollacott, eds., *Mass Communication and Society*, pp. 142–173. London: Edward Arnold, 1977; and Beverly Hills, Calif.: Sage Publications, 1979.

Ellsberg, Daniel. *Papers on the War.* New York: Simon and Schuster, 1972.

Epstein, Edward Jay. *News From Nowhere: Television and the News.* New York: Random House, 1973.

———. *Between Fact and Fiction: The Problem of Journalism.* New York: Vintage Books, 1975.

Fiske, John, and John Hartley. *Reading Television.* London: Methuen, 1978.

Flacks, Richard. *Youth and Social Change.* Chicago: Markham, 1971.

Freeman, Jo. *The Politics of Women's Liberation.* New York: David McKay, 1975.

Fruchter, Norman. "Protest, Power and the People." *Liberation* 15 (February–April 1971): 67–70.

———. "Movement Propaganda and the Culture of the Spectacle." *Liberation* 16 (May 1971): 4–17.

———. "SDS: In and Out of Context." *Liberation* 16 (February 1972): 19–32.

Galtung, Johan, and Mari Holmboe Ruge. "The Structure of Foreign News." *Journal of International Peace Research* 1 (1965): 64–90. Reprinted in Jeremy Tunstall, ed., *Media Sociology: A Reader*, pp. 259–298. Urbana: University of Illinois Press, 1970.

Gans, Herbert. "The Politics of Culture in America." In Denis McQuail, ed., *Sociology of Mass Communications*, pp. 372–385. Harmondsworth, England: Penguin Books, 1972.

————. *Deciding What's News*. New York: Pantheon, 1979.

Garrow, David J. *Protest at Selma*. New Haven, Conn.: Yale University Press, 1978.

Gates, Gary Paul. *Air Time: The Inside Story of CBS News*. New York: Harper and Row, 1978.

Giddens, Anthony. *The Class Structure of the Advanced Societies*. New York: Harper and Row, 1973.

Gitlin, Todd. "Casting the First Stone." *San Francisco Express Times* 1 (September 25, 1968), p. 2.

————. "Fourteen Notes on Television and the Movement." *Leviathan* 1 (July–August 1969): 3–9.

————. "The Dynamics of the New Left." *Motive* (October 1970): 48–59 and (November 1970): 43–64.

————. "Sixteen Notes on Television and the Movement." In George Abbott White and Charles Newman, eds., *Literature in Revolution*, pp. 335–366. New York: Holt, Rinehart and Winston, 1972.

————. "Spotlights and Shadows: Television and the Culture of Politics." *College English* 38 (April 1977): 789–801.

————. "The Televised Professional." *Social Policy*, November–December 1977, pp. 93–99.

————. "Media Sociology: The Dominant Paradigm." *Theory and Society* 6 (November 1978): 205–253.

————. "Prime Time Ideology: The Hegemonic Process in Television Entertainment." *Social Problems* 26 (February 1979): 251–266.

————. Review of John Case and Rosemary C. R. Taylor, eds., *Co-ops, Communes and Collectives: Experiments in Social Change in the 1960s and 1970s*. *The Progressive*, June 1979, pp. 55–56.

Gitlin, Todd, and Nanci Hollander. *Uptown: Poor Whites in Chicago*. New York: Harper and Row, 1970.

Glasgow University Media Group. *Bad News*. London: Routledge and Kegan Paul, 1976.

Goffman, Erving. *Frame Analysis: An Essay on the Organization of Experience*. New York: Harper and Row, 1974.

Goldenberg, Edie. *Making the Papers: The Access of Resource-Poor Groups to the Metropolitan Press*. Lexington, Mass.: Lexington Books, 1975.

Goldsen, Rose K. *The Show and Tell Machine: How Television Works and Works You Over*. New York: Dial Press, 1977.

Gould, Stanhope. "The Trials of Network News." *More* 3 (May 1973): 8–11.

Gouldner, Alvin W. *The Dialectic of Ideology and Technology: The Origins, Grammar, and Future of Ideology.* New York: Seabury Press, 1976.

——. *The Future of Intellectuals and the Rise of the New Class.* New York: Seabury Press, 1979.

Gramsci, Antonio. *Selections from the Prison Notebooks.* Edited and translated by Quintin Hoare and Geoffrey Nowell Smith. New York: International Publishers, 1971.

Greeley, Bill. "Progress in Viet War Coverage (Airing Once-Nixed Film a Sign of the 'Times')." *Variety,* June 28, 1972, p. 1.

Habermas, Jürgen. *Legitimation Crisis.* Translated by Thomas McCarthy. Boston: Beacon Press, 1975.

Halberstam, David. *The Making of a Quagmire.* New York: Random House, 1965.

——. *The Best and the Brightest.* New York: Random House, 1972.

——. *The Powers That Be.* New York: Alfred A. Knopf, 1979.

Hall, Stuart. "Determinations of News Photographs." In Stanley Cohen and Jock Young, eds., *The Manufacture of News,* pp. 176–190. London: Constable, 1973; and Beverly Hills, Calif.: Sage Publications, 1973.

——. "Encoding and Decoding in the Television Discourse." Centre for Contemporary Cultural Studies, University of Birmingham, 1973. Mimeographed.

——. Introduction to *Paper Voices: The Popular Press and Social Change, 1935–1965,* by A. C. H. Smith with Elizabeth Immirzi and Trevor Blackwell, pp. 11–24. London: Chatto and Windus, 1975.

——. "Culture, the Media, and the 'Ideological Effect.'" In James Curran, Michael Gurevitch, and Janet Woollacott, eds., *Mass Communication and Society,* pp. 315–348. London: Edward Arnold, 1977; and Beverly Hills, Calif.: Sage Publications, 1979.

Hall, Stuart, Ian Connell, and Lidia Curti. "The 'Unity' of Public Affairs Television." *Working Papers in Cultural Studies* 9 (Spring 1976): 51–93.

Halloran, James D., Philip Elliott, and Graham Murdock. *Demonstrations and Communication: A Case Study.* Harmondsworth, England: Penguin Books, 1970.

Halperin, Morton H., Jerry J. Berman, Robert L. Borosage, and Christine M. Marwick. *The Lawless State: The Crimes of the U.S. Intelligence Agencies.* New York: Penguin Books, 1976.

Hartmann, Paul, and Charles Husband. "The Mass Media and Racial Conflict." In Stanley Cohen and Jock Young, eds., *The*

Manufacture of News, pp. 270–283. London: Constable, 1973; and Beverly Hills, Calif.: Sage Publications, 1973.

———. *Racism and the Mass Media*. London: Davis-Poynter, 1974.

Hayden, Tom. *Trial*. New York: Holt, Rinehart and Winston, 1970.

Hodgson, Godfrey. *America in Our Time*. Garden City, N.Y.: Doubleday, 1976.

Hoffman, Abbie [Free]. *Revolution for the Hell of It*. New York: Dial Press, 1968.

Hoggart, Richard. *The Uses of Literacy*. Boston: Beacon Press, 1961.

Hoopes, Townsend. *The Limits of Intervention*. New York: David McKay, 1969.

Hughes, Helen MacGill. *News and the Human Interest Story*. Chicago: University of Chicago Press, 1940.

Jacobs, Harold, ed. *Weatherman*. Berkeley, Calif.: Ramparts Press, 1970.

Johnson, Nicholas. "Audience Rights." *Columbia Journalism Review* 18 (May–June 1979): 63–66.

Johnstone, John W. C., Edward J. Slawski, and William W. Bowman. *The News People: A Sociological Portrait of American Journalists and Their Work*. Urbana: University of Illinois Press, 1976.

Joreen. "Trashing: The Dark Side of Sisterhood." *Ms.*, April 1976, p. 49.

Kadushin, Charles. *The American Intellectual Elite*. Boston: Little, Brown, 1974.

Kael, Pauline. *Kiss Kiss Bang Bang*. New York: Bantam Books, 1969.

Kelly, Aileen. "Good for the Populists." *New York Review of Books* 24 (June 23, 1977): 10–15.

Klapper, Joseph T. *The Effects of Mass Communication*. New York: The Free Press, 1960.

———. "Mass Communication: Effects." *International Encyclopedia of the Social Sciences*. Vol. 10, pp. 81–90. New York: Macmillan and The Free Press, 1968.

Knutson, Pete. "Dragnet: The Perfect Crime?" *Liberation* 18 (May 1974): 28–31.

Kornhauser, William. "Mass Society." *International Encyclopedia of the Social Sciences*. Vol. 10, pp. 58–64. New York: Macmillan and The Free Press, 1968.

Lasch, Christopher. *The Agony of the American Left*. New York: Random House, 1969.

———. "The Narcissist Society." *New York Review of Books* 23 (September 30, 1976): 5–13.

———. *The Culture of Narcissism*. New York: W. W. Norton, 1979.

Laufer, Robert. "Radicals and the Life Cycle: A Comparative Analysis of the 1960's Activists in the Netherlands and America." Paper delivered to the American Sociological Association meeting, San Francisco, August 1975.

Levin, Jack, and Allan J. Kimmel. "Gossip Columns: Media Small Talk." *Journal of Communication* 27 (Winter 1977): 169–175.

Levy, Mark R. "The Audience Experience with Television News." *Journalism Monographs*, No. 55 (April 1978).

Lipsky, Michael. "Protest as a Political Resource." *American Political Science Review* 62 (1968): 1145–1158.

Lynd, Staughton. "Coalition Politics or Nonviolent Revolution?" *Liberation* 10 (June–July 1965): 18–21.

———. "The Prospects of the New Left." In John H. M. Laslett and Seymour Martin Lipset, eds., *Failure of a Dream? Essays in the History of American Socialism*, pp. 713–738. Garden City, N.Y.: Doubleday, 1974.

Lyons, Eugene. *David Sarnoff*. New York: Harper and Row, 1966.

McCombs, Maxwell E., and Donald L. Shaw. "The Agenda-Setting Function of the Mass Media." *Public Opinion Quarterly* 36 (Summer 1972): 176–187.

McCormack, Thelma. "Establishment Media and the Backlash." Unpublished paper read to meetings of the American Sociological Association, Washington, D.C., 1970.

McGaffin, William, and Erwin Knoll. *Anything But the Truth*. New York: Putnam's, 1968.

McLeod, Jack M., Lee B. Becker, and James E. Byrnes. "Another Look at the Agenda-Setting Function of the Press." *Communication Research* 1 (April 1974): 131–166.

MacNaughton, Donald S. "Business and the Press—Independent or Interdependent?" The Prudential Insurance Company of America, 1976. Excerpted in the *New York Times*, Business Section, March 7, 1976, p. 12.

Magruder, Jeb Stuart. *An American Life: One Man's Road to Watergate*. New York: Atheneum, 1974.

Mannheim, Karl. "The Problem of Generations." In *Essays in the Sociology of Knowledge*, translated by Paul Keckskemeti. New York: Oxford University Press, 1952.

Marx, Gary T. "Thoughts on a Neglected Category of Social Movement Participant: The Agent Provocateur and the Informant." *American Journal of Sociology* 80 (1974): 402–442.

Millett, Kate. *Flying*. New York: Alfred A. Knopf, 1974.

Mills, C. Wright. *The Power Elite*. New York: Oxford University Press, 1957.

Molotch, Harvey. "Media and Movements." Unpublished paper, 1977.

Molotch, Harvey, and Marilyn Lester. "Accidents, Scandals and Routines: Resources for Insurgent Methodology." *The Insurgent Sociologist* 3 (1973): 1–11.

————. "News as Purposive Behavior: On the Strategic Use of Routine Events, Scandals, and Rumors." *American Sociological Review* 39 (February 1974): 101–112.

————. "Accidental News: The Great Oil Spill as Local Occurrence and National Event." *American Journal of Sociology* 81 (September 1975): 235–260.

Morris, Monica B. "Newspapers and the New Feminists: Blackout as Social Control." *Journalism Quarterly* 50 (1973): 37–42.

Murdock, Graham. "Political Deviance: The Press Presentation of a Militant Mass Demonstration." In Stanley Cohen and Jock Young, eds., *The Manufacture of News*, pp. 156–175. London: Constable, 1973; and Beverly Hills, Calif.: Sage Publications, 1973.

Paley, William S. *As It Happened*. Garden City, N.Y.: Doubleday, 1979.

Park, Robert E. "Natural History of the Newspaper." *American Journal of Sociology* 29 (1923): 273–289.

————. "News as a Form of Knowledge." *American Journal of Sociology* 45 (1940): 669–689.

Pearce, Frank. "How to Be Immoral and Ill, Pathetic and Dangerous, All At the Same Time: Mass Media and the Homosexual." In Stanley Cohen and Jock Young, eds., *The Manufacture of News*, pp. 284–301. London: Constable, 1973; and Beverly Hills, Calif.: Sage Publications, 1973.

The Pentagon Papers. The Senator Gravel Edition. Vol. 3. Boston: Beacon Press, 1972.

Pollak, Richard. "Abe Rosenthal Presents the *New* New York Times." *Penthouse*, September 1977, pp. 49 ff.

Porter, Dennis. "Soap Time: Thoughts on a Commodity Art Form." *College English* 38 (April 1977): 782–788.

Porter, William E. *Assault on the Media: The Nixon Years*. Ann Arbor: University of Michigan Press, 1976.

Powers, Thomas. *The War at Home: Vietnam and the American People 1964–1968*. New York: Grossman, 1973.

Real, Michael R. *Mass-Mediated Culture*. Englewood Cliffs, N.J.: Prentice-Hall, 1977.

Robinson, Michael J. "American Political Legitimacy in an Era of Electronic Journalism: Reflections on the Evening News." In Douglass Cater and Richard Adler, eds., *Television as a Social Force: New Approaches to TV Criticism*, pp. 97–139. New York: Praeger, 1975.

Rockefeller, David. "The Values That Can Serve Mankind." Remarks before the Northern California Region of the National Conference of Christians and Jews, April 7, 1976. Mimeographed by the Chase Manhattan Bank, New York.

Rosenthal, Alan. *The New Documentary in Action: A Casebook in Film Making*. Berkeley: University of California Press, 1971.

Roshco, Bernard. *Newsmaking*. Chicago: University of Chicago Press, 1975.

Ross, Robert J. "Primary Groups in Social Movements: A Memoir and Interpretation." *Journal of Voluntary Action Research* 6 (July–October 1977): 139–152.

Rossman, Michael. *The Wedding Within the War*. Garden City, N.Y.: Anchor Books, 1971.

Rubin, Jerry. *Growing (Up) at 37*. New York: M. Evans, 1976.

Rudd, Mark. "Symbols of the Revolution." In Jerry L. Avorn et al., *Up Against the Ivy Wall: A History of the Columbia Crisis*, pp. 291–297. New York: Atheneum, 1968.

———. "Notes on Columbia." *The Movement*, March 1969, pp. 7–10.

Sahlins, Marshall. *Culture and Practical Reason*. Chicago: University of Chicago Press, 1976.

Sale, Kirkpatrick. *SDS*. New York: Random House, 1973.

———. "Myths as Eternal Truths." *More* 3 (June 1973): 3–5.

———. "Mark Rudd and the Radical Movement." *San Francisco Chronicle*, September 24, 1977.

Schandler, Herbert Y. *The Unmaking of a President: Lyndon Johnson and Vietnam*. Princeton, N.J.: Princeton University Press, 1977.

Schell, Jonathan. *The Time of Illusion*. New York: Alfred A. Knopf, 1976.

Schneider, Bob. "Spelling's Salvation Armies." *Cultural Correspondence*, No. 4 (Spring 1977), pp. 27–36.

Schorr, Daniel. *Clearing the Air*. Boston: Houghton Mifflin, 1977.

Schudson, Michael. *Discovering the News: A Social History of American Newspapers*. New York: Basic Books, 1977.

Sennett, Richard. "The Boss's New Clothes." *New York Review of Books* 26 (February 22, 1979): 42–46.

Shaw, David. "Page 1 News: Press Rarely in Agreement." *Los Angeles Times*, June 24, 1977.

Sigal, Leon V. *Reporters and Officials: The Organization and Politics of Newsmaking.* Lexington, Mass.: D. C. Heath, 1973.

Silk, Leonard, and David Vogel. *Ethics and Profits.* New York: Simon and Schuster, 1976.

Simmel, Georg. *Georg Simmel: On Individuality and Social Forms.* Edited by Donald N. Levine. Chicago: University of Chicago Press, 1971.

Skolnick, Jerome. *The Politics of Protest.* New York: Ballantine Books, 1969.

Small, William. *To Kill a Messenger: Television News and the Real World.* New York: Hastings House, 1970.

Stoller, Nancy. "The Ins and Outs of SNCC." *Studies in Brandeis Sociology,* Brandeis University, n.d.

Talese, Gay. *The Kingdom and the Power.* New York: World, 1969.

Taylor, Arthur R. "Business and the Press: Who's Doing What to Whom and Why?" Remarks before the Financial Executives Institute, October 21, 1975. CBS Inc., New York, 1975.

Thorne, Barrie. "Resisting the Draft: An Ethnography of the Draft Resistance Movement." Unpublished Ph.D. dissertation, Brandeis University, 1971.

————. "Protest and the Problem of Credibility: Uses of Knowledge and Risk-Taking in the Draft Resistance Movement of the 1960's." *Social Problems* 23 (December 1975): 111–123.

Tuchman, Gaye. "Objectivity as Strategic Ritual: An Examination of Newsmen's Notions of Objectivity." *American Journal of Sociology* 77 (1972): 660–679.

————. "Making News by Doing Work: Routinizing the Unexpected." *American Journal of Sociology* 79 (1973): 110–131.

————. "Assembling a Network Talk-Show." In Gaye Tuchman, ed., *The TV Establishment,* pp. 119–135. Englewood Cliffs, N.J.: Prentice-Hall, 1974.

————. "Ridicule, Advocacy and Professionalism: Newspaper Reporting About a Social Movement." Paper delivered at the American Sociological Association meetings, New York, August 1976.

————. *Making News.* New York: The Free Press, 1978.

Tunstall, Jeremy. *Journalists at Work.* London: Constable, 1971; and Beverly Hills, Calif.: Sage Publications, 1971.

Venturi, Franco. *Roots of Revolution.* Translated by Francis Haskell. New York: Grosset and Dunlap, 1966.

Weaver, Paul H. "Newspaper News and Television News." In Douglass Cater and Richard Adler, eds., *Television as a Social Force: New Approaches to TV Criticism*, pp. 81–94. New York: Praeger, 1975.

White, David Manning. "The 'Gatekeeper': A Case Study in the Selection of News." *Journalism Quarterly* 27 (Fall 1950): 383–390.

Whiteside, Thomas. "Shaking the Tree." *The New Yorker*, March 17, 1975, pp. 41–91.

Williams, Raymond. "Base and Superstructure in Marxist Cultural Theory." *New Left Review*, No. 82 (1973): 3–16.

———. "Developments in the Sociology of Culture." *Sociology*, September 1976: 497–506.

———. *Marxism and Literature.* New York: Oxford University Press, 1977.

Winick, Charles, ed. *Deviance and Mass Media.* Beverly Hills, Calif.: Sage Publications, 1978.

Wolin, Sheldon S. *Politics and Vision: Continuity and Innovation in Western Political Thought.* Boston: Little, Brown, 1960.

Wolpert, Jeremiah F. "Toward a Sociology of Authority." In Alvin W. Gouldner, ed., *Studies in Leadership*, pp. 679–701. New York: Harper and Brothers, 1956.

Wright, Charles. *Mass Communications.* 2nd edition. New York: Random House, 1975.

Zeitlin, Maurice. *Revolutionary Politics and the Cuban Working Class.* Princeton, N.J.: Princeton University Press, 1967.

Index

7322